Drawing Boundaries

Drawing Boundaries
Legislatures, Courts, and Electoral Values

EDITORS
John C. Courtney
Peter MacKinnon
David E. Smith

Fifth House Publishers
Saskatoon, Saskatchewan

Cover design by Robert Grey

Printed and bound in Canada
94 93 92 3 2 1

The publisher gratefully acknowledges the assistance of The Canada Council,
the Saskatchewan Arts Board, and the University of Saskatchewan.

Canadian Cataloguing in Publication Data
Main entry under title:

Drawing boundaries

Conference held Nov. 8-9, 1991 at the University of Saskatchewan, Saskatoon, Sask.
Includes bibliographical references.
ISBN 1-895618-03-7

1. Election districts - Canada - Congresses.
2. Election districts - United States - Congresses.
3. Election law - Canada - Congresses. 4. Election
law - United States - Congresses. I. Courtney, John C.
II. MacKinnon, Peter. III. Smith, David E., 1936–

JL193.D72 1992   328.71'07345   C92-098082-1

76212

FIFTH HOUSE PUBLISHERS
620 Duchess Street
Saskatoon, Saskatchewan S7K OR1

Contents

Introduction

In a lead editorial of 30 December 1991 entitled, "How Much is Your Vote Worth?" *The Globe and Mail* argued for a greater measure of voter equality than has historically been the case in Canada. Disputing a recent decision of the Alberta Court of Appeal, in which the province's newest, but controversial, legislation governing electoral boundary redistributions was upheld, the editorial asserted that "there is no excusing what can only be described as widespread, systemic discrimination against city dwellers." Many Canadians, particularly those in traditionally underrepresented urban areas, would no doubt support such a claim. What the editorial and the growing public awareness about "equality of the vote" demonstrated is that questions of representation and electoral fairness of constituency boundaries have entered the political and judicial arenas as never before in Canada.

For the first 100 years following Confederation, the drawing of boundaries of electoral districts had been carried out by legislatures and parliaments themselves. It was a highly partisan activity, as was reflected in the constituencies produced more or less at 10-year intervals by those bodies. A quarter of a century ago this practice began to change with the establishment of the first of several independent extra-legislative commissions to carry out the task of drawing boundaries without regard for partisan advantage. Some, but by no means a majority, of the federal and provincial commissions made their primary goal a substantial measure of population equality among constituencies; others placed greater emphasis on the geographic location, economic links, and historic associations of voters (defined in the main as community of interest), with less regard to equal district populations.

With the introduction of the Canadian Charter of Rights and Freedoms in 1982, the constitutional mechanism existed whereby for the first time these two different approaches to legislative representation could be tested. The growing importance of the Charter as an influence on the values and expectations of many Canadians led voters in some jurisdictions (notably the country's three most westerly provinces) to challenge either the legislation governing the redistribution of legislative seats or the existing boundaries themselves. These challenges of the late 1980s and early 1990s came on the heels of a growing body of scholarly literature examining how independent boundary commissions had come to interpret their mandate and to exercise their powers in Canada. (See the Bibliography). In all, the evidence suggested an increased interest in and awareness of the links between political representation and electoral districts. As had been the case in the United States from the mid-1960s on, the issue generated a debate in Canadian legislatures and courts over the value of "one person–one vote."

Drawing Boundaries is about that debate. Its 11 papers and 9 commentaries explore the arguments for and the consequences of competing representational theories as they have surfaced in political, legal, and scholarly circles in the recent past.

An important if not a prominent theme in many of these presentations is raised by Jennifer Smith's distinction between a procedural concept of representation, and a mirror or ascriptive concept of representation. The latter describes an approach by which it is claimed that effective representation depends upon representatives and constituents sharing one or more characteristics (gender, racial origin, colour) deemed to be critical for this purpose.

While recognizing the importance of diversity in the membership of our institutions of government, Katherine Swinton argues against fixed seats for groups on the basis of a shared characteristic "which ignores the complexity of individual experience and identity." Jennifer Smith herself agrees, asserting that preselection of candidates in the form of quotas is a troublesome limitation on a right to vote that assumes people are entitled to make choices as they see fit. However, she concedes, quotas mandated by ascriptive or mirror theories of representation might be appropriate for a community that defines its relationship with a larger society in terms of sovereignty.

Left undecided in the wake of the *Reference Re Provincial Electoral Boundaries* is the question of the constitutional validity of what Professor Smith called mirror systems of representation. The issue of guaranteed representation for particular groups is a very current one. In the spring of 1991 alone, there were reports of Québec considering a seat for Inuit in the far north, Nova Scotia looking favourably upon a seat reserved for the Micmacs, and Alberta contemplating electoral reforms which could include aboriginal districts. In the national context, the Royal Commission on Electoral Reform and Party Financing has endorsed an allocation of seven or eight parliamentary seats to aboriginal people, a proposal that has been warmly received by some commentators. (See editorial, *Star Phoenix*, [Saskatoon] 15 February 1992, D9).

These proposals merit a closer look. Murray Rankin cites the New Zealand Royal Commission recommendation against retaining separate Maori seats, and asked whether the implementation of mirror or ascriptive representation would "become a nightmare of pluralism gone wild." Professor Rankin asks some of the practical questions which must be addressed in this area. In his discussion of electoral reform in the Yukon, he raises questions about the implications of First Nations partial sovereignty and self-government for the participation of their representatives in the affairs of the Territory: "How many powers of the sort ordinarily enjoyed by the Territory must a First Nation take down before its citizens lose their right to vote in a territorial election?"

INTRODUCTION

Kent Roach is also sceptical about separate seats allocated on the basis of race, gender, ethnicity, or other personal characteristics. He argues that while they might create a more responsive politics at the constituency level, they would make politics more difficult and divisive in the legislature. Professor Roach proposes as an alternative that affirmative districting and active encouragement of women and minorities by political parties is a better way to respond to demands for more representative legislatures.

The papers were presented at a conference on 8–9 November 1991, sponsored by the College of Law and the Department of Political Studies at the University of Saskatchewan. Participants included academics, public servants, lawyers, politicians, students, and the interested public. Each of these brought a different perspective to a topic that was once the preserve of legislators, a fact noted by Patrick Boyer, MP for Etobicoke-Lakeshore and author of a series of scholarly works on electoral law and practices. In an after-dinner speech Mr. Boyer observed that whatever virtues may now attend the nonpartisan and expanded consultation accompanying the drawing of constituency boundaries,

> it is a fact that MPs or members of the legislature do have particular knowledge that can be useful to electoral boundaries commissioners when they are doing their work. If you just see it from the point of view that it's the elected representative who 365 days a year is busy with that bit of territory and who is travelling around it and in and out of it, getting to know the communities and the transportation and all the rest of it, I think there is certainly a role that the elected representative has in making some suggestions about the process. I would not for a minute think that MPs should be excluded from the process. In fact that's why in the amendments introduced in 1986 it was provided that MPs should appear before electoral boundaries commissions at the start of the process ... That was because if you've got something valuable to say about where the boundary should be, those suggestions should be made at the outset where they can have more influence.

There is no need to summarize further the arguments of the papers in *Drawing Boundaries;* their authors are eminently qualified to make their own cases. It is useful to emphasize, however, that the process of redistribution embraces much more than the drawing of constituency boundaries alone. There is, in Patrick Boyer's words, a profound "ripple effect" to the undertaking. The choices made during the redistribution of boundaries ultimately affect the operation of Cabinet and the House of Commons, the organization of political parties from the constituency association level on up, and the functioning of the federal system itself.

It is also worth observing that more than is true of most areas of Canadian politics, modern redistribution evokes a comparative dimension. Canadian political institutions are among the country's most distinctive features; yet the process of redistribution, especially since the advent of the Charter, forces Canadians to take note of the experience of the United States over the last 30 years. The papers by Bernard Grofman and Howard Scarrow should help inform

Canadians as they discuss the competing claims of equality of voting power on the one hand and the representation of group interests on the other. The centrality of that debate in the United States and its more recent emergence in the Canadian context warrants special notice here.

From the time that the United States Supreme Court first agreed in the early 1960s to hear cases argued on the doctrine of one person–one vote, American courts have been drawn into the vortex of a constitutional and representational storm involving voter equality, partisan districting, and affirmative gerrymandering. Changes over the last decade to the federal Voting Rights Act and decisions by the Supreme Court have fundamentally altered the geographic configuration of congressional and legislative districts and their social composition. Racial, ethnic, and religious minorities have successfully persuaded American courts to protect their interests without jeopardizing the principle of one person–one vote. As a consequence, redistricting in the United States has become as much an exercise in computerized map-making and sociology as in protection of partisan interests or voter equality. The resulting configurations of congressional districts defy an adequate justification beyond protection of some group interest, as *The New York Times* noted in describing a recently approved seat:

> While [U.S.] districts do have to be contiguous, they do not have to be compact. The new fourth Congressional District in Illinois stretches 15 miles from the near Northwest Side west to the Cook County line, jogs south and then comes back east another 15 miles to join two Hispanic communities, one Puerto Rican and the other Mexican-American.
>
> In this earmuff-shaped district, the frame connecting these neighbourhoods is often only a block wide. The district was drawn that way because the more compact, north-south approach would have cut through a black district. (*NYT* 30 December 1991, A11.)

The American experience of attempting to ensure the majoritarian presence in a constituency of what is otherwise a minority group interest has some relevance for Canada where, as already noted, the legislative representation of minorities is increasingly discussed.

Thus, as the following papers will attest, the task of drawing boundaries–of creating a system of representation–is infinitely complex both in conception and practice. Recent court cases in British Columbia, Saskatchewan, and Alberta have served, it would seem, only to introduce, not to resolve, the kaleidoscopic interests that envelope the issues of representation. Those who begin this volume with a commitment to the honoured precept of "rep by pop" will soon find themselves drawn into what U.S. Supreme Court Justice Felix Frankfurter once called the "political thicket of reapportionment." The path to realizing voter equality quickly grows less clear as routes to alternative destinations (for example, "effective representation") beckon. Eventually, in the words of one commentator, "the focus is subtly shifted from the voter to the representative," with the paradoxical result, according to authors Richards and Irvine, that "an electoral map which scrupulously adheres to the concept of 'one person-one vote' may be unconstitutional."

JOHN C. COURTNEY
PETER MACKINNON
DAVID E. SMITH

~

The conference and this volume of papers have been made possible by grants from the Social Sciences and Humanities Research Council, the University of Saskatchewan College of Law Endowment Fund, and the Hardy donation to the Department of Political Studies, University of Saskatchewan.

DEMOCRATIC PRECEPTS
AND ELECTORAL VALUES

Representation and the Charter:
Should Rights Be Paramount?

JANET HIEBERT
QUEEN'S UNIVERSITY

The debate in the Saskatchewan electoral boundary case *Carter v. Saskatchewan (Attorney General)* about the proper scope of the right to vote in section 3 of the Charter is particularly revealing of the contribution of entrenched rights to a changing Canadian political culture. Although the case was principally involved with competing views of representation, in particular whether electoral boundaries should be based on a strict adherence to the principle of one person–one vote, the case also provided an opportunity for voicing differing views of the proper role of governments and courts in a political system with entrenched rights.

The entrenchment of rights in the Charter has placed a greater emphasis on courts as the forum for airing and resolving disputes about the desirability of legislative policies. By providing standards to assess legislation in the form of articulated, although generally stated, rights, the Charter has fostered a politics of rights where individuals and groups assert claims of entitlement, often framed in terms of freedom from the interfering effects of particular policies.

One of the most significant political implications of the Charter discourse is the increasing prominence of rights-based assessments in how Canadians evaluate and respond to governments and the policies they defend. Canadians have not traditionally feared government or assumed that government represents a general threat to individual liberty. Rather, Canadian political culture has been characterized by the deference accorded political institutions by the people affected by them. For many this trust is changing rapidly, encouraged in no small part by the Charter which invites scrutiny of legislative and executive decisions in terms of how they affect individual rights. The Charter, and the language of rights it has encouraged, has contributed to a growing distrust of discretionary decision making where government decisions have the effect of conflicting with a perceived right.

1

This distrust stems from the view, widely held by those who advance Charter claims, that the Charter has fundamentally altered the Canadian political system. Many believe that, with the Charter, governments have lost their legitimacy and constitutional capacity to make decisions about the priority of competing values, if protected rights are adversely affected in the process. Accordingly, the entrenchment of rights in the Charter means that any discretionary capacity formerly exercised by governments, about whether to pursue policies that conflict with rights, is suspect. Instead, it is believed that all decisions about the validity of policies that encroach upon rights should be made by courts. It is further assumed by some that judicial decisions are superior to political ones, because they involve principled applications of Charter requirements rather than political decisions involving policy considerations which may include self-interested motivations.

In making decisions about whether legislative objectives warrant limiting a protected right, many believe that the Charter provides courts the necessary and sufficient context for evaluating the constitutional worth of impugned legislation. The reference in the limitation clause to a free and democratic society and the actual enumerated rights in the Charter are often assumed to be one and the same. The specified rights in the Charter are the very ones that are necessary for a free and democratic society and, therefore, exhaust the range of values entitled to limit a protected right. The implication of this for policy is that objectives that cannot be easily accommodated within the language of the Charter are deemed to be of insufficient importance to warrant limiting a protected right. This is because these objectives do not involve matters of rights but merely policy objectives and, therefore, are not entitled to restrict a protected right. By assuming that the Charter is exhaustive of the most fundamental values in society and that the requirements of a free and democratic society consist primarily, if not exclusively, of the enumerated rights themselves, this view offers little recognition that the values essential to a free and democratic society may be contested.

In addition to expectations that courts should consider worthy of limiting a protected right only the narrow range of policy considerations that can be deemed as advancing a specified right (and, therefore, consistent with a free and democratic society), courts are expected to exercise strict scrutiny of these objectives to ensure that they have been demonstrably shown to warrant curtailing a protected right. Often the assumption is that limiting a right can be justified only if the impugned policy is absolutely essential to maintain a free and democratic political system. The fact that the protected rights in the Charter are vague and generally stated and require policy-laden judicial decisions about the proper scope and breadth of rights does not lessen the conviction that rights must nevertheless be protected against governments that seek to limit them. This conception of the Charter, and how it affects governments, will be referred to in this paper as the "rights are always paramount" view.

This view is not uncontested. Some, in particular those defending provincial and federal policies against Charter claims, reject the assumption that governments no longer have the constitutional legitimacy to pursue policies in conflict with protected rights. This belief stems from disagreement with one of the principal assumptions underlying the "rights are always paramount" view of the Charter; namely, that judicial decisions are preferable to legislative ones because they are more objective (being based on principled interpretations of articulated rights). Critics of the "rights are always paramount" view emphasize the general nature of the articulated rights and argue that the determination of what circumstances and activities are actually protected by rights engage justices in philosophical and normative inquiries that are anything but objective exercises. Further, the explicit requirement in section 1 of the Charter, that courts determine the constitutional validity of legislative decisions that impose limits on rights, requires courts to engage in policy-laden deliberations similar to those that have already taken place in the legislatures. Many argue, therefore, that rather than assume that all political decisions encroaching upon protected rights are constitutionally suspect, it is possible that the legislative objectives in conflict with protected rights are worthy of limiting a protected right. Determining the priority that should be given to different values may involve assessing competing philosophical assumptions. Where complex and controversial issues are disputed and their resolution is not amenable to principled judicial resolution, courts should exercise caution before invalidating legislation; in short, in these circumstances, political decisions about the merit of impugned policies should prevail over judicial ones.

Both views of the Charter were represented in the questioning of the Saskatchewan practice of drawing electoral boundaries. Both the population variances in constituencies and the process for determining boundaries were constitutionally questioned. The impugned boundaries were provided for in The Representation Act, 1989, which was produced by the Boundaries Commission in compliance with The Electoral Boundaries Commission Act. Under the terms of the legislation, the commission was required to produce an electoral map which contained 2 northern and 64 southern seats, including 29 urban and 35 rural ridings. The commission was required to determine the base population for each riding by dividing the voter population by the mandated number of constituencies. However, it was empowered to deviate from population equality to accommodate the sparsity, density, or relative rate of growth of any proposed constituency; special geographic features including size and means of communication between the various parts of the proposed constituency; the community or diversity of interests of the residents; or other "similar or relevant factors." There were no specified guidelines as to what weight should be attached to these considerations other than that electoral boundaries could not deviate more than 25% from the base population (or 50% in the two northern ridings).

The constitutional challenge of the way electoral boundaries were drawn in Saskatchewan attracted the attention of 14 interveners representing federal,

3

provincial, territorial, and municipal governments as well as individual citizens and civil liberty and anti-poverty groups. The debate among interveners reflected disagreement about the principles of representation that should guide the drawing of boundaries. The views expressed ranged from an absolute interpretation of the right to vote, which accorded no latitude for objectives in conflict with the principle of one person–one vote, to an interpretation that allows significant deviations from that principle to accommodate a number of concerns entirely unrelated to equality in individual voting strength. The debate also revealed conceptually different assessments of what effect the Charter should have on governments in designing policies and courts in interpreting and enforcing the Charter's standards. The significance of these competing views of how the Charter affects both governments and the policies they pursue is that they provide important insights about the contribution of entrenched rights to a changing political culture: specifically, changes in how the legitimacy and scope of governmental power are viewed.

Of the 14 interveners, 5 argued that the legislation was unconstitutional while 9 argued that section 3 was not violated by the Saskatchewan legislation. The division between those opposing and supporting the legislation was almost exclusively on the basis of whether the intervener represented a government.[1] The 9 interveners supporting the legislation represented the federal, BC, Alberta, PEI, Newfoundland, Yukon, and Northwest Territories governments as well as the Alberta Association of Municipal Districts and Counties. The 5 interveners opposing the legislation were the BC Civil Liberties Association, the cities of Edmonton and Grande Prairie, Equal Justice For All, John Conway, and a coalition of four individuals.[2]

Arguments of Those Opposing the Saskatchewan Boundary Practice

The basic claim of those opposing the legislation was that section 3 includes the right to an equal vote, understood as one in which constituency population sizes are roughly equal. There was little philosophical debate about the merits of different understandings of representation. The interpretation of the right to vote was from an individual perspective where interveners assumed, many without argument, that if an individual has a right to vote, he or she also has the right to an equal vote, defined as constituting a vote in constituencies of equal population size. In the words of one intervener, for an individual to be equal in dignity and in rights, one must accept that "as a right, by being a citizen in a free and democratic society, every person's vote, every person's democratic franchise must count the same."[3]

Given the view that the right to vote assumes constituency population sizes will be equal, many interveners understandably objected to the mandated require-ments for a predetermined distribution of rural and urban seats. In their opinion, not only was The Representation Act unconstitutional because it failed to adopt the principle that constituencies reflect equal population size, but the process for determining electoral boundaries was flawed because the government had illegitimately and unconstitutionally exercised political discretion in advancing policy objectives that conflicted with equality in voting strength. Critics of the legislation saw only equal population size as constitutionally relevant. From this perspective the criteria imposed by the legislation were flawed because they mandated the number of urban and rural ridings and legitimized significant deviations from equality of population size. Thus, the commission was prevented from protecting the individual right to equal voting strength.

> To speak of a standard of 25% above or below the average voter population (or, for that matter, 15% or 10%) as being all that section 3 of the Charter requires is to miss the point. If a proposed redistricting scheme contemplates divergences which exceed a certain point (be it 10% or 25%), the scheme is prima facie unconstitutional.[4]

Because the majority of the protected rights are conceived of and stated in individual terms, a "rights are always paramount" conception of the Charter lends itself to a view that emphasizes the individual rather than community. In this case the assumption that the right to an equal vote is an individual right, one paramount to any other objective, dictated that community of interest, geographical considerations, and serviceability be treated as simply policy considerations, not matters of rights, and as a result of lesser importance. Legislative objectives that impose limits on protected rights are assumed not to represent values of the same magnitude as rights explicated in the Charter. They are based not on "principles" but on "political" considerations such as administrative convenience, or bureaucratic or political self-interest. As such, these are not considerations that warrant limiting a protected right.

> The argument of ... the "historical context" of the right to vote must be rejected. It fails to appreciate that any distortions and abuses heaped on the democratic principle as applicable to voting in the past are not part of the right. Those distortions detracted from the right.
> With the advent of the Charter, every citizen's right to vote and to participate on an equal basis with other citizens in the election process has been given paramountcy over the factors ... which have affected the manner in which electoral districts have been set in the past.[5]

The reluctance to recognize competing objectives that conflict with protected rights was further influenced by the view that with the Charter has come a new political order in which the protected rights are paramount to all other claims and objectives. Under this new order, governments no longer have the constitutional capacity to determine the priority of competing values and objectives, where protected rights are infringed in the process.

> The nature of Canada's political system was fundamentally altered by the ... decision ... to give the Courts the right and responsibility to stop any activity of government which infringes the rights and freedoms of the Charter.[6]

Contributing to the characterization of geographical concerns, community of interest, or serviceability as being constitutionally irrelevant were suspicions that what really motivated the enactment of The Representation Act was electoral self-interest. The mildest version of this claim was that the Saskatchewan government should not be viewed as an impartial arbiter of competing social interests because it has a vested interest in the design of electoral boundaries.[7] More explicit allegations of gerrymandering asserted that the reasons for deviating from equality in constituency population were really nothing more than an arrangement "deliberately planned" to perpetuate the ability of the incumbent administration to win elections[8] by intentionally distorting electoral boundaries to elect more members than it could with a fair electoral boundary system.[9] Thus, the reasons advanced by the Saskatchewan government in defending boundary practices were dismissed as "vague" and "intangible," in part because they made it rather easy to confuse "honourable with dishonourable intentions."[10] Given the view that the government was acting out of self-interest rather than according to principled adherence to rights, interveners argued that it is contrary to the new constitutional order imposed by the Charter to allow the Saskatchewan government to make discretionary decisions that would restrict the quality of the vote:

> ... the constitution requires the Legislature to create an independent body with the power to deal with electoral boundaries and the proper balancing of other considerations with the principle of one person–one vote ...
>
> The point of procedural protection ... is to protect the constitutional right against the tendency of the regulatory process to fail to give adequate weight to it ... (T)he "shackling" of the Commission's discretion (by the mandated number of rural and urban ridings and other criteria to consider) was an unconstitutional procedure because it removed the Commission's ability to exercise independent judgment.[11]

While the majority of interveners opposed to the legislation recognized that rights are not absolute and can be subject to limits under section 1,[12] there was little agreement as to the validity of the conception of representation advanced by those defending the Saskatchewan legislation. For example, those critical of the legislation disagreed strongly with the assumption that rural and urban ridings should vary in population size and noted as mitigating factors changing communication technologies and modern forms of rapid transportation.[13] On the question of whether it is constitutionally appropriate for electoral boundary decisions to include factors other than population equality, opinions ranged from a willingness to consider factors under section 1 as long as the reasons for departing from equality are justified and that the deviation is not too large[14] to categorical rejection of the idea that factors other than population equality are constitutionally relevant. The latter position explicitly rejected the Saskatchewan government's claim that reviewing electoral boundaries involves philosophical and political debates about what assumptions should guide the Canadian approach to representation. In the opinion of one intervener, the

6

issue of what philosophical considerations should prevail has been resolved by the entrenchment of a Charter value that places the individual right to vote in constituencies of equal population ahead of all other considerations.

> There are no profound or complex political philosophy questions involved. The issue of voter equality is unanimously and constitutionally settled. We each have the constitutional right to vote. Since we are free and equal citizens by constitutional decree, it requires intellectual manipulation of section 3 of the *Charter* to suggest that the right to vote is not equally guaranteed to everyone of us.[15]

Not only did those opposing the Saskatchewan boundary practice believe that the Charter imposes a new political order, but they assumed this new order would be an improvement over the previous one, because it would force governments to adhere to the highest principle of a liberal democracy—respect for individual rights. By replacing discretionary political decisions with principled judicial interpretations of the Charter, Canadians would be better protected because individual rights would become paramount to political considerations. In advancing this argument, there was virtually no scrutiny of the contrary proposition: that judicial review is anything but an objective process, that is the substantive content of the rights in the Charter is neither self-defining nor uncontested. The process of improving the Canadian political order will largely be accomplished by providing for a "greater role for fully independent (from government) adjudicators" to guard the Charter principles and ensure "accountable democracy from government action contrary to these."[16] Because the Charter involves the principled application of standards, its purpose, in the view of one intervener, is to ensure:

> ... the movement of our society forward from a society, which can and does have governments which enact laws deemed to be unjust, towards a society which is likely to have governments which enact laws consistent with principles of justice, freedom, equality and democratic accountability.[17]

While many interpreted the Charter as producing a new political order, concerns were expressed that the virtues of this order will only be realized if courts strictly scrutinize government action and invalidate any activities that contravene the protected rights in the Charter. To defer to legislative decisions to limit rights would detract from the possibility "of making post-*Charter* Canada a deeper and more vibrant political democracy"[18] and would be a delegation of constitutional responsibility analogous to giving the government "a legislative licence equal to that of a s. 33 override."[19]

Arguments of Those Defending the Saskatchewan Practice

In defending the legislation, the Saskatchewan government argued that the principle of equal voting weight is only one of several criteria that should guide electoral boundary drawing. In arguing that section 3 "does not compel the creation of ridings of mathematically equal size," the government indicated that its overriding concern when determining boundaries is to ensure a system of effective representation which includes consideration of such factors as community of interest, geography, means of communication, and sparsity of population.[20] In rejecting the claim that electoral boundary decisions should be based exclusively or even primarily on equal population size, the Saskatchewan government argued in favour of an alternative approach to representation, one that emphasizes the concept of effective representation.

> (T)he focus on the "weight" of votes reflects a narrow and rather sterile notion of electoral equality. The root concern of those who advocate equal "weight" in voting is equal "representation." But, a meaningful conception of equal representation should involve matters like the quality of access to representatives once they are elected and the extent to which group and community interests find expression in the legislative process. The advocates of equal sized districts overlook that richness and as a result tend to confuse "equal numbers" with "equal representation."[21]

The Saskatchewan government argued that the core content of section 3 is the "straightforward entitlement to cast a ballot" and that the claim that constituencies should be of equal size is derivative of this right and hence not essential to interpreting and defining section 3.[22]

There were three reasons the government and supporting interveners advanced for wanting courts to resist implying new or different rights from those clearly or readily apparent in the text of the Charter. The first was that an interpretation of section 3 that requires constituencies to be of the same population size would place emphasis on a different interpretation of representation at the expense of traditional and strongly held understandings. It would, in short, delegate constituency service, geographical considerations, and other factors affecting the "quality of representation" to the constitutional backburner and give priority to a different understanding of representation.

Second, many interveners who supported the legislation rejected the assumption that section 3 offers only one interpretation—one that is based on equality of constituency population. It was argued, in fact, that not only is the Charter unclear on this question but there is no single or right answer to the question of what considerations should enter into electoral boundary drawing. In the view of those interveners defending the Saskatchewan boundary practice, conceptions of representation and electoral boundary decisions involve fundamental political questions "about how a society views itself, its conception of democracy, and how it defines those interests which warrant representation in a democratic legislative assembly." These questions are inherently political and not judicial.[23] For this reason, courts should not take it upon themselves to decide which of these many considerations should be acted upon:

> It is outside the Court's legitimate role to question the decision to place value on recognizing and preserving communities of interest within a legislative assembly.

This is a peculiarly political question requiring highly subjective philosophical assumptions. On this question the *Charter* provides no guidance.

It is no answer to say that *Charter* guarantees of "the right to vote," "democracy" and "equality" authorize the substitution of judicial preferences on this question ...

Charter guarantees of "democracy" and "equality" imply no preferences for the "numbers only" version of democracy. Indeed, given the *Charter*'s recognition of the pluralistic nature of our society (ss. 15, 23, 27, 29) and the recognition of existing legislative institutions (ss. 31-33), ... the balancing approach taken in Canada sits very comfortably with a document designed to protect minority interests.

... nothing in the *Charter* suggests that the balancing approach inherent in Canadian apportionment is an illegitimate, undemocratic method of apportioning a legislature. Judicial intervention at this level would indeed be to manufacture constitutional rights out of whole cloth.[24]

The third reason interveners argued for judicial caution in "implying" rights for which there is no solid or obvious Charter foundation was the belief that the Charter has not fundamentally changed the basic institutional division of labour, particularly in matters relating to complex and controversial policies. Decisions about which factors should enter into electoral boundary decisions are fundamentally policy decisions involving a multitude of considerations— community of interest, geography, means of communication, sparsity of population, and serviceability. Given the complexity of the issues involved, and the question of accountability for the nature of decisions taken, it is better that these kinds of decisions continue to be made by legislatures rather than courts. If courts involve themselves in a substantial manner in determining whether the electoral boundary system is constitutionally acceptable, they will be drawn into a complex policy process for which they are not particularly well suited:[25]

The obvious advantage of the "one person-one vote" rule and its easily applied mathematical population standard is that it is judicially manageable. However, the danger is that by applying it to the exclusion of the other very complex issues involved, is that the achievement of equally populated constituencies becomes an end in itself. If the real underlying constitutional objective rule is to guarantee "equal representation," then, that objective cannot be achieved by simply ensuring that all constituencies are of equal population size. Yet, if a relatively strict mathematical standard is abandoned in favour of a more flexible one that takes into account these complex issues, the court will inevitably have to face the question of how it can determine, on any principled basis, whether an electoral boundary system comes within acceptable limits of "equal representation" and whether it is the appropriate forum for making that kind of determination. These questions become even more difficult when one takes into account the fact that "equal representation" is a very subjective concept ...

... A central question that this court must, therefore, address in this case is: is it possible for Canadian courts to set appropriate and principled standards for evaluating electoral districting and which take into consideration and address the complexity of the process, which avoid the adoption of an overly simplistic and rigidly applied rule such as "one person-one vote."? If it can not—if the issues raised are not capable of principled resolution because there are no correct answers to the questions that must be addressed—then electoral districting should be left to the legislatures.[26]

Related to calls for judicial deference was the suggestion that courts should recognize broad latitude for legislatures to determine the considerations that should be acted upon when drawing electoral boundaries.[27] Courts should involve themselves in the issue of electoral boundary drawing, interveners suggested, only when it is clear that electoral distributions are substantially out of step with generally accepted Canadian standards[28] or when there is reason to believe that the boundaries were not drawn on the basis of "good faith."[29]

Assessing the Respective Claims

The divergent opinions on the relationship between section 3 and electoral boundary decisions offer evidence of the effects entrenchment is having on how Canadians evaluate government decisions to promote values that conflict with protected rights. Claims of entitlement grounded in the view that rights are paramount to all other considerations foster attitudes that legislative objectives or policies that conflict with rights are constitutionally suspect. The language of rights encourages the positing of Charter claims in terms of inviolable and non-negotiable principles that supersede alternative "policy" considerations.

This assumption that rights-based claims immediately and unquestionably vault to the head of the line ahead of alternative policy objectives (often interpreted by rights claimants as little more than utilitarian, politically expedient, or institutional self-interest considerations) has significant implications for how governmental power is conceptualized. To those subscribing to this or some similar reading of the Charter's impact on government, it is no longer valid for governments to take it upon themselves to determine the priority of competing values where a protected right is infringed in the process. There simply can be no going back to an earlier political order where legislatures and governments exercised exclusive discretion when determining the issues, interests, values, and rights considerations that should shape policy. It is no longer acceptable, according to this view, for governments to establish alternative values as primary over protected rights. With the Charter we have resolved all questions about the importance and priority that must be attached to rights. While conflicts between competing rights are inevitable and will have to be resolved, the fact of entrenchment has settled all questions about whether other considerations, in this case community of interest, geographical considerations, and serviceability, should be given priority over protected rights. As the intervener Equal Justice For All viewed the issue, there are no profound or complex political or philosophical questions involved when drawing electoral boundaries. The Charter has resolved these disputes about the relative importance of competing values and objectives in favour of the rights provided for in the Charter.[30]

At the same time that the "rights are always paramount" interpretation of the Charter undermines confidence in the discretionary judgment of governments, it heightens the likelihood of divisive political debate. No longer is the question one of which of two or more competing interests or values is the most important or which best achieves the general welfare, the public good or some similar criterion. Instead the debate is shaped by allegations, directed at those who would resist claimants' views of entitlement, of wanting to subvert the fundamental and core values of society. As John Conway argued, if courts do not prevent governments from encroaching upon protected rights "a door will be at least partly closed on the possibility of making post-*Charter* Canada a deeper and more vibrant political democracy."[31] In rejecting the legitimacy of alternative policies, because they do not have the same status as rights and, therefore, do not warrant constitutional protection, the language or terms of the debate are altered to the extent that compromises are more difficult to achieve. How can society, after all, compromise fundamental constitutional principles?

The strength of the conviction that rights are placed ahead of all other policy considerations is not altered by arguments urging judicial deference to complex policy decisions. Nor is it seriously affected by claims that because the rights in the Charter are not necessarily self-evident or self-defining, courts should be cautious before providing them with meanings that would frustrate the promotion and protection of strongly held values. To concede the point would be to undermine the argument that the defence of rights is about principles, not policies.

The importance of giving priority to rights over policy considerations encourages arguments that the sanctity and protection of rights require stringent empirical demonstration of government objectives under section 1, the reasonable limits clause.[32] Since principles should not be compromised by policies, nothing short of evidence, or "proof," that a government objective actually facilitates a free and democratic society or promotes the very rights specified in the Charter, can be entertained as worthy of limiting rights. Here the assumption that rights are self-defining and that their meaning can be objectively determined holds equally true for determining the requirements of a free and democratic society.

This view is not uncontested. There is a different reading of how the Charter affects governmental decision making. But because those who offer this conception of the Charter are often associated with the very governments defending impugned policies, this view may be dismissed as one of self-interest. While there is inevitably a measure of self-interest in attempts to prevent the diminution of government's discretionary capacities to frame policies, it is overly cynical to equate this alternative conception exclusively with political self-interest. The fundamental difference between this interpretation of the political significance of the Charter and the "rights are always paramount" approach is the rejection of the idea that the protected rights in the Charter must be assumed at all times and under all circumstances to

11

be paramount to alternative values or policy considerations.

This rejection is due to disagreement with the premise that the Charter is exhaustive of all values deserving constitutional protection. Underlying this view is the assumption that the rights in the Charter can neither be assumed to be absolute nor presumed to comprise a higher priority than all other values and policy objectives. Unlike the "rights are always paramount" approach which suggests that with the Charter has come the resolution of philosophical and normative questions about the relative importance of different values, proponents of this second understanding of the Charter suggest that the debate about these issues is still very much alive and should take place as much as possible in the political and legislative rather than judicial branches of government.

According to this view, since the rights in the Charter are neither absolute nor self-defining, it remains the responsibility of society, through its elected officials, to determine on a regular and continuing basis the values and objectives that should be given priority at any particular time. While courts serve an important purpose in defining rights and in making decisions about the constitutional worthiness of legislative decisions to impose limits on rights, courts should be prepared to defer to legislative decisions where issues are complex and involve conflicting interpretations of what is best for society, particularly where the language of the Charter does not provide sufficient judicial guidance to resolve these disputes; in short, where these debates are not amenable to judicial resolution on the basis of defined and accepted legal principles. This assumption informed the arguments of the Saskatchewan government and supporting interveners that the issue of drawing electoral boundaries involves the reconciliation of competing and complex policy choices to which there are no obvious or right answers. As a result, it is appropriate that the Court display judicial deference to the process contained in The Representation Act. To do otherwise would not only fundamentally alter the nature of representation, by emphasizing one particular interpretation of representation at the expense of an alternative understanding which accommodates geographical communities or serviceability requirements, but would also engage courts in an exercise that is not amenable to resolution via traditional judicial principles. It would amount to little more than substituting one opinion for another.

While it has been argued here that these two competing views offer conceptually different understandings of what the Charter means for the political process, there is one other factor which contributed to the lack of common ground between these two views. That is the failure of those resisting a "rights are always paramount" interpretation of the Charter to face, honestly and sincerely, the constitutional responsibilities imposed by entrenchment. While it is a contentious claim to view the Charter as representing an entirely new constitutional order (many, including the author, resist the proposition that the Charter is either exhaustive of all fundamental values or that governments no longer have any discretionary capacities to determine the priority of competing values), the fact remains that the Charter has imposed a requirement that governments respect and accommodate the protected rights in the Charter and be prepared to justify the reasons for wanting to impose limits on the protected rights.

The Saskatchewan government can be criticized for not taking this constitutional responsibility as seriously as it should have. This shortcoming was particularly apparent in the reasons advanced for arguing that the legislation did not impose a limit on section 3. Neither the Saskatchewan government nor the nine interveners supporting the legislation were prepared to recognize that section 3 includes the principle that constituencies be of roughly equal population size. Section 3 was interpreted, by those defending the legislation, as being principally concerned with the right to vote—not with considerations that affect the quality of the vote.

The argument that section 3 does not include the right to vote in constituencies of equal population can be criticized from two perspectives: it invites a technical and formal approach to defining section 3 and it is inconsistent. The Saskatchewan government argued that although the Charter "does have some application in respect of the relative size of constituencies," this feature is "entirely derivative" of the right to vote.[33] As a result, claimants pressing for constituencies of equal population size are not entitled to protection which should be restricted to the "core content" of section 3—"the straightforward entitlement to cast a ballot." This reasoning is not only formalistic and inconsistent with the general understanding that protected rights be interpreted in a broad purposive manner, it is also intellectually confusing. For example, while the Saskatchewan government acknowledged that voter population is an important factor to be considered in boundary decisions, indeed "equality in population levels is the prime consideration in setting electoral boundaries,"[34] it nevertheless argued that deviations from this idea do not constitute a restriction on section 3. Neither the Saskatchewan government nor supporting interveners offered sound reasons for why boundary decisions should deviate so significantly from this principle. Either constituency size is an important factor in the right to vote, and therefore must be considered in boundary drawing, or it is not. If it is an important factor, which all parties to the dispute more or less seemed to agree, then it should be included in determining the scope of the section 3 right to vote. Yet the Saskatchewan government and other supporting interveners flatly refused to acknowledge that section 3 had been limited.

It is unclear why the Saskatchewan government or supporting interveners were so reluctant to admit that section 3 had in fact been limited by the Saskatchewan boundary practice. Recognizing the full scope of a section 3 entitlement would not necessarily prejudice arguments for wanting to resist a mathematical approach to representation. It would, however, mean a more intellectually honest approach to interpreting the Charter and at the same time acknowledging that limits on this right must be evaluated under section 1 in the context of arguments about why the government wishes to promote alternative values and objectives.

When arguing in favour of a different approach to representation, one which accommodates factors other than population equality (such as community of interest, serviceability, geography, and the like), it is incumbent on the government to show why these factors warrant imposing a limit on the right to vote in a constituency of equal size. This is particularly true given allegations and concerns of gerrymandering. It is not enough to posit that the issue is of a "political" nature and that judicial deference should be accorded to whatever government decision is taken. The problem with the argument that the boundary decisions are not amenable to principled resolution and that courts should, therefore, exercise deference to legislative decisions, was the existence of legislative criteria that did not have any clear or apparent connection to the reasons for deviating from voter equality. While the Electoral Boundaries Commission Act empowered the commission to deviate from voter equality by as much as 25% in southern and 50% in northern ridings to accommodate a number of considerations, these criteria were not specifically related to the mandated distribution of urban and rural seats. In light of the serious allegations of gerrymandering, it was incumbent on the government to demonstrate why community of interest, geography, serviceability, and related factors warranted not only substantial deviations in population base but also why they required a mandated distribution of urban and rural seats.

Instead of providing arguments to demonstrate the linkage between the alternative representation concerns and the extent of the deviation from population equality and mandated distribution of rural and urban seats, the only justification advanced was that the deviations in Saskatchewan did not differ from general Canadian standards.[35] Thus, the defence was largely based on practices of the past with virtually no attempt to argue that the deviations were necessary for a particular vision of representation or that less restrictive means than these significant deviations could have accomplished the legislative objective.

The Saskatchewan government may have had good reasons for arguing that it would be difficult for the Court to determine the merits of the exact balance struck between the competing objectives of voter equality and effective representation, given the complexity of the issues involved and the inherent arbitrariness of determining the exact balance struck. Nevertheless, it was simply too stark a claim to assert that courts have no legitimacy in reviewing elements of the legislative framework. It is unreasonable to expect judicial deference to legislative decisions in the absence of some demonstration that serious legislative deliberations have taken place about the respective importance of the competing values at stake; that sincere efforts have been undertaken to ensure that the affected right has been treated as generously as practically possible; and that the exercise was conducted in good faith. These conditions were not met and, as a result, it was unreasonable to demand extreme judicial deference to claims that the legislation and its mandated criteria represented the best way of reconciling Charter requirements with the broader societal concerns the legislation claimed to promote.

Conclusions

The entrenchment of rights in the Charter has had a significant effect on how Canadians conceptualize the proper role of government and courts. This paper has shown two different views of how the Charter affects the discretionary capabilities of governments to pursue policies and objectives that conflict with and limit the protected rights in the Charter. There is little common ground between these two views, because they have very different assumptions about the values that are worthy of limiting protected rights or the role of courts and governments in protecting and promoting these competing values.

In this case the Saskatchewan government further widened this gulf by failing to address honestly and sincerely the requirements of the Charter. This was unfortunate for at least two reasons. Despite the assumption of some that the Charter is exhaustive of all fundamental values in society, there is no inherent reason to presume that government will abstain from pursuing a policy objective that limits a protected right—in this case an approach to representation that may impose limits on an aspect of section 3. Section 1, both as conceived and interpreted by the Supreme Court, accommodates values or objectives governments deemed to be important enough to warrant limiting a protected right. The Court often requires, however, that the government provide an indication that it has been sensitive to the protected right at stake and has tried to accommodate it as much as reasonably possible. While this requires more sensitive and careful tailoring or drafting of legislative objectives, it does not prevent governments from pursuing values that are not easily accommodated in the language of the Charter.

Had the Saskatchewan government undertaken a more sincere attempt to abide by the Charter requirements, this may not necessarily have narrowed the conceptual gulf between the two rival views of representation or conceptions of the Charter, as expressed in this case. It is highly likely that there would still have been debate and controversy surrounding government claims about the priority attached to particular values. But there is no reason for fearing and every reason for embracing a debate about the priority a society wishes to attach to competing values and objectives. This debate, however, is not easily fostered where governments engage in technical and manipulative interpretations of rights as a way of avoiding or minimizing the responsibility of openly and honestly evaluating the relative importance of the competing claims.

Notes

1. With the exception of the cities of Edmonton and Grande Prairie, no government opposed the legislation.
2. The coalition included Douglas Billingsley, Wilson McBryan, Leonard Jason, and Daniel Wilde.
3. Factum of Equal Justice For All, 6-7.
4. Factum of the BC Civil Liberties Association, 7.

5. Ibid., 11.
6. Factum of Equal Justice For All, 22.
7. Factum of the Cities of Edmonton and Grande Prairie, 20.
8. Factum of the Respondent Roger Carter, 21-22.
9. Factum of John Conway, see in particular, 7-16.
10. Ibid., 12.
11. Factum of the Respondent Roger Carter, 19-20.
12. One exception was John Conway who argued that the right to vote in constituencies of equal population size should be interpreted as an absolute right. Factum of John Conway, 23.
13. Ibid., 22.
14. Factum of the Cities of Edmonton and Grande Prairie, 18-19.
15. Factum of Equal Justice For All, 9.
16. Ibid., 19.
17. Ibid., 18-19.
18. Factum of John Conway, 5.
19. Factum of Equal Justice For All, 11.
20. Factum of the Appellant, Attorney General for Saskatchewan, 8.
21. Ibid., 12.
22. Ibid., 10.
23. Factum of the Attorney General of BC, 16.
24. Ibid., 14-15.
25. On this point, Saskatchewan counsel reminded the Court of the words of one of its former members, Justice William McIntyre:

    . . . None of these issues (in this case, relating to the right to strike) is amenable to principled resolution. There are no clearly correct answers to these questions. They are of a nature peculiarly apposite to the functions of the legislature . . . It has been said that the courts, because of the Charter, will have to enter the legislative sphere. Where rights are specifically guaranteed in the Charter, this may on occasion be true. But where no specific right is found in the Charter and the only support for its constitutional guarantee is an implication, the courts should refrain from intrusion into the field of legislation. That is the function of the freely elected legislatures and Parliament.

    Cited in Factum of Attorney General of Saskatchewan, 16-17, from *Reference Re Public Service Employee Relations Act* (1987), 1 S.C.R. 313 at 420.
26. Factum of the Attorney General of PEI, 16-17.
27. Factum of the Attorney General of Saskatchewan, 38-39.
28. Ibid.
29. Factum of the Attorney General of BC, 16.
30. Factum of Equal Justice For All, 9.
31. Factum of John Conway, 5.
32. Equal Justice For All, for example, argued that because section 3 is a core right, one which is not subject to the legislative override of section 33, it requires a higher degree of judicial protection than other rights in the Charter. The government must produce "sound evidence, not argument" to support limiting s. 3, pp. 13, 16-17.
33. Factum of the Government of Saskatchewan, 10.
34. Ibid., 8.
35. Ibid., 39.

Federalism, Representation, and Rights

KATHERINE SWINTON
UNIVERSITY OF TORONTO

For Canada's first 115 years, there were two pillars to the constitution: parliamentary democracy and federalism. The constitutional amendments of 1982 added a third: citizens' rights. This imagery of pillars suggests that the elements of the constitution are distinct and separate from one another. Clearly, in Canada, this is not the case, for each influences the others in numerous ways. Our system of parliamentary democracy has long been shaped by the federal nature of the country, whether in the allocation of seats in the House of Commons, the makeup of the Cabinet, or the institution of executive federalism. More recently, the interaction between those two systems has been filtered through the language of citizens' rights. Thus, the image we might better use to describe the major elements of the constitution is not freestanding pillars, but the "living tree" invoked by the Privy Council in *Edwards,* with several branches intertwining with each other, sometimes in a supportive manner, but at others, in a more stressful fashion.[1]

This paper explores some of those interactions through a discussion of representation and the drawing of electoral boundaries in our national institutions of government. Federalism, in the guise of a concern about adequate provincial representation at the national level, has long influenced the allocation of seats in the House of Commons. This solicitude for provinces and regional voices is now challenged by claims rooted in the Canadian Charter of Rights and Freedoms for a system of electoral representation more sensitive to equality for individuals: a claim that leads in more than one direction, to encompass, on the one hand, demands for representation more closely tied to population (equality among voters) and, on the other, for representation on the basis of characteristics other than geography. Charter-based claims may, in the future, influence the drawing of electoral boundaries within constituencies as we have known them. More significantly, the Charter, and the consciousness

17

that it nurtures, will generate claims for representation from groups not necessarily based within the same geographical area, as illustrated by the current discussion of seats for aboriginal peoples in the House of Commons.

Parliamentary Democracy

The first pillar of the constitution, parliamentary democracy, has the deepest footings, for the country formed in 1867 was already familiar with its principles, most importantly representative and responsible government (although those entitled to choose representatives encompassed a much narrower group than the electorate of today).

The hallmark of democracy is the ability of individuals to participate in the institutions that govern them. While direct participation may be possible in small associations, considerations of time, expertise, and efficacy require that participation in government occur through the selection of "representatives." Immediately, we are faced with difficult questions about the meaning of representation, making the design of that selection process a delicate and complex task. A.H. Birch has discussed three meanings of representation: the person who acts as an agent for a principal carrying out a certain mandate, the person who is elected with some general obligation to advance the interests of his or her electors, and the person who bears the characteristics of a group so as to be reflective of them.[2] Leaving aside the first type of representation—since our elected members have not traditionally been seen as delegates[3]—let us focus on the second and third, which Jennifer Smith has described as a "procedural" concept of representation, as distinguished from "mirror" representation.[4]

In Canada, we have emphasized the procedural concept, choosing elected representatives at the national and provincial levels on the basis of territorial constituencies. In theory, those members have a twofold responsibility. First, they are expected to "represent" those who elected them, although, as Birch has noted, they are not expected to be, and cannot be, delegates of their constituents. Obviously, the demands of constituents will often conflict, making trade-offs necessary. Thus, the member must personally make a determination as to the appropriate position to take in light of a multiplicity of considerations, including short- and longer-term policy needs and, more realistically in Canada, the strictures of party discipline. Nevertheless, despite these other considerations, members are expected to voice their constituents' perspectives and to reflect their needs in the policy process—a necessary role if the representative wishes to be re-elected.[5]

The second function of the elected member is to act as an ombuds, assisting the constituent who has problems with the government apparatus.[6] This is an important role which provides a strong underpinning to the current geographical constituency and militates against other electoral systems, such as proportional representation, which may require multiple representatives for much larger geographical areas.

Drawing the boundaries for constituencies might seem a relatively mechanical exercise, especially if there was a significant degree of homogeneity among voters. The aim would be formal equality, or "representation by population," with the objective to accord one person's vote an equal chance with that of another to influence the selection of a representative.[7] However, the task can never be mechanical, for the objective of formal equality must be tempered by concerns for effective representation—more specifically, by the desire to facilitate the two members' functions described above.[8]

Thus, even though we embrace a procedural concept of representation, concerns for mirror representation can influence the boundary-drawing process. There is great diversity in our society, and individuals have multiple identities—with an ethnic or religious group, with those of a similar income level, with their gender, as well as with those who live in a particular region or who share a common party allegiance. The quality of representation and the legitimacy of a decision-making body can be enhanced if boundaries are drawn so as to group those who share certain characteristics, giving them either a majority position or a significant minority position in a constituency, and thus a better chance to influence the selection of representatives. As a result, the boundary drawing becomes a complex exercise of deciding on the appropriate characteristics to cluster together. Clearly, different communities will seek to create constituencies that maximize their ability to elect a representative who shares the characteristic of greatest importance to them.[9]

This exercise is further complicated by other concerns about effective representation, including the fulfilment of the member's ombuds role. Traditionally, it has been assumed that sparsely populated rural and northern ridings are harder to serve than populous urban ridings close to the capital.[10] Travel around the constituency is often onerous, making it more difficult to communicate with the constituents, thus detracting from both the representative and ombuds roles. The member also has a role as representative of his party, especially the government party, to try to explain and defend policy decisions, and that, too, becomes more difficult. As a result, concerns about effective representation may require some adjustment to the size of the constituency to allow other objectives to be met.[11]

Canadian acceptance that the goal of "rep by pop" should be tempered by considerations of effective representation is indicated by, for instance, the provisions of Canada's Electoral Boundaries Readjustment Act, with its explicit permission for electoral boundary commissions, when drawing boundaries, to consider the need for a manageable geographic size for districts in sparsely populated rural or northern regions, as well as any special community of interest or identity among the inhabitants of a region. There is an outside limit, though, for the goal is to have the population of each constituency correspond as close as is "reasonably possible" to the provincial electoral quota. Variations are permitted within a 25% range above and below the quota, except in cases that the commission believes are "extraordinary."[12]

In sum, the appropriate "populations" to group in a constituency will be a subject for debate in any system of government with territorial representation. In Canada, the federal system adds further complications to the drawing of electoral boundaries for seats in the House of Commons.

Federalism and Representation

The constitution created in 1867 added federalism to the constitutional pillar of parliamentary democracy. Federalism is a system of government concerned about communities, although some might argue that its vision is too limited, because the only relevant communities seem to be the regions recognized as units of government.

Federalism is designed to handle pressures for both unity and diversity or, in the words of Daniel Elazar, it is a system with elements of shared and self rule.[13] By providing for both national and regional levels of government, federalism allows communities that have a territorial base to determine their own policies in certain areas—ideally, those important to the preservation and protection of the community or those in which there is some difference in preferences across regions.[14] At the same time, these communities can join with members of other communities in a national government to address matters that seem to require a unified approach.

In the design or reform of any federal system, the challenge is to respond to the claims for both unity and diversity. One obvious technique is through the distribution of legislative powers between federal and provincial governments. While the ideal might be "watertight compartments," the goal is impossible in a modern nation state with two levels of activist government. Inevitably, there is interdependence and overlapping jurisdiction between governments that requires institutional and financial arrangements in order to generate effective public policy. More important for purposes of this article is the fact that policy making at the national level is often vulnerable to attack from voters in regions who do not feel that the output is sufficiently responsive to their needs and aspirations. Majority rule, in a country where the populations of regions are significantly different, undermines the salience of the views of the less populated regions.[15]

Institutional responses to these tensions—managing interdependence and giving adequate voice to regions at the national level—can take a number of forms. One possibility is "interstate federalism"—that is, devising mechanisms for handling relationships between the federal and provincial governments. In Canada, this has been the role of executive federalism.[16] A second possibility is "intrastate federalism"—that is, design of national government institutions so as to amplify the voices of regions within the central government. Classically, this has been through the upper house, which has been structured either to represent the regional governments or the citizens of the regions through elected representatives.[17]

It has often been said that federalism, the second pillar of Canadian constitutionalism, is in tension with parliamentary government.[18] While the latter emphasizes the equality of individuals as a principle of representation—encapsulated in the phrase "rep by pop"—federalism is preoccupied with the representation of regions. When the populations of those regions contrast significantly in magnitude, as in Canada, there is a problem in determining the appropriate weight to give to regions, as opposed to majority rule in national institutions. Obviously, this is fodder for heated debate, especially in the design of the upper house—an issue to which I shall return shortly, after a discussion of the tension between federalism and parliamentary democracy that emerges in the allocation of seats in the House of Commons.[19]

In drawing electoral boundaries for that House, it is not surprising that seats are allocated to provinces in recognition of the degree to which Canadians identify with their provinces. The more difficult question is the appropriate share of seats for each province—more specifically, the degree to which the allocation should deviate from the ideal of representation by population. History shows that departures from the principle of representation of provinces in the House of Commons according to their population are not new in Canada. The original formula for the redistribution of seats, found in section 51 of the British North America Act, 1867, protected provinces with declining populations, ensuring that their allocation of seats would not be reduced in the decennial redistribution following a new census, unless their proportion of the national population had declined by 5% or more since the preceding census.[20]

A further safeguard for provinces with declining populations came with the addition of section 51A to the British North America Act, 1867, (now the Constitution Act, 1867) in 1915.[21] This section enshrined the "Senate Floor Rule," ensuring that no province can be allocated fewer members in the House of Commons than its allocation of Senate seats (as determined by section 22). Its main beneficiaries were meant to be, and have been, the Maritimes.

The concern for provinces with declining populations emerged again in a 1952 amendment to section 51, which guaranteed that a province would lose no more than 15% of the members to which it was entitled at the last redistribution, and it would not have fewer members than a province with a smaller population.[22] Section 51 was further amended in 1974 to add a complicated formula known as the "Amalgam Method" to govern the readjustment of seats between the provinces. Again, one goal was to protect provinces with declining populations, by employing a series of rules revolving around a set number of seats for Québec that differed for small (Newfoundland, Nova Scotia, New Brunswick, Prince Edward Island, Manitoba, and Saskatchewan), intermediate (Alberta), and large provinces (Ontario and British Columbia).[23]

Finally, the current formula, enacted by the 1985 Representation Act, established yet another method for distributing seats among the provinces at the time of the decennial redistribution.[24] The Amalgam Method was deemed unsatisfactory because it would inexorably lead to a dramatic growth in the size of the House of Commons. In contrast, the 1985 amendment started with a fixed number of House seats and then provided certain "add ons." Pursuant to its rules, a national electoral quotient is obtained by dividing the total population by 279. Each province's population is then divided by this quotient to give a number of members. The second principle is key: no province will have fewer members than it had at the time of the previous redistribution (that is, after the 1976 redistribution).[25]

This formula, coupled with the Senate Floor Rule in section 51A of the Constitution Act, 1867, results in a significant degree of overrepresentation for some provinces and underrepresentation of others. The impact of the Senate Floor Rule is most clearly demonstrated by the benefit conferred on Prince Edward Island. That province, with a population of approximately 122,500 at the time of the 1981 census, maintains 4 seats in the House to match its 4 Senate seats. Absent the rule, it would have had, at most, 2 seats.[26] New Brunswick also gains 2 seats from the Senate Floor Rule, which ensures that it will continue to have 10 seats regardless of the number of residents lost.

The Senate Floor Rule need not have a distorting effect on interprovincial equity among voters—provided that the size of the House of Commons is not capped, and provinces with increasing populations are allocated more members in proportion to population growth.[27] However, once a decision is made to fix the size of the House, or at least to restrict the pace with which it will expand, the Senate Floor Rule begins to create problems, for the goal of interprovincial equity among voters is impeded by its operation. As described by Courtney, there has been strong resistance to expanding the size of the House of Commons significantly due to concerns about the impact on time for debate, space in the House, and added cost.[28] The result is serious inequities in the size of constituencies across provinces, best illustrated by a comparison between those in Prince Edward Island and many large urban areas, especially in Ontario and British Columbia.[29]

These problems of interprovincial voter inequity are compounded by the terms of the 1985 Representation Act. The "grandfather clause" described earlier now protects 4 provinces whose populations are declining. Indeed, 6 of the 10 provinces are protected by the grandfather and senatorial floor rules, giving them 12 seats more than those to which they would be entitled on the basis of population. It has been projected that this will increase to 7 provinces and 17 seats after the 1991 census.[30] The only provinces to be governed by the principle of representation by population will be Ontario, Alberta, and British Columbia.

The presence of electoral boundaries commissions at the national level since 1964 prevents politicians from manipulating the allocation of seats within provinces, yet the control over section 51 of the Constitution Act, 1867, still allows members of Parliament to affect the distribution of seats between provinces.[31] The repeal of the Amalgam Method and the substitution of the grandfather clause in conjunction with a relatively fixed number of seats in the House indicates that parliamentarians have been sympathetic to claims from sitting members to protect their provinces' existing level of representation. The result, though, has been greater variation in the electoral quotas of the different provinces simultaneously with an increasing convergence in the electoral quotas for constituencies *within* provinces.[32]

Is there a defensible rationale for this departure from the principle of representation of provinces according to population, or is the system explained largely by the tendency of politicians to protect their own power bases?[33] Most importantly, are there arguments based on a concept of effective representation to support this outcome? The usual claim for departures from equality within provinces comes from residents of northern and rural areas who argue that the difficulties of representation in sparsely populated and isolated areas require some control on the size of the constituency. Clearly, that argument cannot be made to protect provinces with declining populations, yet their claims do rest on concerns about the quality of representation—more specifically, the belief that an effective voice in national parliamentary institutions requires a minimum number of members in order to protect the province's interests adequately in a variety of settings, including the Cabinet, legislative debates, committee proceedings, and party caucuses.[34]

No one would deny the importance of regional voices at the national level in Canada. It is the degree of amplification given to particular provincial voices that is open to debate. Why four seats for Prince Edward Island, when the province's population is not much larger than that of some of the urban constituencies in other provinces?[35] Why should this inequity be compounded by the grandfather clause, which benefits a number of provinces but leaves Ontario, Alberta, and British Columbia chronically underrepresented? Why should province of residence privilege certain voters over those in other provinces?

The explanation lies, in part, in the role played by the Senate in the Canadian parliamentary system. While that House was designed, at least in part, to represent the regions, it has never been an effective element of intrastate federalism.[36] The explanation lies in federal appointment of senators. As a result, they lack legitimacy: they are not effective regional spokespersons, since the basis for the appointment has traditionally been political patronage; and they lack the legitimacy to act as independent decision makers, capable of blocking policy initiatives from the elected House, since they are appointed. Therefore, other institutions have adapted to bring regional considerations more effectively into federal government decision making.

Provincial governments have taken on the major role as regional representatives,[37] although within the national government, other institutions have also adapted to take account of Canada's federal nature. Most important are the House of Commons, the party caucus, and the Cabinet, although they have not always been perceived as effective instruments of regional representation. Still, they provide avenues for expressing regional considerations in national policy making.[38] Therefore, the argument can be made from provinces with declining populations that they need a critical mass of elected members in the House to express the province's concerns in each of these institutions.

As we approach the 21st century, there are likely to be challenges to an electoral system at the national level that favours smaller provinces at the expense of those growing in population. In part, demands for change will be spawned by the debate about the design of other federal institutions, most obviously the pressure for an elected Senate. One *quid pro quo* might well be more equal representation in the House of Commons.

Another pressure for reform comes from Canada's changing demography. The diverse groups that make up the population of many urban centres, especially in British Columbia and Ontario, will demand more equal representation across provinces. More importantly, we will see increasing claims for participation from groups not well "represented" today in the House of Commons, who may challenge not only the distribution of seats among provinces, but the concept of representation on the basis of territory as well. Drawing boundaries for individual-member constituencies is, for some, a problem of the past that does not reflect current conceptions of "representation."

Senate Reform and Electoral Representation

Dissatisfaction with the Senate ranges from those who see no need for an upper house and would cheerfully see it abolished to those who want significant reform. For virtually no one is the status quo of federal appointment acceptable; rather, the goal is to improve regional input into national decision making through the upper house. The debate then centres on whether to adopt "provincialist" or "centralist" models of interstate federalism: the choice is between an upper house selected by provincial governments and one elected by the voters in the province.[39]

Some earlier efforts at constitutional reform in Canada recommended a "House of the Provinces" model, with the upper chamber constituted of individuals selected by provincial governments.[40] However, in an age of voter dissatisfaction with governments and calls for citizen empowerment,[41] that model has been superseded by demands for an elected Senate, most vociferously made by Western Canadian supporters of the "Triple E" model (equal, effective, and elected). Its advocates argue that a popularly elected Senate would be able to provide a much stronger regional voice in Parliament, able to counteract the power of Ontario and Québec derived from their larger share of seats in the House of Commons. As well, it might strengthen citizen ties to the national government, both by reducing the role of provincial governments as the predominant voice of the regions and by increasing the legitimacy of federal government policies that have gained the support of a regionally weighted institution.[42]

The federal government's proposals for constitutional renewal issued in September 1991 are responsive to these demands for better regional representation through elected senators.[43] An elected Senate is recommended, although its ultimate shape is very difficult to determine, since the proposals do not set out a detailed plan on key issues. There is no formula for representation of the provinces (only the suggestion that it be "equitable" rather than equal).[44] This leaves much room for debate about the distribution of seats among the provinces, as well as the powers of the Senate. While the province of Alberta, the major proponent of the Triple E model, insists on provincial equality, the reality is that Ontario and Québec cannot agree to be represented by the same number of seats as Prince Edward Island and New Brunswick, especially if senators are to have strong powers equivalent to, or even slightly less effective than, the present Senate.[45] If the larger provinces are to agree to greater weight for the smaller provinces in the Senate than population would indicate, there are trade-offs to be made—most obviously with regard to Senate powers, but also with regard to a more equitably designed House of Commons. If federalism is to shape the upper house, then the lower house should more accurately reflect the values of majority rule and representation by population.[46]

The problem with this proposition lies, of course, in legal and political realities. The amendment formula necessary to remove the inequities caused by the Senate Floor Rule, found in section 41(b) of the Constitution Act, 1982, requires the unanimous consent of the federal Parliament and the 10 provincial legislatures. The federal government, well aware of the problems of unanimity following the failure of the Meech Lake Accord, has shied away from any unanimity items.[47] And well it might, for it is difficult to see why Prince Edward Island or New Brunswick would agree to such a change. The implication for Senate reform, then, will be increased pressure on the "effective" and "equal" components. "Equity" has already replaced "equality" in much of the parlance, as can only be expected in a country with such a large population difference between the provincial units, coupled with the small number of units.[48]

But while the Senate Floor Rule seems unchangeable, that need not be the case with other rules for the distribution of seats that contribute to interprovincial inequity, where other rules of amendment apply and where the Charter of Rights can have both a legal and moral impact.

Rules of Representation and Rights

The 1982 amendments to the constitution added a third pillar to the constitution, the Charter of Rights, which gave citizens a legal guarantee of certain rights against governments. Although the Charter has had a profound effect on the way citizens think about the constitution and their relationship with governments, it is wrong to see its guarantees in sharp contrast with the other elements of Canadian constitutionalism.[49] Our commitment to parliamentary democracy rooted in the Westminster model influences the interpretation of such rights as freedom of expression (especially the value placed on political speech[50]), just as the rights set out in the Charter will inevitably have an impact on the way in which our parliamentary democracy functions in the future, whether in direct limits on legal rules such as parliamentary privilege or indirectly, as a basis for argument about the values that should shape the way in which we are governed.[51] Thus, many of the arguments that individuals and groups make about the proper distribution of electoral seats and representation are no different than they were pre-Charter. In both periods, we worry about equality among voters, as well as the need to represent various communities fairly. The contribution of entrenchment is the new force behind these arguments, because they can now be made before the courts. This gives them not only important legal force through the litigation process, but also significant clout in lobbying.

The two key provisions of the Charter likely to affect decisions and consciousness about the drawing of electoral boundaries are section 3, the right to vote, and section 15, the guarantee of equality. Before discussing their interpretation, there is a prior issue of their applicability to decisions about electoral boundaries. Most specifically, can the Charter be used to challenge rules for allocating seats when they are part of the Constitution Act, 1982? The answer depends on the kinds of provisions one would like to challenge (although some have argued that anything found in the Constitution Acts is invulnerable).[52]

This last argument relies on the decision of the Supreme Court of Canada in *Reference re Bill 30*, where the argument was made that provincial funding for Roman Catholic separate schools, pursuant to Ontario's power to legislate with regard to education under section 93 of the Constitution Act, 1867, required similar treatment for other denominational schools because of section 15 of the Charter. In rejecting that argument, Wilson J. for the majority stated that the Charter could not be used to invalidate other provisions of the constitution.[53]

This statement is understandable when directed to provisions specially entrenched in the constitution—that is, those requiring something more than the action of either the federal or a provincial legislature alone to change them. The Charter cannot, and should not, reach items in the constitution subject to the amendment rules under sections 38 or 41 (the general amending formula and the unanimity formula, respectively). As a result, the present system of "proportionate representation of provinces in the House of Commons," which is subject to the general formula (but not subject to opting out by section 42), cannot be challenged—for example, by aboriginal groups seeking representation in the House of Commons on a basis detached from the provinces.[54]

Similarly, the Charter cannot constrain amendments to those constitutional provisions—for example, if Parliament and the legislatures adopted an electoral system other than "proportionate representation among the provinces." This conclusion was drawn by the Yukon Court of Appeal in an unsuccessful Charter challenge to the provisions of the Meech Lake Accord in *Penikett*.[55] The Court held that the Charter did not apply to any amendment properly enacted under Part V of the Constitution Act, 1982, which contains the various amending formulae. It relied, in part, on the wording of section 32 of the Charter, holding that the provisions of a constitutional amendment were not "matters" within the authority of either Parliament or the provincial legislatures to which that section refers. Moreover, the Court noted that the amendment formulae created a way to change the constitution, and that process should not be undermined by the Charter (which, itself, can be changed through the general formula).[56]

The language of *Penikett*, and even that of the Supreme Court in the *Bill 30* case, might be taken to mean that *no* constitutional amendment is subject to the Charter. But such a conclusion goes too far. There are good reasons to hold some constitutional amendments (and potentially some existing provisions of the constitution) up to Charter scrutiny, with the criterion for judicial oversight resting on the fact that they have been enacted, or are subject to repeal, under the formulae in sections 44 and 45 of the Constitution Act, 1982. Those provisions confer the power of unilateral amendment on the federal Parliament and provincial legislatures to amend their respective constitutions. Like any other legislative power possessed by those governments under the constitution, the legislative product is the type of activity that section 32 of the Charter sweeps within its scope.

This view has been adopted by the Supreme Court of Canada in cases involving provincial legislation governing electoral boundaries and the distribution of seats in the legislature. In the *Saskatchewan Boundaries* case, McLachlin J., for the majority, held that provincial laws passed pursuant to authority found under section 45 were subject to the Charter.[57] The same conclusion should follow with regard to provisions enacted unilaterally by the federal Parliament under section 44 of the constitution. The fact that they are in the Constitution Act, 1867, makes no difference. There is no magic in the fact that they are found in that document, rather than in freestanding statutes like the provincial laws attacked in the British Columbia and Saskatchewan cases.[58] Some might argue that such provisions are not subject to Charter scrutiny, because they are part of the "Constitution of Canada," said by section 52 of the 1982 act to be supreme. As well, they might point out that the different parts of the constitution are to be read together, not measured against one another. While this is true with much of the constitution (as defined by section 52), provisions subject to repeal under section 44, and thus capable of unilateral amendment, are of a lesser stature than those protected by the more rigid amending formulae. The Charter, as one of those "higher" laws, should take precedence.

But even if the Charter can apply to the formula for distributing seats among the provinces in section 51 of the Constitution Act, 1867, one should not be overly optimistic about the possibility of success in litigation. The Supreme Court of Canada has determined that the right to vote in section 3 is not a guarantee of absolute parity, with all departures subject to scrutiny under section 1. Rather, the right is one to "effective representation," which, in Canada, has always permitted certain deviations from absolute parity to recognize difficulties in servicing sparsely populated ridings, as well as other social and demographic circumstances. Therefore, section 3 guarantees "relative parity" of voting power only.[59] Thus, the Court accepted with virtually no question the allocation of two northern seats in Saskatchewan, because of the difficulty of communication in a sparsely populated region. As well, the fixed number of rural and urban seats was not fatal, because the Court found the discrepancy between rural and urban seats reasonable in light of the greater difficulty in servicing rural ridings. Differences between particular ridings fell within a 25% variance and were justifiable because of considerations of geography, community of interest, and population growth patterns.

The distribution of seats in the present House of Commons in accordance with the grandfather clause benefits four provinces, which gain seven seats.[60] The result of this allocation of seats is to cause the electoral quota for Ontario to rise to 87,122, while that of Saskatchewan, the greatest beneficiary of the clause, is 69,165.[61] There is really no rationale behind this rule, other than that provinces with declining populations should not lose seats.

The result is often to impose a cost on those who have migrated within Canada. Ontario, British Columbia, and Alberta are currently the main beneficiaries of interprovincial migration.[62] A cost is also imposed on those who have immigrated to Canada from other countries, who overwhelmingly settle in these provinces and Québec.[63] The votes of new Canadians, as well as those of others in the three fastest-growing provinces, are discounted to help those losing population.[64] Not only is this inconsistent with the objective of equality among voters, it also undermines the commitment to interpret the Charter in accordance with the preservation and enhancement of Canada's multicultural heritage, as set out in section 27. The provinces most diverse in their ethnic makeup are Ontario and British Columbia, yet they are the ones most disadvantaged by the present formula for the distribution of seats.[65]

This concern about the distribution of seats is not insignificant in terms of the outcome in some elections, especially in minority government situations. One of the best predictors of party support in Canada recently has been province of residence.[66] If that remains true, then the weighting of seats in favour of the Maritime provinces, Saskatchewan, and Manitoba can have an impact on party strength in the House of Commons. Therefore, there is arguably a violation of section 3, since it is difficult to see why this departure is necessary to "effective representation."

Some might argue that the present system is also inconsistent with the equality guarantee in section 15 of the Charter. I am less sanguine about such an argument, since section 15 requires that one demonstrate discrimination against an individual or group on the basis of a characteristic enumerated in the section or one analogous to them.[67] Section 51 of the constitution discriminates among provinces, not individual citizens, and it would be stretching an argument of indirect discrimination significantly to hold that the treatment of the growth provinces is discrimination against groups disadvantaged on racial or religious lines.[68]

But how successful is a section 3 argument likely to be? The Saskatchewan case indicated a strong judicial attitude of deference to legislatures in the process of allocating seats in legislative bodies.[69] Moreover, the fundamental problem in challenging the grandfather clause lies in the fact that we have enshrined an even more egregious departure from the principle of proportionate representation in the Senate Floor Rule. As well, the Court might be influenced by an argument that the allocation of seats under section 51 occurs through a formula enacted by the House of Commons itself in which British Columbia, Ontario, and Alberta have a large number of seats.

Still, there is a problem here that should give a Court cause for concern. In the Saskatchewan case, the Court permitted departures from "rep by pop" because there were real representation concerns underlying the distribution, and the departure from equality was within an acceptable degree of variance. When it comes to the provincial variation, the disparity between provinces is growing, and there is no principled rationale for it. One might, for example, have sympathy if grandfathering was based on a principle such as the following: provinces like Saskatchewan or Manitoba will have no fewer seats than the Maritime provinces receive under the Senate Floor Rule. There is a good argument for fairness here. Why should Saskatchewan or Manitoba end up with 6 seats as their floor, when New Brunswick or Nova Scotia are assured 10?[70]

But there is no rationale here for the grandfather clause. Rather, there is a protection for existing members, and that is not an adequate justification for the current departures from interprovincial equity. Granted there is a need for regional voices in the national institutions of the Canadian federal system—but a reformed Senate is the place to protect those voices, not the House of Commons.[71]

Will the Court be willing to accept such an argument? The Saskatchewan case does not give cause for optimism. In a related case, the British Columbia Court of Appeal in *Campbell* also concluded that Canada's history demonstrates a commitment to a principle of proportionate representation among provinces that does not require mathematical equality. Indeed, the Court noted that Canadian history shows a long-standing sympathy for provinces with declining populations.[72]

Deference in this case can be seen as consistent with certain views about federalism and rights expressed by the Supreme Court in other Charter contexts. Differences in policy between provinces are accepted in many cases, and even deviations in the application of federal laws in different provinces.[73] Diversity in Canada is a fact of life, both across provinces and communities. This is reflected in our interpretation of rights, and it has influenced the design of national institutions. The Court, well aware of the Canadian roots of the Charter, has often tried to marry federalism values with the definition of rights, and it will undoubtedly continue to do so.

Rethinking Representation: The Challenge from the Charter

The Charter provides an opportunity for a second group of challenges, based not on concepts of parity among voters, but on a different vision of equality.

Both sections 3 and 15 may be used by equality-seeking groups to challenge electoral boundaries because a placement does not give them adequate representation. Indeed, one can anticipate that claims will come particularly from those groups Alan Cairns calls "Charter Canadians"—that is, those who identify themselves on the basis of a characteristic recognized in section 15 of the Charter.[74] Thus, women's and ethnic groups may come forward to argue for better representation, with their demands rooted in a concept of mirror representation that puts in question traditional approaches to electoral boundaries.

At a minimum, those with a territorial base will demand that boundary lines be drawn so as to benefit groups who feel that they are not adequately represented in the House of Commons. Therefore, they will argue that boundary lines should be drawn to maximize the voting strength of the group. Some would argue that this claim is fully consistent with the instructions now found in the Electoral Boundaries Readjustment Act to take into account communities of interest, even if the result is to depart from the goal of parity among ridings (subject to the 25% variance limit, which obviously gives much room for manoeuvre).

Our traditional method of drawing boundaries has assumed a fairly compact territory with some degree of rationality in the end result (e.g., attention to municipal limits or geographical obstacles such as rivers). Will pressures for group representation lead, in the future, to boundaries that pay more attention to colour or ethnic origin and less to the shape of the territory? How far should we be prepared to "affirmatively gerrymander" in order to maximize the voting strength of particular groups?

To this point, the discussion has concentrated on the issue of representation of voters grouped on the basis of territory, both local and provincial. While this has long been our tradition, and is characteristic of Westminster-style parliamentary democracy, there are indications that some may no longer accept this principle of representation. Most obvious is the call for aboriginal seats in the House of Commons, using the model of the four Maori seats in the New Zealand Parliament. While there are many ways that this could be achieved, let us work with the suggestion that there be a fixed number of seats, with aboriginal voters allowed to choose inclusion in either the general voters' list or an aboriginal voters' list.[75] Such a claim inevitably generates echoes from other groups for equivalent rights.[76]

These claims hark back to the initial discussion of representation in this paper. No longer is the basis for the legitimacy of the representative based on the method of selection—now the shift is clearly towards "mirror" or ascriptive representation, a move of great significance for the operation of our political institutions. There are some serious issues for debate before we move in this direction. Some of the issues are specific to a particular group calling for representation: for example, when we speak of aboriginal seats, who qualifies as an Aboriginal (status and non-status Indians, Inuit, Métis)? How are seats to be divided—on the basis of province, or through a set of national constituencies that can cross provincial boundaries, or just through selection of the representatives as a group, without tying them to a constituency? If the latter, should we be concerned about the ombuds role of the member foregone by aboriginal voters? And how does this representation harmonize with aboriginal self-government? Should House representatives be precluded from voting on items regulated by self-government agreements?

But there is a prior—and fundamental—question about identity and politics that must be addressed. Is our primary identity as aboriginal peoples, women, Chinese Canadians? Do we see ourselves as separate and apart from those of the other sex and other ethnic backgrounds? For many, the answer would be that such a method of description is too simplistic, for we are complex individuals with multiple identities. Despite the claims of some feminists that women share an essential nature, it is obvious that women are not a homogeneous group. While they will share views with many other women on many issues, they will also identify with men from their region, class, occupation, or ethnic affiliation on issues as well. There is, for example, no "woman's view" on such difficult issues as control of reproductive technology, abortion, daycare policy, let alone the merits of free trade or the distinct society clause in the constitutional proposals. This is true for members of other groups as well. Indeed, increasingly, Canadians are coming to question a politics that emphasizes difference and cleavage.[77]

This is not to suggest that there is no need to encourage representation from women or ethnic groups in the House of Commons. Diversity in the membership of governing institutions should be welcome, since women and members of ethnic groups other than French and English may bring different perspectives and experiences to policy making, just as do those from different regions and occupations.[78] My argument is against fixed seats for groups on the basis of a shared characteristic, which ignores the complexity of individual experience and identity. The present system of territorial representation is designed to aggregate interests and recognize the richness and diversity of views both among groups and within individuals on different issues. We should be reluctant to depart from it, for the result is to emphasize distance rather than dialogue and consensus.[79]

There is clearly a role for political parties to be more active in seeking out candidates from groups who have not been well represented in the House. Indeed, there may be an incentive to do so to the extent that constituency boundaries take into account the makeup of various communities, including ethnic and religious groupings. Unfortunately, this will not create equivalent incentives to select women candidates, but a concern for more women candidates can be met by party activism in the form of targeted recruitment efforts and support systems. Another approach would be to consider a shift to a system of proportional representation, which has usually been considered in the past as a solution to the problems of regional representation in the House of Commons, but may also benefit other interests.[80] The latter systems can be tailored to preserve many of the benefits of the present system, especially territorially based constituencies and a consensus approach to politics. The danger with quotas of seats for groups lies in the emphasis on separation, even though the aim is inclusion.[81]

Conclusion

The three branches of Canadian constitutionalism can both nurture and undermine the others. Our concept of representation of territorially based communities in parliamentary institutions, based on values of equality and participation, is tempered by our federal system, with its sensitivity to the claims of regional units. Those two systems are now affected by the Charter of Rights, which is itself interpreted in light of our long-standing commitment to parliamentary democracy and federalism. The Charter presents opportunities to question the distribution of seats among local communities—whether in challenges to seat distribution among provinces or, more likely, within provinces so as to promote values of equality among voters and among different groups. Even more significantly, the Charter has contributed to a growing consciousness among certain minority groups, who not only dispute the drawing of boundary lines in constituencies, but question the whole system of representation based on territory, rather than shared characteristics. Some of these challenges will be made in the courts; most will play out in political debate, both in our current struggle to reshape confederation and in our continuing effort to determine how to create a society in which citizens from all regions and identities feel included.

Notes

1. *Edwards v. Attorney General of Canada*, [1930] A.C. 124, 136.
2. A.H. Birch, *Representative and Responsible Government* (Toronto: University of Toronto Press, 1964), 14–16.
3. See generally, R. MacGregor Dawson, *The Government of Canada*, 5th ed., rev. by N. Ward (Toronto: University of Toronto Press, 1970), 317–18. Some of the pressure for direct democracy from groups such as the Reform Party, including referenda and recall, might suggest a departure from the traditional view of the member's role.
4. J. Smith, "Representation and Constitutional Reform in Canada" in D. Smith, P. MacKinnon, and J. Courtney, eds., *After Meech Lake: Lessons for the Future* (Saskatoon: Fifth House Publishers, 1991), 75. My colleague Carolyn Tuohy uses the term "ascriptive representation" to describe representation on the basis of a shared characteristic.
5. Often, because of party discipline in a system of responsible government like Canada's, this representation of constituents' interests will occur in caucus or Cabinet, and not openly in public debate, thus hiding an important aspect of the representative role.
6. For a discussion of the MP's role, see J. Reid, "The Backbencher and the Discharge of Legislative Responsibilities" in W. Neilson and J. MacPherson, eds., *The*

Legislative Process in Canada (Toronto: Institute for Research on Public Policy, 1978), 139.

7. "Rep by pop" is a phrase that has echoed throughout Canadian history, most prominently in the demands of George Brown and his Reform Party in Canada West pre-Confederation.

8. There are many other issues relating to effective representation that I shall not discuss, including different methods of electing representatives, such as proportional representation (especially with a list system). Some of these are found in the Macdonald Commission (Canada. Royal Commission on the Economic Union and Development Prospects for Canada. *Report*, vol. 3 [Ottawa: Minister of Supply and Services, 1985], 84–85). See also, W. Irvine, "A Review and Evaluation of Electoral System Reform Proposals" in P. Aucoin, ed., *Institutional Reforms for Representative Government* (Toronto: University of Toronto Press, 1985), 71.

9. Traditionally, we think of drawing boundaries as an exercise rife with the danger of political "gerrymandering," as parties try to group those voters most likely to support them. As the last section of this paper discusses, there are also pressures from other groups for "gerrymandering" or line drawing so as to maximize a group's voting clout, if members choose to vote as a block. See infra, 27.

10. I say "close to the capital" with reason, since there is a range of difficulty in representing urban ridings (and rural ridings) at the national level, with the members from British Columbia able to argue that it is much more difficult to represent a Vancouver riding or northern BC than Toronto or even Fredericton, because of the three-hour time difference from Ottawa and the amount of travel time necessary to service the riding.

11. Of course, there are other mechanisms to assist the member, such as special allowances, as described by J. Courtney, "Parliament and Representation: The Unfinished Agenda of Electoral Redistributions," *Canadian Journal of Political Science* 21 (1988): 682–83.

12. Electoral Boundaries Readjustment Act, R.S.C. 1985, c. E–3, s. 15, as amended R.S.C. 1985 (2nd Supp.), c. 6, s. 2.

13. The phrase is picked up in the federal constitutional proposals: *Shaping Canada's Future Together: Proposals* (Ottawa: Minister of Supply and Services, 1991), v.

14. There are many perspectives with which to evaluate federal systems. The best survey is found in K. Norrie, R. Simeon, and M. Krasnick, *Federalism and the Economic Union in Canada* (Toronto: University of Toronto Press, 1986). The "community" perspective described in chapter 4 has dominated in Canada: that is, powers are generally divided on the basis that we share certain preferences across national or provincial communities with which citizens identify. Nevertheless, the allocation of powers in the federal system has also been guided by concerns of functionalism and economic efficiency, as well as democratic and distributional considerations.

15. The Western provinces have expressed this view most forcefully in reaction to the perceived dominance of Ontario's and Québec's interests. For a brief discussion see R. Gibbins, *Senate Reform: Moving Towards the Slippery Slope* (Kingston: Queen's Institute of Intergovernmental Relations, 1983), 5.

16. A good discussion is found in J.S. Dupré, "Reflections on the Workability of Executive Federalism" in R. Simeon, ed., *Intergovernmental Relations* (Toronto: University of Toronto Press, 1985), 1.

17. The different ways to facilitate intrastate federalism are described by D. Smiley and R. Watts in *Intrastate Federalism in Canada* (Toronto: University of Toronto Press, 1985). Drawing on the work of Alan Cairns, they note that there are two models of intrastate federalism in Canada: provincialist and centralist, with the difference turning on whether it is provincial governments or provincial voters who gain a stronger voice at the national level (at 17). See also A. Cairns, *From Interstate to Intrastate Federalism* (Kingston: Queen's Institute of Intergovernmental Relations, 1979).

18. Smiley and Watts stated that the major problem with intrastate federalism is "the difficulty if not the impossibility of reconciling the majoritarian dispositions of the Westminster model of parliamentary responsible government with the pluralistic and anti-majoritarian impulses . . . that made federalism necessary in the first place and sustain federalism today." (ibid., 29). See as well the Macdonald Commission (see n.8), 70–72.

19. There are many other points of tension: for example, the role of regional considerations in Cabinet appointments, the lack of accountability associated with executive federalism, and the need to protect regional interests endangered by the requirement of party discipline. See generally, Smiley and Watts, *Intrastate Federalism* (see n.17), ch. 5 through 8.

20. Constitution Act, 1867, s. 51. This section was repealed and a new formula for the calculation of provincial seats enacted in the Constitution Act, 1946, 9–10 Geo. VI, c. 63 (U.K.).

21. Enacted by the Constitution Act, 1915, 5–6 Geo. V, c. 45 (U.K.).

22. Constitution Act, 1952, S.C. 1952, c. 15, s. 51(1)5.

23. Constitution Act, 1974, S.C. 1974-75-76, c. 13. The Amalgam Method is described in J. Courtney, "The Size of Canada's Parliament: An Assessment of the Implications of a Larger House of Commons" in *Institutional Reforms for Representative Government* (see n.8), 18–21. Courtney notes that the Amalgam Method would have narrowed the spread between small and larger provinces over time and that voter equity across provinces was more of a feature of this than of all the other schemes tried (at 21).

24. Constitution Act, 1985 (Representation), S.C. 1986, c. 8, Part I.

25. This creates certain floors: British Columbia 28, Alberta 21, Saskatchewan 14, Manitoba 14, Ontario 95, Québec 75, New Brunswick 10, Nova Scotia 11, Prince Edward Island 4, and Newfoundland 7. For a discussion of this formula (and the others preceding it), see J.P. Boyer, *Election Law in Canada*, vol. 1 (Toronto: Butterworth, 1987), 102–8, and N. Ward, *Dawson's Government of Canada*, 6th ed. (Toronto: University of Toronto Press, 1987), 90–92.

26. I am assuming a 25% variance from a provincial quota and the likelihood of rounding up the numbers to give two seats.

27. Indeed, there would be no problem of inequity among the provinces if all were given the same electoral quota as Prince Edward Island–although the size of the House of Commons would be drastically increased.

28. Courtney, "Size of Canada's Parliament" (see n.23) 4–10.

29. A further inequity in size emerges with the comparison of the size of the Yukon and Northwest Territories, where the constitution allocates one and two seats respectively [Constitution Act, 1867, s. 51(2)].

30. Courtney, "Parliament and Representation" (see n.11), 687.

31. There are certain constraints on their discretion, most particularly section 52, which requires that proportionate representation between the provinces be preserved in any increase in the number of members in the House. That section can be changed only in accordance with the general amending formula requiring the approval of both the national Parliament and seven provincial legislatures representing 50% of the population [Constitution Act, 1982, ss. 38 and 42(1)(a)]. The application of this provision is discussed at n.61.
32. Courtney, "Parliament and Representation," (see n.11), 679, 689.
33. Ibid., 686.
34. Obviously, the effectiveness of these provincial voices is enhanced if they are found within the government party—an outcome that our "first past the post" electoral system often confounds.
35. Calgary Centre, for example, had a population of 104,787 as of the 1986 census; Calgary Southeast 102,838; Kitchener, 98,956. In contrast, Prince Edward Island seats ranged from 29,049 to 33,736.
36. John Courtney also develops this point in "Federalism and Representation: Voter Equality and Electoral Reapportionment in Canada and the United States" (mimeo, June 1989).
37. This is one of the major reasons that Gibbins, Senate Reform, (see n.15), suggests an elected Senate: to reduce the role of the provincial governments (6, 11).
38. See Smiley and Watts, Intrastate Federalism (see n.17), ch. 5 and 6.
39. Ibid., 121-33.
40. The examples include the Pépin-Robarts Commission [Canada. The Task Force on Canadian Unity. A Future Together (Ottawa: Minister of Supply and Services, 1979), 97-99, recommending a Council of the Federation], Bill C-60 [Canada. The Constitutional Amendment Bill, 1978, 21-32, which included a House of the Federation], and the Beige Paper [Quebec Liberal Party. Une nouvelle fédération canadienne (Montreal, 1980), ch. 9, recommending a "conseil fédéral"].
41. See, for example, the findings of the Spicer Commission [Canada. Citizens' Forum on Canada's Future (Ottawa: Minister of Supply and Services, 1991), 103-4].
42. See Gibbins, Senate Reform (see n.15), 41.
43. Federal Proposals, Shaping Canada's Future (see n.13), 17.
44. Ibid., 19.
45. The proposals actually contemplate a fairly effective Senate, which would have an absolute veto on all matters except appropriation bills and taxation, as well as those of "particular national importance" (with the examples of national defence and international issues mentioned). On issues of language and culture, a double majority of English- and French-speaking senators would be required (17-21). Roger Gibbins, in a 1983 discussion of Senate reform, suggested that the resolution of these issues of seat allocation and powers is an "intimidating" task (Senate Reform [see n.15], 2). Québec, in particular, has a great deal to lose in Senate reform, especially if we move toward greater provincial equality. This would once again undermine Québec's assertion that it is not a province like the others.
46. Indeed, Prime Minister Mulroney made this point in tabling the proposals in the House of Commons (Canada. House of Commons. Debates, 24 September 1991, 2588): "The Commons would likely become a chamber in which there was stricter adherence to the principle of representation by population..."
47. The Federal Proposals avoid items that cannot be implemented through the general

formula of seven provinces with 50% of the population (s. 38 of the Constitution Act, 1982). There is an oblique discussion of the possibility of unanimity items, but none are proposed [*Shaping Canada's Future* (see n.13), 23].

48. Some point to the fact that the disparity in size between California and Alaska is comparable to the almost 80-fold difference between Prince Edward Island and Ontario, yet both states have two Senators in the U.S. Congress. However, those states are only 2 of 50, in contrast to 2 of 10 in Canada, and there are opportunities for coalitions of large states not available here.

49. Alan Cairns is typical of a number of commentators who see the Charter as a fundamental point of departure from the past, generating a consciousness of group identity among those whom he calls "Charter Canadians" ["Author's Introduction: The Growth of Constitutional Self-Consciousness" in *Disruptions: Constitutional Struggles, from the Charter to Meech Lake*, D. Williams, ed., (Toronto: McClelland & Stewart, 1991), 19-21, and "Political Science, Ethnicity, and the Canadian Constitution" in the same book, 164)] While he is correct that the Charter has had an important impact, it is important to remember the other forces contributing to the mobilization of these groups, not only here, but in many other countries as well.

50. See, for example, *Committee for the Commonwealth of Canada v. Canada* (1991), 77 D.L.R. (4th) 385 (S.C.C.)–right to hand out political pamphlets in airport.

51. There is controversy among constitutional theorists about the relevance of the past in constitutional interpretation, since there is a danger that the values of a dead majority will govern the constitution's application to future generations. Yet a failure to understand a country's history can lead to Charter interpretation that bears no relation to the community's concept of rights. Canadian judges have been sympathetic to arguments from history to date, without showing slavish adherence to its teachings. See, for example, both Dickson J. in *R. v. Big M Drug Mart Ltd.* (1985), 18 D.L.R. (4th) 321, 359-60 and McLachlin J. in *Reference re Electoral Boundaries Commission Act, ss. 14, 20 (Sask.)* (1991), 81 D.L.R. (4th) 16 (S.C.C.) [hereafter *Sask. Boundaries*], where she states at 33:

> The right to vote, while rooted in and hence to some extent defined by historical and existing practices, cannot be viewed as frozen by particular historical anomalies. What must be sought is the broader philosophy underlying the historical development of the right to vote–a philosophy which is capable of explaining the past and animating the future.

52. See the discussion in K. Roach, "One Person–One Vote?: Canadian Constitutional Standards for Electoral Distribution and Districting" in D. Small, ed., *Drawing the Map: Equality and Efficacy of the Vote in Canadian Electoral Boundary Reform* (Toronto: Dundurn Press, forthcoming 1991), 15-23 (mimeo).

53. *Reference re An Act to Amend the Education Act (Ontario) (Bill 30)* (1987), 40 D.L.R. (4th) 18 (S.C.C.), 60.

54. As described in the subsequent section, there have been recent suggestions to provide seats in the House of Commons reserved for aboriginal peoples. Refusal to grant such seats might hypothetically be challenged under s. 15 of the Charter (although I am doubtful of the success). The argument would be that territorial representation deprives certain minority groups, such as aboriginal peoples, of representation because they are almost always a small minority in traditional ridings.

55. *Penikett v. Canada* (1987), 45 D.L.R. (4th) 108 (Y.T.C.A.); leave to appeal to S.C.C. denied [1988] S.C.R. xii.
56. Ibid., 114.
57. *Sask. Boundaries* (see n.51), 31:

> Although legislative jurisdiction to amend the provincial constitution cannot be removed from the province without a constitutional amendment and is in this sense above Charter scrutiny, the provincial exercise of its legislative authority is subject to the Charter . . .

McLachlin J. relied on an earlier decision of the British Columbia Supreme Court, holding the Charter applicable to a provincial law dealing with the allocation of seats in the legislature [*Re Dixon and A.G.B.C.* (1986), 31 D.L.R. (4th) 546].
58. Thus, I disagree with the Ontario Court of Appeal *obiter* statement in the Bill 30 case that the Charter would not apply to s. 51 of the Constitution Act, 1867 [*Reference re An Act to Amend the Education Act* (1986), 25 D.L.R. (4th) 1 (Ont. C.A.) at 54].
59. *Sask. Boundaries* (see n.51), 35. While McLachlin J. focused on the rationale for treating rural and urban voters differently in this case, she also stated (at 36): "Factors like geography, community history, community interests and minority representation may need to be taken into account to ensure that our legislative assemblies effectively represent the diversity of our social mosaic."
60. Lambert J.A.'s dissenting judgment in *Campbell v. A.G. Canada* (1988), 49 D.L.R. (4th) 321 (B.C.C.A.) sets out a useful table at 326, showing the beneficiaries of the senatorial and grandfather clauses: Québec 1, Nova Scotia 1, New Brunswick 2, Manitoba 2, Prince Edward Island 3, Saskatchewan 3.
61. Of course, this problem is further compounded by the Senate floor which gives Prince Edward Island an electoral quota of 30,267 and New Brunswick one of 69,640.
62. Statistics Canada. *Canada Yearbook 1990* (Ottawa: Minister of Supply and Services, 1989), 2-16. Obviously, the rate and pattern of internal migration varies somewhat with economic conditions.
63. Ontario attracts most immigrants, with 47.7% in 1987, followed by Québec (15.6%), British Columbia (15%), and Alberta (12.1%) [ibid., 2-16].
64. The discount is further compounded by the delay in each decennial redistribution. The 1988 election was the first to see the results of the redistribution following the 1981 census.
65. The *Canada Yearbook 1990* notes that Asians are more likely to settle in Ontario and British Columbia and that 85% of blacks are found in Ontario and Québec (at 2-8). Approximately 40% of Metropolitan Toronto's population was born outside Canada, 39.3% of Vancouver's, and only 9.8% in Regina and 4% in St. John's [Ontario. *Changing for the Better* (1991), 22]. One in 4 Ontario citizens was born outside Canada compared to 1 in 12 Québecers.
66. The result to regional voting patterns generated much discussion about electoral reform. See, for example, Irvine, "Review and Evaluation" (see n.8) and Smiley and Watts, *Intrastate Federalism* (see n.17).
67. *Andrews v. Law Society of British Columbia* (1989), 56 D.L.R. (4th) 1 (S.C.C.) at 23.
68. I argue this because the makeup of the immigrant population in a province like

Ontario, while containing a significant number of visible-minority groups, also contains many white immigrants. Moreover, the loss of seats hurts all residents of the province, not just those of a particular race or ethnic group.

69. This is most clearly indicated by the Court's willingness to find that s. 3 is a right with internal limits, which protects governments from having to make a s. 1 defence in many circumstances.

70. Newfoundland is in a similar position because it has six senators.

71. This is especially true if senators can sit in Cabinet, since this ensures a provincial voice in the most important institution of government. Nevertheless, one would want a minimum of one seat per province—as the constitution has acknowledged with the representation of the Yukon and Northwest Territories.

72. *Campbell* (see n.60) dealt with the issue of the appropriate amending formula for the Representation Act, 1985, with the plaintiffs arguing that the grandfather clause was a departure from the principle of proportionate representation of the provinces, and thus must be implemented through the general amending formula because of s. 42(1)(a) of the Constitution Act, 1982, rather than through unilateral federal action under s. 44. There was no discussion of the Charter. Leave to appeal to the Supreme Court of Canada was denied (1988), 27 B.C.L.R. (2d) xxxv.

73. Illustrations are found in *Edwards Books & Art Ltd. v. The Queen* (1986), 35 D.L.R. (4th) 1 and *R. v. S (S.)* (1990), 77 C.R. (3d) 373 (S.C.C.). The interaction of federalism and rights is discussed in K. Swinton, *The Supreme Court and Canadian Federalism: The Laskin-Dickson Years* (Toronto: Carswell, 1990), 338–49.

74. Cairns, (see n.49).

75. Suggestions of this type have come from a group led by Senator Len Marchand, as described in J. Simpson, "Playing the politics of exclusion is a dangerous game," *The Globe and Mail,* 9 October 1991, A16. Various models of aboriginal representation are described in D. Hawkes and B. Morse, "Alternative Methods for Aboriginal Participation in Processes of Constitutional Reform" in R. Watts and D. Brown, eds., *Options for a New Canada* (Toronto: University of Toronto Press, 1991), 178–86.

76. See Simpson, "Playing the politics of exclusion" (see n.75), referring to the demand from the National Action Committee on the Status of Women for 50% of Senate seats; and Beverley Baines, "After Meech Lake: The Ms/Representation of Gender in Scholarly Places" in Smith et al., eds., *After Meech Lake* (see n.4), 211–13; and C. Boyle, "Home Rule for Women: Power-Sharing Between Men and Women" 7 *Dalhousie Law Journal* (1982–83): 790.

77. See, for example, the findings of the Spicer Commission (see n.41), 88–89.

78. A similar argument is made by Isabel Grant and Lynn Smith for gender representation in the judiciary ["Gender Representation in the Canadian Judiciary" in Ontario Law Reform Commission, ed., *Appointing Judges: Philosophy, Politics and Practice* (Toronto: Ontario Law Reform Commission), 66–78]. Indeed, the spectacle of sexist and racist comments from members of the House in the 1991 sessions shows a need for more sensitivity among members, which might be assisted by the presence of more women and visible minorities in the House.

79. Daniel Elazar has argued that a territorial basis for representation is the most neutral of the alternatives, since it permits shifts in power from one interest to another, such as class or ethnic group, as a particular characteristic becomes of

greater political salience—provided, of course, that those who share the characteristic are located within a particular region [D. Elazar, "Federalism and Intergovernmental Relations" in D. Elazar, ed., *Cooperation and Conflict: Readings in American Federalism* (Itasca, Ill.: F.E. Peacock, 1969), 9].

80. Smiley and Watts note that women (and ethnic groups) may do better in a system of proportional representation, for in multimember constituencies, parties may include women and minority candidates in order to broaden their appeal [*Intrastate Federalism* (see n.17), 115].

81. It can be argued that the aboriginal peoples are in a significantly different position than other groups because of their status as the first peoples in Canada and their distinct identity and status.

COMMENTARY

JENNIFER SMITH
DALHOUSIE UNIVERSITY

In their papers, Janet Hiebert and Katherine Swinton discuss representation. Hiebert is interested chiefly in how decisions about it are made, and therefore her discussion of the *Carter* decision focuses on the phenomenon of Charter-based judicial review of legislative policy. Swinton takes up substance as well as process, examining how the issue of representation has been dealt with in the past and how it might be pursued in the context of the institutional changes of our day. Let me begin with Hiebert and process.

Charter-Based Review of Public Policy
Hiebert is troubled by the ramifications of a "rights are always paramount" model of Charter-based judicial review although, as she acknowledges, it did not succeed in the *Carter* case. This model, she argues, limits significantly the freedom of governments to pursue policies that are in conflict with or limit Charter rights. Some would respond—and a good thing, too! But as Hiebert points out, the Charter does not necessarily exhaust the good things of the world, as the model appears to imply. There are other valued public goods, the realization of which might well require limiting a Charter right. So she wants to maintain the distinction between Charter rights and competing values, and avoid collapsing the two into a single "rights" view of the good.

Swinton has a useful point to make here. She reminds us that the Charter is itself interpreted through the lens of Canadian political culture, in particular, our version of parliamentary democracy and federalism. The Charter pillar is not simply an independent variable; it is also a dependent variable. The two-way influence restricts the utility of the "rights are always paramount" model's explanatory force because it suggests that the Charter will never be thought to embody all political goods. Instead judges will continue to find that

40

there are good things that justify limitations on a given right. Indeed, they might even interpret that right in a Canadian way, finding that there is no conflict between it and the impugned law, and therefore not even needing to consider a section 1 defence of the law. This is exactly what the S.C.C. did in *Carter*.

Effective Representation

Utilizing the broad and purposive understanding of a right, Madam Justice McLachlin found that the purpose of section 3 of the Charter, the right to vote, is to guarantee effective representation, something she thinly defines in relation to an elected representative's roles of legislator and ombudsman. The equal vote principle, or voter parity, is only the leading factor involved in effective representation. The other and countervailing factors are: geography, community history, community interest, and minority representation.

McLachlin defends her interpretation of the right to vote as the right to effective representation on the basis of some very Canadian observations that undermine the idea of voter parity: (1) the respectability of the purposive approach is established by the S.C.C.'s Charter-based review; (2) the Canadian historical record on the vote is not one of mighty efforts to attain voter parity—that was nobody's purpose and therefore the framers of the Charter could hardly have had it in mind; (3) other Commonwealth countries have similar records; (4) the vastness of the country makes voter parity impractical; (5) the country's concern with cultural and group identity militates against an easy acceptance of voter parity.

By defining the right to vote purposively, McLachlin enters the nether world of representation. Certainly today the meaning of the term is problematic, and she herself has not much to say about it, although she does demonstrate how foolish it is to talk about representation and avoid any reference to political parties. In the meantime, people could get some funny ideas about the effective part of the phrase. She might have avoided the problem by dividing voting and being represented.

Voting is an isolated, individualistic act that produces measurable institutional repercussions. Voters' decisions in the constituency produce a winner, and that in turn contributes to the determination of the winning party in the country, a party that produces a Cabinet, and so on. The community of interest concept applies here. However, being represented is what happens between elections and this is where the factor of geography looms. It can be resolved by money and staffing because it is an administrative problem. There is no need to "solve" it by diminishing the value of someone else's vote.

Be this as it may, as Swinton reminds us, the Court often tries to marry the values of federalism to the values of rights. And so the trials of the legislator-as-ombudsman, surrogate for the trials of the underpopulated peripheries, receive a sympathetic ear. It is hardly surprising that Swinton moves on to "rethink representation" and get at the principle of voter parity by considering non-geographic electoral systems. Proportional representation is the obvious example;

seat quotas are another. Swinton argues that nongeographic systems imply a different concept of representation, namely, mirror or ascriptive representation.

Ascriptive Representation

I am not so sure. After all, in his recommendation of a complicated system of proportional representation as a means of giving minorities a voice in Parliament, John Stuart Mill contemplated a meeting of like minds rather than like bodies. In any event, Swinton questions an important presupposition of the concept of ascriptive representation, that is, the one-dimensional notion of human identity. As she argues, it is inadequate for those who regard themselves as complex individuals with multiple identities.

There is another problem as well, and it has to do with individual rationality. Voting is an act of individual responsibility that presupposes both rationality and freedom. The assumption is that individuals are entitled to make choices as they see fit. Whether or not those choices are thought to be wrong by someone else is entirely irrelevant. Students of politics know that voters face restraints on their choices—prior restraints, as it were. For example, political parties select the candidates, generally against a background of financial exigency. From time to time, in a fit of reform, Canadians try to counter the effect through the use of regulatory schemes, which means that they understand the problem of pre-selection. The idea of further pre-selection in the form of quotas is troublesome. On the other hand, it might well be a fit model for a community that has a qualitatively different relationship with the larger society, a relationship defined in terms of sovereignty.

To return, then, to Hiebert's discussion of the logic of Charter-based judicial review of an issue like the vote, the foregoing discussion illustrates the kind of discourse not captured by the "rights are always paramount" model. But it is not captured by the *Carter* decision either. The purposive approach to the right to vote turns out not to lead anywhere new. On the contrary, it led the Court right back to the old, Canadian-style chestnuts that have been trotted out against voter parity for decades.

COMMENTARY

MURRAY RANKIN
UNIVERSITY OF VICTORIA

After brief comments on each paper, I would like to illustrate some of my concerns in this context by reference to the particular situation in one Canadian jurisdiction, namely, the Yukon Territory. What are the implications of the *Saskatchewan Reference* case[1] for the electoral redistribution exercise currently under way in that jurisdiction and what, if any, are its implications in the debate over self-government for First Nations in jurisdictions such as the Yukon?

In her paper, Professor Hiebert closely examines the factums of all parties and interveners in the Supreme Court action and provides a useful analysis of their conflicting positions. I share Professor Hiebert's concern as to the "rights are always paramount" position that some say is mandated by the Charter. However, I believe that the majority judgment of McLachlin J. is sufficiently sensitive to balance the factors with which she is concerned. Unlike Professor Hiebert, however, I believe that such a balancing judgment should be made not under section 1 but rather in section 3 of the Charter. I will develop this point below.

What does "right to vote" mean in section 3? As Justice McLachlin points out in her majority judgment, when this right was originally entrenched, there was no one advancing the argument that it meant anything like "one person–one vote." It is my view that the majority opinion in the *Saskatchewan Reference* case illustrates an appropriate degree of judicial deference to legislative determinations in this field, particularly in light of the report of the Saskatchewan Boundaries Commission. The Court found that there was no evidence that this commission acted in a biased fashion.

As noted, I disagree with Professor Hiebert on whether the content of the "right to vote" should be defined broadly, with departures from the broad position to be justified solely under section 1 of the Charter. A "one size fits all" approach to section 3 is simply inappropriate in the widely varying circumstances that apply across Canada. The standard of what a "right to vote" means should be defined as much as possible in the rights-conferring sections of the Charter. For the Charter to be a workable document in the Canadian reality, the rights it confers must take their meaning and be reflective of Canadian history and geography. These rights must accord with our traditions and our experience. As in other Charter adjudication, the right to vote must be read contextually. By analogy, this has been the approach taken by the courts in the administrative search and seizure cases under section 8,[2] the freedom of association cases under section 2,[3] and in the section 15 equality cases.[4] The Supreme Court of Canada has interpreted the meanings of each of these rights in light of uniquely Canadian circumstances. Thus, for example, the meaning of "freedom of association" did not get expansively interpreted and then narrowed by section 1. Rather, in each case, the right itself was given a more limited meaning as the Court held that its meaning had to be determined in its proper context.

To do otherwise would mean that the rights guaranteed in the Charter could be trivialized. As the Court stated in the *Big M Drug Mart* case,[5] to give them a broad, generous meaning would be to trivialize them. It is also submitted that the Court has something akin to a vested interest in not having always to resort to section 1 in order to legitimize what would otherwise amount to violations of rights. It would be an unfortunate result of entrenched constitutional rights in Canada if all legislative exercises in electoral redistribution constantly had to be labelled as violations of the Charter only then, perhaps, to be "saved" by resort to section 1. Such a result would detract from the Court's role as the protector of our rights in the last resort.

However, there remains an important role reserved for section 1 in those cases arising under section 3. As Madam Justice McLachlin said in *Dixon*,[6] section 1 should be applied to resolve unusual, practical difficulties, such as sudden, dramatic changes in population, as would occur where the mine closes in a single-industry town and there is no time to change the electoral map, or where a mine opens and there is a dramatic increase in the local population. In these circumstances, of course, section 1 should properly be triggered.

Turning to Professor Swinton's paper, her reference to Professor Cairns's "three pillars" of the Canadian constitution—namely, parliamentary democracy, federalism, and the citizens' rights consciousness—is a very useful backdrop against which to assess the exercise of drawing electoral boundaries at this time in our constitutional history. At this time of constitutional crisis, it is entirely appropriate that the entire notion of legitimate "representation" be considered. If a significant degree of homogeneity exists among voters, redistribution *can* be fairly uncontroversial. Professor Jennifer Smith's distinction between a procedural concept of representation on the one hand, and a mirror or ascriptive concept of representation on the other, is particularly helpful in this analysis. Under the former, a choice of representatives is made on the basis of territorial constituencies. The latter focuses on whether particular representatives are "like me," as determined by the characteristics that they and I happen to share.

It is in this latter context that the claims of First Nations Citizens to a certain number of guaranteed seats in legislatures may be considered. The argument is advanced in part because our territorial-based approach to representation often leaves First Nations Citizens as a small minority in traditional ridings. Consequently, the legislature does not accurately mirror the population. Nor does it necessarily mirror the two sexes. It is unlikely, as Professor Swinton suggests, that the Court would hold that a refusal to grant a reserved number of seats to women or aboriginal Canadians would be held to amount to a violation of section 15. Should our legislatures nevertheless take radical measures to change our approach to representation?

The experience with reserved seats for Maoris in the New Zealand legislature must be considered, however, before Canadians embrace such a reform. The New Zealand Parliament consists of 4 Maori and 93 "General" seats. In a recent Royal Commission report on the New Zealand experience, a great deal of the relevant evidence was negative.[7] Although the report noted that "[t]he 4 seats have become an important symbol of Maori people of their special status as the indigenous people of New Zealand,"[8] the Royal Commission, which included a Maori commissioner, recommended against retaining this system of separate representation. It concluded that "separate representation works against the development of mutual understanding between the races."[9] Moreover, unlike New Zealand where there is one major aboriginal community, there are many First Nations in Canada with very different languages, cultures, and traditional communities. For instance, do Inuit living in a traditional community see the world like urbanized members of the Musqueam First Nation who reside in Vancouver? Do First Nations women perceive issues in a sufficiently similar manner to First Nations men? If not, should we have designated reserved seats for First Nations men and women? In practical terms, would this vision of Jesse Jackson's "rainbow coalition" be positive or would it become a nightmare of pluralism gone wild?

I will not address Professor Swinton's remarks concerning federalism, at least insofar as federal-provincial relations are concerned. However, I agree that federalism is a system of government that at bottom is concerned about communities and, as she notes, it is a system with elements of shared and self-rule. Quite clearly, resort to narrow majoritarianism is simply not appropriate in modern Canada. Representation by population must be balanced by representation by region.

However, another aspect of "federalism" might come into play if First Nations are given partial sovereignty and effective self-government. What kind of relationship should these First Nations have with the rest of Canadian society? For example, say that in the Yukon a great deal of power is "taken down" by a First Nation, and its powers come to approximate those of the Territory itself. It might be able to legislate in respect of health, education, social services, and so forth. Should the Member of the Legislative Assembly for an electoral district comprised predominantly of First Nations Citizens enjoying such wide legislative powers be entitled to vote in respect of issues on which the First Nation has equivalent legislative authority? Similarly, if a First Nation government has passed laws parallel to those passed by the Yukon legislature, should the First Nations Citizens also be entitled to vote in territorial elections? How many powers of the sort ordinarily enjoyed by the Territory must a First Nation take down before its citizens lose their right to vote in a territorial election? Perhaps some "asymmetrical" notion of federalism will have to be forged in the future to address these issues.

In the *Saskatchewan Reference* case, the permitted variations from the electoral quotient were in the neighbourhood of 25%. Even in the two northern Saskatchewan ridings, the variation from the norm was less than 50%. Mr. Justice Tallis of the Saskatchewan Court of Appeal recently chaired a similar commission in the Northwest Territories.[10] Notwithstanding the *Dixon* case, his commission recommended deviations far in excess of the 25% or even the 50% deviations that were upheld in the *Saskatchewan Reference.*

Consider the Yukon situation in light of the foregoing. It is trite to observe that the Yukon is not the same as Saskatchewan. It has very different realities regarding communication, culture, and aboriginal populations. It has one centre, Whitehorse, with two-thirds of the total population of the Territory—and the Territory only has a population of some 30,000 residents. The non-aboriginal population of the Yukon is comparatively transient, with new towns springing up and dying away, following trends that often follow the prices of natural resources. The Yukon also has a large First Nations population, comprising about 20% of its total population. Eight native languages are spoken. Very different aboriginal communities exist, often in far-flung communities with very small populations. The level of economic development and education in the varying native communities is very different as well. When the term "different communities of interest" is used, therefore, it is submitted that this has special relevance in the Territories.

A particularly poignant illustration is the community of Old Crow. Its total population is perhaps 250. Even "relative parity" of population in the Yukon would destroy the constituency of Old Crow.[11] In the *Saskatchewan Reference* case, Justice McLachlin held that section 3 should guarantee "relative parity" of voting power. What section 3 guarantees, she states, is "effective representation"; differences in geography, sparsity of population, communities of interest, population growth patterns, and minority representation "may need to be taken into account to ensure that legislative assemblies effectively represent the diversity of our social mosaic."[12] She indicates that these factors are mere illustrations and that the list of factors that could be taken into account is not closed.

At the time of writing, Mr. Justice Lysyk of the BC Supreme Court is serving as the Electoral Boundaries Commissioner of the Yukon. It may be that a later court could determine that the right to vote in section 3 must take some meaning and be coloured by other sections of the constitution, such as the interplay between it and sections 25 and 35, containing certain guaranteed aboriginal rights. The task of the Lysyk Commission is to work out the specific accommodations in light of specific evidence about the Yukon: evidence about the settled expectations of the First Nations there and their evolving rights to participate in the electoral and legislative process; evidence about the traditional boundaries of the First Nations; and evidence about the fluctuating populations of certain small communities.

My point is that these electoral exercises should be allowed to proceed and the legislators in these jurisdictions should be allowed to act upon them. They should not be foreclosed from this work by an approach to section 3 that involves a mechanical, mathematical formula applied on a universal basis. The sensitivity of the majority judgment, which contemplated that the balancing exercise would be performed under section 3, offers some hope that the special circumstances found in places like the Yukon may legitimately be considered. But how far can this exercise extend? Only a 5 to 10% deviation from the equal-population norm may be too great where there is absolutely no evidence of justification—say, as between two very similar urban ridings. But how far will a future court allow the deviation for cases such as that of Old Crow? The fact that this question can still be asked in Canada is eloquent testimony to the wisdom of the majority in the *Saskatchewan Reference* case, and suggests that such uniquely Canadian circumstances may indeed be accommodated in future litigation.

Notes

1. *Reference re Electoral Boundaries Commission Act (Sask.)* (1991), 81 D.L.R. (4th) 16 (S.C.C.).
2. *Thomson Newspapers Ltd. v. Canada* (1990), 76 C.R. (3d) 129 (S.C.C.).
3. *Reference re Public Service Employees Relations Act (Alta)*, [1987] 1 S.C.R. 313.
4. See, especially, *Andrews v. Law Society of British Columbia* (1989), 56 D.L.R. (4th) 1 (S.C.C.).
5. *R. v. Big M Drug Mart Ltd.* (1985), 18 D.L.R. (4th) 321.
6. *Dixon v. Attorney General of British Columbia* [1989] 4 W.W.R. 393, at p. 418 (B.C.S.C.).
7. See *Royal Commission Report on New Zealand's Electoral System* (1986).
8. Ibid., 18.
9. Ibid., 19.
10. *Report of the 1989/90 Electoral District Boundaries Commission: Northwest Territories.*
11. Applying 1986 Census data, the total population of the Yukon was 23,040. At present, there are 16 electoral districts, resulting in an "equal population norm" of 1,440. Since the population of Old Crow is shown as 230, this represents a deviation of -84%. Note also that the population of Old Crow is 82.6% aboriginal.
12. 81 D.L.R. (4th) 16 (S.C.C.), 36.

DRAWING BOUNDARIES: THE SASKATCHEWAN CASE

Reference Re Provincial Electoral Boundaries: An Analysis*

ROBERT G. RICHARDS
MACPHERSON, LESLIE & TYERMAN
THOMSON IRVINE
SASKATCHEWAN DEPARTMENT OF JUSTICE

The Supreme Court of Canada decision in *Reference re Provincial Electoral Boundaries*[1] has major implications for the Canadian electoral system. The Court held that the right to vote guaranteed by section 3 of the Canadian Charter of Rights and Freedoms does not include an entitlement to votes of equal "weight" in the sense that constituencies must be of equal population size. As a result, the meaning of the right to vote in Canada has been substantially clarified.

This paper considers *Reference re Provincial Electoral Boundaries* from a legal perspective. It begins with an examination of the history of electoral redistribution and the circumstances that gave rise to the proceedings in the case. The Supreme Court decision itself is then examined and the reasoning of both the majority and dissenting opinions is considered. Finally, the principal implications of the ruling are noted and the questions left unanswered by the Court are identified. Overall, it will be seen that the decision is extremely significant but that a number of relatively key issues remain substantially unresolved.

History of Electoral Boundaries

The history of electoral redistribution in Canada has not been characterized by a close adherence to the notion of "one person–one vote." As John Courtney has said, " . . . the doctrine of representation by population is one that has never been greatly respected in Canada."[2] That observation certainly holds true for the distribution of House of Commons seats *among* provinces. The Senate Floor Rule (which guarantees that provinces will have at least as many members of the House of Commons as they have senators)[3] and section 42(1)(a) of the

48

Constitution Act, 1982, (which entrenches the principle of proportional representation of provinces in the House of Commons)[4] both dilute the concept of voting parity. The rules for allocating seats among provinces reveal a genuine concern for equality but they have consistently been designed to create significant exceptions to the equality rule in order to ensure adequate provincial representation in the Commons.

The distribution of House of Commons seats *within* provinces has a rather similar history. Over time, there has been a trend toward limiting variations in constituency size but the notion of equal voting "weight" has never been the overriding electoral objective. The Commons had no rules for drawing intraprovincial boundaries for roughly the first 100 years of its existence. Variations in riding size were often very substantial and the basis on which boundaries were established was not consistent.[5]

The Electoral Boundaries Readjustment Act of 1964 substantially changed federal boundary drawing.[6] It introduced a system of boundary commissions and imposed limits on the permissible overall amount of variation in intraprovincial constituency size. Variations of +/- 25% from provincial quotients were allowed in order to accommodate a variety of matters such as geographic considerations (including the sparsity of population in an area and the size or accessibility of regions) and special community or diversity of interest. Subsequent federal statutes have taken generally the same approach.[7]

The electoral history of Saskatchewan is similar to that at the federal level. The first Legislative Assembly of the province was composed of 25 members elected to represent constituencies set out in an appendix to the Saskatchewan Act.[8] Subsequently, between 1908 and 1970, boundaries were regularly redrawn by way of government-sponsored legislation. The electoral maps during the period before 1971 did not involve ridings of equal size. For example, in 1905 constituencies varied from the "provincial quotient" (i.e., the number obtained by dividing population by the number of constituencies) by as much as +129% and -64%. In 1934 the range was +82% to -45%. That trend continued after World War II. In 1971, the variance was +91% at one extreme and -50% at the other.[9]

The approach to boundary drawing changed dramatically in the 1970s. The general election of 1971 was conducted on the basis of an electoral map that was widely regarded as reflecting a partisan gerrymander. In reaction to that state of affairs, the new NDP administration introduced a different system for creating constituency maps in The Constituency Boundaries Commission Act, 1972.[10] It provided for independent commissions to make periodic recommendations about the electoral map. Those recommendations were put into effect by way of The Representation Acts of 1974 and 1981.[11]

Background to the Case

The central issue in *Reference re Provincial Electoral Boundaries* was whether The Representation Act, 1989[12] violated section 3 of the Charter by virtue of the variances in the sizes of the constituencies that it established. The ridings described in that act were a function of the electoral distribution system set out in the controversial Electoral Boundaries Commission Act of 1987. It had replaced The Constituency Boundaries Commission Act.[13] Accordingly, an examination of The Electoral Boundaries Commission Act is essential to an understanding of the case.

The Electoral Boundaries Commission Act provided for the periodic establishment of electoral boundaries commissions to review and to make proposals for the areas, boundaries, and names of constituencies for the province. Each commission was to be comprised of a retired or supernumerary judge of the Court of Appeal or Court of Queen's Bench, nominated by the Chief Justice of Saskatchewan; a judge of the Provincial Court, nominated by the Chief Judge; and the Chief Electoral Officer of Saskatchewan.[14]

The act also specified that the Legislative Assembly would consist of 66 constituencies: 29 urban, 35 rural, and 2 northern. It drew a dividing line running from Cold Lake on the Alberta border to a point on the Manitoba boundary south of the intersection of the Saskatchewan River and that boundary. (The line followed the northern limit of surveyed land in the province and had been used in The Constituency Boundaries Commission Act as well.) The area north of that line was to be split between the two northern constituencies. The urban ridings were statutorily required to be confined within the municipal limits of the cities involved. The specific allocation of the urban seats among individual cities was set out in the act. The parts of the province outside the northern and urban areas were to be included in the so-called rural constituencies.[15]

The commission was required to proceed with its work by dividing the total voter population of the province by the number of constituencies. The "electoral quotient" so obtained was to be used in determining the size of the constituencies. Subject to the requirements concerning the division of the southern part of the province into specific numbers of urban and rural seats, the population of southern constituencies was not to vary by more than 25% from the quotient. The population of northern constituencies was not to vary from the quotient by more than 50%. The variance could be used to accommodate matters such as the density of population and rate of population growth, geographic features, community or diversity of interests, and similar factors. The specific language of the statute was as follows:

> 20. A Commission, in determining the area to be included in and in fixing the boundaries of all proposed constituencies:
> (a) shall determine a constituency population quotient by dividing the voter population by the number of constituencies, from which:
> (i) no proposed southern constituency population shall vary, subject to section 14 and subsection 15(1), by more than 25%;
> (ii) no proposed northern constituency population shall vary, subject to section 14, by more than 50%;
> (b) may use the following variation from the population quotient mentioned in clause (a) to accommodate:

(i) the sparsity, density or relative rate of growth of population of any proposed constituency;
(ii) any specific geographic features, including size and means of communication between the various parts of the proposed constituency;
(iii) the community or diversity of interests of the population, including variations in the requirements of the population of any proposed constituency; and
(iv) other similar or relevant factors.

The Electoral Boundaries Commission Act of 1987 differed in a number of ways from the legislation that it replaced. In that regard, four features of the act are important:

(a) the express direction that the province be divided into exactly 29 urban, 35 rural, and 2 northern seats was new. The predecessor legislation simply required the commission to divide the southern part of the province into no more than 63 ridings and the northern part into not less than 2 ridings. The actual number of seats was at the discretion of the commission and there was no statutory injunction as to how they were to be distributed between rural and urban areas.[16]

(b) the requirement that urban ridings could not extend beyond municipal boundaries was also novel. Although previous commissions had generally chosen to draw boundaries that tracked the municipal limits of larger cities, they had never been under a statutory obligation in that regard.[17]

(c) The Electoral Boundaries Commission Act did not expressly state that the commission should attempt to create ridings of equal population. The earlier legislation had specifically obliged the commission to fashion ridings of equal population and it authorized departures from equality only in order to accommodate matters such as community of interest.[18]

(d) the permissible variation in the population of southern ridings under the earlier act was +/- 15%. The 1987 legislation extended that range to +/- 25% and provided that even those limits could be exceeded if that should be necessary to maintain the prescribed division between rural and urban seats.[19]

Those four features of the act attracted considerable criticism from the Official Opposition when the legislation was considered by the assembly.

The Electoral Boundaries Commission Act came into force on 6 November 1987. The Lieutenant Governor appointed an Electoral Boundaries Commission on 31 January 1988. The commission published an interim report in August 1988.[20] It then held public hearings as required by the act and produced a final report which it submitted to the Legislative Assembly.[21] Not unexpectedly, the electoral map ultimately proposed by the commission involved some reasonably substantial deviations in population among ridings. Overall, there was a general tendency for rural seats to have fewer voters than urban seats. There were also some reasonably substantial variations in the size of urban and rural seats themselves. The complete list of ridings with their populations is reproduced as an Appendix to this paper.

The legislature then enacted The Representation Act, 1989. It adopted the findings of the commission and, with the exception of some very minor changes not relevant for present purposes, implemented the electoral boundaries drawn by the commission. The Representation Act, 1989, was to come into force the day after the dissolution or expiry of the Legislative Assembly.[22]

The Court of Appeal

After passage of The Representation Act, 1989, a group called the Society for the Advancement of Voter Equality (SAVE) contested the constitutional validity of the electoral map and threatened litigation. It believed that the introduction of the Charter had marked a watershed in electoral affairs and advocated a strict theory of "one person-one vote" based on section 3 of the Charter. Section 3 reads as follows:

> Every citizen of Canada has the right to vote in an election of members of the House of Commons or of a legislative assembly and to be qualified for membership therein.

The Lieutenant Governor in Council then referred the constitutionality of the act to the Saskatchewan Court of Appeal for consideration. The specific questions presented to the Court were as follows:

> In respect of the constituencies defined in *The Representation Act, 1989:*
> (a) Does the variance in the size of voter populations among those constituencies, as contemplated by section 20 of *The Electoral Boundaries Commission Act* and recommended in the *Electoral Boundaries Commission 1988 Final Report*, infringe or deny rights or freedoms guaranteed by the *Canadian Charter of Rights and Freedoms?* If so, in what particulars? Is any such limitation or denial of rights justified by section 1 of the *Canadian Charter of Rights and Freedoms?*
> (b) Does the distribution of those constituencies among urban, rural and northern areas, as contemplated by section 14 of *The Electoral Boundaries Commission Act* and recommended in the *Electoral Boundaries Commission 1988 Final Report*, infringe or deny rights guaranteed by the *Canadian Charter of Rights and Freedoms?* If so, in what particulars? Is any such limitation or denial of rights justified by section 1 of the *Canadian Charter of Rights and Freedoms?*[23]

The Court of Appeal appointed Mr. Roger Carter, Q.C., to present the case in opposition to the constitutional validity of the electoral boundaries. He had already been retained by SAVE and continued to act for that group. An anti-poverty group and a Regina voter were granted intervener status. The Reference was heard on 4 and 5 December 1990. The Court delivered its unanimous ruling on 6 March 1991.[24]

The Court of Appeal held that the right to vote includes the requirement that "one person-one vote" must be the guiding ideal in evaluating electoral distribution schemes. Some minor deviation in the size of ridings was said to be inherent in section 3 of the Charter but only because voters are mobile and because elections in parliamentary systems can theoretically happen at any time. The Court said that these "inherent" deviations must interfere as little as possible with the controlling concept of "one person–one vote." Considerations such as geography, historical boundaries, and community of interest can only be considered under section 1 of the Charter. That section provides that rights can be limited validly in ways that are reasonable and demonstrably justifiable.[25]

The Court, on the basis of those principles, concluded that The Representation Act, 1989, was unconstitutional. It described the division of seats between urban and rural ridings as "arbitrary" and considered that the variations in the size of ridings was "egregious."[26] It also said that deviations in constituency size of +/– 25% from the electoral quotient for southern ridings could not be justified. However, the Court did uphold the validity of the two northern constituencies by applying section 1 of the Charter.[27]

That decision had rather dramatic implications for Saskatchewan. By advising that the ridings described in The Representation Act, 1989, were unconstitutional, the Court had placed the province in an electoral limbo. The government was well into the fifth year of its mandate and an election call seemed imminent. All parties had nominated large numbers of candidates to contest the ridings described in The Representation Act, 1989. The electoral map that formed the basis of the assembly as it existed at the time of the ruling had been put in place by The Representation Act, 1981.[28] Due to ongoing demographic changes, by the time of the Court of Appeal ruling the 1981 map had population variances even greater than those found in The Representation Act, 1989.[29] There seemed to be no constitutionally sound map on which to base a general election.

The government reacted to this situation by moving simultaneously on two separate tracks. First, it appealed the Court of Appeal decision to the Supreme Court of Canada and asked for an expedited hearing. Second, it put in place a new electoral boundaries commission process to establish constituency boundaries on principles that were consistent with the Court of Appeal ruling.[30] In this way, a valid electoral map would be available in the event that the Supreme Court dismissed the appeal or did not render a judgment on a timely basis.

The Supreme Court Decision

The Supreme Court appeal attracted considerable national attention. The reason is readily apparent. The implication of the Court of Appeal's decision was that, with the possible exception of Manitoba, every electoral map in the country was invalid. The attorneys general of Canada, Québec, British Columbia, Prince Edward Island, Alberta, and Newfoundland, the ministers of justice of the Northwest Territories and the Yukon, and the Alberta Association of Municipal Districts and Counties all intervened in support of the Attorney General of Saskatchewan. The two interveners from the Court of Appeal hearing, the British Columbia Civil Liberties Association, a group of voters from the Northwest Territories, and the cities of Edmonton and Grande Prairie intervened to uphold the Court of Appeal decision.

The appeal was argued on 29 and 30 April 1991. The Court gave judgment on 6 June 1991. It split six to three. Madam Justice McLachlin gave the majority judgment upholding the boundaries. Justices La Forest, Gonthier, Stevenson, and Iacobucci adopted her reasons. Mr. Justice Sopinka wrote a short concurring opinion. Mr. Justice Cory dissented. Chief Justice Lamer and Justice L'Heureux-Dubé endorsed his approach.

Reasons of the Majority

McLachlin J. began her reasons by noting that she was faced with two different views of the purpose of section 3.[31] One approach, suggested by SAVE, was that the focus of section 3 was to require "parity of voting power"–a "one person–one vote" principle. Factors other than population levels could only be considered under section 1 of the Charter as possible "reasonable limitations" of the right itself. The other view of section 3, put forward by the Attorney General, was that the section was not concerned solely with voting parity. Under the latter approach, equality in population levels was conceded to be the prime consideration in setting electoral boundaries. However, concern about the equal "weight" of votes had to be moderated and qualified by other considerations relevant to a system of effective representation. Thus, factors such as community of interest, geography, and communication should be comprehended by the right to vote itself and need not be considered only under section 1 of the Charter.

Before turning to the substance of the problem before the Court, McLachlin J. considered an issue that was a recurring theme throughout the proceedings: is section 3 of the Charter concerned solely with results (i.e., the fairness of the actual distribution) or is it also concerned with the process by which a map is produced? The point is of some importance. Under the second approach, defects in process could lead to a map being struck down even if it reflected an absolutely equal distribution of population. McLachlin J. held that it was the map and its actual population distributions that were at issue. The process by which the map was drawn was a relevant consideration, "but the basic question put to this court is whether the variance and distribution reflected in the constituencies themselves violate the *Charter* guarantee of the right to vote."[32]

McLachlin J. then dealt with the substantive meaning of section 3 of the Charter. She concluded that the purpose of the right to vote was not equality of voting power *per se,* but the right to "effective representation."[33] She arrived at that view by way of reference to a number of factors. First, absolute equality was impossible because voter mobility precluded the establishment of boundaries that guaranteed exactly the same number of voters in each district. Second, there was no evidence to suggest that the framers of the Charter had intended to incorporate an American-style doctrine of voter parity into the Canadian constitution. Third, Canadian history, along with the British and

Commonwealth experience, suggested that the object of section 3 of the Charter was not to enshrine voter equality but rather to guarantee effective representation. Fourth, the practical problems of representing vast, sparsely populated geographical areas also suggested that deviations from a strict "one person–one vote" approach are necessary in Canada.[34] In the final analysis, McLachlin J. considered that "the values and principles animating a free and democratic society are arguably best served by a definition that places effective representation at the heart of the right to vote."[35]

In light of all those considerations, McLachlin J. noted that parity in riding size may actually detract from the primary goal of effective representation. Factors such as geography, community history, and community interests may need to be considered to insure effective representation. The essence of her conclusion on the meaning of section 3 of the Charter was expressed in the following terms:

> It emerges therefore that deviations from absolute voter parity may be justified on the grounds of practical impossibility or the provision of more effective representation. Beyond this, dilution of one citizen's vote as compared with another's should not be countenanced. I adhere to the proposition asserted in *Dixon*, at p. 414, that "only those deviations should be admitted which can be justified on the ground that they contribute to better government of the populace as a whole, giving due weight to regional issues within the populace and geographic factors within the territory governed."[36]

McLachlin J. next turned to the issue of the validity of the electoral map that was before the Court.[37] She began by sounding a significant note of warning that courts must be cautious and restrained when dealing with decisions that involve the balancing of conflicting policy considerations. McLachlin J. reiterated views she had expressed earlier, when on the British Columbia Supreme Court, to the effect that "the courts ought not to interfere with the legislature's electoral map under section 3 of the *Charter* unless it appears that reasonable persons applying the appropriate principles ... could not have set the electoral boundaries as they exist."[38]

She next dealt with the suggestion that the Electoral Boundaries Commission had acted arbitrarily in generating the map because of the statutory constraints placed on it. That argument had been accepted by the Court of Appeal. As noted above, it concluded that the commission could not give proper emphasis to parity of riding size because the governing legislation required it to create 35 rural and 29 urban ridings.

McLachlin J. accepted the Attorney General's invitation to look beyond the simple allocation of seats in the legislation and to review the genesis of those stipulations and the actual population base that underpinned the distribution of urban and rural seats. She concluded that "the allotment of seats to the various urban centres in *The Representation Act, 1989* flows logically from the electoral map that it replaced"[39] and noted that the earlier map had been drawn by an impartial commission under no obligation to create particular numbers of rural and urban ridings. She considered the details of the allocation of urban ridings and related them to the earlier electoral map. Her conclusion was that "the configuration of urban seats in *The Representation Act, 1989* simply reflects population growth in those areas from the time the earlier map was put in place."[40] With regard to the tendency for urban seats to have somewhat more voters than rural seats, she said that the discrepancies were not great, that there were a number of exceptions to the general trend, that the actual allocation of seats between urban and rural areas was very close to the population distribution between those areas, and, finally, that similar overall deviations had occurred in the redistributions proposed by previous commissions.[41]

McLachlin J. then considered the second major line of attack against the Saskatchewan map. It was to the effect that the discrepancies in the populations of particular southern ridings could not be justified. She began by noting that the material before the Court suggested it was more difficult to represent rural ridings than urban ridings and that, accordingly, the goal of effective representation could generally justify somewhat lower populations in rural areas. McLachlin J. also offered the general observation that boundaries will be in place for a number of years and that, as a result, some attention legitimately can be paid to population growth patterns.[42]

The reports of the Electoral Boundaries Commission did not include detailed riding-by-riding explanations or justifications for the population discrepancies among constituencies. However, although The Electoral Boundaries Commission Act did not explicitly address the equality issue, the commission had stated that it considered that it was entitled to depart from strict equality in riding size "only for the reasons set forth in the *Act* [i.e. geography, community of interest and so on] and only to the extent that the special circumstances properly permit, and the legislation requires."[43] The *Final Report* did directly address the reasoning behind the boundaries of the largest and the smallest rural ridings. McLachlin J. quoted those explanations with apparent approval. She also dealt with two adjacent urban ridings in Saskatoon with controversial population variances of +24% and -24% respectively. They had been the subject of special criticism by the Respondent. She observed that those opposing the map had presented no evidence apart from the population figures to support the contention that the variance between those ridings was arbitrary and said that "it may be, as the [Attorney General] suggests, that the potential for future increases in the population . . . is a factor in the discrepancy."[44] Overall, she summarized her views in the following language:

> In summary, the evidence supplied by the province is sufficient to justify the existing electoral boundaries. In general, the discrepancies between urban and rural ridings is *[sic]* small, no more than one might expect given the greater difficulties associated with representing rural ridings. And discrepancies between particular ridings appear to be justified on the basis of factors such as geography, community interest and population growth patterns. It was not seriously sug-

gested that the northern boundaries are inappropriate, given the sparse population and the difficulty of communication in the area. I conclude that a violation of section 3 of the *Charter* has not been established.[45]

In result, McLachlin J. answered both reference questions in the negative and upheld the constitutional validity of the map put in place by The Representation Act, 1989.

Reasons of Sopinka J.

Sopinka J. agreed with McLachlin J. that section 3 of the Charter does not guarantee strict mathematical equality of voting strength. [46] In his opinion, the content of section 3 was to be determined by reference to the history of the right to vote in Canada. The Charter was not intended to create a new right or to alter the concept of the right to vote that existed prior to 1982. Historically, attempts had been made to achieve relative voter equality, but other factors had also been considered necessary to achieve fair and effective representation. In the end, the question was the fairness of the map. In his view, the population deviations in the ridings created by The Representation Act, 1989, were not so great as to deny fair and effective representation.

Sopinka J. also responded directly to the argument, which Cory J. adopted in dissent, to the effect that section 3 of the Charter required boundaries commissions to be completely independent. Sopinka J. observed that there was no obligation on the legislature to create a commission at all. It could have drawn the map itself. Therefore, having created a commission, the legislature was entitled to set tight guidelines for it to follow in the execution of its responsibilities.

The Dissent

Cory J. held that section 3 of the Charter required an analysis of both substantive result and process. In his view, the courts should not restrict themselves solely to the end result of an electoral redistribution:

> We are concerned in this appeal not only with results but also with process. In my view, section 3 scrutiny attaches not only to the actual distribution in question, but also to the underlying process from which the electoral map was derived.[47]

Cory J. said expressly that the boundaries imposed by The Representation Act, 1989, were not as fair as those reflected in the 1981 riding map. He considered the difference between the old boundaries commission legislation and the 1987 statute to be of fundamental importance. The division of the province into set numbers of rural and urban seats and the requirement that urban ridings not extend beyond municipal boundaries resulted in a constitutionally defective product. Cory J. considered that the 1981 redistribution showed that a deviation of +/- 15% could reasonably accommodate geography, community interests, and other relevant matters. That degree of equality should have been maintained. The mandatory rural-urban allocation and the require-ments with respect to municipal limits made it impossible to give proper effect to the ongoing population shift in favour of urban centres and led to greater variances than otherwise would have occurred if the commission had been free to make its own recommendations.[48] Cory J. considered that "the fundamental importance of the right to vote demands a reasonably strict surveillance of legislative provisions pertaining to elections."[49]

In considering the process of redistribution, Cory J. held that "while the actual redistribution map may appear to have achieved a result that is not too unreasonable," the effect of the statutory conditions was interference with the rights of urban voters. He held that once an independent boundaries commis-sion was established, " . . . it was incumbent upon the Saskatchewan legislature to ensure that the commission was able to fulfil its mandate freely and without unnecessary interference." The strictures placed on the commission by the legislature were sufficient interference to constitute a breach of section 3 of the Charter. He held that the province had failed to justify the need to impose restrictions on the commission with respect to the mandatory rural-urban allocation and the confinement of urban boundaries to municipal limits.[50]

Cory J. went on to consider issues arising under section 1 of the Charter.[51] He found that the two northern constituencies were in a class by themselves and that their creation could be justified under section 1 of the Charter. With respect to the southern ridings, he found that the Attorney General had shown no pressing and substantial reason for imposing restrictions on the boundaries commission and, in any event, had not shown that the legislation in question affected the rights of urban voters as little as possible. He concluded that the boundaries could not be justified as reasonable limitations of rights pursuant to section 1 of the Charter.[52]

Implications of the Decision

Reference re Provincial Electoral Boundaries has resolved a number of very substantial issues with respect to the meaning of the right to vote in section 3 of the Charter. Perhaps most significantly, it establishes that a strict doctrine of "one person–one vote" is not constitutionally enshrined in Canada. Rather, the right to vote itself comprehends an accommodation of various factors relevant to effective representation. The case also decides that the Charter does not guarantee any particular kind of process for the establishment of electoral boundaries. Maps need not be drawn by fully independent commissions. Finally, the decision indicates that courts will be very deferential to legislative choice when considering the constitutional validity of electoral boundaries.[53] Each of these determinations is extremely substantial and significant. However, there are still a number of important questions about electoral redistribution and the "right to vote" that remain unsettled.

First, it is not entirely clear what kinds of factors legitimately can be used as a basis for moving away from strict equality in riding size. The majority of the Court did not purport to define exhaustively the list of considerations that would be constitutionally acceptable. McLachlin J. said:

> Factors like geography, community history, community interests and minority representation may need to be taken into account to ensure that our legislative assemblies effectively represent the diversity of our social mosaic. These are but examples of considerations which may justify departure from absolute voter parity in the pursuit of more effective representations; the list is not closed. [54]

Interestingly, The Electoral Boundaries Commission Act itself involves a very fluid list of factors that could be considered in justifying variations from strict equality. Section 20 of the act contains, in paragraphs (b)(i) to (iii), the standard inventory of considerations such as sparsity or density of population, geographic features, means of communication, and community interests. However, section 20(b)(iv) then goes on to add "other similar or relevant factors" to the list. The Supreme Court did not comment specifically on that feature of the act. Thus, it is likely fair to infer that the Court will not be quick to second guess the types of variables that a legislature deems relevant to insuring "effective representation" so long as they are generally consistent with mainstream practice.

The second issue that remains unresolved in the wake of *Reference re Provincial Electoral Boundaries* involves the question of how far ridings can be moved away from strict equality before Charter problems are encountered. The map before the Court in *Reference re Provincial Electoral Boundaries* involved actual deviations in the southern ridings ranging from -24% to +24% from the electoral quotient. McLachlin and Sopinka JJ. obviously found that range of variance to be acceptable but neither commented specifically on the outer limits of variation that could be constitutionally sustained. Accordingly, the decision does not mean that any amount of variation in riding size is acceptable so long as it reflects factors like those noted in section 20 of The Electoral Boundaries Commission Act.

It is perhaps significant that a variance of +/- 25% is something of an electoral norm in Canada. The relevant federal legislation, as well as the governing laws in Alberta, British Columbia, Newfoundland, Ontario, and Québec, all use +/- 25% as the basic parameter for map drawing. [55] Only the Manitoba system, with a maximum variance of +/- 10% for southern ridings, was more strict than the Saskatchewan map. [56] Many of the submissions to the Supreme Court stressed the fact that the Saskatchewan variances were entirely consistent with general Canadian practice and standards. As a result, it may be that (with the exception of especially remote regions) variations much beyond +/- 25% are constitutionally suspect. However, exactly where the lines of constitutional tolerance might be drawn is difficult to predict.

A third point that was not addressed by the Supreme Court concerns the appropriate population base that should be used when determining constituency size. The Electoral Boundaries Commission Act required that boundaries be drawn on the basis of "voter population." However, there is no common view on that point. For example, Australia, the United Kingdom, Québec, and Saskatchewan all draw their maps on the basis of voter population.[57] On the other hand, redistributions in Alberta, Manitoba, and at the federal level in Canada are based on overall population levels.[58]

The choice of population base can clearly have a significant impact on the makeup of an electoral map. If all residents are considered when boundaries are established, then the map will favour those areas with relatively large numbers of children or persons otherwise not entitled to vote, such as landed immigrants. The issue raises often unarticulated questions about the nature of representation. Do legislators represent voters or the total population? If they represent the total population, should the relative "weight" of votes nonetheless be determined as among electors rather than the population at large? These are extremely fundamental issues that are not particularly amenable to judicial resolution. It can be expected that the courts will not impose their view as to how they should be answered. It is highly likely that the judiciary will defer entirely to legislative choice as to the appropriate population basis on which to establish electoral boundaries.

The fourth significant issue left undecided by the Supreme Court ruling is whether the constitutional validity of an electoral map can be eroded over time. The most perfectly drawn map can go rapidly out of date if there are significant population shifts. For example, the Saskatchewan general election of 1975 took place only 13 months after a redistribution under The Constituency Boundaries Commission Act, 1972. Even though that act permitted deviations of no more than +/- 15%, four ridings had already exceeded that maximum—the largest with a population 37% greater than the average.[59] Greater delays in redistribution can create even more acute problems. Prince Edward Island has not redistributed ridings since 1963.[60] In the last general election, all its seats but one varied from the provincial average by more than +/- 30%.[61] Similarly, New Brunswick has not had a redistribution since 1974,[62] and 31 out of 58 seats varied by more than +/- 25% from the provincial average in the 1987 general election.[63]

It seems clear that the actual population distribution created by an electoral map will be the crucial consideration in a constitutional challenge. The fairness of the distribution when the map was first drawn will not be determinative. However, none of the redistribution systems in Canada envisages redistribution after every election. Some require that it be done after every second general election, while others tie it to the decennial census. Either way, current practice reflects an assumption that a map will be in use for several years, even though there may be significant population shifts in the interim. Given the general tone of *Reference re Provincial Electoral Boundaries*, it is unlikely that the courts will force a sharp break from the general Canadian practice. It is probable that, in the absence of some extraordinary circumstance, the Supreme Court would find that a properly drawn map must enjoy some reasonable constitutional longevity notwithstanding the fact that actual population levels in ridings will shift over time. Nonetheless, the problem of locating the limits of judicial tolerance in this regard may be difficult to resolve.

Another aspect of this issue is raised by the Court's recognition that a valid map can reflect anticipated population shifts. Once a commission is allowed to look into the future, on what basis should the map be drawn? Should it create ridings that are of equal size at the moment the map is prepared, or should it be drawn with the idea that ridings will move toward equality in the future? For example, at the Commonwealth level in Australia redistribution committees are required to draw a map that will have ridings that are as close to equal size as possible 3 1/2 years in the future. [64] Overall, this appears to be another area where, in the absence of extraordinary circumstances, the courts will defer to legislative choice.

A fifth issue that remains undecided in the wake of *Reference re Provincial Electoral Boundaries* concerns the constitutional validity of special systems of representation for particular racial, linguistic, or other groups. This may soon become an important consideration because guaranteed representation for aboriginal peoples is now a commonly discussed concept. [65]

Reference re Provincial Electoral Boundaries clearly upholds special representation based on territorial considerations. The Electoral Boundaries Commission Act allowed the northern ridings in Saskatchewan to vary from the provincial quotient by as much as +/- 50%. These two ridings together contain approximately 2% of the voter population of the province but represent approximately one-half of the total land area. McLachlin J. noted that none of the parties to the proceedings took serious issue with the special provisions relating to northern Saskatchewan and found that the electoral map which reflected those provisions did not violate section 3 of the Charter. [66] That result is consistent with a general practice in Canada that has traditionally recognized the special difficulties involved in representing extremely large or remote areas. [67]

The language chosen by McLachlin J. also suggests that the Court may look charitably on special representation regimes based on linguistic or racial considerations. She noted that "factors like geography, community history, community interests and minority representation may need to be taken into account to insure that our legislative assemblies effectively represent the *diversity of our social mosaic.*" [68] She also said that " . . . *the need to recognize cultural and group identity* and to enhance the participation of individuals in the electoral process and society requires that [concerns other than voting parity] also be accommodated." [69] Those views indicate that it may be possible for a legislature to create a special kind of representation for members of a particular group in society who are inadequately represented under an existing electoral system. The unique constitutional and legal position of aboriginal peoples, combined with the fact that they are almost completely absent from legislative assemblies, suggests that the Supreme Court would be inclined to accommodate some kind of guaranteed representation for them under section 3 of the Charter. [70]

The sixth point to note about *Reference re Provincial Electoral Boundaries* is closely related to the issue of special representation. It flows from the decision of the majority of the Court to characterize "effective representation" as the purpose of section 3 of the Charter. That approach to the right to vote may mean, as McLachlin J. herself intimated at one point, that an electoral map that scrupulously adheres to the concept of "one person–one vote" may be unconstitutional for that very reason, i.e., because it fails to reflect the other kinds of considerations necessary to ensure a system of effective representation. There is certainly language in the decision that aboriginal communities, or others, might use in an attempt to force legislatures to give them some special system of representation.[71] The argument would be that, absent such special considerations, those communities would be denied "effective representation" as *per* their rights under section 3 of the Charter.

However, it is by no means certain that McLachlin J. intended her ruling to involve those kinds of results. Key passages in her reasons suggest that she views section 3 of the Charter as allowing legislatures to move away from strict equality in the name of effective representation but that she does not consider that they must do so. That approach would see the Charter as simply accommodating the pursuit of effective representation rather than mandating it. It is quite likely that the somewhat ambiguous wording of the Supreme Court ruling will inspire litigation involving the issue of whether the right to vote actually imposes a positive obligation on legislatures to establish effective representation.

Finally, it should be noted that *Reference re Provincial Electoral Boundaries* does not determine the constitutional implications of partisan gerrymandering. Submissions were made to the Court to the effect that The Representation Act, 1989, was deliberately skewed in favour of the over-representation of rural Saskatchewan and hence in favour of the partisan interests of the government of the day. After reviewing the background of the allocation of rural and urban seats in detail, McLachlin J. said:

> This [background] belies the suggestion that the 1989 Act was an unjustified attempt to adjust boundaries to benefit the governing party.[72]

Therefore, the legal consequences of partisan gerrymandering remain to be considered. It is likely fair to anticipate that the courts will be reluctant to enter into an inquiry with respect to those kinds of issues.[73] However, they will be obliged to grapple directly with the problem if confronted with a situation where gerrymander can be convincingly documented and established. In such circumstances, it is likely that the courts will find that the Charter has been violated.

Conclusion

Reference re Provincial Electoral Boundaries will govern the redistribution of electoral maps in Canada for the foreseeable future. It clearly rejects any effort to read a strict application of the doctrine of "one person–one vote" into section 3 of the Charter. However, the decision leaves a number of other important legal problems unanswered. It is highly likely that more litigation with respect to the meaning of "the right to vote" will be forthcoming.

Notes

* The authors were counsel for the Attorney General of Saskatchewan in the Reference. The views expressed in this paper are their own. The authors wish to thank Lane Wiegers, Student-at-Law with the Saskatchewan Justice Department, for his assistance in preparing this paper for publication.

1. *Reference re Provincial Electoral Boundaries,* [1991] 5 W.W.R. 1 (S.C.C.), 81 D.L.R. (4th) 16 *(sub nom. Reference re Electoral Boundaries Commission Act).* All citations are to the W.W.R. report.
2. John C. Courtney, "Some Thoughts on Redistribution," *Canadian Parliamentary Review,* (Spring 1986): 18.
3. Constitution Act, 1867, s. 51A, as amended by the Constitution Act, 1915.
4. As interpreted by the courts, the "principle of proportionate representation" in s. 42(1)(a) is not equivalent to pure representation by population. Instead, it means "modified representation by population, a principle necessary to protect provinces with declining populations." See the Constitution Act, 1867, s. 51(2), as amended by the Constitution Act, 1985 (Representation), S.C. 1986, c. 8, Pt. I and *Campbell v. Attorney General of Canada* (1988), 25 B.C.L.R. (2d) 101 (B.C.S.C.), 113-14.
5. For example, in 1961, the population of the smallest federal constituency was 12,479 while the largest was 267,252. Urban seats in Montréal ranged from 34,020 to 233,964. Saskatchewan ridings varied from 37,937 to 95,575. The largest riding in Prince Edward Island was more than double the smallest. See Norman Ward, "A Century of Constituencies," *Canadian Public Administration* (1967): 105, 107, 109.
6. Electoral Boundaries Readjustment Act, S.C. 1964-65, c. 31.
7. Electoral Boundaries Readjustment Act, R.S.C. 1985, c. E-3.
8. Saskatchewan Act, S.C. 1905, c. 42, s. 13 and Schedule.
9. Provincial Elections in Saskatchewan 1905-1986 (Regina: Chief Electoral Office, 3rd ed., 1987), 17-158. (Percentages calculated by the authors.)
10. The Constituency Boundaries Commission Act, 1972, S.S. 1972, c. 18.
11. The Representation Act, 1974, S.S. 1973-74, c. 91; The Representation Act, 1981, S.S. 1980-81, c. R-20.1.
12. The Representation Act, 1989, S.S. 1989-90, c. R-20.2.
13. The Electoral Boundaries Commission Act, S.S. 1986-87-88, c. E-6.1. (The Constituency Boundaries Commission Act, 1972 [see n.10], had been consolidated as The Constituency Boundaries Commission Act, R.S.S. 1978, c. C-28.)
14. Ibid., s. 3.
15. Ibid., ss. 2(b), 14-18 and Schedule; The Constituency Boundaries Commission Act (see n.13), s. 4.
16. The Constituency Boundaries Commission Act, s. 13(1).
17. See the maps prepared by the 1974 and 1981 Constituency Boundaries Commissions, in *Provincial Elections in Saskatchewan* (see n.9), 179-88.
18. The Constituency Boundaries Commission Act (see n.13), s. 16(1), rule 1.
19. Ibid., s. 16(1), rule 2; The Electoral Boundaries Commission Act (see n.13), s. 20(a)(i).

20. *Electoral Boundaries Commission 1988 Interim Report.*
21. *Electoral Boundaries Commission 1988 Final Report.*
22. The Representation Act, 1989 (see n.12), s. 4. The Lieutenant Governor dissolved the assembly on 20 September 1991, bringing the act into force the next day.
23. Saskatchewan Order-in-Council 90/0702, 20 July 1990, Schedule A, enacted pursuant to The Constitutional Questions Act, R.S.S. 1978, c. C–29, s. 2.
24. *Reference re Provincial Electoral Boundaries,* [1991] 3 W.W.R. 593 (Sask. C.A.), 90 Sask.R. 174, 78 D.L.R. (4th) 449 *(sub nom. Reference re Electoral Boundaries Commission Act).* All citations are to the W.W.R. report. The Court set a five-judge panel: Tallis, Cameron, Vancise, Gerwing, and Sherstobitoff JJ.A.
25. Ibid., 606–9.
26. Ibid., 613–20.
27. Ibid., 623–27.
28. The Representation Act, 1981 (see n.11).
29. The 1986 election had been conducted on the 1981 map. Even in five years the population had shifted markedly. In 1986 the smallest riding, Morse, had a population of 7,757, while the largest, Saskatoon Mayfair, had a population of 20,741 *(Provincial Elections in Saskatchewan* (see n.9), 151-57). These were variances from the average of –26.7% and +49.0%, respectively. (Calculations by the authors.)
30. The Electoral Boundaries Commission Act, 1991, S.S. 1990-91, c. E-6.11.
31. *Reference re Provincial Electoral Boundaries* (S.C.C.) (see n.1), 11.
32. Ibid., 7.
33. Ibid., 12.
34. Ibid., 15.
35. Ibid.
36. Ibid., 13.
37. Ibid., 16–22.
38. *Dixon v. British Columbia (Attorney General),* [1989] 4 W.W.R. 393 (B.C.S.C.), 419.
39. *Reference re Provincial Electoral Boundaries* (S.C.C.) (see n.1), 18.
40. Ibid.
41. Ibid., 18–19.
42. Ibid., 20.
43. *Final Report* (see n.21), 4.
44. *Reference re Provincial Electoral Boundaries* (S.C.C.) (see n.1), 21.
45. Ibid., 22.
46. Ibid., 22–24.
47. Ibid., 28–29.
48. Ibid., 27–29.
49. Ibid., 28.
50. Ibid., 29.
51. Ibid., 29–31.
52. The Attorney General made several additional arguments in support of the boundaries which the Court did not discuss. In brief, these arguments were as follows. First, the argument for "one person-one vote" is based on the idea of equal "weight" of votes. Yet if this argument is accepted, it casts into doubt the constitutionality of the entire "first past the post" electoral system, which allows a party with a plurality of popular support to win a majority of seats. Arguably, a system of proportional

representation would measure voter opinion much more accurately, and therefore be constitutionally required if voter "weight" was the sole factor to consider. Second, the Senate Floor Rule (Constitution Act, 1867, s. 51A) mandates a certain distribution of seats in the House of Commons amongst the provinces. If Parliament purported to distribute seats strictly according to population, the resulting map would breach this rule and would be unconstitutional. This fact starkly illustrates that s. 3 cannot mandate "one person-one vote," at least at the federal level. Third, although the United States has gone furthest along the road of "one person-one vote," it still has some exceptions to this requirement, notably in the distribution of seats in the House of Representatives amongst the states, the weight of each state in presidential elections, and the different standards used to evaluate federal and state redistributions. Fourth, there were statutory guarantees of the right to vote prior to 1982, but there was no suggestion that this right meant "one person-one vote" (The Saskatchewan Bill of Rights, S.S. 1947, c. 35, s. 7 [carried forward in The Saskatchewan Human Rights Code, S.S. 1979, c. S-24.1, s. 8]; Charter of Human Rights and Freedoms, R.S.Q. 1977, c. C-12, s. 22).

53. The Alberta Court of Appeal recently decided a similar electoral challenge, *Reference re Electoral Boundaries Commission Act (Alberta)*, #9103-0081-AC, 21 November 1991 (unreported). The decision demonstrates just how deferential the courts are likely to be. After quoting McLachlin J.'s standard of review from the *Dixon* case (see n.38), the Alberta Court of Appeal set out its interpretation of the test (at p. 9): "We must therefore ask ourselves whether a boundary rule or decision is clearly wrong. In other words, we should not interfere unless a rule or decision is demonstrably unjustified, palpably wrong, or manifestly unreasonable." This is a very heavy onus. If adopted by other courts, it is one that most challengers will likely be unable to overcome.

54. Ibid., 12–13.
55. Electoral Boundaries Readjustment Act, R.S.C. 1985, c. E-3, s. 15(2), as amended by R.S.C. 1985, c. 6 (2nd Supp.), s. 2; Electoral Boundaries Commission Act, S.A. 1990, c. E-4.01, s. 17; Electoral Boundaries Commission Act, S.B.C. 1989, c. 65, s. 9; The Electoral Boundaries Delimitation Act, 1973, S.N. 1973, c. 44, s. 16; Resolution of the Ontario Legislative Assembly, 16 June 1983, at pp. 97–98, *Journals of the Legislative Assembly, 1983;* Election Act, S.Q. 1989, c. 1, s. 16.
56. The Electoral Divisions Act, R.S.M. 1987, c. E40, s. 11(3).
57. Commonwealth Electoral Act 1918 (Australia), s. 65(2), consolidated to 30 Sept. 1984; House of Commons (Redistribution of Seats Act), 1958 (U.K.), 6 and 7 Eliz. II, c. 26, s. 3; Election Act, S.Q. 1989, c. 1, s. 16; The Electoral Boundaries Commission Act (see n.13), s. 2(i).
58. Electoral Boundaries Commission Act, S.A. 1990, c. E-4.01, s. 12(d); The Electoral Divisions Act, R.S.M. 1987, c. E40, s. 9; Electoral Boundaries Readjustment Act, R.S.C. 1985, c. E-3, s. 15(1)(a), as amended by R.S.C. 1985, c. 6 (2nd Supp.), s. 2.
59. *Provincial Elections in Saskatchewan* (see n.9), 125–30. (Calculations by the authors.)
60. Election Act, S.P.E.I. 1963, c. 11, ss. 165–68.
61. *Report of the Chief Electoral Officer of Prince Edward Island, 1989.* (Calculations by the authors.)
62. An Act to Amend the Elections Act, S.N.B. 1974, c. 92 (Supp.), s. 19; An Act to Amend the Elections Act, S.N.B. 1974, c. 12 (Supp.), s. 31.

63. *Report of the Chief Electoral Officer of New Brunswick, Thirty-First General Election, 1987.* (Calculations by the authors.)
64. Commonwealth Electoral Act 1918, s. 73(4), as amended by the Commonwealth Electoral Amendment Act, 1987, No. 35 of 1987, s. 13.
65. "Shaping Canada's Future Together—Proposals" (Minister of Supply and Services Canada, 1991), 8-9; "Quebec considers seat for Inuit in far North," *The Globe and Mail*, 1 May 1991; "Nova Scotia legislature endorses special seat for Micmacs," Saskatoon *Star Phoenix*, 25 May 1991; "[Alberta] Electoral reform could see aboriginal districts," *Edmonton Journal*, 27 June 1991.
66. *Reference re Provincial Electoral Boundaries* (S.C.C.) (see n.1), 22.
67. In addition to Saskatchewan, Newfoundland, Ontario, and Québec guarantee a set number of seats to sparsely populated or isolated regions [House of Assembly (Amendment) Act, S.N. 1979, c. 2, s. 5; Resolution of the Ontario Legislative Assembly, 16 June 1983, at pp. 97-98, *Journals of the Legislative Assembly, 1983*; Elections Act, S.Q. 1989, c. 1, s. 17]. At the federal level, the two territories have three seats, which a strict "one person–one vote" principle likely would not allow [Constitution Act, 1867, s. 51(2), as amended by the Constitution Act, 1975, S.C. 1974-75-76, c. 28]. In addition, several jurisdictions allow their boundary commissions to exceed the normal maximum deviation in "extraordinary" or "special" circumstances. This wider range normally will benefit more isolated or sparsely populated areas [Electoral Boundaries Readjustment Act, R.S.C. 1985, c. E-3, s. 15(2), as amended by R.S.C. 1985, c. 6 (2nd Supp.), s. 2(2); Electoral Boundaries Commission Act, S.A. 1990, c. E-4.01, s. 17(2); Electoral Boundaries Commission Act, S.B.C. 1984, c. 65, s. 9(c); The Electoral Divisions Act, R.S.M. 1987, c. E40, s. 11(3); Resolution of the Ontario Legislative Assembly, 16 June 1983, at pp. 97-98, *Journals of the Legislative Assembly, 1983; Elections Act, S.Q. 1989, c. 1, s. 17].*
68. *Reference re Provincial Electoral Boundaries* (S.C.C.) (see n.1), 12-13 (emphasis added).
69. Ibid., 15-16 (emphasis added).
70. Note that in the United States, the federal Voting Rights Act of 1965, § 5 (42 U.S.C.S. § 1973c) in some cases requires states to take racial factors into account in an attempt to ensure certain minorities will be represented. The Supreme Court has upheld the constitutionality of distributions under this provision: *United Jewish Organizations of Williamsburgh, Inc. v. Carey*, 430 U.S. 144, 51 L. Ed. (2d) 229 (1977).
71. The Alberta Court of Appeal also sees this type of litigation as a possibility: "We foresee the possibility of minority claims for effective representation that, if accepted, might have an impact not just on the boundaries of specific districts but also on the total number of districts, the idea of single-seat constituencies, and the tradition of contiguous boundaries" *(Reference re Electoral Boundaries Commission Act (Alberta)* (see n.53), 5-6).
72. *Reference re Provincial Electoral Boundaries* (S.C.C.) (see n.1), 19.
73. Significantly, the United States Supreme Court has traditionally been extremely reluctant to review allegations of partisan gerrymanders under the 14th Amendment, citing a lack of judicial standards. At the same time, however, it has reviewed racially motivated gerrymanders, relying on the more specific wording of the 15th Amendment [*Gomillion v. Lightfoot*, 364 U.S. 339, 5 L. Ed. (2d) 110 (1960)]. This position changed in 1986, when a fractured majority of the Supreme Court held that partisan gerrymanders were justiciable [*Davis v. Bandemer*, 478 U.S. 109, 92

L. Ed. (2d) 85 (1986)]. However, a majority of the Court in that case held that the plaintiffs had not proven that the partisan gerrymandering warranted judicial intervention. The Court reversed the District Court, which had held that the map violated the 14th Amendment [*Bandemer v. Davis*, 603 F. Supp. 1479 (S.D.Ind.)]. To date, the Supreme Court has not struck down any plan on the basis of partisan gerrymander, and commentators are apparently divided on the effect of *Bandemer*. The American experience indicates that it may actually be easier to gerrymander under a strict "one person–one vote" standard, as it then becomes possible to ignore natural community and geographic dividing lines. Sophisticated computer programs have assisted U.S. legislators intent on gerrymandering. See *Karcher v. Daggett*, 462 U.S. 725, 77 L. Ed. (2d) 133 (1983), per Stevens J. at p. 156 (L. Ed.), White J. at p. 171, and Powell J. at p. 176, and the decision of the District Court in *Bandemer*, 1483–84. See also: Roger H. Davidson and Walter J. Oleszek, *Congress and Its Members* (Washington: C.Q. Press, 1985), 713; Robert H. Bork, *The Tempting of America* (New York: Free Press, 1990), 88–90.

APPENDIX: SASKATCHEWAN CONSTITUENCIES, 1989

Name of Constituency	Number of Eligible Voters per Constituency	Percentage Deviation from Norm
Northern Constituencies		
Athabasca	6,309	-37.82
Cumberland	7,190	-29.14
Rural Constituencies		
Arm River	9,786	-3.55
Assiniboia–Gravelbourg	8,773	-13.54
Bengough–Milestone	8,128	-19.89
Biggar	9,916	-2.27
Canora	10,373	-5.94
Cut Knife–Lloydminster	12,019	+18.44
Estevan	10,924	+7.65
Humboldt	11,734	+15.64
Indian Head–Wolseley	8,865	-12.63
Kelsey–Tisdale	9,849	-2.93
Kelvington–Wadena	9,885	-2.58
Kindersley	9,354	-7.81
Kinistino	10,947	+7.88
Last Mountain–Touchwood	9,865	-2.77
Maple Creek	9,036	-10.94
Meadow Lake	9,813	-3.29
Melfort	9,864	-2.78
Melville	10,106	-.40
Moosomin	9,719	-4.21
Morse	7,757	-23.55
Nipawin	9,508	-6.29

Pelly	8,581	-7.26
Qu'Appelle-Lumsden	11,100	+9.39
Quill Lakes	9,276	-8.58
Redberry	10,430	+2.78
Rosetown-Elrose	8,596	-15.28
Rosthern	10,453	+3.01
Saltcoats	8,994	-11.36
Shaunavon	8,031	-20.85
Shellbrook-Torch River	9,759	-3.82
Souris-Cannington	8,884	-12.44
Thunder Creek	8,553	-15.70
Turtleford	9,453	-6.83
Weyburn	10,174	+.26
Wilkie	8,775	-13.52
Urban Constituencies		
Moose Jaw Palliser	11,903	+17.30
Moose Jaw Wakamow	12,350	+21.71
Prince Albert Carlton	10,882	+7.24
Prince Albert Northcote	10,393	+2.42
Regina Albert North	9,403	-7.33
Regina Albert South	10,744	+5.88
Regina Churchill Downs	11,008	+8.48
Regina Dewdney	10,721	+5.65
Regina Elphinstone	12,144	+19.68
Regina Hillsdale	10,994	+8.34
Regina Lake Centre	11,794	+16.23
Regina Normanview	8,623	-15.01
Regina Rosemont	11,593	+14.25
Regina Victoria	11,325	+11.60
Regina Wascana Plains	8,237	-18.82
Saskatoon Broadway	11,513	+13.46
Saskatoon Fairview	11,138	+9.76
Saskatoon Greystone	12,567	+23.84
Saskatoon Haultain	10,557	+4.04
Saskatoon Idylwyld	12,364	+21.84
Saskatoon Nutana	12,362	+21.82
Saskatoon River Heights	12,143	+19.67
Saskatoon Riversdale	11,170	+10.08
Saskatoon Sutherland-University	7,684	-24.27
Saskatoon Westmount	12,076	+19.01
Saskatoon Wildwood	9,445	-6.91
Swift Current	10,655	+5.00
The Battlefords	12,316	+21.37
Yorkton	10,833	+6.76

Source: *Electoral Boundaries Commission 1988 Final Report,* 9–10.
Note: The provincial norm was 10,147 (*Final Report,* 3).
[Ed. note: 1) The number of eligible voters in Canora and in Pelly should read 9,544 and 9,410. The percentage deviation is correct.
2) Due to changes as a result of legislation that created the constituencies, the number of eligible voters and the percentage deviation from the norm for Cutknife-Lloydminster became 11,808 (+16.37%), and for The Battlefords 12,527 (+23.46%)]

The Saskatchewan Electoral Boundaries Case and Its Implications[1]

RONALD E. FRITZ
UNIVERSITY OF SASKATCHEWAN

In November 1987 the Saskatchewan Electoral Boundaries Commission Act[2] received royal assent. There were two features of the legislation that attracted the greatest opprobrium:

(i) The commission was directed to redraw the 64 southern constituency boundaries subject to the following constraints. First, each of 7 urban centres was allocated a specified number of seats totalling 29. The area outside of the municipal boundaries of these 7 centres was designated rural and was allocated 35 seats. The commission could not recommend constituencies that mingled these designated urban and rural voters. The fixed allocation of seats resulted in an overrepresentation of the rural areas (from whence the governing party had garnered its electoral support in the previous election) and in an underrepresentation of the urban areas.

(ii) Whereas the previous legislation had permitted deviations to a maximum of +/- 15%, the act permitted deviations to a maximum of +/- 25%.

Both of these changes meant that the principle of "representation by population" was under assault.

In response to requests from individuals and groups such as the Society for the Advancement of Voter Equality (SAVE), the Saskatchewan government referred to the Saskatchewan Court of Appeal the matter of whether the 1987 legislation and the constituency boundaries established by The Representation Act, 1989,[3] infringed or denied rights or freedoms guaranteed by the Canadian Charter of Rights and Freedoms. Counsel for SAVE was appointed by the Saskatchewan Court of Appeal to present the argument against their constitutionality.

The Judgment of the Saskatchewan Court of Appeal

In giving meaning to the "right to vote" contained in section 3 of the Charter, the Saskatchewan Court of Appeal rejected the argument of counsel for the intervener, Equal Justice For All, that the right required absolute equality. Instead, the Court defined the right as requiring "relative or substantial equality of voting power" to take account of such problems as the mobility of the electorate between when the constituency boundaries were established and when the elections were held based on those boundaries. It rejected an approach that was based on a specified percentage of deviation as constituting an acceptable *de minimus* limit on the right.[4]

After concluding that the electoral population differentials exceeded the notion of "relative or substantial equality of voting power," the Court went on to consider whether the differences could be justified under section 1 of the Charter. Following the approach articulated by the Supreme Court of Canada in *R. v. Oakes*[5] and *R. v. Keegstra*,[6] the Court considered whether "the impugned state action has an objective of 'pressing and substantial' concern in a free and democratic society."[7] It was particularly concerned, in this regard, about the commission's discretion being limited vis-à-vis the southern constituencies. Although counsel for the Attorney General of Saskatchewan had presented argument regarding the representational difficulties experienced in rural constituencies, no evidence had been presented to support the position. The Court concluded this part of its judgment by saying:

> Representative democratic government should neither be nor be seen to be a fight between rural and urban interests. We have no evidence that members of the legislature from "rural" areas are insensitive to concerns and community interests of urban or northern people. Likewise we have no evidence that "urban" members of the Legislative Assembly are insensitive to concerns and community interests of rural or northern people.
>
> In earlier times travel and communication in rural Saskatchewan were limited. But the court may take judicial notice of the fact that that is no longer so. Saskatchewan has an impressive network of provincial highways and gridroads—an "all weather" road system in every sense of the word—and the means of travel are many and efficient. Our communications systems are equally impressive. People in both rural and urban areas have ready access to those systems.
>
> It is true that in Saskatchewan today, the interests of those residing in rural constituencies are varied and broad; but so too are the interests of people living in urban constituencies. And the cultural, political, economic, social and other interests of the citizens of southern Saskatchewan do not much differ.
>
> Furthermore, strong links exist between rural and city interests in this province. Quite apart from significant interrelated economic interests, we recognize that people in rural and urban Saskatchewan have strong ties with one another. Most city residents have rural "roots" and still maintain strong rural ties. Likewise, many rural residents have strong ties with the cities—that is where their children go for advanced education and training as well as employment. Indeed their interests often directly overlap because the major cities are surrounded by a number of so-called "bedroom communities" where people live but commute to work in the city.

Our conclusion with respect to the arbitrary apportionment in ss. 14 and 15 of the Electoral Boundaries Commission Act . . . , as adopted in the Representation Act *does not foreclose reasonable consideration of valid geographic, regional and other relevant matters in drawing constituency boundaries. Such leeway is necessary to achieve equal and effective representation* but, speaking generally, effective representation can be nurtured by other, non-infringing and equally effective methods. For example, Members of the Legislative Assembly who represent larger geographic areas might be provided with additional travel allowances, support staff and "up-to-date" communication services.[8] [Emphasis added]

This analysis appears to overlap with the second aspect of the *Oakes* approach, namely the proportionality requirement. Indeed, the Court did not find it necessary to consider it, having found that the legislation did not meet the first aspect of the *Oakes* approach.

Regardless of whether parts of the analysis were misplaced, it is important to step back and form an overall picture of the Court's approach. The Court of Appeal clearly recognized that the guiding principle was "one person–one vote" but that the principle could be tempered by other factors to ensure "effective representation." These other factors, however, had to be reasonable in the sense of being the least obtrusive means of promoting "effective representation."

One other part of the judgment deserves comment. With respect to the two northern constituencies, the Court concluded that "the exigencies of geography, very sparse population, transportation and communication warrant deviation from the ideal"[9] and thus satisfied the requirements of the *Oakes* case.

The Judgments of the Supreme Court of Canada

In giving the decision for the majority in the Supreme Court of Canada, Justice McLachlin defined the right to vote enshrined in section 3 of the Charter as entailing the right to "effective representation."[10] By so defining the right she attempted to recognize that elected representatives perform two functions, one legislative (i.e., through whom one has a voice in the deliberations of government[11]) and one service (i.e., through whom one brings problems and concerns to the attention of the bureaucracy). For her, "effective representation" was comprised of a number of aspects:

The first is relative parity of voting. A system which dilutes one citizen's vote unduly as compared with another citizen's vote runs the risk of providing inadequate representation to the citizen whose vote is diluted. The legislative power of the citizen whose vote is diluted will be reduced, as may be access to and assistance from his or her representative. The result will be uneven and unfair representation.

But parity of voting power, though of prime importance, is not the only factor to be taken into account in ensuring effective representation . . .

[S]uch relative parity as may be possible of achievement may prove undesirable because it has the effect of detracting from the primary goal of effective representation. Factors like geography, community history, community interests and minority representation may need to be taken into account to ensure that our legislative assemblies effectively represent the diversity of our social mosaic ...

It emerges therefore that deviations from absolute voter parity may be justified on the grounds of practical impossibility or the provision of more effective representation. Beyond this, dilution of one citizen's vote as compared with another's should not be countenanced.[12]

If one were to ignore whether the analysis was occurring under section 3 or section 1 of the Charter there appears little difference between Justice McLachlin's general approach and that of the Court of Appeal. Justice McLachlin's recognition that "parity of voting power" was "of prime importance" is similar to the Court of Appeal's view that "one person–one vote" was "the controlling principle." Both recognize "effective representation" as a legitimate concern in drawing constituency boundaries. However, when one places these concepts into the analytical framework of section 3 and section 1 of the Charter, the differences become significant. By placing the consideration of "effective representation" within section 1, the Court of Appeal has simply left it to the discretion of those responsible for establishing constituency boundaries whether to take into account those factors that nurtured "effective representation." Justice McLachlin, on the other hand, by defining the section 3 right to vote as meaning "effective representation," has mandated the consideration of such factors as community of interests, etc., where they are present. The implications of her decision will be explored more fully below.

The two levels of court also differed significantly on their analysis of the facts. Justice McLachlin found that, on the facts, there had been no infringement of section 3. Whether the facts did, indeed, justify the constraints placed on the commissioners and the deviations in the electoral populations of the constituencies that were created will be addressed below.

The judgment of the dissenting judges[13] was cast quite narrowly. Justice Cory for the dissenters agreed "with many of the principles" Justice McLachlin set out in her judgment[14] but he came to a different conclusion on the facts.

One difference came in the minority's consideration of whether the degree of permissible variation could be justified. In this regard Justice Cory expressed the view that, in relation to the southern ridings, the additional burdens faced by MLAs in representing rural ridings had been and could be accommodated within a maximum deviation of +/- 15% of the electoral quotient.[15] Later in his judgment he observed that the permissible deviation had to be dependent on the particular characteristics of each province.[16] This approach should be contrasted with that taken by the Court of Appeal and by Justice McLachlin who focused on the factors that justified the variation and not on some percentage limitation delineating what was an acceptable variation.

The second concern that Justice Cory had with the Electoral Boundaries Commission Act was the legislated straight-jacket that was imposed in the case of the drawing of the boundaries for the southern constituencies. The prohibition of intermingling certain urban and rural voters not only led to greater variances than would otherwise have been the case but prevented the commissioners from adequately recognizing the continuing movement of people from the rural areas of Saskatchewan into the urban centres.[17]

Having found that section 3 of the Charter had been infringed, the minority concluded that the government had failed to justify the infringements under section 1 of the Charter vis-à-vis the southern ridings.[18]

It should be emphasized that both Justice McLachlin and Justice Cory viewed the two northern seats as justifying special consideration. They appeared to view it as self-evident that major deviations from the electoral quotient could be justified on the basis of that region's sparsity of population.[19]

The Majority Decision: Revisionist History?

In giving meaning to the Charter-protected right to vote, Justice McLachlin indicated that one must approach the question "in a broad and purposive way, having regard to historical and social context."[20] Her account of history was, however, very brief, referring only to a self-serving statement made by Sir John A. Macdonald in 1872 and to the negotiations surrounding the adoption of the Charter which made no reference to adopting the narrower American electoral model. Despite the brief account, it served as the foundation for her defining the Charter-protected right as a right to effective representation.

Perhaps she considered this description of Canadian constitutional history as being without controversy. After all, this was the description presented by the Attorney General of Saskatchewan and most of the governmental interveners who supported the appellant's position. However, this view of Canadian constitutional history represents only a superficial account, giving a patina of respectability to the true political motivations that drove the historical developments (what Norman Ward has described as "theories masquerading as principles"[21]).

Although there are dangers in trying to look at such history at the national level and then attempting to equate it with the local Saskatchewan scene, one has to recognize that the decision rendered in the Saskatchewan context had national implications and that it could not have been decided in isolation from those national developments. As well, Saskatchewan's history is part of the national interprovincial history, and it has similarities with the national intraprovincial history of drawing electoral boundaries.

The issue of "representation by population" was a contentious one during the negotiations that led to Confederation. Representatives from Canada West made it very clear that they would not be prepared to participate in Confederation if "representation by population" was not the principle used in the interprovincial allocation of seats in the lower house. Prince Edward Island, on the other hand, indicated that it was not prepared to participate if Canada West's position was adopted. Canada West won out and the principle was enshrined in sections 51 and 52 of the British North America Act, 1867. The one exception was the "one-twentieth clause" which was designed to give some protection to the Maritimes, although Norman Ward has suggested that it was not anticipated that it would ever have to be applied.[22] Except for manipulations by the Conservative government in the 1870s surrounding the admission of Manitoba, British Columbia, and Prince Edward Island, the principle was adhered to until 1915.[23] The redistributions following the 1891 and 1901 censuses resulted in each of the three Maritime provinces losing seats despite the "one-twentieth clause."[24]

Two constitutional references were submitted to the Supreme Court of Canada in 1903. The first related to Nova Scotia and New Brunswick[25] and the second related to Prince Edward Island. The essence of both references involved whether section 51 of the British North America Act, 1867, required a reduction in their respective numbers of representatives. In deciding the issue in the affirmative, Chief Justice Taschereau, in giving the judgment of the Court in the Prince Edward Island case, observed that "it has to be taken as a settled proposition . . . that the representation in the federal House of Commons is . . . based on population."[26]

The "Senate Floor Rule" in 1915[27] represented a significant breach of the principle. The amendment was not apparently motivated by any concern about ensuring that Prince Edward Island's voice was heard in Ottawa but was simply designed to placate Prince Edward Island. Even then, Prince Edward Island's MPs continued to argue for their long-standing claim for six guaranteed seats, but were rebuffed.

The repeal of the "one-twentieth clause" in 1946[28] was designed to bring the House of Commons *more* in line with the principle of "one person–one vote." It is submitted that until the constitutional amendments of 1974[29] that principle played the dominant role in allocating seats in the House of Commons to the various provinces.

Once it has been determined how many representatives each province is to have for the purpose of effecting a redistribution of the House of Commons seats, it then requires the actual constituency boundaries to be established. Political opportunism has been the hallmark of that history despite the reassuring words of Sir John A. Macdonald quoted by Justice McLachlin in her judgment.

Until the establishment of independent federal electoral boundaries commissions by the Electoral Boundaries Readjustment Act, 1964,[30] redistributions tended to favour the party in power, with some redistributions being more infamous than others. Although the politicians who were responsible for the redistributions tried to justify the disparities in constituency sizes on the basis of ensuring the representation of all segments of the Canadian mosaic in Parliament, few were naive enough to buy the rhetoric.

Of particular relevance to the *Saskatchewan Reference* case was the theory that the populations of urban constituencies should be larger than rural constituencies. Norman Ward has suggested that at the outset the theory developed by accident because the process of urbanization took place at a pace faster than the process of redistribution.[31] J.R. Mallory was not as charitable in describing the roots of the "principle." He suggested that the politicians were concerned about their inability to control the articulate and organized urban masses who were clamouring for social change whereas the rural dwellers held traditional values and were unorganized and weak.[32] Sir Wilfrid Laurier, during debate on the 1892 redistribution, argued against increasing Montréal's representation from three to five members, basing his position on the fact that many MPs representing rural constituencies lived in Montréal.[33]

Even when the independent commissions were employed after 1964 to devise federal electoral boundaries, politicians complained when the commissions adhered too closely to the principle of "representation by population."[34] Two redistributions were never implemented because of parliamentary intervention. The commissions in the early 1970s and the early 1980s had been viewed as being out-of-step with the political masters by proposing, in the 1970s, constituency boundaries where 65% of the seats were within +/- 10% and, in the 1980s, constituency boundaries where 77% of the seats were within +/- 10% of the applicable quotient.[35] The federal Saskatchewan commission proposed that *all* of the Saskatchewan seats could be brought within +/- 5% of the provincial electoral quotient in the never-implemented 1983–84 redistribution[36] and a reconstituted federal Saskatchewan commission implemented, despite fierce parliamentary opposition, a redistribution where all of the seats were within +/- 5% of the provincial electoral quotient.[37]

Saskatchewan history relating to the redistribution of the seats in the legislature bears many similarities to Canadian intraprovincial history. That political considerations weighed heavily in the redistribution process prior to 1970 cannot be denied; the Liberal Party gerrymander preceding the 1971 provincial election is infamous. The victorious New Democratic Party kept its campaign promise to reform the system by having future redistributions done by independent commissions. Although the Constituency Boundaries Commission Bill garnered nonpartisan support, two MLAs representing northern constituencies voted against the bill at second reading. The focus of their concern was the setting aside of at least two seats in an area described as Northern Saskatchewan. The area designated formed parts of five provincial ridings and it was the view of those MLAs that the representation of the North was being weakened, not strengthened. They wanted the commissioners to have an unfettered discretion.[38]

The first commission carried out its mandate working closely to the principle of "representation by population." Sixty-nine percent of the seats were within +/- 5% of the southern electoral quotient, 95% of the seats were within +/- 10% of the southern electoral quotient, and 3% (the two northern constituencies to which an electoral quotient did not apply) of the seats exceeded the southern electoral quotient by more than -15%.[39]

The second redistribution was not quite as committed to the principle. Fifty-five percent of the seats were within +/- 5% of the southern electoral quotient, 80% of the seats were within +/- 10% of the southern electoral quotient, and 3% (the two northern constituencies to which an electoral quotient did not apply) of the seats exceeded the southern electoral quotient by more than -15%.[40]

The 1987 amendments which were the focus of the reference case not only meant that the urban centres received three seats fewer than their electoral populations justified but that the impact was unevenly felt. For example, the Battlefords' one constituency was 23.46% above the electoral quotient while Swift Current's one constituency was 5% above the quotient. In addition, where the commission had discretion, it exercised it to the maximum allowed by the legislation. Only 24% of the new constituency boundaries were within +/- 5% of the quotient and only 52% were within +/- 10% of the quotient. Fully one-third of the constituencies exceeded the quotient by more than +/- 15%, a degree of deviation allowed only to the two northern seats under the previous legislation.

It is submitted that Justice McLachlin unfortunately viewed Canadian constitutional history through rose-coloured glasses. She failed to see how politicians had manipulated the system for partisan political reasons to thwart the principle of "representation by population" rather than being motivated to ensure effective representation.

The Majority Decision: Factors Which Nurture Effective Representation

Although all the judges who heard the reference case acknowledged that deviations could be accepted if justified on the basis that such deviations were necessary to promote effective representation, they came to different conclusions on the facts. Unfortunately, a reference case is an entirely unsuitable vehicle for considering fact-sensitive questions.

This problem is exemplified by what Justice McLachlin said in regard to the allocation of seats to the urban and rural areas:

> [I]t may be useful to mention some of the factors other than equality of voting power which figure in the analysis. One of the most important is the fact that it is more difficult to represent rural ridings than urban. The material before us suggests that not only are rural ridings harder to serve because of difficulty in transport and communications, but the rural voters make greater demands on their elected representatives, whether because of the absence of alternative resources to be found in urban centres or for other reasons. Thus the goal of effective representation may justify somewhat lower voter populations in rural areas.[41]

In this passage she confused "fact" with argument. No party adduced evidence establishing that it was more difficult to represent a rural constituency than an urban constituency. Unfortunately, political scientists in Canada have not done the necessary empirical work to establish whether this is in fact correct. Her comments regarding transport and communication systems in Saskatchewan should be contrasted with those made by the Court of Appeal.[42] One would have thought that local judges would have a greater knowledge of such a fact than judges in Ottawa.

77

Although I accept that factors such as community of interest, rate of growth, the condition of communication and transportation networks, and special geographic features should be considered in drawing electoral boundaries, one has to take care in ensuring that the facts warrant the deviation from electoral equality for each and every constituency, be they urban, rural, or northern. It is submitted, however, that when closely examined they will seldom justify major deviations.

Community of Interest

Probably the factor that garners the most discussion in this context is community of interest. Some argue that, in order for politicians to carry out their roles as representatives of their constituents and as intermediaries in helping constituents in their dealings with government, elected officials can be an effective voice for constituents only where the group of electors is composed of a homogeneous collective.

The factor of community of interest has received strong endorsement from Canadians such as Alan Stewart and Professors Morton and Knopff. Ironically, however, these proponents are unable to give us a working definition of the concept.[43] One would have thought that, if it is to be used as a tool in drawing constituency boundaries, there would be some generally accepted notion of what it entails.

An example that Alan Stewart gives in a paper in support of recognizing community of interest is instructive in highlighting the problems associated with the concept. His example from a 1986 Ontario redistribution involves the adjacent counties of Bruce and Grey and the town of Hanover. By putting the voters of Hanover with the voters of the adjacent county instead of leaving them with the voters of the county within which they resided, both electoral districts would have been roughly equal in number and would have been close to the provincial electoral quotient. He, however, argues that, by artificially grouping the town voters with those in the other county, the natural community of interest that is developed within the county structure would have been lost.[44] Although he devotes a large portion of his paper to describing "indicia of community interest," he does not attempt to apply them to the example. We are not told anything else about Hanover. How did it relate to the surrounding area in the other county in terms of transportation patterns, general economic ties, shopping patterns, school catchment areas, recreational ties, telephone catchment areas, work-residence patterns, and so on? Also left unsaid in his paper is how one would deal with a situation where a number of factors (e.g., schools, health facilities, etc.) are organized on a county basis but other factors (e.g., place of work, shopping patterns, media coverage, etc.) cross over county boundaries. Are some factors more important than others or is it simply a matter of counting up the most connecting factors and attaching the town to the county with which it has the most real and substantial connection?

Proponents also recognize that, although there may be a grouping of individuals that could be said to have a community of interest, their numbers may be too small to set up a discrete constituency. Although one might be able to point to pockets of individuals who share a common ethnicity (e.g., French in the Gravelbourg area, Ukrainians in the Hafford area), socioeconomic background, or place of work, their overall numbers may be insufficient to justify the necessary deviation from the electoral quotient.[45]

Community of interest does not usually present sharp lines between the groupings. For example, teachers in a rural part of Saskatchewan may have a closer community of interest with teachers in an urban part of Saskatchewan. A person with a particular socioeconomic background in Saskatoon may have a greater community of interest with someone with a similar background in Regina than she or he has with a person with a different socioeconomic background who lives on the next street. As well, a point is reached where boundary lines just have to be drawn either because representation by population cannot be totally ignored or because a natural barrier or provincial boundary necessitates it. In such cases, people either side of the boundary may have a greater community of interest than they do with others with whom they are grouped in the constituency. Just as those who strongly adhere to the principle of "representation by population" are better served by a proportional representation rather than a "first past the post" electoral system, so too are those who strongly emphasize community of interest. Reality is that areas are not populated in sufficient numbers by those who could be considered to have a community of interest. In order to draw those people together in sufficient numbers, it would be necessary to set up separate electoral rolls, for example, for Natives,[46] gays and lesbians,[47] teachers, and the poor.

The underlying assumption behind the concept also fails to recognize a number of political realities. Canadian politics is heavily oriented to party politics. Candidates in Canada stand for election as representatives of parties with a platform developed from the top down. Once elected, the classical Burkean theory is that elected officials are not the mouthpieces, delegates, or ambassadors of their constituents. A common complaint heard from the electorate is that the elected representatives are not governing in accordance with the wishes of the majority (e.g., on the death penalty, Free Trade, the GST). The irony is that, although MPs and MLAs assert their independence, they usually subordinate it to the system of party discipline. In carrying out their function as a representative, they more often do so as the representative of her/his party and not of her/his constituents.

Parties themselves downplay the importance of representing the electorate when it comes to holding by-elections to fill vacancies. In the province of Saskatchewan there is no requirement that a vacancy be filled within any particular time (ed. note: legislation to set a time limit passed the Saskatchewan legislature in December 1991). When the provincial election was held on 21 October 1991, constituents in 4 constituencies had been without representatives for periods varying from 15 to 22 months. Parties also downplay the importance of representing the electorate when they prorogue the legislature without passing a budget or when they meet infrequently in legislative session.

It has been argued by some that in order to speak for a community you must be of the community. Yet, there is nothing in electoral law that requires candidates to reside in the community or to have the ethnic, economic, social, or occupational background of the majority making up the community.

One cannot, however, ignore the fact that MPs and MLAs also perform as intermediaries between constituents and government departments. Most perform the task admirably, either because they are truly concerned about the plight of the constituent or because they want to curry favour with that individual for the next election. Often this role is performed on behalf of an individual and not on behalf of a community.

So long as "representation by population" is the controlling principle, some adjustments could be tolerated where the facts establish that such a community of interest exists. An example might be the avoiding of drawing a boundary that would place a homogeneous ethnic community into two separate constituencies. Major deviations would not be justifiable.

Rate of Growth

Relative rate of growth is an important factor to consider in devising constituency boundaries. If the boundaries are to have any lasting utility, anticipated population shifts should be taken into account.

It is clear that in 1988 the commissioners took account of relative rate of growth in devising some of the urban constituencies. In their *Final Report,* they specifically referred to that being a consideration in drawing the two Prince Albert constituencies.[48] Although not expressly stated in their reports, it likely guided their recommendations in respect of a number of the proposed constituencies in Saskatoon and Regina. Saskatoon Sutherland-University was 24.27% below the southern electoral quotient but this was the area of Saskatoon where growth was expected to occur.

Rate of growth has both positive and negative connotations. It is the writer's opinion that the commission did not adequately take the fact of rural depopulation into account. During an exchange between the author and one of the commissioners on this point, the commissioner asked how such information could be garnered for the rural areas. The fact that rural depopulation had been a continuing process in Saskatchewan for the last half-century (as federal electoral history attests to) was widely known and projections could have been made by studying long-term census, electoral population, and/or Saskatchewan Health data.

Circumstantial evidence also supports the claim that the commission did not seriously take the factor into account. In its *Interim Report,* the commission recommended no changes to the existing boundaries of 32 constituencies, including 28 of the 35 designated rural constituencies. Of these 28, 25 were below the southern electoral quotient. Thirteen of the 25 were below the quotient by greater than 10%, 6 of the 25 were below the quotient by more than 15%, and 2 of the 25 were below the quotient by more than 20%. In my presentation to the commission, I pointed out that a number of these constituencies that were significantly below the quotient had likewise experienced significant reductions in electoral populations between 1978 and 1986. Yet, with the exception of one minor change, the *Final Report* did not result in changes to the recommendations contained in the *Interim Report*.

There are limits, however, as to how far one should go in estimating movements in population. For example, the recession has meant that growth in Saskatoon Sutherland-University has been far below what had been anticipated in 1988. Ongoing monitoring would appear to be justified if "representation by population" is to be paramount, with the redistributions triggered by need and not the simple effluxion of time.

Communication and Transportation Networks

Although not specifically mentioned in the Electoral Boundaries Commission Act as a factor to be considered in devising constituency boundaries, transportation is often linked with communication networks. Both relate to the ability of constituents to be in contact with their MP or MLA, either in the latter's representative or intermediary capacities.

When Canada was a frontier society, such networks were sadly deficient. In designing constituencies, major differences in constituency populations could be justified. What of today?

Justice McLachlin found as a fact that "rural ridings [are] harder to serve because of difficulty in transport and communication."[49] This should be contrasted with the Saskatchewan Court of Appeal's finding of fact that Saskatchewan's transportation and communications systems were "impressive," with the result that rural residents would not be disadvantaged in having access to their MLA.[50]

Who was correct? The facts support the judges in the Court of Appeal. The most recent Statistics Canada information regarding highways and roads is for 1976. In that year 23.3% of Canada's highways and roads were located in Saskatchewan, the most extensive system in the country. Alberta came second with 20.4% and Ontario third with 18.25% (over 45,000 fewer kilometres than in Saskatchewan).[51] Some settlements are not connected to the road system but they are located in the north. Over 97.8% of Saskatchewan households have telephones.[52] Telephone service is available throughout the province. Information is extensively available to the populace with 99.4% having radios and 96.9% having colour televisions.[53]

If "parity of voting," although of "prime importance," must be tempered to ensure "effective representation," surely that infringement should be as little as reasonably necessary to achieve the goal. Investing in toll-free telephone numbers to aid MLA-constituent contact, in full-time constituency help, in travel supplements, etc., may still leave gaps in service. In those instances, it should be incumbent on governments to justify on an individual constituency basis how, in fact, communication or transportation deficiencies necessitated a lower-than-average electoral or census population. Although all judges assumed that special allowances had to be made for the North, it is submitted that they too should be assessed on the same basis and that deficiencies should be established as a matter of fact.

Special Geographic Features

Generally speaking, when one refers to "special geographic features" one usually is alluding to such natural features as rivers, mountains, forested areas, etc. For the purpose of analysis, however, I also include human-developed features such as highways and arterial roads.

The most dominant natural feature of Saskatchewan is the number of major river systems passing through the province. Although crossing points are few and far between and a number of ferry services do not run after freeze-up, rivers do not necessarily dictate that constituency boundaries should not cross them. For example, Saskatoon, "The Bridge City," is bisected by the South Saskatchewan River but multiple bridge crossings mean that the natural feature does not represent a barrier. Even where bridges do not exist or where there are major mountain ranges, good communication links can surmount the barrier.

Rivers, like highways and arterial roads, represent easily identifiable reference points for boundaries. If the thrust is to ensure "effective representation," then constituents should be able to identify which MP or MLA is their representative. Clearly delineated reference points enhance that comprehension.

Leeway, thus, is justified to take into account natural and human-developed special geographic features. This does not mean that such features should lead to significant departures from the quotient. Although a river may represent a natural boundary, a highway or some other feature on the other side of the river can likewise serve as a reference point. Where such features are considered to justify major departures from the principle of "representation by population," the drawer of the boundaries should set out what alternatives were also canvassed and why they were rejected. As with the other factors that constrain the discretion, the justification should be based on the facts and not on some perceived conventional wisdom.

The Majority Decision: Lessons from Other Countries?

Justice McLachlin's judgment made reference to judicial decisions rendered by courts in the United States and Australia. Although these along with other countries such as the United Kingdom and New Zealand could be said to represent "free and democratic" societies, their approaches to the issue of representation in the lower houses of their legislatures have to be put into the context of their constitutional and legislative history. Although we can learn from their experiences and approaches, they must be adapted to meet Canadian values and needs.

The United States

The United States Supreme Court has adopted one position in respect of the redistribution of seats for the Congressional House of Representatives and another in respect of the redistricting of state legislatures. The difference in approach is best demonstrated by two decisions rendered by that court on 22 June 1983. In *Karcher v. Daggett*[54] the majority struck down a federal redistricting plan for New Jersey where the maximum deviation from the average was 0.6984%. The majority rejected a *de minimis* approach reasoning that "If we accept that argument, how are we to regard deviations of 0.8%, 0.95%, 1%, or 1.1%?"[55] In *Brown v. Thomson*, however, the majority upheld a Wyoming state redistricting plan where the average deviation from equality was 16% and the largest deviation was 90%.[56]

The basic elements of the United States Supreme Court's approach to state redistricting can be summarized as follows:

> (i) Where the maximum deviation exceeds 10%, a *prima facie* case has been made out and the state has the burden of justifying the proposed redistricting plan.
> (ii) Where the maximum deviation is less than 10%, the court considers it to be a "minor deviation" which is insufficient to make out a *prima facie* case. The burden of proof rests with the party challenging the validity of the proposed redistricting plan to establish that the plan is "invidiously discriminatory." The maximum deviation is not capable of establishing that, in and of itself. Examples of what would meet the burden is proof that the plan was developed "to minimize or cancel out the voting strength or political elements of the voting population."[57]

It should be emphasized that the state may, as it was able to do in the *Brown* case, be able to justify very substantial deviations.

Although Justice McLachlin expressly declined to follow the approach taken by the American court in the *Karcher* case,[58] she made no reference to cases such as *Brown*. I will address later how this approach can be adapted to Canadian needs.

Australia

Australia's approach to effecting the redistribution of electoral boundaries by way of electoral boundaries commissions operating under the guidance of legislated criteria served as the model adopted first federally in 1964 and later in Saskatchewan in 1972.[59] With the adoption of the "eye of the needle" principle in 1983, Australia became a strong adherent of the principle of "representation by population." Under this innovation, although initially constituencies could be established that varied by a maximum of +/- 10%, the commissions had to " . . . as far as practicable, endeavour to ensure that, 3 years and 6 months after the State or Territory has been redistributed, the number of electors enrolled in each proposed Electoral Division in the State or Territory will be equal."[60] Criticisms of the approach led to a slight relaxation of the requirement in 1987 when the section was amended to set the mid-term target of not "less than 98% or more than 102% of the appropriate quotient."[61]

As has been the case in Canada, the Australian approach to redistributions has been subject to political machination.[62] Although Australia is similar in terms of too much geography with people concentrated in urban areas, the urban/rural divisions are much more pronounced. Unlike Canada, an urban-based Labor Party has achieved political dominance federally during the past two decades and it has been successful in bringing to the fore its philosophy emphasizing "one person–one vote." The changes have been brought about through ordinary legislation.

In the course of her judgment, Justice McLachlin made a brief reference to the case of *Australia (Attorney General) v. Commonwealth,*[63] apparently using it to bolster her interpretation of section 3 of our Charter.[64] In so doing, however, she failed to recognize not only that the constitutional provision that was before the Australian Court was quite different from what was before the Supreme Court of Canada but that there were a number of other features of the Australian constitution that further distinguished it from the Canadian constitution.

Just as the Australian decision was a reflection of Australian constitutional and legislative history, decisions rendered by Canadian courts should reflect Canadian constitutional and legislative history.

The United Kingdom

Challenges have been brought against United Kingdom boundary commissions for paying insufficient attention to the principle of "representation by population." The most significant was *R. v. Boundary Commission For England, Ex Parte Foot and Others.*[65] The case revolved around whether the rules governing the commission's discretion made other factors subject to the overriding factor of electoral equality. The Court of Appeal, in interpreting the appropriate legislative provisions, concluded that electoral equality was simply one of many factors that had to be balanced in constructing electoral boundaries and that the differentials from electoral equality would have to be "grotesque" before it could be said that the commission had carried out its *administrative* function in an unreasonable fashion.

It is submitted that the United Kingdom's legislative and judicial history has limited pertinence in the Canadian context. First and foremost, the United Kingdom does not have a written constitution or charter of rights serving as a brake on parliamentary sovereignty. It is for this reason that court challenges employ an administrative law, as opposed to a constitutional law, approach. Second, its electoral boundaries commission legislation, unlike, for example, the federal legislation and the pre-1987 Saskatchewan legislation, has not given prime importance to electoral equality. Somewhat related to this is the equal importance expressly given to municipal and county boundaries in effecting redistributions, a factor that appears in the Canadian context only inferentially at best under "community of interest." And finally, Canadian constitutional history has, especially in the context of the interprovincial allocation of seats in the House of Commons, emphasized electoral equality.

The Implications of the Supreme Court Decision

A number of people have viewed the decision as representing a major hurdle that would effectively block any successful court challenges in the future except in cases of extreme disparities in the voter populations of constituencies. To some extent this pessimism stems from Justice McLachlin's observation that:

> This court has repeatedly affirmed that the courts must be cautious in interfering unduly in decisions that involve the balancing of conflicting policy considerations ... These considerations led me to suggest in *Dixon* ... that "the courts ought not to interfere with the legislature's electoral map under s. 3 of the Charter unless it appears that reasonable persons *applying the appropriate principles* ... could not have set the electoral boundaries as they exist."[66] [Emphasis added]

Those who wish to challenge constituency boundaries in the future must devote their efforts to establishing that "the appropriate principles" were either not considered or were unreasonably applied.

On the face of it, this appears to present a daunting obstacle. However, such an appearance can be deceiving. In defining the Charter-protected right as requiring "effective representation," the Court has mandated the consideration of such factors as community of interest, rate of growth, special geographic features, etc., where they are present. This has altered significantly the job of those who draw constituency boundaries in the future. Each constituency's boundaries must be measured against those factors and failure to consider them will open the boundaries to challenge. Justice McLachlin's comment related to giving deference to the conclusion but only where the proper balancing of considerations is shown to have taken place. Those who are responsible for the drawing of the boundaries, be they commissioners, members of legislative committees, representatives of the governing party, or members of the bureaucracy, may find themselves being called to testify about how they carried out their task. Ideally the detailed reasons should be provided in any reports that they produce. Failing that, prudence would suggest that such reasons should be available in records detailing their deliberations.

This emphasis on effective representation may have implications for how often constituency boundaries must be revised. Significant population shifts affect the ability of MPs and MLAs to act as intermediaries between constituents and government departments, thus undermining their ability to provide effective representation. It may force legislatures to give greater attention to the resources provided to MPs and MLAs that enable them to effectively represent their constituents. It may also necessitate that vacancies must be filled within a reasonable time.

One irony of Justice McLachlin's approach is that constituency boundaries having regard only to parity of voter numbers would be unconstitutional. Unlike the Court of Appeal's judgment, which viewed effective representation as a reasonable qualification to "relative or substantial equality of voting power" *if* a legislature decided to pursue that goal, her judgment mandates effective representation as the touchstone.

Legislatures may decide that the risks of potential litigation and the attendant uncertainties are not worth running. However, by emphasizing effective representation and the factors that promote that goal, Justice McLachlin's judgment will constrain what the legislatures can do.

The criteria established to guide the work of those who draw constituency boundaries may become the subject of judicial scrutiny. Even establishing tighter limits on the maximum permissible percentage deviation from the electoral quotient, thus ensuring closer adherence to the principle of "representation by population," may open the door for challenges based on the argument that insufficient emphasis is being given to the other factors. This would suggest that, if a body such as an electoral boundaries commission or a committee made up of elected members of the legislature is given the task to establish or recommend constituency boundaries subject to specified criteria, numerical guidelines should be avoided. As well, although Justice McLachlin's judgment would not require that such drawers of constituency boundaries would have to set out detailed reasons in a report justifying each constituency's boundaries, it might be wise to require such reasons to be set out, either in a report or in records detailing their deliberations.

Conclusion

Although the *Saskatchewan Reference* case was the first electoral boundaries case to reach the Supreme Court of Canada, it is unlikely to be the last. Far from erecting a barrier to such litigation in the future, except in cases of extreme disparities in the voter populations of constituencies, the Supreme Court's emphasis on effective representation in defining the Charter-protected "right to vote" is likely to have just the opposite affect.

It is likely that the Supreme Court did not intend this result. By defining the section 3 right as a right to effective representation, however, no verbal gymnastics will allow the Court to logically reinterpret "the conditions" as nonrequired factors. If the Court intended these factors to be permissive rather than mandatory, it must either redefine the section 3 right or adopt the approach of the Saskatchewan Court of Appeal.

Should the Supreme Court decide to readdress the questions starting with a *tabula rasa*, I submit that the approach taken by the Saskatchewan Court of Appeal represents a good starting point. However, a balance has to be struck between ensuring that sufficient emphasis is given to the principle of "representation by population" and not opening the floodgates to litigation. The American approach to redistricting state legislatures appears to strike that balance.

Where a constituency's electoral population varies from the provincial electoral quotient by more than +/- 5%, a meaningful onus should be imposed on the state to justify that such a deviation is necessary to ensure effective representation or that there is some other legitimate state interest involved. If all constituencies are created with electoral populations within +/- 5% of the provincial electoral quotient, the burden should be on the person challenging the constitutionality of the redistribution to establish bad faith in the redistribution process. Admittedly, the 5% figure is arbitrary but I submit that it can be justified on several grounds. The first is that it balances the need to ensure that "relative or substantial equality" is the "controlling principle" with the other legitimate concerns relating to effective representation. Second, the standard is a flexible one which allows for greater variation where it can be justified on the evidence. By placing the burden on the state to justify greater variations, it will force the drawers of the boundaries to either give or be prepared to give reasons for such variations that can be scrutinized. Third, it recognizes the reality that federal and most provincial redistributions are preceded by the work of an independent commissioner or commissioners. It appears unnecessarily restrictive to expect such a person(s) to have to provide detailed reasons for each and every constituency, explaining, for example, why this arterial road as opposed to that arterial road was used as a boundary. The provision of detailed reasons is a legitimate expectation for deviations greater than 5%. Finally, the bad-faith standard applicable to challenges relating to deviations of less than 5% acts as a check so as not to indirectly necessitate the providing of detailed reasons for all constituencies and to focus the issue on the process of redistribution as opposed to the actual boundaries themselves.

If such an approach is adopted by the Court and if legislatures turn to a third party(ies) to either set or recommend the constituency boundaries, legislatures should require such a person(s) to provide justification in her/his report for deviations greater than +/- 5%.

Notes

1. A paper entitled "A Citizen's Fight: The Saskatchewan Electoral Boundaries Case and Its Implications" which was presented at the 7-9 November 1991 conference served as the basis of this paper and would be more useful for litigation purposes.
2. S.S. 1986-87-88, c. E-6.1.
3. S.S. 1989-90, c. R-20.2.
4. *Reference re Electoral Boundaries Commission Act* (1991), 78 D.L.R. (4th) 449 (Sask. C.A.), 462-66; *sub nom Reference re Provincial Electoral Boundaries,* [1991] 3 W.W.R. 593.
5. [1986] 1 S.C.R. 103.
6. [1990] 3 S.C.R. 697. [1991] 2 W.W.R. 1.
7. *Reference re Electoral Boundaries Commission Act* (see n.4), 477.
8. Ibid., 479-80.
9. Ibid., 481.
10. *Reference re Electoral Boundaries Commission Act* (1991), 81 D.L.R. (4th) 16 (S.C.C.), 35; *sub nom Reference re Provincial Electoral Boundaries* [1991] 5 W.W.R. 1.

11. Ibid., 35, 38.
12. Ibid., 35–36.
13. The decision of Justice Sopinka who concurred in the decision of the majority is omitted from the analysis of the decisions.
14. *Reference re Electoral Boundaries Commission Act* (see n.10), 22, 27.
15. Ibid., 23.
16. Ibid., 28.
17. Ibid., 26.
18. Ibid., 28–29.
19. Ibid., 45, 27–28.
20. Ibid., 32.
21. Norman Ward, *The Canadian House of Commons: Representation*, 2d ed. (Toronto: University of Toronto Press, 1963), 35.
22. Ibid., 23.
23. Ibid., 22–26.
24. Norman Ward, "A Century of Constituencies," 10 *Canadian Public Administration* (1967): 108.
25. In *Re Representation In the House Of Commons*, [1903] 33 S.C.R. 475 (S.C.C.); aff'd. [1905] A.C. 37 (P.C.).
26. In *Re Representation of Prince Edward Island In The House of Commons*, [1903] 33 S.C.R. 594 (S.C.C.), 665; aff'd. [1905] A.C. 37 (P.C.).
27. 5–6 Geo. V, c. 45 (U.K.).
28. 9–10 Geo. VI, c. 63 (U.K.).
29. The British North America Act, 1974, S.C. 1974–75–76, c. 13.
30. S.C. 1964–65, c. 31.
31. Ward, *Canadian House of Commons* (see n.21), 32.
32. J.R. Mallory, *The Structure of Canadian Government* rev. ed. (Toronto: Gage Publishing Ltd, 1984), 22.
33. Ward, *Canadian House of Commons* (see n.21), 34.
34. Ward, "Century of Constituencies" (see n.24), 119–20.
35. J.C. Courtney, "Parliament and Representation: The Unfinished Agenda of Electoral Redistributions," 21 *Canadian Journal of Political Science* (1988): 680.
36. J.C. Courtney, "Theories Masquerading As Principles: Canadian Electoral Boundary Commissions and the Australian Model," in *The Canadian House of Commons: Essays In Honour of Norman Ward*, J.C. Courtney, ed., (Calgary: University of Calgary Press, 1985), 157.
37. Courtney, "Parliament and Representation" (see n.35), 684.
38. 12 *Saskatchewan Debates and Proceedings* at 1528 (6 April 1972) and at 1679–80 (12 April 1972).
39. These calculations are based on figures provided in the *Final Report: Constituency Boundaries Commission* 9 November 1973, Appendix 2, and the *Interim Report: Constituency Boundaries Commission* 18 July 1972, 9–32.
40. *Final Report: Constituency Boundaries Commission* 1 September 1980, Appendix III.
41. *Reference re Electoral Boundaries Commission Act* (see n.10), 43–44.
42. See p. 2 of the text.
43. A. Stewart, "Community of Interest in Redistricting," Unpublished, December 1990, 25, found at Tab 10 of the *Appendix and Authorities of the Intervenor the Attorney*

General of Canada; F.L. Morton and R. Knopff, "The Right to Vote, Electoral Distribution and Boundary Adjustment in Alberta," 34, found in *Authorities of the Intervenor Cities of Edmonton and Grande Prairie.*

44. Stewart, "Community of Interest," 18, 21.

45. Ibid., 94.

46. New Zealand established four separate electoral districts for its Maori population: Electoral Act 1956, S.N.Z. No. 107 consolidated to 1 April 1984, s. 23. See also, "Group Wants Federal Seats Designated For Natives," Toronto *Globe and Mail,* 13 August 1991, A3.

47. See "San Francisco Gays Gaining Political Clout," Toronto *Globe and Mail,* 12 August 1991, A1, A7.

48. *Final Report: Electoral Boundaries Commission 1988,* 5-6.

49. *Reference re Electoral Boundaries Commission Act* (see n.10), 43-44.

50. *Reference re Electoral Boundaries Commission Act* (see n.4), 479-80.

51. *Canada Year Book 1980-81* (Ottawa: Minister of Supply and Services, 1981), Table 15.9, 574.

52. *Household Facilities and Equipment 1990* (Ottawa: Minister of Supply and Services, 1991), 20-21.

53. Ibid.

54. 462 U.S. 725, (1983).

55. Ibid., per Brennan, J., 732.

56. 462 U.S. 835, (1983).

57. *Gaffney v. Cummings* 412 U.S. 735, (1973) per White, J., 751.

58. *Reference re Electoral Boundaries Commission Act* (see n.10), 36-37.

59. See Courtney, "Theories Masquerading as Principles" (see n.36), 157.

60. Commonwealth Electoral Act 1918, Reprint No. 2 consolidated to 30 September 1984, s. 66(3).

61. Commonwealth Electoral Amendment Act 1987, S. Comm. of Aust. 1987, No. 35, s. 7.

62. Courtney, "Theories Masquerading as Principles" (see n.36), 140-44; Joint Standing Committee on Electoral Matters: Parliament of the Commonwealth of Australia, Report No. 1, *One Vote One Value* (Canberra: Australian Government Publishing Service, 1988), 39-41.

63. 135 C.L.R. 1, 50 A.L.J.R. 279, 7 A.L.R. 593 (Aust. H.C.).

64. *Reference re Electoral Boundaries Commission Act* (see n.10), 37-38.

65. [1983] 1 All E.R. 1099 (C.A.); leave to appeal denied [1983] 1 All E.R. 1118 (H.L.).

66. *Reference re Electoral Boundaries Commission Act* (see n.10), 39-40.

COMMENTARY

ANDREW SANCTON
UNIVERSITY OF WESTERN ONTARIO

Although both papers obviously derive from efforts to prepare legal arguments on opposite sides of the same question, they have a great deal in common. They tell the same story, analyse many of the same issues, and arrive at remarkably similar conclusions about the implications of the Supreme Court's decision.

Both papers refer early on to the ways in which House of Commons electoral districts have been allocated among the provinces. Although I believe the issue is fundamentally irrelevant to the Saskatchewan *Reference re Provincial Electoral Boundaries,* I cannot resist the temptation to begin on this point because I know far more about why Saskatchewan has 14 electoral districts in federal elections than I do about why the boundaries of the 66 provincial constituencies were drawn as they were.

As defenders of the Saskatchewan provincial boundaries, Richards and Irvine argue that "The history of electoral redistribution in Canada has not been characterized by a close adherence to the notion of 'one person-one vote.'" They go on to claim that this is especially true concerning the allocation of House of Commons seats among the provinces. To support this statement they point to the Senate Floor Rule, originally enacted by the Imperial Parliament in 1915 and now entrenched in section 41(b) of the Constitution Act, 1982. They then make the astonishing claim that the entrenchment of "the principle of proportionate representation of the provinces in the House of Commons prescribed by the Constitution of Canada" in section 42(b) of the Constitution Act, 1982, also dilutes "the concept of voting parity."

I have argued elsewhere[1] that it was not until 1986 that the Parliament of Canada amended section 51 of the Constitution Act, 1867, in such a way that the principle of representation by population for the provinces was eroded. The 1952 amendments provided only a temporary cushion for provinces with

90

relatively declining populations and the 1974 amendments actually enhanced the principle. I still maintain that the amendments made to section 51 by the Representation Act, 1985, can be shown to violate "the principle of proportionate representation of the provinces in the House of Commons as prescribed by the Constitution of Canada." I am arrogant (or foolish) enough to maintain that Thomas Berger simply did not present the strongest arguments possible when he attacked the constitutionality of the Representation Act, 1985, in the *Campbell* case. [2]

Except for provisions concerning the entry of new provinces, the effects of which turned out to be temporary, there have been only two occasions since 1867 when the principle of representation by population of the provinces has been eroded by legislative enactment. The first was in 1915 when the Imperial Parliament implemented the Senate Floor Rule and the second was in 1986 when the Canadian Parliament approved the Representation Act, 1985 . "Rep by pop" was a central principle of the Confederation settlement in 1867 and in my view it remains so. Indeed, Prime Minister Mulroney, when tabling the most recent package of federal constitutional proposals in the House of Commons, pointed out that, if the government's plans for Senate reform were implemented, "the Commons would likely become a chamber in which there was stricter adherence to the principle of representation by population . . .[3]

The Saskatchewan decision is, of course, only relevant to drawing boundaries *within* provinces, for both provincial and federal electoral districts. But, together with certain provisions of the federal Representation Act, 1985, it sends out a strong message that unequal representation is constitutionally acceptable, that it could even be desirable in some circumstances, and that it might be part of what sets our political system apart from that of the Americans.

From 1964 to 1986 the federal Electoral Boundaries Readjustment Act provided for the creation of independent commissions in each province which were mandated to establish electoral districts, the populations of which had to be within 25% of the provincial average. In many ways this 25% rule itself came to be regarded as a kind of quasi-constitutional objective, if not requirement, that applied to both levels of government. It is ironic that those challenging the Saskatchewan decision did so in part on the grounds that a 25% variation was excessive.

Provisions of the Representation Act, 1985, amended the Electoral Boundaries Readjustment Act to enable the commissions to violate the 25% rule "in extraordinary circumstances." In the 1987 federal redistribution, commissions in three provinces established five extraordinary electoral districts. In light of the Saskatchewan decision it is difficult to see how in the future they will be able to resist establishing more. Commissioners will not be able to insist that their prime purpose is to promote equal representation. Indeed, both papers point out that in the future it might be possible to challenge redistributions on the grounds that they implemented *only* the "one person–one vote" principle and did not pay sufficient attention to some of the other principles that the

Supreme Court has identified as being part of "effective representation."

Both papers also point out that, as a result of the Saskatchewan decision, the job of future boundary-drawers is going to be considerably more difficult. For example, what if they accepted a demand for special representation from one group but rejected a similar request from another one on the grounds that granting it would create adverse effects on adjoining constituencies? What if they decided instead to reject all such requests on the grounds that they did not want to get involved in the kind of problems suggested in the previous question? Perhaps the Supreme Court would accept almost any reasoned defence of a set of boundaries. If so, it would appear that "effective representation" is little more than what the boundary-drawers say it is.

Might the Supreme Court have struck down the Saskatchewan redistribution if the case presented by those challenging it had been different? Neither paper explicitly addresses this question. However, I believe that once one accepts the proposition, as the Saskatchewan Court of Appeal did,[4] that legislatures are entitled to create constituencies with significantly smaller populations for people living in sparsely populated areas, then it is inconsistent to argue that they should be prevented from responding in a similar way to those who make claims for special representation based on language, ethnicity, economic status, local-government boundaries, or other particular factors related to alleged community of interest.

By claiming that deviations of 39 and 28% from the provincial average were acceptable for the North but deviations approaching 25% were not acceptable elsewhere, the Court of Appeal defied common sense. The Supreme Court's doctrine of "effective representation" is in my view little more than a logical extension of the notion that the North deserves special treatment.

Richards and Irvine claim that the creation of the two northern constituencies "is consistent with general practice in Canada which has traditionally recognized the special difficulties involved in representing extremely large and/or remote areas." This is generally true at the provincial level and was true at the federal level as well until 1964. However, it is important to re-emphasize that, until it was amended by the Representation Act, 1985, the federal Electoral Boundaries Readjustment Act provided that *all* electoral districts within a province (including northern ones) had to fall within the 25% limit. Except for Labrador, all federal electoral districts at the northern extremities of the provinces still do.

Fritz somehow thinks we are not yet able properly to address the issue of sparsely populated areas because we do not know whether it is "more difficult to represent a rural constituency than an urban constituency." This is because "political scientists in Canada have not done the necessary empirical work." I hereby promise to begin such a research project as soon as Professor Fritz begins one to determine whether it is more difficult to be a circuit-court judge or a judge on a court of appeal. Learning more about how our MPs do their jobs is a meaningful objective; determining which ones face the "more difficult" working conditions is not.

The Court's decision seems to have been written in such a way as to encourage extensive future litigation, or at least threats of such litigation directed at the hapless boundary-drawers. Numerous groups will inevitably want to argue that "effective representation" means that boundaries must be drawn to take account of their particular concerns. Others, with similar objectives as the SAVE group in Saskatchewan, will still want to use the courts to try to enforce equal representation. Richards and Irvine point out that there are a number of provinces in which there is much less voter parity than in Saskatchewan after the last redistribution. Even federal electoral districts are not immune to this kind of challenge. For example, as a result of the 1987 federal redistribution in Newfoundland, the population of the Labrador constituency was 61.4% below the provincial average and St. John's West was 28.8% above. Such figures make the architects of the Saskatchewan redistribution appear as vigorous defenders of urban political strength.

Although the Saskatchewan decision is hardly a ringing endorsement of the principle of representation by population, its effect, when considered in combination with the *Dixon* case in British Columbia, could well cause officials in other jurisdictions to want to eliminate their most glaring inequities so as to insure that they come within the Saskatchewan parameters. Paradoxically, the overall effect of the decision could be both to provoke further demands for special representation from various groups having alleged communities of interest and to prompt at least some governments to introduce legislation eliminating some of the more dramatic examples of such representation, particularly if it has been inadvertent. In these circumstances, redistributions at both levels could become much more politically explosive, especially after the release of the 1991 federal census figures.

In conclusion, I should like to introduce one final question that might not have occurred to others attending this conference: To what extent does the Saskatchewan decision apply to electoral systems within *municipal* government? The short answer is that it does not, because section 3 only applies to the House of Commons and legislative assemblies and not to municipal councils. However, another possible way of challenging redistributions is to claim that they violate other sections of the Charter, notably section 15, which guarantees to each individual "the equal protection and equal benefit of the law." Such a claim was made in the *Dixon* case, but Chief Justice McLachlin did not address it on the grounds that " . . . having found that the existing system violates s. 3 of the Charter, it is unnecessary to consider whether it also violates other sections of the Charter."[5]

Any provincial law or territorial law that allows the establishment of unequal municipal electoral systems is subject to challenge under section 15 of the Charter.[6] An objection to this claim might be that, had the framers of the Charter meant to include guarantees concerning municipal voting, they would have been included in section 3. It is important to note, however, that section 3 is not subject to "the notwithstanding clause" (section 33), but section 15 is. Federal and provincial legislatures cannot override the courts on section 3 but they can on section 15. To the extent that equal municipal voting rights are arguably protected by section 15, they are not immune from "notwithstanding" legislation in the way that section 3 voting rights are.

One obvious implication of the argument that municipal voting arrangements are subject to section 15 is that ward boundaries within any given municipality must be redrawn on a fairly regular basis so as to ensure that the populations of each are roughly equal. Perhaps the degree of inequality permitted in the *Saskatchewan Reference* case can serve as a rough guide as to what might be acceptable, although the reasons justifying the deviations permitted for the two northern Saskatchewan electoral districts are unlikely to find analogues within a single municipality.

Representation in two-tier metropolitan or regional structures raises even more interesting issues. As recently as 1989, the Ontario legislature approved legislation establishing a new two-tier system for Lambton county. The City of Sarnia, comprising 58% of the new county's population, was allocated only 15 of 37 votes (41%) on its council.[7] Are residents of Sarnia receiving "the equal protection and equal benefit of the law"? It would seem not.[8] Similarly, in the Region of Peel, the City of Mississauga in 1990 comprised 62.8% of the Region's population, but Mississauga is entitled to only 10 representatives on Peel's 21-member council.[9] In both Lambton and Peel, major urban municipalities are dramatically underrepresented within units of local government that include large tracts of rural land. There is little in the Saskatchewan decision to give comfort to people who might think that such arrangements are constitutionally acceptable. It is only a matter of time until they too are subject to judicial review.

Notes

1. "Eroding Representation-by-Population in the Canadian House of Commons: *The Representation Act, 1985*," *Canadian Journal of Political Science* 23 (1990): 441–42.
2. For details, see ibid., 449–52.
3. Canada, House of Commons, *Debates*, 34th Parliament, 3rd Session, Number 34 (24 September 1991): 2588.
4. Richards and Irvine point out that Mr. Justice Cory also accepted special treatment for the North in his dissenting Supreme Court opinion.
5. *Dixon v. British Columbia (Attorney General)*, [1989] 4 W.W.R. 393.
6. For a discussion of the relevance of section 15 to electoral boundaries, see the paper by Kent Roach in this volume.
7. Byron J. Montgomery, *Annexation and Restructuring in Sarnia–Lambton; A Model for Ontario County Government?*, Local Government Case Studies #4 (London, Ontario: University of Western Ontario, Department of Political Science, 1990), 71.

8. Such an argument would be especially compelling if it could be shown (which it no doubt can) that certain voters vulnerable to systemic political, legal, or social discrimination (such as county welfare recipients) tended to live disproportionately within the City of Sarnia. See Kent Roach's paper in this volume.
9. Bonnie J. Zeran, "Should Peel's Regional Chairman be Directly Elected?" Unpublished Diploma in Public Administration research paper, University of Western Ontario, March 1991, 34.

DRAWING BOUNDARIES: THE ALBERTA AND BRITISH COLUMBIA CASES

Charter Politics in Alberta: Constituency Apportionment and the Right to Vote*

RAINER KNOPFF

UNIVERSITY OF CALGARY

F.L. MORTON

UNIVERSITY OF CALGARY

In *Dixon* (1989) Justice McLachlin, then of the BC Supreme Court, interpreted the right to vote in section 3 of the Charter as requiring "relative equality of voting power."[1] By this she meant that electoral divisions must be relatively equal in population size. Using this criterion, she found that British Columbia's existing electoral divisions violated the Charter. Although Justice McLachlin did not define or impose a precise numerical definition of "relative equality," she indirectly endorsed the Fisher Commission's recommendation of a maximum permissible deviation from the provincial average of no more than +/- 25%.[2] Thirty-two percent of British Columbia's electoral districts exceeded this limit.

The *Dixon* decision raised questions in other Canadian jurisdictions concerning the constitutionality of their own districting systems. Alberta's electoral system seemed particularly vulnerable. Under Alberta's existing legislation, the province was divided into urban and rural categories, with an almost equal division of constituencies (42 urban and 41 rural) between the two categories. Since 60% of Albertans live in urban centres, however, urban ridings were on average much larger than their rural counterparts. Moreover, considerable variation was allowed within the two categories. Urban ridings were not supposed to exceed the *urban* average by more than 25% (though in 1989 five did), but were allowed to fall below the *urban* average by more than 25% (in 1989 three had fallen below this limit). No deviation limit was specified for the rural category, but if the 25% rule were applied, 15 of the 41 divisions would have been in violation. Eight were more than 25% above the rural average and 7 more than 25% below it.

Even constituencies that did not depart from their category's average by more than 25% nevertheless varied considerably: the standard deviation of urban constituencies from the urban average, for example, was 17%. Needless to say, many constituencies that did not vary from their within-category average by as much as 25% would differ by more than that amount from the *provincial* average. In fact, fully 51% of Alberta's constituencies exceeded the latter standard. If British Columbia's electoral system, with only 32% of constituencies varying by more than 25% from the provincial average, was too unequal to withstand a Charter challenge, Alberta's would surely suffer the same fate.

It thus comes as no surprise that in August of 1989 the Province of Alberta responded to *Dixon* by striking an all-party Special Committee on Electoral Boundaries to review "the implications of the Charter of Rights and Freedoms for electoral boundaries and the distribution of constituencies."[3] The committee's report was tabled in November 1990. The following month the Government of Alberta introduced Bill 43, the "Electoral Boundaries Commission Act." After several weeks of debate and some minor amendments, Bill 43 became law.

The new law embodied a number of changes relevant to the issue of "relative equality of voting power." Total population replaced the old standard of enumerated voters as the basis for distributing constituencies. The total number of divisions remained at 83, but a 25% maximum permissible deviation from the *provincial* average was established, a fairly obvious attempt to "Charter-proof" the new act by bringing it within the reach of the *Dixon* ruling.[4] Nevertheless, 5% of the seats are allowed to deviate from the average by up to 50% in order to accommodate problems of especially large size and small population. Most controversially, the former distinction between urban and rural divisions was replaced by the new categories of "single-municipality" and "multi-municipality" divisions. Forty-three single-municipality divisions were allocated to Alberta's five major cities,[5] while the rest of the province received 40 "multi-municipality" districts.

The new categorization into urban and multi-municipality constituencies is not airtight. The electoral boundaries commission is permitted to create multi-municipality constituencies combining parts of the designated urban centres and the surrounding rural areas. Indeed, in five cases (including such centres as Red Deer and Grande Prairie), the commission is required to construct such "hybrid" urban-rural districts. Obviously, the more urban voters are drawn into hybrid districts, the smaller the average size of the 43 wholly urban districts, the larger the average size of the 40 multi-municipality ridings, and thus the greater the overall equality among ridings. Most constituencies cannot vary from the provincial average by more than 25%, but much greater equality is possible through aggressive creation of hybrid districts.

While Alberta's opposition parties certainly favoured more equal constituencies, they did not like the idea of achieving equality through the construction of hybrid districts. They did not, in short, wish to purchase increased equality at the cost of blurring the traditional urban-rural categorization. For example, the NDP, as a predominantly urban party, stood to benefit from the traditional categorization if urban ridings increased to reflect their share of the population. Such interests obviously preferred to achieve greater equality of constituencies simply by increasing the relative number of urban districts. They worried that the hybrid districts envisaged by the new legislation would be used to swamp slices of urban population in predominantly rural constituencies, thus benefiting rurally based Conservatives at the expense of urban New Democrats and Liberals. In mock honour of Premier Don Getty, potential gerrymanders of this sort became known as "Gettymanders."

Canadian governments have learned that constitutional litigation is not just available to those who would challenge their policies. It can sometimes also be used proactively by governments to promote their own agendas. Reference cases are particularly useful in this respect. They can be used either as a tactic of "avoidance," deflecting unwanted political hot potatoes into the courtroom, or to confer the aura of constitutional legitimacy on otherwise controversial policies.[6] The Alberta government employed the latter tactic in this case. Hoping that a judicial imprimatur of constitutionality would help to forestall criticism of the new act, it referred it to the Court of Appeal in February 1991, well before the Electoral Boundaries Commission had a chance to embody the new legislative requirements in a revised electoral map. The province's major cities as well as representatives of the opposition parties intervened to oppose the legislation, while the Alberta Association of Municipal Districts and Counties intervened in its support.

Governments cannot control judges, of course, so when a government seeks a judicial stamp of approval in this manner it always runs the risk of losing. In this case the risk was considerably diminished, however, by the fact that the Court would be asked to comment only on the bare framework of the legislation as such, not on an actual electoral map drawn pursuant to the legislation, which did not yet exist. Without a map, the charge of Gettymandering would be entirely hypothetical and abstract, and the judges might be expected to ignore it. After all, hybrid districts could as easily be constructed to swamp rural voters in predominantly urban voting populations as the reverse.

Given this serious obstacle, one is compelled to wonder why the cities and opposition parties agreed to participate in a case at this early stage. In doing so, did they not risk dignifying a process stacked against them? Wouldn't it have been strategically sounder to reject the legitimacy of such an abstract reference, refusing to participate until a map had been drawn? But this assumes that the Gettymandering issue was their only concern. It seems likely that they participated in the case because they hoped to have the legislation invalidated on other grounds. For example, it was still possible that the 25% variation limit was too great to satisfy the requirements of the section 3 right to vote. True, Justice McLachlin in *Dixon* had seemed to endorse such a limit, but that was only the judgment of one lower court judge. Neither the provincial courts of appeal nor the Supreme Court had had the opportunity to consider the issue. It thus remained possible to argue that Canada should adopt the American rule of "one person-one vote."

Certainly this is what litigants were then arguing before the Saskatchewan Court of Appeal, which was also hearing a reference on new electoral legislation. Like Alberta's previous act, the new Saskatchewan law divided the province into fixed urban and rural categories, though constituencies within neither category could vary from the provincial average by more than 25%. (Two "northern" districts constituted a third category, and were permitted to fall below the provincial average by as much as 50%; for convenience we include these within the "rural" category in most of the subsequent analysis.) The Saskatchewan allocation of seats to the two categories was not nearly as skewed as Alberta's, however. Whereas the rural 40% of Alberta's population received virtually half of the seats under the old Alberta law, rural Saskatchewan, which constitutes 52.4% of the province's population, received 37 or 56% of the seats, an overrepresentation of less than 4 percentage points. Similarly, the 29 urban seats in Saskatchewan represent 43.9% of the total, less than 4 percentage points under the rural share (47.6%) of the population. With the exception of the two northern districts, the differences between the average size of urban and rural constituencies imposed by this categorization could thus easily be accommodated within the overall 25% deviation limit. Such a standard might be sufficient to invalidate the old legislation in British Columbia or Alberta, but it would not invalidate the much smaller overrepresentation of rural areas in Saskatchewan. Thus opponents of the Saskatchewan law found themselves promoting a much closer approximation to the "one person-one vote" standard.

Proponents of "one person-one vote" were delighted by the Saskatchewan Court of Appeal's unanimous decision on 6 March 1991 to strike down the Saskatchewan law.[7] Although the Court did not require constituencies to be absolutely equal, it argued that departures from strict equality were compatible with section 3 only to the extent that they were "inherent in a representative, parliamentary democracy." Such "inherent" limitations on equality included the mobility of modern populations and the unpredictable timing of elections, factors making it unlikely that even constituencies drawn to achieve strict equality would in fact be equal on voting day.[8] Noninherent limitations, such as the attempt to accommodate the different interests of regionally skewed populations, were prima facie violations of section 3, which could stand only if "demonstrably justified" as "reasonable limits in a free and democratic society" under section 1 of the Charter.[9] Noninherent limitations included what the Court called the "arbitrary division of the province" into fixed urban and rural categories. They also included Saskatchewan's generous 25% deviation limit because the "inherent" limitations of parliamentary representation clearly did not require nearly so much leeway. The 25% deviation limit was thus a Charter violation subject to the requirement of section 1 justification. The Court found that it could not be so justified.[10] If the Alberta Court of Appeal could be persuaded to come to a similar conclusion, Alberta's law could be struck down without having to rely on the Gettymandering charge, simply because it too embodied a deviation limit far larger than needed to accommodate the "inherent" limitations of parliamentary democracy.

The Saskatchewan government immediately appealed the decision of its Court of Appeal to the Supreme Court of Canada. In the normal course of events this appeal would have taken considerable time, and the next major judicial consideration of these issues would have been the Alberta reference, scheduled for 17 June 1991. By the time the Supreme Court would normally be expected to hear the Saskatchewan case, it would have the benefit of the considered opinion(s) of another provincial court of appeal. But this was not a normal situation. With the legislature nearing the end of its five-year term, the Saskatchewan government faced the prospect of imminent elections without valid electoral legislation or constituencies. In urgent situations, the Supreme Court sometimes expedites its proceedings–the *Daigle* case comes to mind[11]– and it did so in this case, granting leave to appeal on 17 March, just days after the Saskatchewan Court of Appeal handed down its decision, and setting 29 and 30 April as the dates for oral argument. What the Supreme Court said about the Saskatchewan case could obviously settle some of the central issues in the Alberta litigation. The June hearing of Alberta's case thus suddenly seemed a sideshow, perhaps even redundant.

This turn of events posed a problem for the parties to the Alberta case. Considerable time, energy, and money had been devoted to preparing evidence and arguments for that case, and now the locus of action had suddenly shifted to Ottawa in another case. Naturally, most of the Alberta litigants quickly applied for, and received, status to intervene in the Saskatchewan appeal. This did not entirely dispose of their difficulties, however. Intervener status gave them the right to make legal arguments relevant to the Saskatchewan case, but not to introduce the "social fact" evidence they had commissioned for their own case. The law firm representing the Alberta government, for example, had commissioned the authors of this paper to prepare a study addressing historical, comparative, and philosophical issues relevant to the question of apportioning constituencies.[12] Seven other academics were hired by the other parties to respond to or further develop the evidence and arguments in this study.[13] This considerable body of research was to have been entered into evidence in the Alberta reference, but as material that had not been considered by the lower court in the Saskatchewan case, it could not be directly entered into the Supreme Court appeal of that case.

Although this caused some initial consternation among government lawyers in Alberta, a loophole was soon found to enable at least our study to be placed before the Supreme Court. While new "evidence" specific to the case cannot be introduced at an appeal, previously "published authorities" can be. As it turned out, we are associated with the University of Calgary's Research Unit for Socio-Legal Studies, which publishes a series of "occasional papers." The obvious answer was to publish our study in this series, and to do so quickly.

This required turning a study obviously directed to the Alberta litigation into a general paper entitled "Does the Charter Mandate 'One Person, One Vote'?" With the aid of computerized word processing, this was an overnight job, and the required publication was duly released the next morning, ready to be appended to the Alberta government's submissions to the Supreme Court. The manoeuvre was sufficiently transparent that it occasioned objections from counsel for the City of Edmonton during the oral hearing of the case, but to no avail.

Edmonton's objection was not entirely misplaced. While we had managed to slip our study in under the wire, much of the other work prepared for the Alberta case was not so lucky. Nor had equivalent material been amassed for the trial of the Saskatchewan case under appeal. As R.E. Fritz points out, that case was also rushed, with the bulk of "the research effort ... compressed into a 6 week period."[14] This was only enough time to do the necessary legal research, and no significant "social fact" studies were undertaken. Thus, not only did the Supreme Court decide its first electoral districting case in a hurry and under pressure, but it did so in a case for which little social fact evidence had been prepared, and with access to only a small part of the considerable body of such evidence developed for the Alberta case. The potential pitfalls of judicial policy making were glaringly evident.

The Supreme Court rendered its decision in *Carter v. Saskatchewan* on 6 June 1991.[15] In a six to three decision, it allowed the appeal and reinstated the Saskatchewan act and boundary map. The majority judgment was written by Justice McLachlin, the same judge who, before her elevation to the Supreme Court, had decided *Dixon* in 1989.

McLachlin rejected the Saskatchewan Court of Appeal's assumption that the purpose of section 3 of the Charter was to guarantee "equality of voting power," and that all "noninherent" departures from such equality were thus suspect. She did not deny the importance of "parity of voting power" but insisted that it was only one of many factors relevant to fair and "effective representation," the true purpose of section 3.[16] The achievement of fair and effective representation required giving "distinct interests"–such as the interests of sparsely populated territories or cultural and ethnic minorities–"an effective voice in the legislative process as well as ... effective assistance from their representatives in their 'ombudsman' role."[17] Often this could not be done without compromising the ideal of equality to a degree greater than required by the "inherent limitations" emphasized by the Saskatchewan Court.[18] Since a balance between equality and "noninherent limitations" was often required by the very purpose of section 3, inequalities substantially greater than the Saskatchewan Court would have allowed were, for Justice McLachlin, perfectly compatible with section 3 and did not necessarily need to be justified under section 1.

Justice McLachlin thus concluded that neither the Saskatchewan legislation nor its attendant electoral map infringed section 3, despite considerable variations in constituency size. Some of the size discrepancies were caused by the legislatively mandated under- and overrepresentation of urban and rural voters. Justice McLachlin noted that under the previous legislation, which did not impose a similar urban-rural categorization, the Electoral Boundaries Commission had established one in practice, with similar implications for discrepancies in constituency size. The new act thus simply gave legislative expression to an established practice. [19] She was persuaded, moreover, "that not only are rural ridings harder to serve because of difficulty in transport and communications, but that rural voters make greater demands on their elected representatives, whether because of the absence of alternative resources to be found in urban centres or for other reasons." She thus concluded that "the goal of effective representation may justify somewhat lower voter populations in rural areas."[20] Furthermore since the number of seats allocated to each category differed from its share of the population by less than 4% in either direction, the variation in constituency size attributable to this feature of the legislation was "relatively small." The legislative allocation of fixed numbers of seats to the urban and rural areas, out of proportion to their share of the overall population, was thus compatible with section 3 and did not need section 1 justification.

Justice Cory, joined by Chief Justice Lamer and Justice L'Heureux-Dubé, dissented on this point—not, however, because he supported a "one person, one vote" interpretation of section 3, but because he preferred the necessary inequalities to flow from the judgment of the Electoral Boundaries Commission rather than being imposed by the legislature. While Cory thought that "any body charged with creating an electoral map should commence with the proposition that, to the extent that it is reasonable and feasible, the voter population of each constituency should be approximately equal," he agreed that departures from equality could be justified by such "noninherent" factors as "geography, demography and communities of interest."[21] Instead of being free to start from the assumption of equality, however, the commission had to begin its deliberations from a legislatively mandated inequality. That this mandated inequality was minimal was beside the point. "[N]o explanation has been given," Cory wrote, "as to why the balancing of the relevant factors could not, as it was previously, be left to the commission rather than being mandated by the legislature. The province has failed to justify the need to shackle the Commission with the mandatory rural-urban allocation and the confinement of urban boundaries to municipal limits."[22]

Justice Cory's views make sense if one assumes that a completely independent electoral boundaries commission is constitutionally required. Alternatively, he might believe that, though not required, a commission, once established, must be given a free hand. The latter was Justice Sopinka's reading of Cory's opinion. Sopinka could not agree.

> It was not necessary for the Saskatchewan legislature to create an independent commission, and, had it simply legislated the impugned boundaries, the process

itself would not have been subject to judicial scrutiny. Having chosen to delegate the task to the commission, there is no reason why the legislature should be prohibited from laying down tight guidelines delineating the powers to be conferred on the commission.[23]

In fact, the discrepancies in size among Saskatchewan constituencies were not all caused by the urban-rural categorization. For all the discussion of this categorization, it cannot be blamed for more than relatively minimal size variations. Certainly it cannot be blamed for variations within each category. For example, Saskatoon Greystone, the largest urban constituency, had 12,567 voters as compared with only 7,684 in the adjacent urban riding of Saskatoon Sutherland–University. Indeed, even the smallest rural constituency, Morse, had slightly more voters (7,757) than Saskatoon Sutherland–University. Within the rural category, Cut Knife–Lloydminster, with 11,800 voters, was significantly larger than not only Morse but also the adjacent constituency of Wilkie (8,775 voters).[24] The commission had obviously tried to accommodate a variety of nonpopulation-based considerations that fell into the Saskatchewan Court of Appeal's "noninherent" category. Unlike the Saskatchewan Court, the Supreme Court had no difficulties with these discrepancies. For Justice McLachlin, they were generally justified by such legitimate considerations as "natural community dividing lines" (e.g., rivers and municipal boundaries). Some discrepancies were also justified by projections of differential population growth. Thus a seat might be allocated to a locality with relatively few voters in the expectation that it would experience relatively high population growth.[25] This may have been the case in Saskatoon Sutherland–University. Nor did Justice Cory's dissenting judgment challenge these discrepancies. After all, they flowed not from legislative "shackling" of the commission, but from the very commission discretion Cory was concerned to bolster.

From the point of view of the parties to the Alberta litigation, the disagreements of the Supreme Court judges were less important than their consensus about fundamentals. Although the judges had carefully avoided endorsing a specific numerical deviation limit, they had agreed in upholding Saskatchewan's 25% standard. The American standard of "one person–one vote," having gained partial entry into Canada with the Saskatchewan Court of Appeal decision, was clearly being pushed back across the border. The parties challenging the Alberta legislation had little to hope for on this score. Furthermore, although the Court had upheld Saskatchewan's urban-rural categorization, there were some indications that the similar categorization in the former Alberta legislation might not have passed constitutional muster, and that the Supreme Court would consider the new act a distinct improvement. Justice McLachlin emphasized the minimal variation caused by the Saskatchewan categorization, and Justice Sopinka added that some urban-rural categorizations might produce variations "so extreme as to amount to a breach of the right to vote." This had obviously not happened in Saskatchewan because the urban and rural populations were close to equal, but it might well happen in Alberta if the old system of dividing seats equally between the two-thirds urban and one-third rural populations had been continued. Alberta had obviously been wise in abandoning its fixed urban-rural categories.

There were strong indications, in short, that the Supreme Court panel that decided the Saskatchewan case would also have upheld Alberta's new legislation. Indeed, the decision might well have been unanimous. The three dissenters in the Saskatchewan case disliked the law they were reviewing not only because it "shackl[ed] the Commission with the mandatory rural-urban allocation," but also because of "the confinement of urban boundaries to municipal limits." It seems that both the lack of an urban-rural categorization *and* the provision for hybrid "multi-municipality" districts in the Alberta legislation would have pleased the dissenters.

The Alberta Court of Appeal had, for obvious reasons, postponed the scheduled June hearing of its own reference until after the Supreme Court decided the Saskatchewan case. With the latter case in hand, however, it was no longer obvious why the parties challenging the Alberta legislation would wish to continue their participation. Prior to the Supreme Court decision they might have hoped to defeat the legislation in the abstract on one person–one vote grounds, but that hope had been dashed. Without an electoral map in place, moreover, the charge of "Gettymandering" remained purely hypothetical. Not surprisingly, therefore, the challengers withdrew from the litigation. Only the Alberta Association of Municipal Districts and Counties, which had intervened in support of the legislation, decided to stay the course. Despite the lack of opposing parties, the Alberta government decided to proceed with the reference, and the case was heard on 30 September.

Courts are supposed to be arenas for adversarial combat, but this courtroom was bereft of opposing parties. The normal judicial role of relatively passive impartiality thus did not make much sense in this case. If any semblance of even-handed consideration of both sides was to be maintained, the judges themselves would have to play part of the role of opposing counsel, assuming a posture more akin to the inquisitorial role of judges in the European civil law tradition. Thus the judges were unusually aggressive and probing in their questioning of government lawyers, giving them a particularly rough ride on the matter of hybrid districts. Perhaps because the dissenters in *Carter* had indicated that they favoured sufficient discretion to create hybrid districts, the Alberta judges focused especially on those few instances in which the electoral boundaries commission was legislatively required to create hybrid districts. If the dissenters in the Supreme Court appeal of *Carter* disliked legislative shackles that prevented hybrid districts, the Alberta judges seemed sceptical about shackles that required them. In fact, this seems the only point in the Alberta legislation that might attract some support among Supreme Court judges. It is difficult to see, however, why the Supreme Court's majority would react any differently to this restriction on commission discretion than they did to the Saskatchewan restrictions. It thus seemed unlikely that the Alberta Court of Appeal could find a way to invalidate the legislation before them, and, indeed, when it handed down its judgment on 26 November it upheld the act, recognizing that it was "of the sort approved by the Supreme Court of Canada in *Carter*."[26]

This does not mean, however, that there could not be future challenges to an actual electoral map drawn pursuant to the legislation. While the Supreme Court rejected the one person–one vote standard, it insisted on a continuing supervisory role over the requirements of "fair and effective representation." While the Canadian ideal of "fair and effective representation" embodied a balance between equality and nonpopulation-based limits on equality–a balance that required considerable leeway in apportioning constituencies–Justice McLachlin nevertheless insisted that "[d]epartures from the Canadian ideal of effective representation may exist," and that "[w]here they do, they will be found to violate s. 3 of the Charter."[27]

It is significant, in this respect, that the Supreme Court laid down no hard and fast deviation limit, within which discrepancies of constituency size might be considered immune from judicial scrutiny. In *Dixon* Justice McLachlin had indirectly endorsed the 25% standard, but in the Saskatchewan case she carefully avoided constitutionalizing this rule, although, obviously, she upheld a statute employing it. In fact, Justice McLachlin carefully considered whether size variations clearly within the 25% limit were justified. She found that they were, but this exercise would have been unnecessary if variations of less than 25% were enough to immunize constituencies. Although the 25% standard probably remains a good rule of thumb, even variations within that limit remain open to judicial scrutiny if they impede "fair and effective representation." As the Alberta Court of Appeal put it, *Carter* did not "mandate the use of [the 25% rule] or any deviation in a case where it is not needed."[28] Furthermore, although exceeding the 25% standard invites invalidation, as in *Dixon*, it does not guarantee it. Thus Justice McLachlin had no difficulty upholding the Saskatchewan provision allowing the two "northern" districts to fall below the provincial average by as much as 50%.[29] Clearly the Court sees no magic in numerical tests; the touchstone of constitutionality is the more judgmental formula of "fair and effective representation."

The formula of "fair and effective representation" is clearly designed to accommodate identifiable group interests in political representation. A set of numerically equal constituencies, whose boundaries are drawn at random in cookie-cutter fashion, would adequately represent people in their purely abstract individuality. But individuals tend to identify themselves politically with a variety of group or collective interests. From the perspective of these interests, it makes a great deal of difference how and where boundaries are drawn, and whether constituencies are of equal size. The Supreme Court has agreed that group interests must receive effective representation and has signalled that it will play a supervisory role in ensuring that they get it.

This might give some hope to those critics of the Alberta legislation who fear that it will lead to Gettymandered constituencies in which urban influence will be diluted, thus undermining the "effective representation" of urban voters. Such "urban dilution" critics often support the principle of one person-one vote, but only so long as constituencies remain wholly urban and rural in practice. This shows that their concern for one person-one vote is subordinate to their promotion of urban interests. If one person-one vote were the only concern, they could not possibly object to the greater equalization of constituencies through the construction of hybrid, urban-rural districts. As long as constituencies are equal, individuals, qua individuals, are well represented, and one person-one vote is achieved. One can object to such constituencies only by bringing in group considerations—for example, by lamenting the dilution of the collective interest of urban voters. The urban-dilution critics support the individualistic principle of one person-one vote because they see it as the necessary condition of effective urban influence—after all, urban votes are diluted most obviously by constituency size discrepancies that favour rural areas—but they understand that it is not a sufficient condition of the collective interest they favour. Even equal constituencies can be Gettymandered to the detriment of that collective interest. The urban-dilution critics clearly would have preferred to maintain the old urban-rural distinction while bringing urban representation into line with its share of the population, either by reducing the number of urban seats, or, more likely, by increasing the size of the legislature to accommodate more urban seats.

Since the Supreme Court has suggested that the effective representation of group interests might be undermined even by constituencies that fall within the 25% variation standard, Alberta's urban-dilution critics might still be able to challenge actual hybrid constituencies when the electoral map is drawn. Still, the prospects do not appear good. If it could be shown that constituency boundaries had been intentionally Gettymandered to favour the Conservative Party, a legal challenge might well succeed. Since constituency boundaries are drawn by a nonpartisan commission, however, it might be difficult to prove such an allegation. By itself, the unadorned charge of urban dilution may not be enough to overturn an electoral map. The Supreme Court has already indicated that the effective representation of rural voters justifies their overrepresentation, something that can be done only at the expense of urban influence. Is it likely to come to a different conclusion in the context of Alberta's hybrid districts?

The fact is that the Court seems anxious to provide constitutional scope for the more effective representation of "disadvantaged" groups, and that it does not seem to situate urban voters as such within that category. In addition to the "distinct interests" of those inhabiting "vast, sparsely populated territories," Justice McLachlin also refers to "minority representation" and "cultural and group identity" as concerns that must be accommodated to achieve "effective and fair representation conducive to good government." Indeed, it might not be going too far to suggest that Justice McLachlin upheld an "affirmative gerrymander" (in the form of variable-size apportionment) for rural dwellers in Saskatchewan in order to open the door for future affirmative gerrymanders on behalf of racial and ethnic minorities. Indeed, it might well be open to such groups to seek constitutional requirements for such affirmative gerrymanders in their favour. The Alberta Court of Appeal gave some indication of the kinds of issues looming on the horizon: "We foresee the possibility of minority claims for effective representation that, if accepted, might have an impact not just on the boundaries of specific districts but also on the total number of districts, the idea of single-seat constituencies, and the tradition of contiguous boundaries."[30] The Alberta Court also foresaw litigation under sections 15, 27, and 28 of the Charter.[31] The bottom-line judicial restraint in the Saskatchewan case has clearly not closed the door to future activism on such issues. Indeed, all the signs suggest that racial, cultural, and ethnic representation, not urban dilution, is where the action is likely to be in the future. In short, while the Court did not slam the door on Alberta's urban-dilution critics, it appeared to leave it only slightly ajar.

The Alberta Court of Appeal has tried to force a wider opening, however. With the exception of the handful of mandated hybrid districts, the Court saw the act as retaining the essence of the forced, and unbalanced, urban-rural categorization of the previous legislation. Assuming that the 43 single-municipality urban districts would incorporate the entire population of the specified urban centres, the Court pointed out that the average population of these seats would be 33,090 (or 16% above the provincial average), while the average population of the remaining seats would be 23,573 (or 17% below the provincial average). Saskatchewan's mandated urban-rural categorization had forced much smaller discrepancies, and the Alberta Court was "troubled" by the larger deviations required by its own province's legislation. True, *Carter* meant that some deviation was justifiable, but why did it need to be so large? The Court could see no justification for the substantial deviation required by the urban-rural categorization other than history, which was inadequate. Conceding that reducing the number of rural constituencies in an 83-seat legislature might make many of them too large and "isolated from other population" to provide effective representation—i.e., that "we may be near the minimal number of divisions that can adequately serve these areas"[32]—the Court nevertheless insisted that "no argument for effective representation of one group legitimizes under-representation of another group."[33] This led it openly to wonder whether the "minimal number" of rural constituencies required for effective representation could be maintained without underrepresenting the urban areas simply by enlarging the size of the legislature. "No doubt a Legislature can be too large," it wrote, "but it also can be too small."[34]

Such comments are usually preliminary to invalidating the act under consideration, but the Alberta Court drew back from the brink. "In light of the rule in *Carter*," it concluded, "the overall size of the Legislature will, in the future, inevitably come under Charter scrutiny."[35] In the future, not now! For now, despite its activist rhetoric, the Court was prepared to adopt a posture of judicial restraint, concluding that, "in all the circumstances, we cannot say [the legislative] choice is clearly wrong."[36]

A more compelling reason for restraint, of course, is that the legislation did *not* force the discrepancies reported by the Court, because it allowed the commission to reduce the average size of the 43 urban ridings, and correspondingly to increase that of the other 40 ridings, by creating hybrid districts in addition to the 5 required by the legislation. That the act provides the discretion to pursue this option is nowhere addressed, or even acknowledged, in the Court's opinion. This is surprising because the Court, in its discussion of the five mandated hybrids, ultimately approves of such districts in principle, asserting that "a division of all Alberta into rural and urban tends to be simplistic."[37] It is all the more surprising because the creative use of the hybrid-district option is an alternative to increasing the size of the legislature as a way of increasing voter parity without reducing the number of non-urban districts. By slighting the alternative implicit in the legislation and recommending the alternative preferred by the urban-dilution critics, the Court provides some solace to the latter, without, however, finding in their favour in this case. All things considered, the Alberta Court's attempt to enhance the prospects of future urban-dilution challenges seems rather lame, and although judicial ingenuity should never be underestimated, we persist in thinking that most of the action on the electoral apportionment front will concern disadvantaged racial or ethnic minorities. However that may be, *Carter* is clearly far from the last chapter in the story of Charter challenges to electoral districting.

Notes

* The research reported in this paper was financially supported by the Social Sciences and Humanities Research Council of Canada, grant #410-91-1396.

1. *Dixon v. British Columbia (Attorney General)*, [1989] 4 W.W.R. 393, 413.
2. Ibid., 431-32.
3. *Report of the Special Select Committee on Electoral Boundaries*, November 1990, 38.
4. An exception from this rule was made for up to four rural divisions, which are allowed to have as much as 50% less population than the average, if certain specified criteria are met.
5. Calgary (19), Edmonton (17), Lethbridge (2), and one each to Medicine Hat, Red Deer, Saint Albert, Sherwood Park, and Fort McMurray.
6. See F.L. Morton, "The Political Impact of the Canadian Charter of Rights and Freedoms," *Canadian Journal of Political Science* 20/1(1987).
7. *Reference re Saskatchewan Electoral Boundaries* (unreported at time of writing), Sask. C.A., decision rendered 6 March 1991, file no. 639, draft judgment.
8. Ibid.
9. Ibid.

10. Ibid., 51.
11. *Tremblay v. Daigle*, [1989] 1 S.C.R. 342. In this case the Supreme Court expedited the hearing of an appeal of an injunction requested by Daigle's ex-boyfriend, and granted by lower courts, preventing Daigle from having an abortion. When the Quebec Superior Court first heard the case, Daigle was 18 weeks pregnant. The Supreme Court heard and decided the case a mere 4 weeks later. Such speed is almost unheard of, but the reasons for the urgency are obvious.
12. The authors prepared a report for the Edmonton law firm of Field and Field, Perraton Masuch, who represented the Alberta government.
13. Barry Cooper (Political Science) and David Bercuson (History) of the University of Calgary prepared a study for the City of Calgary. Allan Tupper (Political Science) of the University of Alberta did the same for the City of Edmonton. Keith Archer (Political Science) and Sheilah Martin (Law) of the University of Calgary were retained by the New Democratic Party. Peter McCormick (Political Science) of the University of Lethbridge prepared a study for the Liberal Party, while Roger Gibbins (Political Science) of the University of Calgary provided advice for the Alberta Association of Municipal Districts and Counties. By our rough estimate, between January and May 1991, consulting costs alone for the Alberta case were at least 50 thousand dollars. (One can be assured that legal fees were at least double this figure.) If nothing else, this explains why the "People's Package" is so popular with lawyers and academics!
14. Reference R.E. Fritz's paper in this volume.
15. *Carter v. Saskatchewan (A.G.)*, S.C.C., decision rendered 6 June 1991, unreported at time of writing, draft judgment.
16. Ibid., 8–11.
17. Ibid., 16.
18. Ibid., 11.
19. Ibid., 21.
20. Ibid., 24.
21. Ibid., draft judgment of Cory J., 11.
22. Ibid., 12.
23. Ibid., draft judgment of Sopinka J., 3.
24. *Saskatchewan Reference* (see n.7), 38–39.
25. *Carter*, draft judgment of McLachlin J., 24.
26. *Reference Re Section 27 of the Judicature Act, R.S.A. 1980*, Chapter J-1, unreported, file #9103–0081–AC, draft judgment.
27. *Carter*, 15.
28. *Reference re Section 27*, 11.
29. Following this lead, the Alberta Court of Appeal upheld the provision in its legislation permitting 5% of constituencies to deviate by up to 50%.
30. *Reference re Section 27*, 6.
31. Ibid., 5.
32. Ibid., 13.
33. Ibid., 14.
34. Ibid., 15.
35. Ibid., 15.
36. Ibid., 14.
37. Ibid., 11.

Electoral Boundaries: An Obstacle to Democracy in Alberta

DAVID J. BERCUSON

UNIVERSITY OF CALGARY

BARRY COOPER

UNIVERSITY OF CALGARY

Since 1867, Canada has evolved from a decidedly nondemocratic constitutional monarchy into a quasirepublic within which the people are effectively sovereign. Notwithstanding the current debate regarding the place of Québec within the existing constitutional regime, Canada is a mature, federal liberal democracy. The evolution of laws governing both the drawing of electoral boundaries and the exercise of the franchise has been directly affected by the march to liberal democracy and has, in turn, affected that process. So has the evolution of the concept of Canadian citizenship and associated rights and duties. The adoption of the Canadian Charter of Rights and Freedoms in 1982 was a major turning point in this emergence of democracy in Canada. Alberta has not been immune to these broad, general, and well-known developments. If Canada had not evolved in the direction just indicated, there would be no reason for electoral reform to be an item on the political agenda of several provinces or of the national government. Nor would political scientists and lawyers be concerned with the question, or conferences such as this one be held.

One of the implications of this political change is that most Canadians no longer find it morally, politically, or constitutionally acceptable for voters to be discriminated against because of their place of residence, whether place is understood in the larger interprovincial context—hence the controversy over the constitutional status of Québec—or in terms of intraprovincial locale. Our assumption, that the free and equal exercise of the franchise is a legitimate objective in a liberal democracy, is not at variance with current attitudes. The objective of electoral boundaries legislation in Canada and in Alberta today is the protection of democratic political rights. That is why the government of Alberta saw fit to establish an Electoral Boundaries Commission and charged it with the responsibility of drawing up new electoral boundaries. In principle, any attempt to cater to special-interest groups in the drawing of electoral boundaries would violate the political rights of citizens living in a modern liberal democracy. That can hardly be a legitimate objective of any government. In more direct language, we believe that Canadian democracy must be based on the principle of one person–one vote, one vote–one value among all electors, which we refer to in a shorthand way as the equality principle. In Canadian terminology, representation by population, "rep by pop," is the slogan that best expresses what is meant by the equality principle. By this principle, votes are equal not merely within a single constituency but among all constituencies. "Rep by Pop," said Balinski and Young, "remains the constitutional aim and is the popularly accepted view of what is fair."[1] Fair and effective representation, we believe, means that electoral boundaries must cleave as closely as possible to the requirements of the equality principle. We will argue, however, that the current Electoral Boundaries Commission Act does not effectively institutionalize the equality principle within the electoral system and to that extent and degree constitutes an obstacle to democracy in Alberta.

The term "fair and effective representation of all citizens" was used in the judgment of the Court of Appeal of Saskatchewan in the 1991 reference subsequently overturned on appeal to the Supreme Court of Canada. It was used by the Saskatchewan Court to construe a remark by Chief Justice McLachlin, as she then was, in *Dixon* regarding "relative equality of voting power." In law, of course, the Saskatchewan Court erred; in fact or in reality, perhaps Justice McLachlin changed her mind upon elevation to the Supreme Court. However that may be, the phrase "fair and effective representation of all citizens" is very close to a statement by Chief Justice Earl Warren of the United States Supreme Court. In *Reynolds v. Sims,* Warren declared: "The achieving of fair and effective representation for all citizens is concededly the basic aim of legislative apportionment." The goal of fair and effective representation is achievable in a way that the mathematically strict but impossible adherence to the equality principle is not. In this regard, it would seem that Chief Justice Warren was also correct in his assessment that the reapportionment rulings were the key judicial decisions of his era because they nourished democracy at its roots.[2] Indeed, deliberate variation from the aim expressed in the equality principle, or significant practical failure to achieve fair and effective representation, amounts to starving democracy at its roots; or rather, it is to lay an axe to the roots of liberal, constitutional, and democratic politics.

Political scientists and historians have, in their more practical moments, made arguments similar to those of their colleagues on the bench. Balinski and Young, early in their critical analysis of the so-called "Amalgam Method" of apportioning representation in the Canadian House of Commons, observed that "equitable representation is at the heart of democracy."[3] Similarly, Carty declared that "concern for regular revisions of the electoral map stem from a basic commitment to fairness and to equity." He immediately added that "the impulse [to revise electoral boundaries] has been vague and uneven in Canada because there has been little consensus as to what constitutes fair representation."[4] And Robert Dixon, the premier student of electoral representation, made essentially the same argument with regard to the United States:

> One of the major ideals, here as well as in Europe, is to have the political parties, who after all still organize and run our legislatures, win seats in legislatures roughly proportional to their share of the popular vote. That ideal is the very core of the term *fair representation*. To the extent that other interests can be factored in, we probably would like that also.[5]

This is not to say that compromises with the "ideal" will not be imposed by the workings of the electoral system. But just as Aristotle's javelin thrower does not hit the target with each attempt, that fact does not mean he should take no aim at it. And likewise, just because there is an inevitable slippage between the "ideal" embodied in the equality principle and the electoral system that implements it, that fact does not mean we should abandon our principles. Fair and effective representation is implied by the very meaning of liberal democracy, and by the institutionalization of the equality principle toward which Canadian political life has been moving. Accordingly, we believe that fair and effective representation must be the aim and goal of the electoral system in any liberal democracy, including Alberta. Unfortunately, as we shall indicate, this is unlikely under the subject legislation.

Canada is not, however, simply a liberal democracy. It has a constitution that includes a nondemocratic element that is usually discussed in terms of federalism. However that may be, no province, and certainly not Alberta, is a mini-federation. Accordingly, arguments made with respect to the federation that have the effect of increasing deviation from the equality principle must be made on other grounds. We do not dispute those grounds here. Nor are we concerned with questions of within-constituency equality, which flows directly from the definition of the franchise. In other words, even though one may distinguish *conceptually* between an equal right to vote and the right to an equal vote (as other contributors to this volume have done), *in practice* the two concepts must be allied for the regime properly to be identified as a liberal constitutional democracy.

If there existed but a single province-wide constituency and one or another form of proportional representation, equality guaranteed by suffrage would be sufficient to ensure the fair application of the equality principle. That the electoral system necessarily derogates from the equality principle has long been observed. The single-member constituency with a plurality only needed to elect has helped contribute to the oft-observed pattern, that successive Alberta governments have enjoyed relatively large majorities in the legislature.[6] This discrepancy is one of the inevitable consequences of the electoral system.

The problem of establishing an electoral system that adequately reflects the equality principle has been expressed with aphoristic pungency by Taylor: "all organization is bias."[7] This means that the electoral system has consequences that affect the political agenda and is not merely a means of deciding on pre-established items on that agenda. Accordingly, nonpartisan districting is a myth.[8] The "districting problem," as it has been called, simply means that "no system of distribution of constituencies is neutral in its effects."[9] These observations have led some political scientists to formalize the logic of the "districting problem" and to arrive at rules to determine what *fair* (if not mathematically *equal*) representation means. In short, they have attempted to determine democratically permissible deviations from a mathematically strict but impossible adherence to the equality principle.[10]

Political scientists do not go to the effort of establishing formal rules and criteria of fairness and equality purely as a kind of mental gymnastics. Their speculations have an application to the real world of democratic electoral politics. Specifically, liberal democratic politics requires not merely that every citizen is allowed to vote the same number of times, but that each voter has virtually the same statistical probability of casting the deciding vote in an election and that votes are cast with relative anonymity, which means that the geographical position of the voter in the electoral system has no bearing on the outcome. What counts, in short, is votes, not who casts them.

That the electoral system has a direct effect on the meaning of political equality has been observed by many political scientists, starting perhaps 40 years ago with the classic work of Maurice Duverger and André Siegfried. One may, therefore, speak confidently of electoral-system bias, that is, of the difference between the percentage of the vote a party receives and the percentage of seats it wins in an election. This is true for virtually all electoral systems and is most assuredly true for single-member constituency plurality systems.[11] Accordingly, it is true for the Canadian and the Alberta electoral systems. In addition to the inevitable derogation from the equality principle that follows from the operation of the electoral system, there exist two additional ways of intentionally and deliberately undermining the goal of fair and effective representation, namely gerrymandering and maldistribution or malapportionment. These distortions to the equality principle are, unlike the ones just discussed, *not* inevitable. Also, unlike the distortions that flow from the operations of the electoral system, they *do* jeopardize the overriding principles of liberal democracy.

There are bound to be inexact correlations between popular voting and legislative representation any time there exist single-member (or, for that matter, multimember) constituencies and a plurality rule for election. Nonpartisan electoral cartography is indeed a myth because even the most nonpolitical procedures have political results.[12] A mathematically equal vote that is nevertheless politically worthless, whether the result of deliberate or inadvertent gerrymandering, is not evidence of a fair and effective franchise. One implication of the limitation of objective mathematical measures of gerrymandering that attempt to gauge its existence by electoral results is important in the context of Alberta, namely that there are a large number of unknowns in the causal chain and these can only be very imperfectly specified: (1) the electorate does not always vote the same way in the same constituency from one election to the next; (2) constituency populations are unstable; (3) voting rates, even within stable constituency populations, can fluctuate; (4) new issues and new candidates can have an independent effect on voting. In 1882, Dawson pointed out, the Conservatives gerrymandered extensively but their opponents made gerrymandering such an issue that it probably cost them seats![13]

One must, therefore, know the *intentions* of the people who draw up constituency boundaries in order to determine if gerrymandering is going on. If, indeed, "gerrymandering is essentially a matter of intent,"[14] it would follow that the conventional criteria, which stress the importance of drawing compact, contiguous constituencies with nearly equal populations, are not necessarily going to inoculate the electoral system against the virus of gerrymandering.

Let us then make a second sailing. Gerrymandering is better understood as the manoeuvring of constituency boundaries for partisan advantage, and more specifically to "waste" as many of the opposition's votes as possible either by concentrating them in a few districts, "stacking," or by spreading them as minority segments among many constituencies, "cracking." By considering the intentions of persons who draw up electoral boundaries, we are invoking a political not a mathematical principle. It was well expressed by James Madison in *Federalist* 10:

> No man is allowed to be a judge in his own cause because his interest would certainly bias his judgment, and, not improbably, corrupt his integrity. With equal, nay with greater reason, a body of men are unfit to be both judges and parties at the same time.

To remedy the temptations of gerrymandering that may indeed bias one's judgment and corrupt one's integrity, but without resorting to the pseudo-solution of searching for objectivity through neutral experts or computers, Dixon concluded that the most acceptable form of boundary commission was explicitly political. In American terms, he advocated a "bipartisan" and *nonlegislative* agency as the most promising way to achieve both fairness and representativeness. His reasoning exhibited both tough-minded realism and an overriding commitment to democratic government. As evidence for the latter, one need refer only to his comment on Justice Felix Frankfurter's statement in *Baker v. Carr* that the apportionment plaintiffs were asking the U.S. Supreme Court to choose between competing political philosophies. Dixon raised a highly pertinent question: "Difficult though it may be, what is wrong with a court commitment to a democratic political philosophy?"[15] What, indeed? Rather, in a democratic regime is the Court not so obliged?

Dixon's realism lay in proposing a politically sensitive committee. Whether appointments to boundary commissions need themselves be partisan may be doubted. What is less doubtful, however, is the fact that nonlegislators should not be used to staff such committees. There is no reason to increase the temptations of logrolling so that legislatures are in a position to gerrymander plenty of safe seats all around. Formally, logrolling that resulted in gerrymandering would violate the principle that each voter has the same statistical probability of influencing the outcome of an election.

There remains the nagging problem of constituencies with irregular shapes. "Gracie's finger," which provided British Columbia MLA Grace McCarthy with a long thin strip of Social Credit voters, is a well-known Canadian example. The most obvious way to deal with noncompact or strangely shaped constituencies is to rely as far as seems reasonable on preestablished political boundaries, which does not mean that subconstituency-level political boundaries should be maintained at all cost. Most municipal and other subconstituency boundaries were drawn up much earlier in the century; but socioeconomic and demographic changes since that time mean that only occasionally will they express current social realities. This is particularly true in Alberta where acreages, which are essentially upper-class suburbs outside city limits, are common. Accordingly, dogmatic reliance on existing political subdivisions may amount to a gerrymander for the preservation of the *status quo,* which in Alberta means rural overrepresentation. In any event, this is a political difficulty that can be dealt with only in a political way.

A second and more general way of dealing with strangely shaped constituencies is to use the rule of compactness and contiguity "merely to force an explanation for odd-shaped districts."[16] This use of the rule would ensure that presumption of fairness lay with the boundary commission and would require plaintiffs to show not that any particular boundary resulted in *unequal* constituencies but that the inevitable inequalities were so gross as to be *unfair* as well. In the Alberta context, "Gettymandering" would have to be publicly defended, which has hardly occurred to date.

The second major way of intentionally and deliberately undermining the goal of fair and effective representation is maldistribution or malapportionment. Maldistribution is simply numerical discrimination, the drawing of constituency boundaries so they enclose different numbers of voters. It is designed to give one party more seats by ensuring that, in areas of the voting strength of that party, there are a large number of constituencies. As Gudgin and Taylor observed:

> Malapportionment is an easily understood electoral abuse. If one voter resides in a constituency twice as large as a neighbouring constituency, he may claim that his vote is worth only half that of a voter in the other constituency.[17]

There are several ways of measuring maldistribution or malapportionment. The most common and least satisfactory is to compare the population of the largest and smallest constituencies. This pretentiously named "maximum population variance ratio" tells us very little in the absence of knowledge of whether the extremes are typical or isolated instances. One must, therefore, ensure proper weighting for the number of constituencies that approach the extremes as compared to the number that approach the mean. A second, and slightly improved, measure is the mean variance ratio. This is commonly used to measure maldistribution and to establish a norm for redistribution. The procedure is simple enough: a mean size for a constituency is calculated by dividing the number of electors (or the total population) by the number of constituencies. This establishes a numerical quota. The population of each constituency is then compared with the quota. Norms for redistribution are set in terms of permissible fluctuation around this quota. Restrictive quotas have the effect of limiting the opportunity for maldistribution but again, unless one has a way of measuring the distribution of constituencies within the limits, mean variance limits are not very informative indicators of maldistribution either.

There are, however, two measures of maldistribution that take into consideration the actual variations in the populations of all constituencies. In this way they make use of information ignored in the previous two measures. These are the Dauer-Kelsay Index and the Gini Index of Concentration.[18] The former measures the disparity in population size of constituencies; the latter measures how far the sizes of constituencies deviate from the quota. A Dauer-Kelsay Index approaching 50%, or .50, indicates a close approximation to the one person–one vote principle; with the Gini Index, complete equality would result in a measure of 0 and complete inequality in a measure of 1. We discuss the significance of the measures provided by these indices for Alberta below.

Unanimity in social science is exceedingly rare, but it exists regarding at least one matter: perfect or arithmetic equality in constituency population size is impossible. The reason for this otherwise remarkable event is not hard to find: there is always a gap between enumeration day and election day. The real problem of maldistribution, however, has very little to do with what might be called demographic slippage. As is well known, the most obvious form of maldistribution is to underrepresent urban voters and overrepresent rural voters. This is done by ensuring that urban constituencies contain more, usually many more, voters than rural ones. The significance of this fairly common form of maldistribution is plain, clear, and simple. As Taylor and Johnston remarked, malapportionment is

a rural defence mechanism which has been used in countries all over the world. It is a convenient way by which formerly dominant groups and areas can maintain their political power long after their numerical majority has been lost to new areas of population growth. It is convenient in the sense that it requires no direct action on the part of the formerly dominant groups; they just have to make changing the *status quo* difficult.[19]

When tolerance limits are set (such as the +/– 25% figure established by the Government of Alberta), it is theoretically possible for boundary commissions to provide for below-quota populations in urban constituencies and above-quota populations in rural constituencies. In fact, it has hardly ever worked out that way. In the 1964 debates over the federal electoral boundaries legislation, for example, several MPs intervened to indicate the way the deviations should go.[20] Sometimes MPs disguised their intentions by pleading for the preservation of "historic ridings." But, like the "historic Boston Gardens," these ridings were old, obsolete, and contained too few people for an equitable franchise. More often, however, such self-interested arguments took the form of drawing the attention of the House to problems of accessibility, transportation, and communications in rural constituencies that MPs from rural ridings encountered. All of these arguments assumed the validity of the proposition that constituencies were created chiefly to assist the politicians who must campaign in them. In a democracy, however, constituencies are units of political representation, not party organization. They exist to satisfy the demands of citizens, not the convenience of politicians. In fact, however, historically speaking, boundary commissions have followed the wishes of the elected politicians. Only in recent years have the actions of independent boundary commissions "shifted the grounds for redistribution in Canada from the more traditional territorial and geographic ones to a more egalitarian one."[21] As we remarked at the outset, Canada has, over the past generation, grown both increasingly democratic and increasingly republican.

As a postscript to this section, we would make two additional points: (1) The effects of the two forms of deviation from the equality principle, namely gerrymandering and maldistribution, are additive. That is, relatively small degrees of maldistribution can produce major electoral advantages when combined with a skilful gerrymander. One may go even farther: having a tolerance of +/– 25% is an invitation to gerrymander fully as generous as anything the Americans have discovered through strict adherence to the zero-tolerance doctrine. The two forms of electoral distortion are, therefore, connected. Legislation that establishes the rules for constituency boundaries should, accordingly, take this reality into account when establishing rules for the conduct of electoral boundaries commissions. (2) "The only proper remedy for bad single-member districts is good single-member districts."[22] In other words, if maldistribution has created bad single-member districts, the solution is not to get rid of single-member districts. There is, in short, no need to consider major changes in the electoral system in order to remedy problems associated with gerrymandering and maldistribution. In general, revisions of the electoral map stem from a fundamental commitment to fairness and equity as guiding principles of the political regime—however vague those terms initially appear to be. What that means, in practice, is adhering as closely as possible to the equality principle. In light of the foregoing remarks, let us now examine the Alberta data and proposed electoral boundary legislation.

For the past generation, political scientists have developed and applied various means of measuring maldistribution to the Alberta electoral data. Their findings have been consistent.[23] It is, therefore, surely beyond doubt that Alberta's

electoral districts are significantly, substantially, or even grossly malapportioned. This is, simply, a fact.

Consider, first, the basic statistical data. It is common knowledge that the
rural and farm population of Alberta is declining both as a percentage of the
total population and in absolute terms. Between 1931 and 1986, for example,
the farm population of Alberta was halved, falling from 370,899 to 178,115. At
the same time the provincial population rose from 731,600 to 2,375,278. In
other words, in 1931, 1 out of every 2 Albertans lived on a farm. By 1986, only
1 Albertan in 14 lived on a farm. Since 1971 in particular, Alberta has
consistently experienced population growth well above the national average.
By far the overwhelming increase was in urban areas.[24]

In order to come close to actualizing the equality principle and thus to
ensure fair and effective representation, constituency boundaries must reflect
these well-known, unambiguous, and significant demographic facts. It is clear
from the political science literature that constituency boundaries have not done
so to date in Alberta. If the current constituency boundaries legislation is to
achieve fair and effective representation, that would constitute a major and
fundamental change in Alberta's electoral history. It would amount to a genuine
reapportionment revolution. In straight demographic terms, if all constituencies in Alberta were equally represented, the urban ridings would be increased
by approximately eight constituencies.[25]

It is true, of course, that every measure of inequality among populations is
based upon assumptions that may or may not be met by the evidence. Every
measure has its limitations. What is significant, however, is that whatever measure
is used, it tells the same story. The data and the application of standard indices to
that data indicate the following: (1) maldistribution in Alberta is by any standard
of judgment substantial or gross; (2) it has not become any better over the last
generation, in spite of increased knowledge of the problems of maldistribution—indeed, by some measures maldistribution has grown worse. Furthermore, the new
legislation holds no promise of rectifying this unsatisfactory situation.

We mentioned earlier two spectacular but not particularly informative ways
of indicating maldistribution. To know, for example, that a vote in Edmonton
Whitemud or Calgary North West is worth about a quarter of what a vote is
worth in Cardston or Little Bow doesn't tell one very much about the
distribution of very large and very small constituency populations. Such
indicators simply provide information about the degree to which electors in any
particular constituency are over- or underrepresented. Such information is of
interest to the electors in those constituencies, but it does not address the larger
question of *systematic* over- and underrepresentation. Accordingly, such indicators are more useful to headline writers than to people concerned with the
general problem of malapportionment in Alberta.

There does exist, however, a measure that takes into account both
distributions of malapportionment and the particular weight or value of a vote
in any specific constituency. Following Schubert and Press, we may call this

measure a Type I Index.[26] We calculated what David and Eisenberg called "the relative value of the right to vote" or "vote-values" for a selection of recent Alberta elections.[27] The data clearly indicates the great range in vote-values across the provincial constituencies.

One obtains additional information from the Dauer-Kelsay Index, which measures the smallest proportion of the electorate that could theoretically elect a legislative majority. In other words, this index measures the disparity in population sizes of constituencies and constitutes a reliable indicator of the prevalence of inequalities in representation. Between 1955 and 1989 it has ranged between 30 and 38, which means that consistently over the past generation only around a third of the electorate was required to elect a majority government. More to the point, however, it indicates that over the last generation there have been very small changes in the maldistribution of seats in Alberta.

The Gini Index of Concentration also measures how far constituencies deviate from the equality principle. Gini Index values for provincial elections over the same period have ranged from .278 in 1959 to .170 in 1986. Considering only recent elections, the introduction of an independent electoral boundaries commission had an effect insofar as the index fell from .269 in 1967 to .191 in 1971. There is, however, a cyclical tendency of the index to climb as the census data upon which it is based grow more out of date. A comparison of Gini indices for Alberta and other Canadian provinces[28] indicates that, whereas in its early history, Alberta's constituencies were distributed more in line with the principles of "rep by pop" than on average were the other provinces, in recent years Alberta's maldistribution has increased relative to other provinces.

The conclusion to which we are drawn, on the basis of the quantitative data and the application of standard measures of maldistribution, is more or less identical with the judgments rendered *sine ira et studio* by 30 years of political science. The data show without question that Alberta constituencies are maldistributed now, and that they have been in the past. Whether they remain so in the future depends in part at least on the response of Alberta's electors.

At the time of writing, the Alberta Electoral Boundaries Commission Act has been referred by the Attorney General of the province to the Alberta Court of Appeal for a ruling on its constitutionality. By the date of publication these remarks may well be moot. Nevertheless, analysis of the act and the factum of the Attorney General does bring to light a number of significant factors that in one way or another dilute the impact of the equality principle. These will be discussed in point form, with reference to specific sections of the subject legislation.

1. Section 2: Appointment and Composition

The Alberta legislation contemplates the appointment of a five-person board, two of whom must be and three of whom may be resident outside a city.

If place of residence is considered an important criterion for appointment, as it seems to be, then it should more closely reflect the four-to-one difference in urban versus rural residents in Alberta. That is, a demographically accurate requirement for the composition of the commission would be *one* rural member and *four* urban ones.

2. Sections 5-8: Time of Appointment and Duration of the Reapportionment Process

Alberta has a rapidly changing population. It has, in fact, experienced more demographic changes in the past 20 years than any other Canadian province. Adequate technology is available to supply commissions with up-to-date statistics and accurate data. The time of appointment contemplated by the subject legislation, namely 8 to 10 years, practically ensures its efforts will be obsolete at the time of the election subsequent to its work. This has been a problem with the Canadian electoral boundaries commissions but not with the Australian. There is no reason, save to guarantee continued rural overrepresentation, of proceeding at so leisurely a pace. Likewise the process of accepting representations from interested parties is too lengthy. Moreover, experience of other commissions has shown that when a lengthy and extensive process of public hearings is undertaken, commissions are subjected to demands they are ill-equipped to deal with. In plain language, they are pressured to compromise and, in consequence, are seen to lose their independence and integrity.

3. Sections 9-10: Action by the Legislature

There is no doubt that debate in the legislature and the option of amending the commission's report erodes the independence of the commission. This has been shown beyond the shadow of a doubt with the experience of the Canadian commissions, to say nothing of the deplorable politicization in the United States. In contrast, the Australian commissions are genuinely independent. In short, while there is nothing inherently unconstitutional in providing for legislative alteration of the work of boundaries commissions, provision for such alteration is an open invitation to legislatures to destroy the independence of the commission and to ensure litigation because of the malapportionment and, possibly, of the gerrymandering that are bound to result.

4. Sections 12-15: Definitions and Provisions of Electoral Divisions

The entire purpose of these sections, from an allegedly noncontroversial section 12 set of definitions to the explicit provisions of sections 12-15, which provide for single- and multimunicipality electoral divisions, in fact is designed to ensure rural overrepresentation and urban underrepresentation.

This intent can be brought into focus by a simple mental experiment. Supposing there were listed not 43 single-municipality electoral divisions, which is to say, urban constituencies, but rather, rural ones. Once these (let us call them) purely rural constituencies were identified, all the remaining ones could be called nonrural. The effect, in theory, would be the same. The result, however, would be to ensure that urban ridings had attached to them subordinate tracts of rural Alberta. It would amount to a gerrymander favourable to the cities and directed against the rural areas.

Now, if this reversal is clear and plain for all to see, why is the intent of the subject legislation not also transparently obvious? What is sauce for the goose is sauce for the gander. If explicit definition of rural constituencies amounts to a gerrymander that benefits cities, it is certainly true that the explicit definition of urban constituencies benefits rural votes.

5. Section 16: Other Factors to be Considered by the Commission

Population density   There is no reason to take population density into account. If Australia can deal with constituencies the size of Ontario and Québec combined, large constituencies (but considerably smaller than the Australian examples) will prove to be but a minor irritant to legislators in Alberta and no irritant at all to their constituents. There are ample means, from fax machines to toll-free telephone numbers, to deal with communication between low-population-density constituencies and their MLAs. We will discuss the related question of community of interest later.

6. Section 17: The +/− 25% Permissible Deviation, with Exceptions for +/− 50% Permissible Deviation

This provision is unjustifiable in this province under current conditions of democratic commitment to the equality principle and with the technical and material ability to put that principle effectively into practice. There is simply no reasonable justification for so generous a deviation allowance. It is a virtual guarantee of maldistribution.

We recognize that zero deviation is impossible for reasons already stated. If it is necessary to provide for permissible variation (and there has been no justification for it), then it should be considerably smaller than the allowances contemplated by the subject legislation.

7. Factum of the Attorney General of Alberta

Without going into excessive detail regarding the evidence cited in the factum accompanying the reference, we would make only two points: (1) no mention is made of the Australian evidence in spite of the fact that it is an apt model by which to measure Canadian and Alberta law and practice; like this country, Australia is a federation whose major institutions have been derived from the Westminster model; (2) the notion of "balancing" population against places is based on a false analogy between an alleged "federal need" and provincial maldistribution; the distortions to the equality principle imposed by Canada's status as a federal regime, while in many respects unsavoury and an insult to the democratic nature of our country, are minor as compared to the systematic overrepresentation of rural voters contemplated by the subject legislation. As previously mentioned, Alberta is not a federation.

Generally speaking, the Attorney General has made a virtue out of necessity. We would submit that virtues and necessities are to be distinguished. More particularly, taking into account "a blend of factors" is inevitable when boundaries are drawn to constituencies. There is no virtue in doing so. Virtue consists in hewing as closely as possible to the line established and laid down by the equality principle: one person–one vote, and one vote–one value for all electors. Anything else simply increases the inevitable variation on the value of each elector's vote. In a democratic regime, such variation is to be minimized. We would conclude, therefore, that the degree of maldistribution is not tolerable. Accordingly, in these circumstances what is interesting is less an explanation of the fact or the significance of maldistribution but an account of the real and alleged reasons for it.

There are, we believe, five reasons that together or severally help account for the fact that rural overrepresentation became an accepted norm for electoral boundary determination in Canada: (1) the myth of the greater virtue of rural voters; (2) the alleged danger of majority urban tyranny; (3) the historical legacy of the greater difficulties inherent in rural representation; (4) the continuing success of rural voters (and their representatives) who were once, but are no longer, a majority in protecting their interests; (5) the absence, until 1985, of any constitutional imperative to disallow that practice.

(1) Scholars in North America have long known of the "myth of the garden." In this myth, most effectively analysed by U.S. historian Henry Nash Smith, nature has been held to be beneficent, healing, the source of all virtue, the place from which democracy sprang and which nurtures democratic ideals.[29] One variation on the myth of the garden was the so-called frontier thesis of Frederick Jackson Turner, another U.S. historian. Turner held that the frontier of settlement, and the interaction of migrants with it had shaped the United States into an egalitarian democracy.[30] These myths had their counterparts in Canada, of course, because Canada, too, was a North American nation, had a frontier of settlement, was the scene of a large homesteading enterprise, and received hundreds of thousands of American farm dwellers seeking land. The impact of this romanticism on myth building in Canada has been well documented by recent Canadian literary analysis and historical writing.[31]

If the country was taken to be a place of democracy and virtue, peopled by honest, clear-thinking farmers, the city, by contrast, was a place of iniquity, crime, dishonesty, and corruption. It was the home of immigrants who did not understand democratic ways and resisted assimilation. It was the home of shifty bankers and capitalists who exploited the hard-working farmer. It was the home of greedy workers who formed socialistic unions and who threatened the virtuous life of the countryside with strikes and civil disorder. These negative views of urban life are also well documented in Canadian historical writing.[32] Such views are quite clearly an anachronism in a modern, technologically advanced nation, and electoral boundaries legislation in a liberal democracy cannot in any way be based on, or give heed to, such archaic prejudices. The myth of rural virtue, in short, is self-serving moralistic rationalization. The fact is, cities are not simply places of perdition for unfortunate country folk who answer its siren's call and succumb to its corrupting charms; the fact is, corruption is not simply an urban phenomenon and virtue does not appear in the world as a consequence of country living. It will not come as a great shock to learn that, in recent years, the party that has formed the Government of Alberta has been the chief beneficiary of this myth.[33]

(2) A second rationalization is that rural voters need to be overrepresented in order to prevent "tyranny of the majority." The assumption is, apparently, that legislators from urban constituencies would take no notice of rural interests and act tyrannically toward them. There are two responses to this rationalization: in the ringing words of the Honourable Member from Danforth, Mr. Reid Scott, during the 1964 debate in the Canadian House of Commons of Bill C-72, which passed into law as the Electoral Boundaries Commissions Act: "rural tyranny must be ended." At the very least Scott introduced the possibility of minority as well as majority tyranny. And tyranny in general is almost always minority rule in its own interest. A second and more pertinent response, however, is to refuse to undertake the rhetorical escalation that invokes the imagery of tyranny in the first place. Sidney Hook was surely correct to observe that the feared majority tyranny in liberal democracy is a "bugaboo which haunts the books of political theorists but has never been found in the flesh in modern history."[34]

(3) It has long been held that legislators representing rural areas have an inherently greater difficulty representing their voters than do those in urban areas and, conversely, that rural voters would *effectively* be underrepresented if their constituencies contained the same number of voters as did those in urban areas. This is alleged to be so owing to the greater distances involved in reaching rural voters or in giving rural voters access to their elected representatives. The belief was well expressed as late as March 1991 by the president of the Alberta Association of Municipal Districts and Counties:

> In rural Alberta we have a great deal of distance, we have a large number of boards, councils and other groups an MLA has to deal with so it's impossible if we go to the one person, one vote system . . . Even now you city people have easier access to your MLA than we do in rural Alberta . . . a city MLA can walk across his whole constituency quicker than a rural MLA currently can drive across his . . .[35]

As already mentioned, however, the major point at issue in questions of representation is not ease of communication between an elected representative and his or her constituents. The major point at issue is voter equality and inequality and the principle of liberal democracy that lies behind it, namely the equality of citizens before the law. We are not unmindful of the possibility that rural MLAs may have a more difficult time staying in touch with their constituents, but there are ways of remedying this difficulty that do not at the same time undermine the democratic principle of one person–one vote. Is it costlier for a rural MLA to cover his or her riding, for example? If it is, let the legislature apportion greater travel allowances to the rural MLA. Is it too time-consuming for a rural MLA to consult his or her constituents in person on some key subject? Then let greater time for consultation be built into the legislative process. Does it take too much time and expense to campaign in a rural constituency? Then let rural MLAs spend more money on their elections and build more time into the election campaign for all MLAs. Finally, there are presently technologies to expedite communication throughout the province. For many years the Alberta government has operated a free long-distance telephone service (the "Rite Line") for Calgary residents who wish to speak to government offices in Edmonton. There is no reason why this service or a similar toll-free service should not be extended throughout the province. Similar arrangements could be made for fax machines, for free cellular car phones for rural MLAs, and so on.[36]

One of the most prevalent and most neutral-sounding terms used to defend rural overrepresentation is "community of interest." The term appears in the federal Electoral Boundary Commissions Act and an equivalent term, "common community interest," appears in the corresponding Alberta legislation. In neither place, however, is the term defined. Nor is it defined in the British legislation whence, in all likelihood, it originated. When a term such as "community of interest" is invoked with great regularity and passion but when at the same time it has been given virtually no content, we have good grounds to suspect we are dealing with ritual and incantation, not argument. If, on the other hand, rural voters constitute a "community of interest" similar in principle to, say, Lutherans, Sikhs, or millionaires, there is no possible justification in a liberal democracy to grant them "group rights" unless at the same time it makes sense to extend such "group rights" to equivalent, and no less real, religious, ethnic, and economic communities of interest. In fact, of course, it is improper to recognize "group rights" in a liberal democracy, whether they be millionaires, Lutherans, or rural voters.

(4) When constituency boundaries were first drawn in Canada, rural dwellers vastly outnumbered urban dwellers. It was not until roughly 1924 that a majority of Canadians as a whole lived in cities. In western Canada the swing from rural to urban took longer. In Alberta the 1951 census counted 489,826 people living in both farm and nonfarm rural areas, and 449,675 people living in urban areas. The 1956 census revealed that the balance had tipped. In that year 487,292 Albertans lived in farm and nonfarm rural areas, and 635,824 Albertans lived in urban areas. The change occurred not only because of urban growth, but also because of rural depopulation—a phenomenon that has been ongoing in Canada since the turn of the century. According to the 1981 census, the ratio of urban to rural dwellers in Canada as a whole was approximately 3:1. In Alberta the ratio as measured by the 1986 census was 5:1, second only to Ontario.

Since rural dwellers dominated politics in Canada until the mid-1920s, and in the province of Alberta until the early 1950s, it was understandable that they would give themselves more representation in the legislatures than they would have been entitled to under the rule, one person–one vote. More representation meant more political power to serve their own social and economic interests.[37] It also meant more power to perpetuate overrepresentation.

It is clear from the statement of the president of the Alberta Association of Municipal Districts and Counties mentioned above that it is still the rural voters and their representatives who argue against one person–one vote and in favour of wide margins of variability. It is clear that the Alberta legislation serves the interests of rural voters at the cost of urban voters. It is also clear why it does so: because of rural overrepresentation. In short, it is a vicious circle.

We would conclude with the following observation. Canada, including Alberta, has become a mature liberal democratic regime, one of the implications of which is that electoral representation aims at fairness and equity. We have also seen that an electoral system based on single-member constituencies with only a plurality required to elect introduces certain and inevitable distortions. These distortions are aggravated by three factors: (1) demographic shifts; (2) malapportionment; (3) gerrymandering. They can, in principle, be ameliorated by three remedies: (1) constituency boundary adjustments responsive to demographic trends; (2) commitment by boundary commissions to the equality principle with judicial enforcement of low constituency size deviation; (3) politically sensitive boundary commissions aware of partisan interests but composed of nonlegislators. Until these remedies are more perfectly embodied in provincial electoral boundaries legislation, and until the current electoral boundaries legislation ceases to be an obstacle to democracy in Alberta, fair and effective representation in the province will remain a desideratum.

Notes

1. M.L. Balinski and H.P. Young, "Fair Electoral Distribution," in Johnson and Pasis, eds., *Representation and Electoral Systems: Canadian Perspectives*, (Scarborough, Prentice-Hall, 1990), 240–44. Similar statements are found in Michael Coulson, "Reforming Electoral Distribution," in ibid., 233–39, as well as in standard texts on Canadian government.
2. Chief Justice Warren made this remark upon his retirement from the U.S. Supreme Court; see *The New York Times*, 27 June 1969, 17.
3. M.L. Balinski and H.P. Young, "Parliamentary Representation and the Amalgam Method," *Canadian Journal of Political Science* 14 (1981): 797.
4. K.C. Carty, "The Electoral Boundary Revolution in Canada," *American Review of Canadian Studies*, 15 (1985): 274.
5. Robert G. Dixon, "Fair Criteria and Procedures for Establishing Legislative Districts," in Bernard Grofman, et al., eds., *Representation and Redistricting Issues* (Lexington: Lexington Books, 1987), 9.

6. S.A. Long and F.Q. Quo, "Alberta: One-Party Dominance," in M. Robin, ed., *Canadian Provincial Politics: The Party Systems of the Ten Provinces* (Scarborough: Prentice-Hall, 1972), 1–26; Terrence J. Levesque and Kenneth H. Norrie, "Overwhelming Majorities in the Legislature of Alberta," *Canadian Journal of Political Science* 12 (1979): 451–70.

7. P.J. Taylor, "All Organization is Bias: The Political Geography of Electoral Reform," *The Geographical Journal* 15 (1985): 339.

8. P.J. Taylor and R.J. Johnston, *Geography of Elections* (London: Croom Helm, 1979), 389.

9. Terrence H. Qualter, *The Election Process in Canada* (Toronto: McGraw-Hill, 1970), 81.

10. Arend Lijphart,"Criteria of Fair Representation," in *Representation and Electoral Systems* (see n.1), 201–6; Jonathan W. Still, "Political Equality and Election Systems," in ibid., 21–27.

11. Douglas W. Rae, *The Political Consequences of Electoral Laws* (New Haven: Yale University Press, 1967); Richard S. Katz, *A Theory of Parties and Electoral Systems* (Baltimore: Johns Hopkins University Press, 1980); Arend Lijphart, "The Political Consequences of Electoral Laws, 1945–85," *American Political Science Review* 84 (1990): 481–96.

12. Taylor and Johnston, *Geography of Elections,* 389; see also S.S. Nagel, "Computers and the Law and Politics of Redistricting," *Polity* 5 (1972): 77–93.

13. R. MacGregor Dawson, "The Gerrymander of 1882," *Canadian Journal of Economics and Political Science* I (1935): 197–221.

14. Carty, "Electoral Boundary Revolution in Canada," 275.

15. Robert G. Dixon, *Democratic Representation: Reapportionment, Law and Politics* (New York: Oxford University Press, 1968), 136; Taylor and Johnston, *Geography of Elections,* 407; see also David R. Mahew, "Congressional Representation: Theory and Practice in Drawing the Districts," in N. Polsby ed., *Reapportionment in the 1970s* (Berkeley: University of California Press, 1971), 249–85; E.R. Tufte, "The Relationship Between Seats and Votes in Two-Party Systems," *American Political Science Review* 67 (1973): 540–54; Graham Gudgin and Peter Taylor, *Seats, Votes and the Spatial Organization of Elections* (London: Piori, 1979), 127–31.

16. Robert G. Dixon, "What is Gerrymandering?" in *Representation and Electoral Systems* (see n.1), 245.

17. Gudgin and Taylor, *Seats, Votes, and the Spatial Organization of Elections,* 55.

18. The first was invented by Manning J. Dauer and R.G. Kelsay in "Unrepresentative States," *National Municipal Review* 44 (1955): 571–75, 587, and corrected in *National Municipal Review* 45 (1956): 198; see also Qualter, *The Election Process in Canada,* 89–93; for an account of the Gini Index as well as the Dauer-Kelsay Index, see Hayward R. Alker, Jr., and Bruce M. Russett, "On Measuring Inequality," *Behavioral Science* 9 (1964): 207–18; see also Glendon Schubert and Charles Press, "Measuring Malapportionment," *American Political Science Review* 58 (1964): 302–27; Harvey E. Pasis, "The Inequalities of Distribution in the Canadian Provincial Assemblies," *Canadian Journal of Political Science* 5 (1972), 433–36, and Pasis, "Electoral Distribution in the Canadian Provincial Legislatures," in *Representation and Electoral Systems* (see n.1), 251–53.

19. Taylor and Johnston, *Geography of Elections,* 360.

20. See Norman Ward, "A Century of Constituencies," *Canadian Public Administration* 10 (1967): 107; William E. Lyons, *One Man–One Vote* (Toronto: Prentice-Hall,

1970), 38ff; *House of Commons Debates*, 13 November 1964, 10056.

21. John C. Courtney, "'Theories Masquerading as Principles,' Canadian Electoral Boundary Commissions and the Australian Model," in J. Courtney, ed., *The Canadian House of Commons: Essays in Honour of Norman Ward* (Calgary: University of Calgary Press, 1985), 157.

22. APSA, Committee Report, "The Reapportionment of Congress," *American Political Science Review* 45 (1951): 156. This report was commissioned in 1950 by several U.S. government agencies who approached the president of the American Political Science Association and asked his advice regarding the redistribution of congressional seats.

23. S.A. Long, "Maldistribution in Western Provincial Legislatures: The Case of Alberta," *Canadian Journal of Political Science* 2 (1969): 345, 348-49, 354; Qualter, *The Election Process in Canada* (see n.9), 91-93, 110-11; Carty, "The Electoral Boundary Revolution in Canada" (see n.4), 280; Pasis, "Electoral Distribution in the Canadian Provincial Legislatures" (see n.18), 251-53; see also Pasis, "The Inequalities of Distribution" (see. n.18), 433-36.

24. All these data are readily available from such standard sources as the *Canada Year Book* and the *Census of Canada*.

25. See Keith Archer, "Voting Rights in Alberta Under the *Electoral Boundaries Commission Act, 1990*" (Manuscript, University of Calgary, May 1990), 7.

26. Glendon Schubert and Charles Press, "Measuring Malapportionment," *American Political Science Review* 58 (1964): 302-7.

27. P.T. David and R. Eisenberg, *The Devaluation of the Urban and Suburban Vote* (Charlottesville: University of Virginia Press, 1961), 12-16.

28. The data are collected in Pasis, "Electoral Distribution in the Canadian Provincial Legislatures" (see n.18), 252.

29. Henry Nash Smith, *Virgin Land: The American West as Symbol and Myth* (New York: Vintage, 1950).

30. Frederick Jackson Turner, "The Significance of the Frontier in American History," in *Annual Report of the American Historical Association*, 1893.

31. See, for example, R. Douglas Francis, *Images of the West: Responses to the Canadian Prairies* (Saskatoon: Western Producer Prairie Books, 1989); Dick Harrison, *Unnamed Country: The Struggle for a Canadian Prairie Fiction* (Edmonton: Hurtig, 1977).

32. See Doug Owram, *Promise of Eden: The Canadian Expansionist Movement and the Idea of the West, 1856–1900* (Toronto: University of Toronto Press, 1980), 192ff.

33. See Archer, "Voting Rights in Alberta" (see n.25), 11-12.

34. Sidney Hook, *The Paradoxes of Freedom* (Berkeley: University of California Press, 1962), 66.

35. *Edmonton Journal*, 28 March 1991.

36. See John C. Courtney, "Parliament and Representation: The Unfinished Agenda of Electoral Reform," *Canadian Journal of Political Science* 21 (1988): 682.

37. American evidence, for example, indicates that closer adherence to the equality principle in the aftermath of *Baker v. Carr* has, in fact, led to a reallocation of policy benefits. See Matthew D. McCubbins and Thomas Schwartz, "Congress, the Courts and Public Policy: Consequences of the One Man, One Vote Rule," *American Journal of Political Science* 32 (1988): 388-415.

The Right to Vote and Inequality of Voting Power in British Columbia: The Jurisprudence and Politics of the Dixon Case

NORMAN J. RUFF
UNIVERSITY OF VICTORIA

With the hindsights of the past 30 months, it might be argued that the 1989 British Columbia Supreme Court application of the voting-equality provision of the Canadian Charter of Rights and Freedoms had significance only in the immediate context of British Columbia politics *circa* 1989–90. Although important as the first application of section 3 of the Charter (the Right to Vote) to an electoral map, Justice McLachlin's reasoning in the BC Supreme Court *Dixon* case might, for example, be seen as superseded by her subsequent 1991 "McLachlin II" reading of that section in the Saskatchewan *Reference re Provincial Electoral Boundaries*[1] after her appointment to the Supreme Court of Canada. In assessing the consequences of judicial decisions, Robert G. Dixon observed, "All apportionment being fully political, any order made by a court has a significant political impact."[2] But how does one weigh any impact that the post *Dixon* case electoral boundaries might have had on half a dozen or so competitive districts when everything is dwarfed by a sweeping province-wide realignment of voting patterns such as occurred in the 17 October 1991 electoral defeat of the BC Social Credit government? It is easy to neglect the consequences of judicially enjoined boundary changes, when a long-entrenched governing party drops from 49 to 24% of the popular vote and as a result is reduced to a third-party status.

Such views, however, also have to make room for a careful assessment of the force of the 1989 *Dixon* case which demonstrated that electoral boundaries can be deemed contrary to the Charter of Rights and Freedoms and only provisionally in place pending remedial legislation. This paper addresses the reasoning and findings of what may be termed McLachlin I in her BC Supreme

Court judgment *Dixon v. British Columbia (Attorney General)*, 1989, and the companion judgment by Justice Meredith. Alongside an examination of the political and legislative responses of the provincial Cabinet and legislators, it attempts to draw lessons from the immediate political context of British Columbia's electoral map and the wider implications which they might continue to have both for and beyond British Columbia.

The British Columbia Redistribution Context

The pre-1989 history of redistributions in British Columbia was not dissimilar to that of most other provinces.[3] The accumulation of boundaries enshrining urban-rural inequities reinforced by delayed redistributions by one-time commissions and accompanied by accusations of gerrymandering are not unique to British Columbia. Only the lateness of the government's 1984 relinquishment of total control over electoral boundaries and the timing of redistributions, plus the retention of multimember districts, makes its experience a little more remarkable. A 1979 redistribution by a provincial court judge (formerly a defeated government party candidate) proved highly controversial. A second 1982 commission appointed to provide more acceptable boundaries led not to a new map but the 1984 Constitution Amendment Act, creating an electoral commission consisting of the chief electoral officer, the clerk of the Legislative Assembly, and a provincial court judge appointed by the chief justice. Redistributions were to be held by the commission every six years or after two provincial general elections.[4] Representation would increase under a formula based on eight regional zones with weighted population quotas. The first redistribution under these provisions was chaired by Judge McAdam in 1984.[5] The formula took account of population growth within each zone through additions to the total existing number of dual-member ridings and, where necessary, the further splitting of rapidly growing dual-member districts into three single districts where they were 60% above their zone quota. Any new drawing of boundaries thus took place only within the existing territory of dual-member districts and all districts were protected against any change due to population decline. The province had only partially moved out of the 19th century in its redistribution process.[6] Table 1 at the end of this paper illustrates both the province-wide inequalities and the zonal inconsistencies embodied in the 1986 electoral district populations. The provincial districts ranged in population per member from 5,511 in Atlin and less than 30,000 in Columbia River, Prince Rupert, Peace River (North and South), and Omineca to over 61,000 in the three new Surrey districts, Esquimalt, and Coquitlam–Moody. Putting the most remote Atlin district to one side with a population 87% below the provincial 1986 average of 41,873, the deviation from the average size per member ranged from –45% to +63%. It was the continuation and the perpetuation of such extreme disparities that prompted the BC Civil Liberties Association to begin its court challenge in 1986.

Justiciability

Throughout the constitutional reform process of 1978-81, British Columbia had been a most vocal proponent of the principle of parliamentary supremacy and an opponent of an entrenched charter of rights that would diminish legislative powers.[7] The provincial government's fears that a charter could interfere with provincial electoral law were subsequently confirmed in respect of voter disqualification and absentee voting provisions.[8] Those fears were now being fully realized in a more fundamental aspect of the province's political framework. The BC Civil Liberties Association petition *Dixon and Attorney General of British Columbia* argued that "one person-one equal vote" was guaranteed by the Charter protections for Fundamental Freedoms: Freedom of Expression (section 2b); Democratic Rights: Voting (section 3); Mobility Rights (section 6); Legal Rights: Liberty (section 7); and Equality Rights (section 15); and that the provisions of the British Columbia Constitution Act governing electoral districts (section 19 and schedule 1) were inconsistent with this principle. If so, they had no force or effect under section 52 (1) of the Constitution Act, 1982. The association sought an order with a time limit for the legislature to conduct a new redistribution or, in the event of default, a further order for a redistribution of seats by the courts. The justiciability of this principle had a special aspect in the case of British Columbia since the province entered Confederation in July 1871 with its own Constitution Act previously enacted by the Legislative Council of the colony of British Columbia.[9] Section 19 of the British Columbia Constitution Act set out the composition, duties, and other terms of reference of the electoral commission, and the names and boundaries of the electoral districts continued to be described and defined in metes and bounds in its Schedule 1, just as they had been in the original 1871 Schedule A.

Before proceeding further with the petition, it had to be first established that *this* Constitution Act for British Columbia was subject to the Charter as a provincial constitutional statute. In October 1986, Chief Justice McEachern of the BC Supreme Court was not persuaded by the arguments put forward by the BC Attorney General. He found the provincial statute was not part of the Constitution of Canada, as defined in section 52(2) of the Canadian Constitution Act, 1982, and thus subject to section 52 (1) supremacy of the constitution. McEachern would not accept narrow technical arguments to avoid the Charter nor accept the view that the 1867 electoral arrangements and British Columbia's 1871 Terms of Union gave the Constitution Act of British Columbia "a larger constitutional complexion."[10] But there was still more at stake. If the act was part of the Constitution of Canada, it still did not follow that it was immune from Charter scrutiny. It was open to the application of the Charter both under section 32 (1)(b) and 52(1).[11] He concluded that the legislature had the "constitutional" authority to enact or amend the Constitution Act of British Columbia but:

How the legislature exercises this authority, and the validity of such provisions in the sense of conforming to the Charter, is quite a different matter. It is the court's reluctant responsibility to examine the result of the exercise of such authority to ensure that it conforms with the Charter. Thus, although the constitutional tree may be immune from Charter scrutiny, the fruit of the constitutional tree is not. If the fruit of the constitutional tree does not conform to the Charter, including s. 1, then it must to such extent be struck down.[12]

As the Chief Justice himself pointed out, at this stage, his ruling neither affected the validity of the 1986 general election nor imposed any obligation on the legislature. He had, however, opened the door to the possibility of future "judicially mandated action."

Government Initiatives

The following review of the petition is best understood in the context of its convergence with the redistribution initiative commenced by Premier Vander Zalm after the October 1986 general election. During the campaign, Premier Vander Zalm had repeatedly promised to end the province's dual-member districts.[13] He was himself a candidate for election in the largest dual-member district (Richmond) with a population per member 30% above the average. Six months after the return of the Social Credit government, a county court judge Thomas Fisher was appointed as a commissioner to replace the 17 electoral districts and given the power to recommend boundary adjustments to "contiguous electoral districts" where this was considered desirable. It was not clear how this would be eventually reconciled with the 1984 redistribution framework nor whether the membership of the Legislative Assembly was to remain at 69. The terms of reference in drawing boundaries included:

(a) the principle of the electoral quota . . . ;
(b) historical and regional claims for representation;
(c) special geographic considerations including the sparsity or density of population of various regions, the accessibility to such regions, or the size or shape thereof;
(d) special community interests of the inhabitants of particular regions; and
(e) the need for a balance of community interests.[14]

The "principle of the electoral quota" and the lack of a precise number of members as its denominator might be seen to imply significant movement toward the principle of one vote–one value through more equality in district populations, but it was not the only criterion. Its scope appeared particularly limited by confining the redefinition of districts to dual-member and "contiguous" districts—assuming a narrow interpretation of what was contiguous. However, given a broader construction and the cumulative effects of continuing boundary changes beyond those of the 17 dual-member districts, virtually all of the electoral districts might be redefined.[15]

At the conclusion of the first round of public hearings in mid-August 1987, the commissioner obtained an amendment to his mandate to allow consideration of "all electoral districts in the province to ensure proper representation for British Columbians in the Legislative Assembly."[16] The number of districts and hence the size of the population quota was left to the commissioner to determine. After two days of special hearings on this subject in November, a preliminary ruling set the number of districts at 75, prior to a January-April 1988 second round of province-wide hearings. This number was reaffirmed in the commissioner's May 1988 interim report on the grounds that an increase from 69 to 75 seats was the minimum required and offered "the only way to deal with the problem of underrepresentation of the urban areas without exacerbating the problems experienced in northern and remote areas."[17] This increase in seats reduced the average population (1986) per district from 41,873 to 38,523. The "principle of the electoral quota" was refined by placing a limit of +/- 25% variation from strict population equality.[18] The report took 25% tolerance to be a Canadian standard and discounted smaller United States tolerances as due to interstate variations and bicameralism. While sensitive to the communicative role of the representative, it nevertheless warned that the legitimacy of the political system might be undermined "if there are great discrepancies in the numbers of people represented by members of the legislature." Departures from strict equality were nonetheless necessary to meet the other criteria in the commission's mandate, i.e., historical and regional claims plus special communities of interest and geographic barriers. The +/- 25% range was put forward as "the limit to which the other representational claims may legitimately modify the principle of one person-one vote."[19]

The +/- 25% tolerance permitted a deviation of up to 9,631 persons from the quota and a range of 19,262 which would be as much as two-thirds of the population of the smaller districts. It may be argued that the Fisher process protected at least two northern seats at the expense of an adequate recognition of population-based claims of the Lower Mainland. Nevertheless, the commissioner managed to combine that sensitivity to regional claims with an extensive reduction in population inequality.[20] In the preliminary report, the population size of districts (1986 census) ranged from 23% below the electoral quota (North Peace River and North Coast-Stikine) but set only two at the +16% mark (Burnaby-Willingdon and Kensington-Riley Park in Vancouver). The final December 1988 Fisher Report (as implemented by the legislature and with some changes in constituency nomenclature) used the 25% tolerance more fully, with four electoral districts (Bulkley Valley-Stikine, North Coast, Okanagan-Boundary, and North Peace River) at more than 23% below and added two additional districts (Comox Valley and Vancouver-Hastings) at more than 16% above, while pushing Vancouver-Kensington still higher. The old 1986 McAdam-Eckardt electoral map ranged from lows of 86.8 (Atlin) and 44.7 (Columbia River) below the provincial average population per MLA (41,873) up to highs of 63.2 (Surrey-Newton) and 62.9 (Coquitlam-Moody) above (see table 1). This spread was to be reduced to 23.6 below (North Coast) and 17.4 above (Vancouver-Kensington) the average 1986 district population.

Twin-Track Route to Redistribution

While the 1987–88 Fisher Commission proceeded with its mandate, the BC Civil Liberties Association case again surfaced in March 1988 when the province's Chief Justice (McEachern) ruled that the commission should be allowed to complete its work so that the legislature would "have the benefit of both Judge Fisher's recommendations and the judgment of this Court." A mid-October to mid-November hearing date was set to facilitate this. Although the trial was not held until January 1989, with a new Chief Justice (McLachlin), the complementary relationship originally contemplated was achieved. The Fisher Report went to Cabinet before Christmas 1988 and judgment was delivered the following April, hard on the heels of the tabling of the report in the legislature and McLachlin's own appointment to the Supreme Court of Canada. Their symbiotic relationship can be seen as a major factor both in shaping the judgment itself and in realizing the Fisher boundaries.

Beyond Justiciability

At the January hearing, the Attorney General conceded that electoral apportionment was justiciable but contended that the petition required the court to "enter into fundamental questions of social and institutional policy where it does not belong" and confronted it with "a litany of policy choices with no clear solution."[21] Nonetheless, he recognized that "the legislature must act in accordance with the Charter and if it fails to do so, the legislation is void . . . The court has no discretion to avoid the question of the constitutionality of the legislation."[22] Simply put, the choice for the court was one of political taboo versus constitutional duty in a Canadian version of *Baker v. Carr*'s 1962 activism. In McLachlin's words:

> The question before me is which of the two views should prevail—the view that the courts should not enter on the question of electoral reapportionment because it is essentially a political matter, or the view that the courts cannot avoid their duty to pronounce on a constitutional violation, no matter how political the issue or how difficult the problem of fashioning the remedies.[23]

With the support of Canadian, American, British, and Australian precedents,[24] she concluded that "the Court can and should intervene." Electoral districting was "first and foremost the task of the legislature" and "best undertaken by our elected representatives":

> However, the mere fact that the Legislature was better suited to weigh the myriad factors involved in electoral apportionment, does not remove from this court the ultimate responsibility of weighing the product of the exercise of the Legislature's discretion against the rights and freedoms enshrined in the Charter and from examining the justification for any infringement that the courts are required to undertake under s.1.[25]

At the outset, she confirmed her predecessor's ruling in 1986 that section

32(1)(b) of the Charter governed the case and rejected the Attorney General's argument that the 1987 Ontario *Reference re Bill 30* could support a general provincial legislative authority (in the Constitution Act) beyond Charter scrutiny. She held that there was more at issue than the question of the authority of the legislature to act. The right to vote was entrenched and beyond the Charter's section 33 override power.

> Viewed in its textual context, the right to vote and participate in the democratic election of one's government is one of the most fundamental of the Charter rights. For without the right to vote in free and fair elections all other rights would be in jeopardy.[26]

If legislative efforts fall short when measured against the standard of a "certain degree of proportionate representation," they must be declared unconstitutional. As discussed below, not only did the BC legislation violate Charter rights beyond any Charter section 1 "reasonable limits," but the court had a duty to rule on the validity of the enactments establishing Canada's electoral boundaries subject to the availability of a remedy.[27]

Canadian Principles: Relative Equality and Better Government

For Chief Justice McLachlin, British Columbia's existing electoral boundaries suggested a "gross violation of the fundamental concept of representation by population which is the foundation of our political system."[28] She noted the substantial deviations from an equal population norm and placed them in a comparative context. If a deviation of +/- 10% were taken as an acceptable limit (as in Australia), then 65% of the districts would offend that limit. Thirty-two percent failed the Canadian federal standard of 25%. The effect of the disparities was to "enhance the power of the rural voter." This inequitable weighting was justified by the Attorney General on several grounds, including special rural interests and communication difficulties.

In applying section 3 of the Charter—the Right to Vote—she was defining "the standard or reference of what, if anything, a vote should be worth."[29] The American experience of population standards was placed in the context of a unique history and conception of democracy. Canadian democratic history is different, with its tradition of evolutionary democracy and pragmatism. The *Durham Report* and John A. Macdonald were marshalled to support the view that "while the principle of population may be said to lie at the heart of electoral apportionment in Canada, it has from the beginning been tempered by other factors."[30] Justice McLachlin found no evidence that the Charter intended to confer a new right of an absolute, or as near as practicable to absolute, equality of voters within each electoral district. The dominant principle of representational democracy lay in a right to vote based on a "relative equality of voting power."

The amount of deviation was to be determined by the legislature acting "in accordance with such legal principles as may be found inherent in the Charter guarantee of the right to vote." Although absolute equality was not required, equality of voting power was "the single most important factor to be considered in determining electoral boundaries" and population must be "the dominant consideration in drawing electoral boundaries." It was "appropriate to set limits beyond which it cannot be eroded by giving preference to other factors and considerations."[31] She argued that equality of voters per representative was essential to the proper conduct of both the legislator and ombudsman role of the elected representative. The majority of elected representatives should represent the majority of the citizens entitled to vote or the legitimacy of the system might be undermined. Good government also required "relative electoral parity" to ensure relatively equal constituency burdens among members.

In a second proposition, she added that "only such deviations from the ideal of equal representation as are capable of justification on the basis of some other valid factor may be admitted." Without being exhaustive, the Chief Justice advanced a "better government" proposition:

> Only those deviations should be admitted which can be justified on the ground that they contribute to better government of the populace as a whole, giving due weight to regional issues within the populace and geographic factors within the territory governed. Geographic considerations affecting the servicing of a riding and the representation of regional interests meriting representation may fall in this category and hence be justifiable.[32]

This approach in McLachlin I prepared the ground for a more open notion of "effective representation" of the "diversity of our social mosaic" in McLachlin II, Saskatchewan 1991 *Reference re Provincial Electoral Boundaries.*[33]

In McLachlin I, the Chief Justice referred to appropriate limits on the erosion of equality of voting power such as the 25% applied to Canada's federal districts and the Australian 10% limit but refrained from any direct unequivocal statement on precise limits. Justification for deviations from an electoral quota thus remain open to judicial examination. Her *Dixon* case statement–that an outside limit might be appropriate to ensure dominance of equality of voting power but was not alone sufficient, "particularly if the outside limit is relatively generous"–implied a close scrutiny of *all* deviations.

Despite the absence of a precise population parameter, in the immediate case at hand it was clear that British Columbia's electoral boundaries did not meet her test. Anomalies in the number of voters, where one riding had 15 times as many voters as another and where there was a resultant disparity in the votes of the respective winner and runner-up, suggested "a gross violation of the fundamental principle of representation by population." Some insight into how she thought nonpopulation factors might be appropriately applied can be seen in the treatment of the factors relied on by the Attorney General. While history, for example, probably played a large part in the boundary anomalies, she gave it short shrift–there were "better ways of fostering a sense of history among people of different regions than perverting the electoral process." Geographical and regional concerns played a role in ridings embracing "vast territory and sparse populations," but "the degree of discrepancy actually tolerated seems far out of proportion to the problems posed." It is important to note here that she drew on the demonstration effect of the Fisher Report boundaries with their maximum divergence of 25% and on a submission to Fisher that gave weight to geographical and regional concerns within 10% limits for the whole province, save for one district at -24%.[34] She used the example of a number of neighbouring ridings to illustrate her observation that "there is no explanation, geographical or otherwise, for some divergences." The zoned quota system also introduced a sliding scale against large urban centres and in favour of rural areas quite apart from any particular regional or geographical considerations for particular ridings.

The question of the possible application of other Charter sections referred to by the petitioner (section 2(b)—Freedom of Expression; section 7—the Right to Liberty; or section 15—Equality Rights) was redundant given a section 3 violation decision. The findings that the boundaries violated the right-to-vote guarantee of the Charter and that the legislation on which they were based was invalid, might, however, be set aside by an appeal to practicality under the "reasonable limits" of section 1 of the Charter.[35] Could population disparities incapable of being supported on regional or geographic grounds to ensure better government be seen as reasonable and "demonstrably justified in a free and democratic society"? Here it must be established first that the objective was "pressing and substantial" and the means to that end "proportional or appropriate."[36] McLachlin believed that it was

> clear that considerable leeway must be given to the legislature and the Cabinet to enact what appear to them to be reasonable measures to ensure that valid geographic and regional considerations are taken into account in establishing electoral boundaries in the interests of better government.[37]

She argued that adjustments for nonpopulation factors were not capable of precise mathematical definition and the better-government objective ought not to require an "optimal scheme." Furthermore, the courts were not to substitute their views, since "in such matters, the court should defer to the legislature." Her general good/better-government test was that there should be no interference with an electoral map under section 3 of the Charter

> unless it appears that reasonable persons applying the appropriate principle —equal voting power subject only to such limits as required for good government—could not have set the electoral boundaries as they exist. In other words, departure from the ideal of absolute equality may not constitute breach of s. 3 of the Charter as long as the departure can be objectively justified as contributing to better government.[38]

Despite the apparent latitude permitted under the "good government" criteria, the importance of equality of voting power was still paramount and could not be "lightly undermined." In the case of British Columbia, the infringement appeared to her to be considerable. She found that in "too many cases grossly disproportionate riding populations cannot be justified on the basis of regional and geographic factors either at all or in their extent." Short-term fluctuations or valid differences could not excuse the divergencies. Since "no good end seems to be served," the legislative enactments for the inequities could not be saved by section 1 of the Charter.[39]

Remedies

If McLachlin took a "liberal and generous" interpretation of the Charter section 24(1) remedial provisions, she was also sensitive to the special constitutional significance of electoral machinery. At a minimum, the Court could grant a "declaration that the impugned legislation infringes the constitutional right to vote and to the extent of the inconsistency with the Charter is of no force or effect."[40] In this instance, i.e., in a parliamentary system without fixed elections, such a declaration could undermine the democratic process since the electoral districts would have vanished. What if an election was required? She placed this on the same magnitude as a suspension of all provincial legislation. McLachlin, however, also asserted an obligation for the executive and legislature to conform to the requirements of the constitution and assumed that there would be prompt steps to remedy the deficiencies.[41] In practical terms she argued

> the court must proceed on the premise that, just as the court does what it must do under the Constitution, so will the legislature. This proposition has repeatedly been affirmed by our courts ...
> It may thus be assumed that the legislature will promptly enter on the question of what remedial steps should be taken to remedy the deficiencies in the existing legislation.[42]

She thus reduced the problem to one of timing and temporary relief and drew on the solution in the Manitoba Language Rights case (*Re Manitoba Language Rights* [1985]). It was "open to the court to specify a temporary period during which the existing legislation remains valid and during which the legislature enacts and brings into force an apportionment scheme which complies with the Charter." Rather than speculating on what would transpire if remedial legislation were not forthcoming, she simply added an enjoiner "that just as courts have a duty to measure the constitutionality of legislative acts against Charter guarantees, so they are under an obligation to fashion effective remedies in order to give true substance to these rights."[43] As she later acknowledged after her appointment to the Supreme Court of Canada, McLachlin had decided to "defer the really difficult question" as to what would happen if the government ignored her judgment. She chose to rely on mutual deference and cooperation.[44]

The Legislature and Fashioning the Remedies

The April 1989 judgment set the stage for submissions on what was a reasonable time period to remedy the legislation and for the electoral boundaries provisions of the Constitution Act to "stay provisionally in place to avoid the constitutional crisis which would occur should a precipitate election be required."[45] Since the Attorney General accepted the basic logic as "somewhat compelling," the provincial government did not appeal the decision and in May 1989 arguments were made before Justice Meredith when the BC Civil Liberties Association sought an end to the stay of the 18 April 1989 order. Some of the judicial momentum given to the redistribution process was lost in Justice Meredith's June ruling. He argued that he was "to consider simply whether an order should be made to terminate the stay"[46] and that the reasons of the Chief Justice neither should nor could require an order. Meredith concluded that "an order fixing a date beyond which the legislation will not 'stay in place' cannot be made," and thus declined John Dixon's petition to bring the existing electoral map to an end on 30 June 1989 or any other date deemed "just" by the BC Supreme Court. In what Professor Kent Roach critically characterized as "an act of judicial activism in the name of judicial restraint,"[47] Justice Meredith held that such an order would itself "violate or threaten the violation of very fundamental constitutional rights" and go beyond the remedial powers of the court. If the legislation did not stay in place, there would be "an annulment of the Legislative Assembly itself." To require the majority of the legislature to "agree on a course of action" was to deprive members of their right and obligation to vote according to conviction. It was beyond the inherent power of the court, since it would be to "effectively legislate."

> So I conclude that the establishment of a deadline would be in direct violation of the rights and obligations of the members of the Legislative Assembly, would threaten the violation of the right of people of British Columbia to the existence of a Legislative Assembly, and would threaten the violation of the right of citizens of Canada to vote for members of a Legislative Assembly, to say nothing of eradicating the right to vote, whether equal or not.
> I think it must be left to the legislature to do what is right in its own time.[48]

The Attorney General welcomed the Meredith decision in preventing the imposition of "a kind of jurocracy."[49] The ball had been volleyed back into the legislature's court, relying on Meredith's assumption that the convictions of the MLAs "will be within constitutional bounds."[50] The judgment of McLachlin had already pointed not only to those bounds but to something more substantial in the actual Fisher Report. Acknowledging the decision was for the legislature to make, she volunteered that the final report of the Fisher Commission appeared reasonable and the proposed districts justified "even though the permitted deviations may be greater than have been accepted in some other jurisdictions." The maximum deviations from the quota appeared to be within a tolerable limit "given the vast and sparsely populated regions," while individual deviations appeared justified by "proper application of geographic and regional consider-ations." Thus,

> if the legislature acts to adopt a scheme similar to that proposed in the Fisher Commission Report within the time specified by the court for amendment of section 19 of the Constitution Act and Sched. 1, the court's involvement will be at an end.[51]

If the legislators' convictions approximated the Fisher boundaries, then Justice Meredith's supposition was well founded, but fears that this might not be the case were only fully assuaged in mid-July 1989.

Six months earlier, in 1988, while the BC Civil Liberties Association petition still lay before the Court and the Fisher Commission pushed forward with its expanded mandate, it had become clear that the prospects of new boundaries had agitated a government caucus already restless at other initiatives emanating from the Premier's Office. Rather than direct the submission of any redistribution report to the Premier or Cabinet, it had been decided that the Fisher Commission's preliminary report would be sent to a nine-member special committee of the Legislative Assembly, which was given the onerous charge of preparing a unanimous report on the Fisher proposals.[52] The Fisher Commission targeted the end of the year for completion of its work, a full year longer than had been contemplated under its original April 1987 terms of reference. Deadlines for final submissions were extended till 17 October, by request of the Special Committee on Electoral Boundaries, to allow a response on the preliminary boundaries from MLAs.[53] The political procrastination became still more evident when the Speech from the Throne on 16 March 1989 made no reference to new electoral boundaries. The commission's final report had been submitted to Cabinet before Christmas 1988 but was not made available to the public until after it was tabled in the legislature on 29 March 1989. An attempt to secure a last-minute rejection of the preliminary report by the special committee's deputy chair and solicitor general, Angus Ree, was thwarted by its unanimity rule, although the committee's final report in fact made no recommendations on the grounds that its work had been superseded by the final Fisher Report.[54] Further delay ensued when the final Fisher Report was tabled in the legislature and then referred to the Select Standing Committee on Labour, Justice, and Intergov-ernmental Relations chaired by Larry Chalmers. Here it languished pending consideration of the Builders' Lien Act and the salaries of provincial court judges. One week after the McLachlin judgment, the select committee estab-lished a subcommittee on agenda and procedures. Its terms of reference required it to "report to the House as soon as possible, or following any adjournment, or the next following session, as the case may be." The official New Democratic Party opposition accepted the Fisher Report, but several government members were opposed to any increase in the size of the legislature and the Premier himself seemed to have second thoughts on additional seats. Not to accept them, however, would have effectively destroyed all of the commission's work.[55]

Shortly before Justice Meredith's ruling, the select committee had commenced a review of the administrative aspects of redistribution,[56] but it was not until the spring session of the legislature neared its adjournment that any significant movement took place. On 15 June, an NDP member, G. Hanson, had moved that the select committee adopt the Fisher Report but had been countered by a motion to adjourn the debate. Three weeks later this motion to adopt was approved as a result of a government-sponsored amendment requiring a committee report by 14 July which would include as well recommendations for an increase in the size of the legislature to 75 single-member ridings, the establishment of an independent electoral boundaries commission, and the adoption of the Fisher map.[57] Only one government back-bencher, J. Kempf, voted against the resultant Bill 87, the Electoral Boundaries Commission Act, when it speedily went through its second reading, committee stage, and third reading on 18 July.[58] This was not quite the end of pressure from incumbent legislators, however, since the select committee still wanted to pursue with Judge Fisher possible boundary changes as a result of its discussions with individual MLAs concerning the impact on community interests in Saanich and the Islands and Cowichan–Malahat.[59]

The Dixon Legacy? Institutions and Process

The 11th-hour rush to proceed with the implementation of the Fisher Commission's boundaries and an accompanying new redistribution process resulted in a succession of instruments dealing both with immediate exigencies and long-run redistribution needs. Bill 87, the Electoral Boundaries Commission Act, provided for adoption of the Fisher boundaries by 31 January 1990. For the immediate redefinition of electoral districts, the provincial Cabinet was empowered to establish the names, areas, and boundaries of the 75 new electoral districts by regulation subject to receipt of a unanimous report from the Select Standing Committee on Labour, Justice, and Intergovernmental Relations due 15 January. In the meantime, Fisher found that, in the absence of any new information or obvious oversight, there was no justification for alterations in his recommended boundaries. The select committee's third report in October 1989 adopted his December 1988 electoral boundaries map modified only by changes in eight electoral district names it had agreed on earlier in July.[60] Unlike previous BC redistribution commissions, full metes and bounds legal descriptions of the recommended boundaries had not been prepared for the Fisher Commission by the Surveyor General and were not begun until August for a 31 October 1989 deadline. Their completion ended the last major procrastination in the redistribution process. Cabinet approved the regulation to establish the new names and boundaries at the end of January 1990.[61] Since this became effective on dissolution of the 34th Legislature, it ensured that an election could be held on the new boundaries any time after February 1990. In fact, Premier Vander Zalm delayed the call and a further 20 months passed before the legislature was dissolved near the end of its five-year term. Therefore there was ample time for the new names and boundaries to be approved in the schedules to a new 1990 Electoral Districts Act[62] by the Legislative Assembly at its 1990 session.

All future redistributions were to follow the regimen put forward through the select committee. The existing Constitution Act provisions were replaced by a Cabinet-appointed three-member boundaries commission, composed of a judge or retired judge of the Supreme Court or Court of Appeal nominated by the Cabinet, the Chief Electoral Officer, and a nominee (not an MLA or government employee) of the Speaker after consultation with the Premier and Leader of the Opposition. Redistribution of seats would occur after every second general election and follow a process not dissimilar to that followed by the 1987–88 Commission with public hearings, followed by a report, further representations and amendments, and a final opportunity for submissions by MLAs. In a reassertion of the role of the Legislative Assembly—and unlike Fisher—the redistribution report and amendments are to be submitted to the Speaker. Section 14 of the Electoral Boundaries Commission Act requires the government to bring in legislation for new districts in the same session as a redistribution commission's proposals or modified proposals receive the approval of the legislature.

The new criteria to govern the drawing of boundaries were defined in the following terms:

(a) that the principle of representation by population be achieved recognizing the imperatives imposed by geographical and demographic realities, the legacy of our history and the need to balance the community interests of the people of the Province;
(b) to achieve that principle, the commission be permitted to deviate from a common statistical provincial electoral quota by no more than 25%, plus or minus;
(c) the commission would be permitted to exceed the 25% deviation principle where it considers that very special circumstances exist.[63]

This wording suggests that British Columbia's "reapportionment revolution" was relatively modest and contained. The new electoral map and the adoption of a statutory +/– 25% tolerance limit in deviations from a population-based electoral quota constituted a significant advance, however, in the context of the old 1986 map and the 1984 redistribution procedures. The province, nonetheless, was content to conform to existing Canadian standards rather than attempt any innovations of its own. The tolerance of 50% variation in population size considerably depreciates the weighting of population criteria and permits broad interpretations of other criteria to accommodate a wide range of boundary options. As Bruce Cain has demonstrated, all such good government criteria are controversial and an apolitical ranking is impossible.[64] Furthermore, the "very special circumstances" subsection, as an escape from the quota levels, may mirror that given Canadian federal redistribution commissions but it also gives future BC commissions far more latitude than that considered necessary and adopted by the Fisher Commission.[65] The map drawn by the Fisher Commission demonstrated that claims of community, geography, and history could be achieved within a 24 to 18% range under only a minimal increase in seats.[66] Assuming a reversion to a three-year election cycle, the BC boundaries commission in 1997 will be able to go beyond these limits and will almost certainly do so if constrained by a strict limitation on any addition to the number of seats. Those who agree with Robert Dahl that "citizens ought to be political equals [and that this] is a crucial axiom in the moral perspective of democracy," may find in all this a sense of going two steps forward and three steps back from this democratic objective.[67]

The exercise of the new statutory latitude will, however, still be subject to Charter review. In the *Dixon* case McLachlin found that an optimal scheme and absolute equality were not required. Nevertheless, other boundary criteria were subordinate in her conclusion that the dominant consideration "must be population."[68] Thus, full use of the 25% range may still be subject to challenge if McLachlin I "better government" or McLachlin II "effective representation" reasons are not forthcoming. The most fundamental lesson to be derived from the British Columbia experience is to confirm Robert Dixon's paradox that, for all their defects, the courts may prove the "best" and "necessarily the ultimate" backstop should political processes fail. In this instance they did not entirely fail but clearly did require a jump start.[69]

Finally, beyond theory and in terms of *realpolitik*, it should be noted that future boundaries will also largely depend on whether future commissions and the legislature are permitted to maintain or reduce their electoral quota by adding legislators. This may be a compelling political option by 1997. The population of British Columbia is forecast to increase by 24% over 1986 to reach 3,576,500 at that date.[70] With 75 seats, the electoral quota would be 47,686 and a 25% deviation of 11,922 would require the smallest riding, save for "very special circumstances," to include 35,764 persons. If no additional seats are added and the quota grows in this way, some eight smaller districts will have to experience population growth of 16 to 21% to escape absorption and/or extinction. This is an unlikely prospect given current regional population growth patterns which continue to favour the Lower Mainland. Some indication of the disparities in rates of growth since 1986 are shown by the range in the number of registered voters at the time of the October 1991 provincial general election. Even keeping in mind that under its continuous voter registration system British Columbia excludes those under 19 years old, noncitizens, and nonregistrants, the 1991 registration statistics reveal a remarkably different picture to the one derived from the current electoral map's 1986 census population base. With an average number of registered voters per district of 26,521, the districts ranged from a high of 38,523 in Okanagan West down to 15,407 in North Peace River.

As of 16 October 1991 the range in *registered voters* per district thus stood at +45.25% to -41.91% from the average. While it must again be emphasized that the province's electoral quota was calculated from 1986 census populations and not voters, variations of this magnitude cannot help but erode some of the sense of progress in equality of voting power since 1986.

No reinterpretation or reordering of the criteria will entirely ease the regional political impact of the economic and social changes of the 1990s. British Columbia has begun the decade with the most fundamental realignment in its voting patterns in nearly 40 years. The abrupt emergence of three-party competition in the 1991 vote and entirely new patterns of regional support for the Liberal and Social Credit parties[71] have added more brambles to the province's political thicket and make it difficult to assess the medium-term electoral significance of the 1990 redistribution. The Fisher-McLachlin I experience had probably already planted the seeds for an entirely different dynamic to the mobilization and articulation of regional interests at the next redrawing of the boundaries. New political party concerns in the 1990s might conceivably encourage a still more radical response toward the very basis of the system itself.

TABLE 1

1986 DEVIATION OF POPULATION PER MLA FROM PROVINCIAL AVERAGE BY CONSTITUTION ACT ZONES AND ELECTORAL DISTRICTS

Electoral District	Population Per MLA	Deviation From Average
Mainland: Metropolitan		
Vancouver East*	46,438	+10.90
Vancouver Centre*	45,123	+7.76
Vancouver South*	44,769	+6.92
Vancouver-Little Mountain*	42,543	+1.60
Vancouver Point Grey*	39,124	-6.57
Island: Metropolitan		
Oak Bay-Gordon Head	44,656	+6.65
Victoria*	40,988	-2.11
Mainland: Suburban		
Surrey-Newton	68,347	+63.22
Coquitlam-Moody	68,203	+62.88
Surrey-White Rock-Cloverdale	66,785	+59.49
Surrey-Guildford-Whalley	61,075	+45.86
Burnaby North	56,647	+35.28
Richmond*	54,246	+29.55
North Vancouver-Seymour	53,502	+27.77
North Vancouver-Capilano	51,776	+23.65
Maillardville-Coquitlam	47,302	+12.97

Burnaby Willingdon	45,784	+9.34
Burnaby Edmonds	42,730	+2.05
New Westminster	39,973	-4.54
Delta*	39,894	-4.73
Mainland: Urban-rural		
West Vancouver-Howe Sound	54,943	+31.21
Chilliwack	49,281	+17.69
Okanagan South*	41,388	-1.16
Langley*	35,229	-15.87
Dewdney*	34,706	-17.12
Central Fraser Valley*	34,126	-18.50
Island: Urban-rural		
Esquimalt-Port Renfrew	61,316	+46.43
Comox	58,951	+40.79
Cowichan-Malahat	44,132	+5.39
Saanich and the Islands*	38,818	-7.30
Nanaimo*	34,661	-17.22
Mainland: Interior-coastal		
Okanagan North	50,753	+21.21
Prince George South	49,954	+19.30
Shuswap-Revelstoke	49,942	+19.27
Skeena	43,436	+3.73
Prince George North	39,710	-5.17
Mackenzie	38,206	-8.76
Kamloops*	37,380	-10.73
Kootenay	37,123	-11.34
Nelson-Creston	36,960	-11.73
Yale-Lillooet	33,834	-19.20
Boundary-Similkameen*	32,181	-23.15
Cariboo*	31,253	-25.36
Rossland Trail	30,910	-26.18
Omineca	29,623	-29.26
North Peace River	29,529	-29.48
South Peace River	27,284	-34.84
Prince Rupert	23,721	-43.35
Columbia River	23,144	-44.73
Island: Interior-coastal		
North Island	48,095	+14.86
Alberni	30,341	-27.54
Mainland: Remote		
Atlin	5,511	-86.84
TOTAL	2,889,207	

Average per MLA (69 seats in 52 districts) = 41,873
* identifies 1986 dual-member electoral district.

Notes

1. *Dixon v. British Columbia (Attorney General)*, [1989] 35 B.C.L.R. (2d) 273, 59 D.L.R. (4th) 247, 4 W.W.R. 393 (C.A.); and *Reference re Provincial Electoral Boundaries*, [1991] 81 D.L.R. (4th) 16, 5 W.W.R. 1 (S.C.C.).
2. Robert G. Dixon, *Democratic Representation: Reapportionment in Law and Politics* (New York: Oxford University Press, 1968), 19.
3. See N. Ruff, "Cat and Mouse Politics of Redistribution: Fair and Effective Representation in British Columbia," *BC Studies* 87 (Autumn 1990): 48-84; and Elections British Columbia, *Electoral History of British Columbia, 1871-1986* (Victoria: 1988), 497-509.
4. British Columbia, Constitution Amendment Act, 1984, s. 19.
5. British Columbia, *First Report of the British Columbia Electoral Commission*, September 1984. The legislature increased in size from 57 to 69 seats while the number of districts grew by 2 to 52.
6. See comparative discussion in R.K. Carty, "The Electoral Boundary Revolution in Canada," *American Review of Canadian Studies* 15/3 (Autumn 1985): 273-87.
7. See, for example, *British Columbia's Constitutional Proposals, Paper 6: A Bill of Rights and the Constitution of Canada* (1978); and *Submission of the Government of British Columbia to the Foreign Affairs Committee of the House of Commons, London, England* (1981), 25-27.
8. *Reynolds v. British Columbia (Attorney General)*, [1984] 53 B.C.L.R. 394, 5 W.W.R. 270, 11 D.L.R. (4th) 380 (C.A.); and *Hoogbruin v. British Columbia (Attorney General)*, [1986] 70 B.C.L.R. 1, 2 W.W.R. 700, 24 D.L.R. (4th) 718 (C.A.).
9. See Campbell Sharman, "The Strange Case of a Provincial Constitution: The British Columbia Constitution Act," *Canadian Journal of Political Science* 17/1 (March 1984): 87-108.
10. *Dixon v. B.C. (A.G.)*, [1987] 7 B.C.L.R. (2d) 186.
11. Unless excluded by a section 33 *non obstante* override, ibid., 187-88.
12. Ibid., 188.
13. See, for example, interview given reporters and editors of the Vancouver *Sun*, "Ridings give Socreds an edge, premier says," Vancouver *Sun*, 18 October 1986, A11, for a statement he subsequently repeated in television interviews.
14. Order in Council 690, (8 April 1987) in British Columbia, Royal Commission on Electoral Boundaries, *Preliminary Report of Proposed Boundaries for British Columbia Electoral Districts* (Victoria: May 1988), 22.
15. See Norman J. Ruff and William M. Ross, "People and Election Districts," submission to the British Columbia Royal Commission on Electoral Boundaries (Victoria: 8 July 1987), 5-7.
16. *Preliminary Report* (May 1988), Schedules B and C, 24-26.
17. Ibid., 5.
18. Both decisions were reaffirmed in the final December report. British Columbia, The Honourable Judge Thomas Fisher, Commissioner, *Report of the Royal Commission on Electoral Boundaries for British Columbia, 1988 (Fisher Report)*, 4-5.
19. *Preliminary Report* (May 1988) 5, 6.
20. Norman J. Ruff and William M. Ross, "Reflections and Refinements: An Appraisal of the Preliminary Report of the Royal Commission on Electoral Boundaries," submission to the Fisher Commission (Victoria: 9 August 1988), 2-3.

21. *Dixon v. British Columbia (Attorney General)* (see n.1), 301.
22. Ibid., 302.
23. Ibid., 304.
24. *Operation Dismantle v. the Queen,* [1985] 1 S.C.R. 441; *Attorney-General of the Commonwealth (ex rel. McKinlay) v. The Commonwealth of Australia* (1975), 135 C.L.R.1; and *R. v. Boundary Commission for England, ex parte Foot and others* (1983), 1 A11 E.R. 1099.
25. *Dixon v. British Columbia (Attorney General)* (see n.1), 305-6.
26. Ibid., 284.
27. Ibid., 307.
28. Ibid., 295.
29. Ibid., 282.
30. Ibid., 290-91.
31. Ibid., 293-95.
32. Ibid., 294. Alan Stewart observes in his case comment on *Dixon v. British Columbia (Attorney General)* that this agenda would replicate the U.S. "rational plan" constitutional standard for apportionment offered by Justice Clark in *Baker v. Carr* and later rejected in *Reynolds v. Sims*; see *The Canadian Bar Review* 69 (1990): 362.
33. [1991] 81 D.L.R. (4th) 36.
34. *Dixon v. British Columbia (Attorney General)* (see n.1), 296.
35. Ibid., 297.
36. See *R. v. Oakes,* [1986] 26 D.L.R. (4th) 200 and *Dixon v. British Columbia (Attorney General)* (see n.1), 298.
37. *Dixon v. British Columbia,* 299.
38. Ibid., 299.
39. Ibid., 300.
40. Ibid., 308.
41. As affirmed in *Hoogbruin v. B.C.(A.G.),* [1986] and *Air Canada v. B.C.(A.G.)* [1986] 2 S.C.R. 539, 8 B.C.L.R. (2d) 273, [1987] 1 W.W.R. 304, 32 D.L.R. (4th) 1.
42. *Dixon v. British Columbia (Attorney General)* (see n.1), 309-10.
43. Ibid., 311, 312.
44. B.M. McLachlin, "The Role of the Court in the Post-Charter Era: Policy-Maker or Adjudicator," *UNB Law Journal* 39 (1990): 62; and "The Charter: A New Role for the Judiciary?" *Alberta Law Review* 29 (1991): 557-59.
45. *Dixon v. British Columbia (Attorney General)* (see n.1), 312.
46. *Dixon v. British Columbia (Attorney General),* [1989] 37 B.C.L.R. (2d) 233.
47. Kent Roach, "Case Comment: Reapportionment in British Columbia," *UBC Law Review* 24 (1990): 100.
48. *Dixon v. British Columbia (Attorney General)* (see n.46), 235.
49. British Columbia, *Debates of the Legislative Assembly,* 2 June 1989, 7194.
50. *Dixon v. British Columbia (Attorney General)* (see n.46), 234.
51. *Dixon v. British Columbia (Attorney General)* (see n.1), 312.
52. British Columbia, Legislative Assembly, *Votes and Proceedings,* no. 87, 22 June 1988.
53. Letter from Mr. Jim Rabbitt, MLA to Honourable Judge Thomas K. Fisher, (8 September 1988).
54. For further details on this stage, see Norman J. Ruff and William M. Ross, "Towards a More Equitable Distribution of Seats in British Columbia," *Canadian Parliamentary Review* 12/1 (Spring 1989): 21-23; *Times-Colonist,* 16 March 1989, p. A; and

British Columbia, *Debates of the Legislative Assembly*, 3rd. Session, 34th Parliament, 29 March 1989.

55. "Socreds balk at implementing 6 more MLAs," *Times-Colonist*, 29 April 1989. See also Rita Johnston and D. Mercier's concerns at the increase in MLAs and members of constituents per riding in British Columbia, Select Standing Committee on Labour, Justice and Intergovernmental Relations, *Report of Proceedings*, 15 June 1989.

56. On 30 May 1989, it met with the deputy chief electoral officer, the surveyor general, and the chief administration officer of the Royal Commission. Select Standing Committee, *Report of Proceedings*.

57. British Columbia, Legislative Assembly, Select Standing Committee On Labour, Justice and Intergovernmental Relations, *Minutes*, 6 July 1989 and *First Report: Report of the Royal Commission On Electoral Boundaries for British Columbia, December 1988*, 14 July 1989.

58. The debate featured a brief exchange between N. Loenen and L. Guno on the loss of the smallest northern riding of Atlin and its implications for the representation of aboriginal people, but the latter had not reached the same level of interest it was later to attain in submissions to the federal Lortie Commission. British Columbia, *Debates of the Legislative Assembly*, 3rd Session, 34th Parliament, 18 July 1989 afternoon sitting.

59. See proposals discussed in Select Standing Committee, *Report of Proceedings*, 11 July 1989.

60. Ladner to Delta North, Tsawwassen to Delta South, Richmond North to Richmond Centre, Richmond South to Richmond-Steveston, Kelowna East and West to Okanagan East and West, Duncan-Ladysmith to Cowichan-Ladysmith, and Cowichan-Malahat to Malahat-Juan de Fuca.

61. Electoral Boundaries Regulation, BC Reg. 25/90, deposited 26 January 1990.

62. S.B.C. 1990, c. 39. This repealed the interim regulation BC Reg. 25/90.

63. Electoral Boundaries Commission Act, S.B.C. 1989, c. 65, s. 9.

64. Bruce E. Cain, *The Reapportionment Puzzle* (Berkeley: University of California Press, 1984), 74.

65. See Andrew Sancton, "Eroding Representation-by-Population in the Canadian House of Commons: The *Representation Act, 1985*," *Canadian Journal of Political Science* 23 (1990): 441-57.

66. As noted in the *Dixon* judgment, this author with W. Ross went further to show how an electoral map for BC could have been drawn respecting claims of geography and community with all but one seat within a +/- 10% range.

67. Robert A. Dahl, *Democracy, Liberty and Equality* (Oslo: Norwegian University Press, 1986), 9.

68. *Dixon v. British Columbia (Attorney General)* (see n.1), 294.

69. Dixon, *Democratic Representation* (see n.2), 21.

70. British Columbia, Ministry of Finance and Corporate Relations, *British Columbia Population Forecast 1990–2016*, rev. July 1990.

71. While the New Democratic vote fell by 1.90% of the total valid votes to 40.70 and by not more than 5% in any one region, the Liberal vote rose from 6.74 in 1986 to 33.25. The Social Credit vote was more than halved in a fall from 49.32 to 24.05% of valid votes.

COMMENTARY

MUNROE EAGLES
STATE UNIVERSITY OF NEW YORK AT BUFFALO

If Canada is on the verge of a "reapportionment revolution," future historians will note that the first shots were fired in British Columbia and diffused eastward quickly thereafter. The three papers considered here present complementary perspectives on important and formative reform processes regarding the drawing of riding boundaries in Canada's westernmost provinces. Professor Ruff's paper on the British Columbia case, along with the analysis of Professors Knopff and Morton on unfinished developments in Alberta, aim primarily to reconstruct the complicated, irregular, and seemingly haphazard process whereby electoral maps were evaluated and modified by judicial scrutiny. Professors Bercuson and Cooper also refer to recent developments in Alberta, but they do so while advocating a stricter application of what they call the "equality principle" in Canadian electoral cartography.

These five authors are uniquely able to advance our understanding of the questions at hand. All have been participants in the political and legal processes about which they write and this lends both credibility and richness to their analyses. In the limited space available here, I will attempt to characterize the contributions made by the papers to our understanding of the current state of electoral cartography in western Canada. The authors identify a number of significant flaws in the practice and process of boundary determination in the two provinces, and this prompts me to offer some general suggestions in conclusion as to how political scientists might continue to contribute to the ongoing process of electoral boundary determination.

Professor Ruff's paper helps us understand the outcome and impact of the *Dixon* case in British Columbia by carefully untangling the dense and complicated matrix of politicians (both legislators and executives), commissioners, reformers, and judges who played a role over the roughly four years that the constitutional challenge was before the province's court system. Reading his account of the interactions over time of the diverse actors who were variously motivated by adherence to specific districting principles, by considerations of crass political advantage, and/or by matters of personality and temperament, one cannot help but be struck by the *ad hoc* and highly contingent quality of the process. Professor Ruff is not an alarmist, however, and an incrementalist reading his well-told account would likely be gratified by the ability of authorities to muddle through such important decisions. The good news at the end of the tale is the widespread agreement that the decision produced by then Chief Justice McLachlin was itself a significant and worthwhile compromise that is consistent with Canadian political traditions. However, the bad news is that demographic trends resulting in an exacerbated population imbalance between (roughly) north and south in the province ensures that the achievement of relative vote equality by the 1990 boundaries will not long survive. The paper convincingly concludes with a prediction that the electoral map in British Columbia will almost certainly continue to be an object of fierce debate in the near future.

Procedural complexities and contingencies affecting reforms to the boundary determination process also figure prominently in the Knopff/Morton paper. In the wake of the *Dixon* decision, authorities in Alberta quickly initiated a reform process designed to bring the electoral map into line with Charter provisions. In essence, the Electoral Boundaries Commission Act that was passed by the provincial legislature late in 1990 saw the replacement of the old system of classifying ridings as either rural or urban with a new distinction between single and multimunicipality ridings. The Act also makes special provision to allow for, and occasionally to require, some hybrid ridings. Perhaps significantly, however, the rural-urban dichotomy survives as a criterion of appointment to the new five-person boundary commission. Two members of the commission must be, and three members may be, drawn from rural areas. The paper explores some of the potential for "Gettymandering" provided by these new regulations. It also details a number of interesting legal twists as they arose in the Alberta reform process. These reveal all too clearly how courtroom schedules, legal intrigue, and other such minutia can crowd out reasoned and principled argument in the evaluation of districting cases.

By contrast, Professors Bercuson and Cooper's objective is more explicitly evaluative and they present a forceful critique of Alberta's districting experience on the basis of its failure to achieve equality of voting power. They recognize that some deviations from "one person–one vote–one value" may arise from the normal operation of nonproportional systems of electoral representation but choose to direct their criticisms primarily at districting abuses such as gerrymandering and malapportionment. Of special concern in their analysis is the tradition of malapportionment that has produced a consistent pattern of rural overrepresentation in Alberta. According to these authors, the tradition will continue undisturbed under the recently passed Alberta Electoral Boundaries Act.

Written by academics who have been participant-observers in the process of reforming the boundary determination process, these provocative analyses invite further speculation as to how political scientists might continue to contribute to the future debates over districting (either within or outside the legal system). The analyses clearly reveal that the achievement of "relative vote equality" in Canada's westernmost provinces has been complicated primarily by the increasing concentration of population in urban areas. Legislators from less densely populated areas, seeking to preserve their ridings in the face of unfavourable demographic trends, advanced "community of interest" arguments to justify the maintenance of representation in legislatures beyond that warranted by numbers alone. A major objective of the Bercuson/Cooper paper is to criticize the tradition in Alberta (and, by extension, elsewhere) of classifying ridings using a rural/urban dichotomy and allocating a fixed number of seats to each category in such a way as to favour rural voters. Though the terms used in the classification are new, it is not clear that the current Alberta Electoral Boundaries Commission Act marks a real departure from this tradition in its distinction between single and multimunicipality districts. Similarly, in the pre-*Dixon* British Columbia case, eight regional zones with weighted population quotas were employed to produce the patchwork map that was pronounced unconstitutional by Justice McLachlin's landmark 1989 decision.

Professors Bercuson and Cooper forcefully advance a number of objections to the idea of rural overrepresentation, to which I would simply like to add a more general comment regarding the manifest inadequacy of the current practice of representing complex community of interest considerations in the electoral-mapmaking process by means of a simplistic formula based on the assumed homogeneity of crudely defined types of communities. Whatever community of interest may mean (and this most assuredly is a subject requiring full debate), its formulistic operationalization in electoral cartography by means of some variant of a rural/urban classification scheme does gross violence to the complexity of human settlement patterns. It is virtually self-evident that rural types of communities are far from homogeneous; urban settlements are similarly diverse. As was clear to one of the founders of the subfield of urban sociology, Louis Wirth, " . . . cities represent a vast continuum shading into non-urban settlements. The same is true of rural settlements . . . To lump the great variety of cities and rural settlements respectively together obscures more than it reveals the distinctive characteristics of each."[1] Political scientists might usefully play a role in the unfolding reform process by urging the adoption of more intellectually defensible incarnations of community of interest.

In addition to community of interest defenses for preferential treatment of rural areas, servicing considerations are also frequently given as reasons for having fewer voters in rural ridings. Proponents of this view argue that rural members must work harder to move around their ridings, and generally face a more difficult task in performing the "ombuds" dimension of representation. Regrettably, little empirical research is available in Canada with which to confirm or disconfirm this generalization. Therefore, it is premature to conclude that rural representatives hold a monopoly on challenges to effective constituency service, or that representatives of remote or sparsely populated ridings are always uniquely disadvantaged in the complex business of representing electors and winning reelection.

Indeed, on some accounts it seems plausible to argue that it is the representatives of populous, ethnically, and socioeconomically diverse urban/suburban ridings who face particularly vexing representation challenges. Such districts, probably comprised of large immigrant populations whose native language is different from the member's, may present thorny problems of communication. Additionally, it has been argued that politicians from more rural ridings may enjoy an especially cozy relationship with local media that can enhance their reelection prospects.[2] Finally, extant research from other systems suggests that elected representatives have a good deal of discretion when it comes to adopting a representational style. Badly needed empirical work into the correlates and challenges of constituency service across the wide variety of ridings in Canada would, I suspect, help debunk many of the familiar deterministic arguments concerning inequalities in servicing burdens in the country's legislatures.[3]

Clearly, many questions germane to the drawing of electoral maps remain unanswered in Canada. By their collective example as well as through their arguments, the authors encourage social scientists to become more involved in the drawing of electoral maps, if only to ensure that districting not fall completely into the hands of the "gerrymandarins."

Notes

1. Louis Wirth, "Rural-Urban Differences," in Albert J. Reiss, Jr., ed., *Louis Wirth on Cities and Social Life: Selected Papers* (Chicago: University of Chicago Press, 1964), 222–23.
2. Lawrence Grossman's analysis of rural-urban differences in safe seats in Ontario, for example, identified this as a factor accounting for the higher retention rates of rural MPs. See his "'Safe Seats': The Rural-Urban Pattern in Ontario," in John C. Courtney, ed., *Voting in Canada*, (Scarborough: Prentice-Hall, 1967), 99–103.
3. Harold Clarke's somewhat dated research into the correlates of constituency service among provincial legislators in Canada suggests that time allocated to constituency service decreases with the urbanization of ridings. However, as Clarke notes, it is unclear whether this pattern is attributable to differences in the representational styles of members elected from diverse types of ridings, or to the level of difficulty inherent in performing such duties in different constituency contexts. See his "Determinants of Provincial Constituency Service Behaviour: A Multivariate Analysis," *Legislative Studies Quarterly* III, 4 (November 1978): esp. 622 and 625 (n.14).

COMMENTARY

R.K. CARTY
UNIVERSITY OF BRITISH COLUMBIA

One is struck in reading these three papers at just how far the agenda has moved in recent years. Not so long ago, most Canadians saw partisan gerrymandering as the most important electoral boundary drawing problem. Now, rightly or wrongly, it seems taken for granted that it is no longer a problem, that it has been solved, only to have been replaced by the American fixation with the question of equality.

In shifting the agenda in this way, however, it is not just the problem that is altered, for we also redefine the players involved and the language and level of abstractness with which the character of the electoral map is discussed. So, with apportionment not gerrymandering seen as the issue, the courts have supplanted partisan legislatures as the battle ground, and the principles and rights of the Charter rather than traditional claims to representation have become the telling arguments. And when the agenda inevitably returns to questions of gerrymandering (for purposes of affirmative representation), it will be in this new, recast way so that our past experience with the issue may offer only limited guidance.

Just how far these changes have taken us can be seen in the papers that chart the Alberta experience over the past two years. Albertans are now fighting reference cases in the courts, apparently at considerable expense and effort, over a map that doesn't exist, indeed has yet to be drawn. This seems to have moved the whole issue to an abstract realm that would have mystified Canadian politicians of an earlier age who dealt with these issues in the most pragmatic and particularistic fashion.

In their analysis of what has gone on in Alberta, Bercuson and Cooper give several reasons for the continuing overrepresentation of rural areas. However, I think it is important to remember that the single-member plurality system is fundamentally a territorial system, and therefore, almost inevitably, some of the biases it will engender will themselves be territorial. When place is being represented, it is difficult for mapmakers not to be aware of and sensitive to spatial considerations. It is this impulse that leads politicians, and now judges, to reject the absolutist equality position of Bercuson and Cooper. It is this that is now taking us into a court-led debate over how much of a departure from the principle of "equal votes" we are prepared to accept as the price for maintaining our territorial representational system.

As Norman Ruff points out, Chief Justice McLachlin (of the BC Supreme Court) finessed the question nicely when she ruled the BC electoral map unconstitutional. This she accomplished not by defining an acceptable level of interconstituency variation, but by broadly hinting that the map prepared by the Fisher Royal Commission would likely be acceptable to the Court. That commission, having to deal with a very badly malapportioned map, had said the equality principle must be paramount but a variation of up to +/- 25% to accommodate local factors was acceptable. The BC ruling gave a judicial imprimatur to this standard and, as circumstance would have it, the judge who made it (Chief Justice McLachlin) was, within days, elevated to the Supreme Court of Canada where she was soon given the opportunity (in the Saskatchewan case) to confirm her endorsement of the Fisher Commission's definition of the Canadian standard.

Parenthetically, it ought to be noted that the language of constituency size variation can be misleading for those not used to working in numbers. Thus +/- 25% does not make for a maximum range of 50% (as commentators often assert) for that is to confuse percentages with percentage points. If one was to use the full range, from –25 to +25 around the equal point, then the largest constituency would actually be 66% larger than the smallest. But to talk of a variance of 66% is to imply something considerably greater (and perhaps less legitimate?) than does a language of +/- 25. As this debate moves into the courts, part of the struggle will be to define the way we think and talk about these issues.

There seems to be agreement on the proposition that constituency size will cluster around some norm and the debate is about just how big or small the acceptable cluster range is. Bercuson and Cooper argue for as near to zero as possible; the Court has, for the moment, identified +/- 25% as the standard. But there are two ways of thinking about this notion of a range and it seems to me the courts have not yet confronted which they lean to.

On the one hand we can argue that the entire area from –25 to +25 (or whatever the number) is a space that can legitimately be occupied and electoral mapmakers ought to exploit it to the full. We might call this the "full range" conception. On the other hand there is the perception that the mapmakers should aim as far as possible for equal-sized constituencies but, where necessary to accommodate local problems, might deviate up to +/- 25% from the quota. This we can call the "deviation" conception.

Though the formal rules may be the same in both cases, the spirit underlying them is fundamentally different and leads to quite different approaches to the exercise of mapmaking. Thus under the first (full range) scenario it would not be a particularly worrisome problem if one ended up with rather a lot of constituencies near the extremes of the range. But, on the other hand, if one assumes the second (deviation) conception ought to be the guiding principle then such a map, even if no cases actually exceeded the limits, would be subject to fair criticism as unacceptable.

Fisher, in his BC Royal Commission, held strongly to the first view. Indeed, as Ruff notes, he had more cases near the extremes in his final report than in his preliminary proposals. He did not regard that as a problem for he believed the full range was there to be used. But, at the same time, the Fisher Commission assumed that this understanding of what the range meant implied a principle of no exceptions. As a consequence, the commission rejected the very idea of a set of special seats that would fall outside the standard. Thus, guaranteeing some seats to the northern parts of the province (as in Saskatchewan) was not an option, for it would appear to make a mockery of a conception of a standard set of limits that could embrace needed variation.

The deviation principle may have much less difficulty with the issue of exceptional cases. After all, if the basic thrust is one of minimizing constituency variation, with the allowable range simply identifying deviations that needn't be individually justified, then a few exceptional instances (be they in northern Saskatchewan or Labrador) need not cause the judges a significant problem. To this point the Court has not addressed the issue of the exceptional cases. When it does so, it will, at least implicitly, have to choose between these two conceptions of what the range means. In doing so it may set off another round of litigation, for if it tolerates exceptions to the limits, then it may strengthen the hand of those who argue the range itself ought to be narrowed.

Ultimately we are led to the hard question raised by all these papers of why deviations anyway? In British Columbia, Fisher talked about the need for fair and balanced representation: fair was the equality principle, balanced referred to the rest of the traditional considerations that justified deviations from the quota. In her decisions Justice McLachlin has transformed this notion of balancing other considerations into that of effective representation.

So the right to vote is translated into the right to effective representation and the focus is subtly shifted from the voter to the representative. And from this point it is but a short step to the problems of governing, for Justice McLachlin tells us that effective representation is important because it is conducive to good government.

The notion of effective representation in this sense, as opposed to Fisher's of balanced representation, seems to me an adoption of American notions that are not appropriate given our constitutional system. We do not want effective representation for good governing in anything like the same sense those using a congressional system might. This is because our parliamentary representatives are not involved in governing in the same way elected representatives in the congressional system are.

Parliamentary representatives have, as one of their most important duties, to constitute themselves an "electoral college" to create, support, and, if necessary, remove governments. In this sense Canadian elections only indirectly connect voters to the governing function, and the continued use of the plurality system, with all its well-known distortions, is tolerable because it is being used to elect parliamentarians. As Bagehot reminds us, Parliament is there to choose a government, articulate grievances, debate public policy, educate the body politic, and sometimes legislate, but it is not the government and MPs are not our governors.

This leads me to wonder whether Justice McLachlin's discussion of permissible limits for electoral districts in terms of effective governance is not fundamentally misguided. Do we not need to think much more carefully about the constitutional role of Parliament and the legislatures, and what that implies about the appropriate character of representation, as well as the character and meaning of the citizen's constitutionally enshrined right to vote? In the few court cases already decided, we have apparently begun to move down a much more government-focused path as if to ask the quintessential Canadian question: "What sort of vote will produce peace, order, and good government?" I suggest that we need to ask whether this is where we want the debate, and our constitutional evolution, to go.

LESSONS FROM
THE AMERICAN EXPERIENCE

What Happens After One Person-One Vote? Implications of the United States Experience for Canada*

BERNARD GROFMAN

UNIVERSITY OF CALIFORNIA, IRVINE

ABSTRACT

An important part of the history of representation is the ongoing struggle between those who argue for representation of persons and those who argue for representation of interests. In the U.S., as in most democracies, the principles of representation embedded in both the federal Constitution (the "Connecticut compromise") and in the majority of state constitutions prior to 1962 reflect a compromise between these two concepts of representation. At stake is whether voters ought to be regarded as faceless and interchangeable (one person-one vote carried to its most mindless extreme) or, whether, instead (or, more plausibly, in addition) they should be seen as appropriately distinguishable on the basis of key characteristics such as place of residence, ethnicity, race, or political beliefs or affiliations.

The initial concern of this paper is to review the history of the post-*Baker* debate over districting standards. I argue that, in the 1970s and the 1980s, the focus has been primarily on fair representation of racial and linguistic minorities, as defined by the aim of avoiding "minority vote dilution." At the same time, a numerically strict one person-one vote standard has come to be taken for granted—with the standards for Congress far harsher than those for state and local redistricting. Moreover, with *Bandemer v. Davis*, a remarkably ambiguous 1986 decision without a majority decision, the issue of political (i.e., partisan) fairness has been declared by the Supreme Court to be, in principle, justifiable. But as yet, no legislative plan has been held unconstitutional, and the two lower court cases subsequent to *Bandemer* suggest that partisan gerrymandering challenges may be impossible to win.

I conclude my essay with a look at the relevance of U.S. redistricting practices and constitutional jurisprudence to the Canadian debate over one person–one vote. In the debate over representation in the United States, the pendulum swung away from territorially based representation and toward voter interchangeability in the 1960s, with *Baker v. Carr* and subsequent cases. However, on the one hand, it did not swing nearly as far as toward perfect equality across districts as some Canadian jurists seem to believe and, on the other hand, the discontinuity with previous practices created by the emphasis of the post-*Baker* Supreme Court decisions on population equality was much greater than Canadian jurists seem to recognize. Indeed, the parallels between U.S. and Canadian redistricting practices in the early history of these countries are far greater than recent Canadian court cases have recognized. Also, as we look to the future, given the language of the Charter of Rights, we can anticipate Canadian courts confronting the same types of challenges to boundary redistributions as U.S. courts have seen in the 1970s and 1980s based on the 14th Amendment—to wit, challenges based on claims of racial, linguistic, and partisan vote dilution. In the U.S., many of those challenges have been successful, especially challenges to at-large elections at the local level.

Types of Vote Dilution

Roughly speaking, we can divide voting rights litigation into two types: the first has to do with issues directly concerning the right to vote (e.g., barriers to registration or practices of voter intimidation); the second has to do with broader questions that fall under the rubric of what is commonly called "vote dilution." Vote dilution has been defined as the minimizing or cancelling out of the voting strength of a given group through practices such as submergence in multimember districts or by practices of electoral gerrymandering that unduly fragment or unnecessarily concentrate that group's voting strength.[1] In the United States, issues of the first type often arise under the 15th Amendment; issues of the second type customarily are brought under the 14th Amendment's "equal protection" clause.

In the United States, most of the legal issues dealing with denial of access to the ballot have long since been resolved, so we shall focus on vote-dilution cases, where there remain important controversies, especially with respect to defining and measuring partisan gerrymandering.[2] For purposes of discussion, and because there are important differences that make the tripartite distinction a sensible one, we may usefully divide recent vote-dilution litigation into three major subareas: one person–one vote issues, issues having to do with racial vote dilution, and issues having to do with partisan vote dilution.

I will characterize an area of law as mature if there are few outstanding legal issues (and these mostly minor ones). I will characterize case law as mechanical to the extent that the determination of which party will prevail can be determined more or less routinely by the application of a well-defined algorithm to a set of objectively definable case characteristics. One index of the maturity and mechanicity of an area of the law is a lopsided pattern of victories and defeats in the cases that are brought. When the case law is both clear and relatively mechanical, almost all challenges that are brought will be successful, since cases likely to be unsuccessful will be screened out in advance. The only exceptions will be cases seeking to extend the frontiers of the case law and mistakes. Nonetheless, even in mature areas of the case law, until issues of operationalization of standards have been fully resolved, there may be a great deal of disputation. Moreover, if the stakes are high, litigants who can project near-certain defeat have an incentive to be ingenious in trying to find ways to recast the case law or "interpret away" case facts that, on their face, appear to be irredeemably damaging.

One Person–One Vote: From Reynolds v. Sims *to* Karcher v. Daggett,
The Mechanistic Jurisprudence of Simple-minded Quantitativism

In the United States, the original impetus for federal courts to involve themselves with reapportionment was what has been called the "silent gerrymander," i.e., the failure of states to redraw legislative and/or congressional district lines when new census data became available. In the early and middle part of this century, the decision not to reapportion was used as a means to maintain rural dominance of state legislatures in the face of dramatic population growth in the nation's urban areas. *Baker v. Carr*[3] held that the failure to periodically reapportion gave rise to a violation of the 14th Amendment's equal protection clause. However, subsequent cases held that periodic reapportionment was not sufficient; equal protection (and the constitutional provisions specifying population-based apportionment of Congress) also required that attention be paid to the degree of population equality. Beginning with *Reynolds v. Sims*,[4] the United States Supreme Court considered when deviations from strict population equality would exceed permissible limits. In *Reynolds*, the Court was very reluctant to set any strict numerical threshold; rather it identified a variety of factors that a jurisdiction might use to legitimate population deviations. "A state may legitimately desire to maintain the integrity of various political subdivisions, insofar as possible, and provide for compact districts of contiguous territory, in designing a legislative apportionment scheme ... Indiscriminate districting, without any regard for political subdivision or natural or historical boundary lines, may be little more than an open invitation to partisan gerrymandering ... [But] the overriding objective must be substantial equality among the various districts ... [D]ivergences from a strict population standard ... based on legitimate considerations incident to the effectuation of a rational state policy ... are constitutionally permissible with respect to the apportionment of seats in either or both of the two houses of a bicameral state legislature."[5] However, in subsequent cases, each of these reasons (e.g., maintenance of the integrity of county borders) was held to be inadequate to justify more than minimal population deviation.

The evolving one person–one vote standard drew on statistical concepts such as total deviation[6] introduced to the courts in the form of expert witness testimony by social scientists. Over the course of three decades of redistricting litigation beginning with *Reynolds*, the Supreme Court has evolved a dual standard for legislative and congressional cases. For Congress, deviations were to be as low as "practicable";[7] for state legislative redistricting,[8] total population deviations below 10% were held to be "prima facie constitutional,"[9] but, except for the aberrant decision in *Brown v. Thompson*, no total deviation above 16.4% has ever been accepted by the Supreme Court.[10] Thus, while *Reynolds v. Sims* invited courts to consider rational state purposes and to balance off competing interests, subsequent cases developed along the lines of strictly numerical standards—the very model of mechanical jurisprudence.

Because the basis for deciding one person–one vote challenges is now so well established in the United States, few jurisdictions draw plans that could successfully be challenged on one person–one vote grounds, and one person–one vote challenges occur (as a procedural device to obtain standing) mostly in jurisdictions that have been unable to agree on a new plan and are being sued to compel a timely redistricting.[11] Hence, we can certainly characterize one person–one vote case law in the United States as a mature area of the law. Indeed, if we look at the one person–one vote case law, we might characterize this area of vote-dilution case law as well past maturity. In fact, to characterize it as in an advanced stage of senility would not be far off. That is to say it repeats itself endlessly and mindlessly with no particular point,[12] and having largely lost track of whatever it was that motivated courts to get into the business in the first place.[13] The limits on acceptable deviations that have been imposed are *far* stricter than what was either foreseen (or advocated) by the early supporters of *Baker v. Carr*,[14] especially when we look at congressional districting.

Racial Vote Dilution: From White v. Regester *to* Thornburg v. Gingles, *From Gestaltism to Number-crunching*

The 1970s and 1980s have seen minority vote dilution replace one person–one vote as the principal basis of redistricting litigation in the United States. Preliminary evidence from the 1990s suggests that vote-dilution cases will be even more important than ever before as a result of two important recent changes in the voting-rights case law standard of proof for minority vote dilution: (1) the shift from the purpose test, required in *City of Mobile v. Bolden*,[15] to the effects-based standard embodied in section 2 of the Voting Rights Act of 1965 as amended in 1982;[16] and (2) the shift from a "totality of circumstances" approach to proving effects to one based on the three prongs of *Thornburg v. Gingles*, enunciated in 1986.

Drawing on the standard of proof outlined in *White v. Regester*,[17] until 1980, when *City of Mobile* enunciated a purpose test, federal courts had looked at a number of factors (e.g., lingering effects of past discrimination, racial campaign appeals, patterns of racially polarized voting, usual absence of minority success, presence of election methods such as runoffs or unusually large election districts held to depreciate the likelihood of minority electoral success) that, in the "totality of the circumstances," were used to determine whether or not there was vote dilution.[18] In seeking to reverse the impact of *City of Mobile*, as part of the 1982 extension of the Voting Rights Act of 1965,[19] Congress passed revised language in section 2 of the act designed to create an effects-based statutory standard for vote dilution based on the "totality of circumstances" approach that *City of Mobile* had rejected as an inappropriate constitutional test. When this "totality of circumstances" approach was codified in a report of the Senate Committee on the Judiciary on the proposed 1982 extension of the act, the Judiciary Committee report asserted that no single factor was necessary for a finding of dilution, and that "point-counting" methods were to be discouraged. Moreover, the report downplayed the importance of certain factors (e.g., proof of responsiveness of elected officials to minority concerns) that some earlier cases had held to be important.[20]

The first case before the Supreme Court involving the proper interpretation of the new section 2 provisions was *Thornburg v. Gingles*, a challenge to a number of multimember legislative districts in North Carolina.[21] In *Gingles*, Justice Brennan set forth a new and considerably simplified effects-based test of vote dilution in the context of challenges to multimember or at-large elections. There are three prongs of the *Gingles* test. First, plaintiffs must show that minority population is sufficiently large and geographically concentrated so as to constitute a majority in at least one district of a potential single-member-district remedy plan. Second, they must show that voting is racially polarized, with the minority community politically cohesive. Third, they must show that minority candidates of choice usually lose. With respect to each of these factors, especially the first two, quantitative analysis and expert witness testimony has proved to be critical. Both the "totality of the circumstances" approach that once characterized voting-rights case law and the *Gingles* three-pronged test look for objectively identifiable indicators of vote dilution. However, while the former approach can be characterized as holistic, eschewing precise directions to lower courts as to either necessary or sufficient conditions for a finding of vote dilution,[22] by contrast, Justice Brennan's approach in *Gingles* is far more tightly reasoned, based on what he refers to as a "functional" analysis of the electoral process.

When we look at the vote-dilution case law with respect to racial questions, at least if we confine ourselves to challenges to at-large or multimember district plans,[23] I would characterize the case law as mature. While there is dispute in the lower courts about whether the three prongs of *Gingles* provide either necessary or sufficient evidence for a finding of vote dilution in an at-large or multimember plan, as of July 1991, every case that has been decided since *Gingles* in which the three prongs of the *Gingles* test were held to be satisfied has been decided in favour of plaintiffs.[24] Moreover, even courts that have not treated the *Gingles* factors as in and of themselves determinative have generally begun with the three-pronged test before going on to consider other aspects of the totality of the circumstances.[25] Most importantly, the Supreme Court has repeatedly refused to revisit *Gingles,* and has dealt with subsequent section 2 challenges to at-large or multimember district elections either by refusing to hear them or by summary affirmance.[26]

Thus, in my view, at present, the question of whether a jurisdiction's use of multimember district or at-large elections can withstand challenge can be relatively straightforwardly ascertained by looking closely at a delimited number of objectively discernible case facts. In the case of at-large or multimember district elections taking place in jurisdictions with a minority population sufficiently large and concentrated enough to satisfy the first prong of *Gingles,* challenges brought by minority plaintiffs almost never lose.[27] The maturity of the U.S. case law in this area is further shown by the fact that the plaintiffs' bar is consolidating its gains in looking for those relatively few places that have not yet been sued (e.g., in California, where plaintiffs are likely to be Hispanic) in order to mop them up,[28] and looking for new frontiers to conquer (e.g., racial gerrymandering in single-member-district plans)[29] while the defendants' bar is primarily looking for loopholes and, by and large, not finding them. Of course, given recent changes on the Supreme Court, this rosy picture of a settled voting-rights case law may be subject to change without notice.

Partisan Gerrymandering: From Bandemer v. Davis *to Who Knows What, An Idea in Search of an Operationalization*

If section 2 challenges to at-large or multimember district elections are in a mature (i.e., fully developed) stage of case law, and case law in the one person–one vote area might be characterized as so mature as to be almost senile, how do we characterize the case law with respect to partisan gerrymandering? My answer to that question is straightforward. Partisan gerrymandering case law is in the toddler phase. How do we characterize the toddler phase? What do toddlers do? They make mudpies. They throw things. What has happened in the political gerrymandering cases heard so far, and what will continue to happen until the Supreme Court provides a resolution to partisan gerrymandering questions more definitive than the plethora of opinions in *Bandemer v. Davis*[30] or the denial of certiorari in *Badham v. Eu,*[31] is that lawyers and expert witnesses are throwing legal theories and statistical models "up against the wall" in the hopes that some of them will stick and make a pretty picture that judges will believe. Let me be clear, however, that this characterization is not meant to be pejorative. It is a necessary part of the evolution of case law that what had been an inchoate area be developed through the active competition of ideas.[32]

Continuing and Emerging Controversies in Minority Vote Dilution: A Look to U.S. Jurisprudence in the 1990s

One Person–One Vote

While one person–one vote issues of the type that had concerned courts in the immediate aftermath of *Baker v. Carr* are no longer of great moment now that population-equality standards are so precisely defined, two interlinked issues related to but yet distinct from the old population-equality standards disputes remain matters of dispute. On the one hand, there is the question of what is an appropriate population base for reapportionment (e.g., total population versus total *citizen* population); on the other hand, there is the problem of how to cope with census undercount, especially insofar as that undercount differentially affects black, Hispanic, and Asian populations.

One Person–One Vote or One Citizen–One Vote?

Litigants concerned with changing the apportionment base to one that would exclude noncitizens unsuccessfully sued in the 1980s to compel the U.S. Census to enumerate only citizens.[33] With respect to congressional apportionment, it seems reasonably clear that the language of the U.S. Constitution (Article I) requires apportionment on the basis of persons.[34] At the state and local level there is some room for flexibility, but only to the extent that jurisdictions make use of what the Supreme Court in *Burns v. Richardson* referred to as a "permissible" apportionment base.[35] While two demographers have recently claimed that the one person–one vote standard must be interpreted as requiring districts that are equal in *citizen voting age* population,[36] that claim has never been accepted by any court and was specifically rejected in *Garza v. County of Los Angeles* at both the trial and the appellate level. As the Ninth Circuit majority opinion said with respect to this issue, basing districts on voting population rather than total population would "abridge the rights of aliens and minors to petition that representative. For over a century, the Supreme Court has recognized that aliens are 'persons' within the meaning of the 14th Amendment to the Constitution, entitled to equal protection. This equal protection right serves to allow political participation short of voting or holding a sensitive public office."[37] Moreover, virtually all jurisdictions at all levels of government use total population as the basis of reapportionment. If only citizens were to be counted for apportionment purposes, then the representation of Hispanics (and also Asians) would be dramatically diminished. The likely net consequences would be reduced Democratic representation.

What To Do About the Census Undercount?

Experts generally agree that the census is not perfectly accurate and that it tends to somewhat understate the total U.S. population. Moreover, there is little dispute that census errors are not evenly distributed. For example, on balance, the undercount is greater for minorities such as Hispanics, Asians, and blacks concentrated in urban areas of high poverty than it is for non-Hispanic whites. After both the 1980 and the 1990 census, there were numerous suits filed on behalf of various states and political subdivisions challenging the accuracy of census figures. The most important census-related case so far in the 1990s has been *Ridge v. Verity*.[38] As part of an out-of-court settlement of that case, the

Census Bureau agreed to convene a panel of experts to consider the question of whether statistical adjustment of the census to correct for undercount,[39] by making use of information about the magnitude of undercount among different population subsamples obtained from a Post-Enumeration Population Survey, was desirable.[40] This panel reported a positive recommendation for adjustment. However, Robert A. Mossbacher, U.S. Secretary of Commerce, while noting that "there are strong equity arguments both for and against adjustment," concluded that the evidence in support of an adjustment was "inconclusive and unconvincing,"[41] and opted against adjustment. That decision appears (as of October 1991) unlikely to be reversed by Congress.

Unfortunately, while the Secretary of Commerce has rejected adjustment, the bureau's advisory panel has indicated a preferred model for statistical adjustment, and the application of that model to the actual census data can, in principle, be duplicated by other experts. I foresaw a litigation nightmare when I wrote about the possibility of undercount adjustment in 1990.[42] What's happened so far is that some jurisdictions, where the claim can be made that adjustment improves accuracy, have been suing to demand that what will be referred to as "bureau-sanctioned" adjustments be done or at least that the adjusted data be made available to them to review. While district courts have required the census to release the adjustment data, the Supreme Court has vacated these writs.

Racial Vote Dilution

Definition and Measurement of Racial Bloc Voting

As noted above, the *Gingles* three-pronged test for vote dilution requires plaintiffs to establish that voting is polarized along racial lines, and cases even earlier than *Gingles,* such as *U.S. v. Marengo,*[43] had already made racial-bloc-voting analysis a "keystone" of any dilution claim. This has led to a great deal of controversy as to how racial bloc voting is to be defined.

Adapting the Gingles Standard to the Single-Member-District Context

Because *Gingles* dealt exclusively with vote dilution that occurred as a result of minority submergence in a multimember district system, there are questions not resolved by *Gingles* having to do with how to judge vote dilution in the context of single-member districts. If there are already single-member districts in place, some of these districts may be configured in a fashion that makes minority success likely, but there may also be concentration or dispersal of minority population so as to dilute minority voting strength. How do we judge whether a single-member-district plan that is being challenged (or one that is being proposed as a remedy) provides minorities an equal opportunity to participate in the political process and elect candidates of choice and thus satisfies the Voting Rights Act?

Relatively few cases involving racial gerrymandering claims in a single-member-district plan have been decided and only a handful of these have been appealed all the way to the Supreme Court; as yet (October 1991) none have generated other than a denial of certiorari or a per curiam decision by the Supreme Court. Lower courts have differed in their approaches to single-member-district challenges, with some relying on the three-pronged *Gingles* test with only minimal modification (e.g., looking at whether an alternative plan exists that would provide at least one *additional* district in which the minority group would be a majority), and others looking to some variant of a "totality of circumstances" test. I have recently written at length on how to adapt *Gingles* to the single-member-district context.[44] In that essay, my co-authors and I assert:

> In the context of providing a full and effective remedy for vote dilution . . . , we begin with a district-specific analysis. In the liability phase we wish to know whether the group has a realistic potential to elect one or more (additional) candidates of choice (over the course of a decade) under an alternative plan, and we may take a 50 percent voting age share district as presumptive evidence (albeit not the only possible evidence) of such a potential. In contrast, in the remedy phase, we are concerned with whether the plan provides minorities an equal opportunity to elect candidates of choice. But before we can define "equal" opportunity in a plan, which requires us to compare both across groups and across districts, we must understand what it means to talk about a *given* group having a realistic opportunity to elect a candidate of its choice in a *given* district. Only after we have conducted a district-specific analysis are we then in a position to begin evaluating the overall fairness of a plan, i.e., whether or not it provides minorities an "equal opportunity to participate in the political process and to elect candidates of choice."
>
> In conducting our analyses [at the remedy phase] we must be attentive both (a) to differential levels of minority and non-minority eligibility, registration, and turnout, and, perhaps even more importantly, (b) to a realistic appraisal of the totality of local political circumstances, such as campaign finance, incumbency advantage, level of white crossover, etc.[45]

Because of space constraints and because I have recently reviewed the subject thoroughly elsewhere, I refer the reader to that work for a more detailed discussion of questions such as how to measure realistic potential to elect candidates of choice.[46]

Partisan Gerrymandering

I now turn to a discussion of the concept of political gerrymandering. One question is whether gerrymandering must be intended. In the racial context, because of the language in the 1982 amendments to section 2 of the Voting Rights Act, as noted above, the answer is no; although for there to be a constitutional violation, intent must still be proved. In the partisan context, where constitutional rather than statutory interpretation is at the basis of the court's judgment, *Davis v. Bandemer* requires that gerrymandering be shown to be intentional. But what is a gerrymander? A key distinction is between definitions that focus on geographic characteristics of plans such as ill-compactness, and those that focus on a plan's actual or expected political/racial consequences.

One approach to defining a gerrymander relies solely on visual inspection, perhaps aided by some type of numerical analysis of compactness. Other approaches derive from different ways to operationalize the political consequences that the second type of definition of gerrymandering requires us to look at. One such approach uses statewide elections as a measure of partisan predispositions and then looks at the extent to which partisan voting strength has been packed (i.e., concentrated) or cracked (i.e., fragmented); another looks at what has been called *seats-votes relationships*[47] and then judges whether or not there is partisan *bias* (i.e., asymmetry in the way the voting strength of each party can be expected to translate into seat share in the legislature [see below]); yet another approach focuses on the extent to which there is a difference in the way that incumbents of each party have been treated in a given plan. These latter three approaches need not be mutually exclusive. Indeed, some scholars (e.g., Gordon Baker) advocate combining a variety of types of political analysis with "visual" analyses, giving rise to a fifth approach that is conceptually very similar to that of the "totality of circumstances" approach to measuring racial vote dilution.

Basically there are three lines of attack or counterattack with respect to claims of political gerrymandering. The first line of rebuttal to a partisan gerrymandering claim is to say: "That's not a gerrymander, that's just politics as usual." The second is to suggest that: "There is no such thing as a partisan gerrymander because there is no such thing as partisan identification in today's world of split-ticket voting." The third line of argument is to dismiss the evidence (e.g., about bias in seats-votes relationships) by saying that: "That's not proof, it's just statistics." With respect to the first point, my view is that courts should confine themselves to only the most egregious types of partisan gerrymanders. With respect to the second point, while who wins and who loses a particular election may vary and the margin of victory or defeat may vary, the *relative* levels of party support are remarkably consistent, i.e., there are certain precincts (certain areas of the state) where candidates of a given party do well and other areas where those same candidates do less well. Thus, I see no reasons to doubt that the probable partisan consequences of alternative districting schemes can be known with some degree of reliability, at least in the short run. Even over the course of a decade, especially if there are few competitive seats, which party can be expected to control a given branch of the legislature can often be anticipated. With respect to the third line of attack on claims of partisan gerrymandering, my own view, quite simply, is that the most powerful statistical test for partisan gerrymandering is (as it is in so many other areas) the interocular test, i.e., "Does the evidence for gerrymandering leap up and hit you between the eyeballs?" While the case law remains unclear (see below), I think it very unlikely that any plan that passes this interocular test will be overturned by the courts as an unconstitutional partisan gerrymander.[48]

Political Gerrymandering as the "Wild Card" of the 1990s Redistricting Game

The case law on partisan gerrymandering can best be described as opaque. No plan has yet been struck down as an unconstitutional gerrymander even though *Bandemer* now makes partisan gerrymandering justifiable. *Bandemer* upheld Indiana legislative plans that were pointed to by some scholars (but not by me)[49] as among the worst instances of 1990s gerrymandering. The first court decision subsequent to *Bandemer*, the challenge to California's congressional plan, *Badham v. Eu*, upheld what many (myself included) believed to be *the* most egregious gerrymander of the decade, and did so without even requiring a trial on the merits. The appeal of that three-judge panel's dismissal of the case for want of a substantial federal question was denied certiorari by the Supreme Court. In the second post-*Bandemer* case, *Republican Party of Virginia v. Wilder*,[50] the district court denied a motion for preliminary injunction against a plan that paired 14 Republicans and no (nonretiring) Democrats.[51] That decision rested in part on the grounds that paired incumbents could run in other districts or run for other office—and by the time the case was filed, many already had.

I believe you can make sense of the Supreme Court's decision in *Bandemer*, but as far as I am aware I am one of only two people who believe that *Bandemer* makes sense.[52] Moreover, the other person, Daniel Lowenstein, has a diametrically opposed view as to *what* the plurality opinion means.[53] I do not believe you can make sense of the Supreme Court's refusal to consider the appeal of *Badham v. Eu*, especially the fact that Justice White did not vote to grant certiorari. I find the majority opinion in *Badham* totally unsatisfactory as to its standard for when gerrymandering is unconstitutional, since it seems to imply that successes of a party's candidates for statewide office rule out any challenge to a redistricting plan for Congress or a branch of the state legislature. By that line of reasoning, Douglas Wilder's election to the Virginia governorship would immunize the legislative plans in the state of Virginia from constitutional challenge as racial gerrymanders.[54] I also find the district court opinion in *Republican Party of Virginia v. Wilder* to be poorly reasoned. By its standards, the fact that an incumbent who had been paired chose to move or chose to run for other offices would vitiate any claim that incumbent pairing had had partisan consequences.

What is going to happen in the 1990s in the U.S. with respect to political gerrymandering is anybody's guess. Unfortunately, so far it appears that *Bandemer* has no teeth.[55]

The U.S. and Canada

I conclude my essay with a look at the relevance of U.S. redistricting practices and constitutional jurisprudence to the Canadian debate over one person–one vote.

In the debate over representation in the United States, the pendulum swung away from geographically based representation and toward voter interchangeability in the 1960s, with *Baker v. Carr* and subsequent cases. However, on the one hand, it did not swing nearly as far toward perfect equality across districts as some Canadian jurists seem to believe and, on the other hand, the swing away from previous practices was much greater than Canadian jurists seem to recognize. I argue that Canadian judges who've written about U.S. redistricting experience and constitutional history, like most scholars in the U.S.: (a) take too seriously the views of the Supreme Court majorities in *Baker* and subsequent cases as to what the U.S. theory and practice of representation had actually been, and in so doing construe constitutional provisions such as Article I and the 14th Amendment in ways that have virtually no historical justification; (b) neglect the role of apportionment in constraining the population equality of congressional districts *across* states by looking at population equality only in terms of the equality among the congressional districts in a single state; (c) frequently conflate the very different standards of equal population applied to congressional as opposed to state and local redistricting in the U.S.; (d) are victims of the mistaken belief that, representation by population is, like being pregnant, something you either have or do not have, rather than a principle whose implementation ranges along a continuum with no obvious "bright lines"; and (e) appear to write in ignorance of the relevant U.S. case law on vote dilution and on partisan gerrymandering that makes a mockery of the claim that U.S. jurisprudence is fixated with one person–one vote to the exclusion of group-based concerns.

Turning to the first of these points, neither Supreme Court judges (nor their clerks) make very good historians, especially when they have incentives to read the record selectively to support a statutory or constitutional interpretation. For example, while the record certainly sustains the claim that the House is intended to be the seat of the popular principle, that does not mean that all (or even any) of the Founding Fathers advocated the standards of strict numerical population equality that the Court now regards as constitutionally compelled by Article I. Indeed, if we look at congressional redistricting in 1792 we find that, if we exclude the 6 states of the 16 that achieved equipopulous districting by the simple expedient of electing all members of Congress at large, while the ratio of largest to smallest district was 1.06 in Vermont, 1.07 in Kentucky, and 1.19 in Maryland, it was 1.33 in Virginia, 1.42 in New Hampshire, 1.46 in Pennsylvania, 1.68 in Massachusetts, 1.76 in North Carolina, 1.78 in South Carolina, and a whopping 2.71 in New York. In New York the total deviation was 88.2%! If this is population equality as close as practicable, somebody is confused. Similarly, if we look at equality among the congressional districts within each state in, say, 1872–a time when, presumably, it was as clear what the 14th Amendment was intended to achieve as one might hope, given that its proponents and opponents were all alive and active–we again find a striking range of variation in congressional district sizes within a given state.

In like manner, if the 14th Amendment forbids that state legislative districts should be apportioned on any basis other than population, it took over 80 years after its passage before anybody noticed that fact. Even today, some 25 state constitutions still have provisions in them for some form of nonpopulation-based districting—provisions which are, of course, null and void insofar as they conflict with the Supreme Court's interpretation of what the 14th Amendment commands. Prior to *Reynolds v. Sims,* numerous states violated "rep by pop" in a drastic fashion. For example, the State of California has constitutional provisions capping potential representation from its urban centres which, by the 1960s, had created population discrepancies on the order of magnitude of 140 to 1 between the smallest and the largest legislative district.

Turning to the second point, even if we had perfect equality within the congressional districts of a given state, if we look across the U.S. as a whole we find striking variations in district size that are generated by the apportionment rule that guarantees each state at least one seat regardless of size and the vagaries of the "rounding" process required by the fact that congressional districts cannot overlap state lines. From the 1790s to the 1990s, the ratio of largest congressional district to smallest congressional district has averaged 2.65, with a range from 1.16 in 1810 to 6.77 (no, that's not a misprint) in 1900. The total deviation for the U.S. House of Representatives as a whole has averaged around 70% across the nation's history. The principal culprit was Nevada which was by a considerable margin the smallest state from its admittance in 1870 through 1950, and again won that distinction in 1980. (In 1960 and 1970, Alaska, newly admitted, was the smallest state; in 1990 that honour has fallen to Wyoming.)[56]

Turning to the third point, it is quite striking to me how the opinions in both *Dixon* and *Carter* neglect the very different standards of equal population applied to congressional as opposed to state and local redistricting in the U.S., despite the fact that the Factum submitted by the Province of Saskatchewan informed the *Carter* court about the use of *de minimis* standards in U.S. legislative districting as well as about the fact that U.S. congressional districts were not nearly as equal across states as they were within them. The absence of attention to the U.S. *de minimis* approach is particularly puzzling since it is the state-level one person-one vote standards, based on the 14th Amendment, rather than the standards for Congress, based on Article I of the U.S. Constitution, that would appear to be the most relevant basis of comparison with provincial boundary redistribution in Canada.[57]

With respect to the fourth point, it is useful to distinguish three approaches to application of criteria such as "rep by pop" that can be used to guide legal decision making. For mnemonic purposes I will refer to these approaches as defeasibility, de minimis, and Die Nothing. By *Die Nothing,* I mean the view that the only acceptable plan is one that *optimizes* some given criterion (such as one person-one vote) by creating the plan with the highest (or lowest) value on that criterion. By *defeasibility,* I mean the view that a particular criterion (such as one person-one vote) is the single most important criterion to be applied, but that other criteria can justify deviations from strict adherence to it, or otherwise outweigh it.[58] By a *de minimis* approach, I mean one that says that outcomes on a criterion that are within a certain range are *ipso facto* constitutional unless the plan violates other constitutional or statutory standards.

As I read *Reynolds v. Sims*, it suggested that one person–one vote would be applied as a defeasible standard. However, in subsequent cases such as *Connor v. Finch*, the U.S. Supreme Court opted for a *de minimis* standard for state legislative districting;[59] while in *Kirkpatrick v. Preisler*, it opted for a "Die Nothing" standard for congressional redistricting. My view, quite simply, is that "rep by pop" is not an either-or proposition. How far from zero deviation one can get and still say that concern for one person–one vote is being observed is not a matter admitting of precise resolution on grounds of abstract principle. Rather it must reflect a realistic sense of historical practices, as well as commonsense appreciation of the inherent inaccuracies in census estimates and the fact that those estimates are a "snapshot" of a continually changing world.

Recognition that "rep by pop" is not an either-or principle allows us to save Chief Justice McLachlin from the accusation that she is schizophrenic in deciding *Carter* for the Province of Saskatchewan and *Dixon* against the Province of British Columbia, as well as from the accusation (made by several participants at the Saskatchewan conference) that in *Carter* she has repudiated the principle of "rep by pop." As J. Paul Johnston of the University of Alberta has argued,[60] the case facts are very different in the two jurisdictions. The total deviations in Saskatchewan, with the exception of the two northern districts, are only barely above the +/- 25% standard set down for federal ridings. The population deviations in BC, in contrast, are over twice as great. Thus, it is, I submit, not unreasonable for Chief Justice McLachlin to assert that the guiding principle of her opinion in *Dixon* is that "the *dominant consideration* in drawing electoral boundaries must be *population*,"[61] and to similarly assert that the guiding principle of her opinion in *Carter* is that "*relative or substantial equality* of the number of voters per representative *is essential.*"[62, 63]

Turning to the fifth point, I was dismayed to see the U.S. case law on redistricting standards reviewed by Canadian courts without any mention of the relevant U.S. case law on vote dilution and on partisan gerrymandering—case law that makes a mockery of the claim that U.S. jurisprudence is fixated with one person–one vote to the exclusion of group-based concerns.[64]

More generally, the notion that the United States is a country whose entire history bespeaks a one person–one vote tradition, while Canada is just the opposite, distorts both U.S. and Canadian history. In trying to determine whether either Canada or the U.S. has a tradition of "rep by pop," it matters greatly whether one emphasizes asserted principles or actual practices. If by representation by population we mean the view that districts should be created that are, *literally, identical* in size, that notion has no historical support in American practice and can be thought of as purely an invention of the U.S. Supreme Court in *Kirkpatrick v. Preisler*,[65] which was then reaffirmed in subsequent cases such as *Karcher v. Daggett*.[66] In the earliest period of U.S. history, there was a strong tradition of territorial representation, with an attempt to maintain townships or counties whole, although, as noted previously, some states opted for at-large representation in Congress.[67] Such a territorially based notion of representation persisted in state constitutional provisions for legislative apportionment.

The claim made in *Connor v. Finch* that a 10% total deviation (roughly a +/- 5% standard) is *de minimis* for state legislative districting in the United States has just as much historical support and textual support in the language of the 14th Amendment and the discussions surrounding its passage as the political compromise[68] that resulted in the +/- 25% standard for parliamentary ridings in Canada has in Canada's previous electoral practices and traditions. Both are practical compromises that seek to expediently reconcile the principle of one person–one vote with concern for other factors and with deference to legislative balancing of such concerns. Even now U.S. courts are unwilling to impose nonterritorially defined remedies for minority vote dilution and, absent intentional discrimination, have not yet definitively recognized voting-rights claims of groups not large enough to constitute the majority in a single-member district.[69]

There are, however, two differences between present practices and jurisprudence in the U.S. and Canada to which it is important to call attention. First, with the exceptions of the nine states that have some form of commission for legislative redistricting, the handful of states that refer redistricting to state courts in the event of the failure of the legislature to act in a timely fashion, the few states that assign the governor's office a prominent role, and a handful of other exceptions, the drafting of new legislative boundaries (whether these be congressional, legislative, or local) is in the hands of the legislature (or county board or city council) itself. In contrast, in recent years, Canada, at least at the federal level and increasingly at the provincial level, has opted for boundary commissions along the British model.[70] Second, Canadian case law permits a constitutional violation to be found without a determination that there has been intentional discrimination; arguably, U.S. case law does not, although the Supreme Court has held that Congress has statutory power to remedy discrimination under the 14th Amendment by passing legislation that relies on an effects test, and Congress has done so with respect to voting rights.[71]

Where Canadian boundary-distribution case law can be expected to proceed post-*Carter* is an intriguing question. With respect to one person–one vote issues, U.S. precedents do not have a clear answer. While hindsight might suggest that the eventual replacement of the vague guidelines in *Reynolds v. Sims* with more precise numerical standards was inevitable, and thus would likewise suggest that the comparably vague standards in the majority opinion in *Carter* will eventually be replaced by something like a +/- 25% *de minimis* approach, U.S. scholars at the time of *Reynolds* simply did not anticipate how far the Supreme Court would eventually carry the one person–one vote doctrine, nor did they anticipate the evolution of the Supreme Court's double standard with respect to population equality at the state or local as opposed to at the congressional level. Given what I see as the relative arbitrariness of the U.S. Supreme Court's enunciation of constitutional standards for one person-one vote, I would be chary of predicting how Canada's courts will eventually come out with respect to this issue, although it does appear clear that they will not be as insanely insistent on absolute population equality as the U.S. Supreme Court has been with respect to congressional districting.[72] I can expect, however, that Canadian courts will eventually be forced to resolve the discrepancy between apportionments based on voters and those based on population suggested by the language in *Carter* that refers at some points to representation by population and at other points to representation of voters, in the same way that such issues have been confronted by U.S. courts in cases such as *Garza*.[73] I am also quite confident in predicting that Canada can look forward to a wave of future challenges to boundary distributions on the grounds that they discriminate against particular racial, linguistic, or political groups.[74, 75] Moreover, it is likely that these challenges will take place at the local as well as at the federal or provincial level. Because such vote-dilution challenges require much more intensive use of social science evidence than one person-one vote cases, Canadian political scientists can look forward to having their day in court.[76]

Notes

* An earlier version of this paper was presented at the "Drawing Boundaries" Conference, University of Saskatchewan, 8–9 November 1991. Portions of this paper were presented at the continuing education workshop on "Voting Rights and Reapportionment" organized by the Stetson University College of Law and the Tulane University Law School, Clearwater Beach, Florida, April 1991. That conference paper is forthcoming in the *Stetson University Law Review* under the title "Continuing and Emerging Controversies in Voting Rights Case Law: From One Person, One Vote to Political Gerrymandering." This research was partially supported by National Science Foundation Grant SES # 88-09392, Program in Law and Social Sciences (joint with Chandler Davidson) and by a grant from the Ford Foundation to study 1990s redistricting. I am indebted to Ziggy Bates and the staff of the Word Processing Center, School of Social Sciences, UCI, for manuscript typing and to Dorothy Gormick for bibliographic assistance. The discussion is an abbreviated one that draws in part on my previously published work. That work should be consulted for a complete and fully nuanced portrait of my views.

1. Chandler Davidson, *Minority Vote Dilution* (Washington, DC: Howard University Press, 1984), 4. Similarly, Richard Engstrom, "Racial Vote Dilution: The Concept and the Court" in Lorn F. Foster, ed., *The Voting Rights Act: Consequences and Implications* (New York: Praeger, 1985), defines vote dilution as "the practice of limiting the ability of blacks [or other minorities] to convert their voting strength into the control of or at least influence with elected public officials."

2. In the United States, the seminal case for the latter type of dilution is *Bandemer v.*

Davis, 603 F. Supp. 1479 (S.D. Indiana, 1984); 478 U.S. l09 (1986). I was the sole expert witness for the State of Indiana in that case.

3. *Baker v. Carr,* 369 U.S. 186 (1962).

4. *Reynolds v. Sims,* 377 U.S. 533 (1964).

5. Ibid., 579.

6. The total deviation (which has a variety of other names in the literature, see Andrea J. Wollock, ed., *Reapportionment; Law and Technology* [Denver: National Conference of State Legislatures, June 1980]) can be defined as the sum of the absolute value of the difference between the largest district and ideal district size and the absolute value of the difference between the smallest district and ideal district size, as normalized by (i.e., divided by) ideal district size.

7. See e.g., *Kirkpatrick v. Preisler,* 394 U.S. 526 (1969); *Karcher v. Daggett,* I 462 U.S. 725 (1983); II 466 U.S. 910 (1984).

8. One person–one vote districting standards at the local level are essentially the same as those applied to state legislative redistricting. See e.g., *Abate v. Mundt,* 403 U.S. 182 (1971).

9. See e.g., *Connor v. Finch,* 431 U.S. 407 (1977).

10. The Supreme Court accepted a total deviation of 16.4% in *Mahan v. Howell,* 410 U.S. 315; a total deviation of 16.5% for the Mississippi Senate and 19.3% for the Mississippi House was rejected in *Connor.* While the Supreme Court accepted a total deviation in excess of 80% in *Brown v. Thomson,* 536 F. Supp. 780 (D. Wyo. 1982) aff'd 103 S Ct. 2690; 462 U.S. 835 (1983), there are very special circumstances in that case that render it of little precedential value. First, the excessive deviation appeared to rest solely on the unequal treatment of one small county; second, Wyoming could argue that its state legislators had been given a unique role in the affairs of counties contained in their districts; third, it is arguable that the jurisdictional statement was so narrowly focused that the Supreme Court never actually reviewed the constitutionality of the entire plan. While federal courts have focused on the total deviation,which is a range, they have sometimes also paid attention to the average deviation as well. See my discussion in "Criteria for Districting: A Social Science Perspective," *UCLA Law Review* 33/1 (October 1985): 77–184.

11. See e.g., *Flateau v. Anderson,* 537 F. Supp. 257 (S. D. New York, 1982).

12. In particular, the strict standard of population equality across congressional districts insisted on by the Supreme Court considerably exceeds the limits of census accuracy and thus makes little sense from a statistical standpoint. (Grofman, "Criteria for Districting" [see n.10].)

13. Presumably that initial motivation was to assure "fair and effective representation." See Bernard Grofman, *Voting Rights, Voting Wrongs: The Legacy of Baker v. Carr,* "A Report of the Twentieth Century Fund" (New York: Priority Press [distributed through the Brookings Institution] 1991), 11. It is hard for me to believe that there would have been the same concern with lack of strict population equality if that inequality was randomized rather than giving rise to a predictable political "bias" in favour of certain groups within the society, e.g., rural interests and white voters. Moreover, while districts that are (within reason) equipopulous may be *necessary* to achieve fair representation, it is quite clear that equipopulous districts are not *sufficient* to assure either the fairness or the effectiveness of representation. The Supreme Court has failed to develop a general theory of equal protection with

respect to representation that would subsume decisions in areas such as one person–one vote, racial vote dilution, and partisan gerrymandering. Academics, however, have not been much better in this regard. See, however, Jonathan Still, "Political Equality and the Election System," *Ethics* 91/3 (April 1981): 375–95; Bernard Grofman, "Fair and Equal Representation," *Ethics* 91/3 (April 1981): 477–85; Charles R. Beitz, "Equal Opportunity in Political Representation," in Norman E. Bowie, ed., *Equal Opportunity* (Boulder: Westview Press, 1988), 155–76; Nancy Maveety, *Representation Rights and the Burger Years* (Michigan: University of Michigan Press, 1991); Bernard Grofman and Howard Scarrow, "The Riddle of Apportionment: Equality of What?" *National Civic Review* 70/5 (May 1981): 242–54; Bernard Grofman, "Toward a Coherent Theory of Gerrymandering: *Thornburg* and *Bandemer*," in B. Grofman, ed., *Political Gerrymandering and the Courts* (New York: Agathon Press, 1990): 29–63.

14. For example, former Attorney General Nicholas Katzenbach only advocated that total deviations of greater than 30% be forbidden. Also see discussion in Twentieth Century Fund, *One Man, One Vote* (New York: the Twentieth Century Fund, 1962).

15. *City of Mobile v. Bolden*, 466 U.S. 55 (1980).

16. Of course, strictly speaking, *City of Mobile* set the standards for vote dilution for cases brought directly under the 14th (or 15th) Amendment while section 2 of the Voting Rights Act only specified a statutory standard. In practice, since section 2 was enacted in 1982, most plaintiffs bring their voting-rights challenges under the section 2 provisions, and even if constitutional questions are also raised, courts decide the case on statutory grounds without needing to consider the more-diffi-cult-to-prove constitutional standard. Moreover, in *Rogers v. Lodge*, 458 U.S. 613 (1982) the Supreme Court backed away from its seeming insistence in *City of Mobile* that the only way to establish intent was by direct evidence that discrimination was purposeful. In *Rogers*, the Court accepted a variety of types of circumstantial evidence (including evidence of foreseeable effects) as proof of purpose. For a more detailed discussion, see Laughlin McDonald, "The Effects of the 1982 Amendments of Section 2 of the Voting Rights Act on Minority Representation," in B. Grofman and C. Davidson, eds., *Controversies in Minority Voting* (Washington, DC: The Brookings Institution, 1992 forthcoming).

17. *White v. Regester*, 412 U.S. 755.

18. See especially *Zimmer v. McKeithen*, 485 F. 2d 1297 (5th Cir 1973) (en banc) aff'd on other grounds *sub nom East Carroll Parrish School Board v. Marshall*, 424 U.S. 636 (1976).

19. The act had previously been renewed in 1970 and 1975. In 1975 persons of Asian ancestry, American Indians, and persons of Spanish heritage were added as groups specially protected by the act—whose coverage previously had extended only to blacks.

20. *Report of the U.S. Senate Committee on the Judiciary on S. 1992*, 1981.

21. I testified on behalf of the black plaintiffs in that case.

22. See more detailed discussion in Bernard Grofman, Michael Migalski, and Nicholas Noviello, "The 'Totality of Circumstances Test' in Section 2 of the 1982 Extension of the Voting Rights Act: A Social Science Perspective," *Law and Policy*, 7/2 (April 1985): 209–23.

23. See below for discussion of vote-dilution standards in racial and political gerrymandering challenges to single-member-district plans.

24. See detailed discussion in Lisa Handley, "The Quest for Voting Rights: The Evolution of a Vote Dilution Standard and Its Impact on Minority Reporting," Ph.D. dissertation, George Washington University, 1991. Also see Bernard Grofman, and Lisa Handley, "Identifying and Remedying Racial Gerrymandering," *Journal of Law and Politics*, 1992 forthcoming.
25. For a detailed discussion of all appellate cases since *Gingles* involving section 2 issues, see references cited above.
26. We might also note that, in the United States, judges at various levels are elected officials. In 1991, in a case consolidating challenges to judicial elections in Texas and Louisiana, the U.S. Supreme Court affirmed that the *Gingles* vote-dilution test applied to judges who were elected at large. That case is the only section 2 litigation since Gingles that has led to a written Supreme Court opinion.
27. Analysis of data from the seven southern states originally covered by section 5 of the Voting Rights Act suggests that minorities prevail in over 90% of the cases that are brought. See Chandler Davidson, and Bernard Grofman, *Voting Rights in the South* (title tentative), 1992 forthcoming.
28. Case facts permitting, of course.
29. See Grofman and Handley, "Identifying and Remedying Racial Gerrymandering," (see n.24).
30. *Bandemer v. Davis*, 603 F. Supp. 1479 (1984), S.D. Indiana.
31. *Badham v. Eu* (N.D. California, No. C-83-1126, dismissed 21 April 1988).
32. See Editor's Introduction in Bernard Grofman, ed., *Political Gerrymandering and the Courts* (New York: Agathon Press, 1990).
33. *Federation for American Immigration Reform (FAIR) et al. v. Philip M. Klutznick*, 486 F. Supp. 564 (1980).
34. See, however, my discussion of this point in *Voting Rights, Voting Wrongs* (see n.13).
35. Precedent in the Supreme Court is quite clear that, for state and local redistrictings, the decision to apportion on the basis of population or citizen population is a discretionary one. "The decision to include or exclude [aliens or other nonvoters] from the apportionment base involves choices about the nature of representation with which we have been shown no constitutionally founded reason to interfere" [*Burns v. Richardson*, 348 U.S. 73 at 91 (1966)]. Nonetheless, were a jurisdiction to shift to apportioning on the basis of citizen population or citizen voting-age population rather than total population, it would seem to me to invite a lawsuit under the 14th Amendment, especially if there were the possibility that a claim could be made that the shift had taken place in order to reduce expected minority representation.
36. William A.V. Clark, and Peter A. Morrison, "Demographic Paradoxes in the Los Angeles Voting Rights Case," *Evaluation Review* 1991 forthcoming.
37. *Garza v. County of Los Angeles*, 9115 F. 2d. 763 (1990). At p. 8142, internal citations omitted.
38. *Ridge v. Verity*, Civ. No. 88-351 (W.D. Pennsylvania 1991).
39. The issue is far more complex than a simple choice of whether to adjust or not. Indeed, certain types of statistical adjustment already take place, e.g., imputation of missing values on incompletely filled-in census forms. Arguably, however, the extant nature of adjustment is qualitatively far different than what would be contemplated if PES data were used in the fashion contemplated by bureau statisticians.
40. The PES is an attempt to go back to selected areas of the country and, by blanketing each area, find out who had been missed.

41. Statement of Secretary of Commerce Robert A. Mosbacher on Adjustment of the 1990 Census, U.S. Department of Commerce Press Release, 15 July 1991.
42. See my discussion of census undercount in *Voting Rights, Voting Wrongs* (see n.13).
43. *U.S. v. Marengo County Commissioners,* 731 F. 2d 1546 (11th Cir. 1984).
44. Grofman and Handley, "Identifying and Remedying Racial Gerrymandering" (see n. 24).
45. Ibid.
46. Ibid.
47. See e.g., Edward R. Tufte, "The Relationship Between Seats and Votes in Two-Party Systems," *American Political Science Review* 67 (1973): 540–47; Graham Gudgin, and Peter Taylor, *Seats, Votes and the Spatial Organization of Elections* (London: Piori, 1979); Rein Taagepera, and Matthew Shugart, *Seats and Votes: The Effects of Determinants on Electoral Systems* (New Haven: Yale University Press, 1989).
48. For a more elaborated discussion of these three points see Bernard Grofman, "Continuing and Emerging Controversies in Voting Rights Case Law: From One Person, One Vote to Political Gerrymandering," *Stetson Law Review,* 1992 forthcoming. My own most important early work on redistricting ("Criteria for Districting" [see n.10]) is found in an October 1985 issue of the *UCLA Law Review* largely devoted to a symposium on political gerrymandering. The issue contains essays that I would call to the reader's attention by Bruce Cain, Richard Niemi, Daniel Lowenstein, and a number of other specialists. This set of essays is an excellent introduction to political gerrymandering issues as they were viewed by social scientists and lawyers just before the Supreme Court issued its decision in *Davis v. Bandemer.* Because partisan gerrymandering questions remain so open, much of what was said in 1985 remains relevant today. Another mini-symposium on political gerrymandering of continuing relevance is that on *Badham v. Eu* in the Summer 1985 issue of *PS.* It contains essays by Bruce Cain, myself, and others. Of course every reader interested in political gerrymandering should consult my edited book, *Political Gerrymandering and the Courts* (see n.13). That volume contains essays by most of the leading authorities on political gerrymandering, representing the complete spectrum of views on the topic. It is intended to be a comprehensive and self-contained source book of readings on political gerrymandering.
49. See my expert witness testimony in the case on behalf of the State of Indiana in *Bandemer.*
50. *Republican Party of Virginia v. Wilder,* Civ. No. 91-0424-R (W.D. Va., 1991).
51. The 1991 plan for the lower house of the Virginia legislature paired over a third of all 1990 Republican incumbents with other Republican incumbents.
52. In particular, I believe that it imposes a test that partisan gerrymandering be intentional, severe, and predictably long lasting before it can be held to be unconstitutional. See Bernard Grofman, "Toward A Coherent Theory" (see n.13).
53. See Daniel Hays Lowenstein, "*Bandemer's* Gap: Gerrymandering and Equal Protection," in Grofman, *Political Gerrymandering and the Courts* (see n.13).
54. In fairness, of course, the *Bandemer* Court did distinguish between the appropriate standard in a racial claim and that in a partisan suit, with the latter having to meet a higher threshold.
55. This view has been most forcefully enunciated by UCLA Law Professor Daniel Lowenstein. See especially his essay in Grofman, *Political Gerrymandering and the Courts,* (see n.13).
56. This point was called to the Court's attention in the Factum submitted by the

Attorney General of Saskatchewan in *Carter*. I am indebted to Crown Solicitor John Thomson Irvine for providing me a copy of the factums submitted by Saskatchewan to the Court of Appeal and the Supreme Court of Canada in the Saskatchewan boundaries case.

57. As an outsider, I am struck by the general insistence among Canadians to distinguish their customs and practices from those in the U.S. This insistence may have led to a kind of cognitive distortion of U.S. case law by the jurists that emphasized its most extreme one person-one vote aspects. Alternatively, the jurists may not have been sensitive to the view that "rep by pop" could be thought of as a principle subject to "more or less" rather than as an absolute zero population deviation standard (see below).

58. At issue, still, would be whether the burden of proof would be on defendants to justify exceptions as necessary, or whether the burden would be on plaintiffs to show that such deviations were unreasonable. See Lawrence Tribe, *American Constitutional Law*, 2d ed. (Mineola: Foundation Press, 1988) for an excellent discussion of related issues in U.S. "equal protection" case law.

59. In some of the early one person-one vote cases in the United States, federal courts asserted that acceptability in a given instance of some given population tolerance could not be used in a talismanic fashion to validate any discrepancies below that range in other jurisdictions—rather, legislatures would have to *justify* deviations in terms of legitimate state purposes. However, in *Connor*, the principle of a *de minimis* standard seems rather clearly set forth.

60. Personal communication, November 1991.

61. *Dixon*, Slip opinion at p. 30, emphasis added.

62. *Carter*, Slip opinion at p. 22, emphasis added.

63. We may think of this approach, with its emphasis on relative equality within the primacy of "rep by pop" as Justice McLachlin's *Carter-Dixon* line—one that she claims separates Canada from its southern neighbour.

64. The developments in U.S. case law that I refer to having to do with racial and partisan vote dilution are, of course, relatively recent ones—some in place only since 1986; most post-1973 (see discussion earlier in my paper). There appears to be a certain time warp aspect to the discussions of U.S. case law in *Dixon* and *Carter*, as if Canadian judges learning about U.S. constitutional and statutory jurisprudence stopped about 20 years ago—perhaps when they were in law school taking courses in comparative law. In fairness, however, these recent developments are also little known and little understood in the U.S., and it takes a peculiar kind of U.S. parochialism to critique judicial decisions in another country for a failure to grasp the nuances of U.S. jurisprudence.

65. 89 S. Ct. 1225, 394 U.S. 526 (1969).

66. 103 S. Ct. 2653, 462 U.S. 725 (1983). Of course, now congressional plans do strive for almost perfect population equality. For example, the congressional plans (peculiarly, there were more than one) passed by the California legislature in 1991 had a total deviation of +/- five—*five persons, that is!*

67. See Rosemarie Zagarri, *The Politics of Size: Representation in the United States, 1776-1850* (New York: Cornell University Press, 1987).

68. In commentary remarks at the Saskatchewan conference, this is how John Courtney characterized the statutory provision of the +/- 25% standard.

69. A potential exception is a recent federal district court ruling, *Armour v. Ohio*, that

seems to permit an "influence" claim by a group not large enough to constitute the majority in a single district. However, this is both a confusing decision and one that seems certain to be appealed to the U.S. Supreme Court. See discussion of this case in Grofman and Handley, "Identifying and Remedying Racial Gerrymandering" (see n. 24).

70. It is at least conceivable that the composition of these commissions, themselves, may come under challenge. In the U.S., one commission was actually challenged for being too representative. In New York City, there was a challenge to the New York City Districting Commission on the grounds that the requirements for representation of minorities among its members set down in the statute that created it violated the ostensibly colour-blind standards of the U.S. Constitution. However, that statute had been precleared by the United States Department of Justice under section 5 of the Voting Rights Act.

71. The requirement that discrimination under the 14th Amendment's equal protection clause must be intentional to be unlawful, at least for a constitutional violation, is a controversial proposition. For example, the Supreme Court did not initially assert this doctrine when it first ruled on school desegregation, although it did so in subsequent cases. Similarly, it is quite controversial whether the earliest vote-dilution cases contained a requirement that discrimination be shown to be intentional, although recent cases such as *Mobile v. Bolden*, 446 U.S. 55 (1980) and *Rogers v. Lodge*, 458 U.S. 613 (1982) claim that they did. Moreover, at no time have the one person–one vote cases been held to require proof of intentional discrimination. Yet, at least for legislative and local cases, they too are decided under the 14th Amendment. For vote-dilution cases, the intent test is largely irrelevant in that the 1982 Amendments to the section of the Voting Rights Act of 1965 specified that a statutory violation required only evidence of dilutive effect given the "totality of the circumstances." As noted above, this statute was given its definitive interpretation by the U.S. Supreme Court in *Thornburg v. Gingles* in 1986.

72. Like many other U.S constitutional scholars, I am sceptical of the legal and historical support for the U.S. Supreme Court's "double standard" for state and congressional districting. Moreover, as one leading scholar, Lawrence Tribe, has put it, regardless of whether there is a justification for distinguishing between state and congressional districting when "considering how far a state may stray from exact equality in pursuit of a legitimate objective, no such rationale supports a distinction concerning the appropriateness or extent of the *de minimis* defense. An appropriately formulated standard of interdistrict equality, allowing minor deviations, could well be applied to both types of cases." Tribe, *American Constitutional Law* (see n.58), 1071, (footnote omitted).

73. Based on my conversations with Canadian political scientists at the Saskatchewan conference, it appears that one difference in likely sources of litigation between the U.S. and Canada is that in Canada there is not dissatisfaction with the accuracy of the census count of minorities.

74. Indeed, since it took the U.S. 90 years to go from the 14th Amendment to *Reynolds v. Sims,* but it has taken Canada only 9 years to go from Charter to *Carter,* it might seem plausible to expect Canada to do in 2 years what has taken the U.S. nearly two decades, namely replace concern for one person–one vote issues with concern for issues of minority vote dilution.

75. Whether the majority opinion in *Carter* was written to actively encourage such challenges is a matter about which I am more sceptical.

177

76. This can be a mixed blessing. See A. Wuffle, "Advice to the Expert Witness in Court," *PS* (Winter 1984): 60-61; Bernard Grofman, "The Role of Expert Witness Testimony in the Evolution of Voting Rights Case Law," in Bernard Grofman and Chandler Davidson eds., *Controversies in Minority Voting* (see n.16); Bernard Grofman, "A Critique of Freedman et al. and Clark and Morrison," *Evaluation Review* (1991 forthcoming); Bernard Grofman, "Multivariate Methods and the Analysis of Racially Polarized Voting: Pitfalls in the use of Social Science by the Courts," *Social Science Quarterly* (1991 forthcoming); Bernard Grofman, "Straw Men and Stray Bullets, A Reply to Bullock," *Social Science Quarterly* 72/4 (December 1991), 838-43.

"One Man–One Vote":
Tracing Its Roots and Consequences

HOWARD A. SCARROW

STATE UNIVERSITY OF NEW YORK AT STONY BROOK

Next year will mark the 30th anniversary of the Supreme Court's historic decision in the case of *Baker v. Carr*. Also, the United States is now beginning the fourth round of congressional and state legislative reapportionments that have been affected by the *Baker* decision and the decisions that stemmed from it, most notably *Wesberry v. Sanders* and *Reynolds v. Sims*, both delivered in 1964. It seems an appropriate time, therefore, to reflect on these early Court pronouncements and their consequences.

The Demand for Equal Population Districts

To begin the analysis, it is useful to recall the nature of the grievances that resulted in the *Baker*, *Wesberry*, and *Reynolds* decisions. The grievances in these cases were stated in terms of the overrepresentation of rural areas to the detriment of representation of urban and suburban areas. Thus the initial *Baker* decision addressed the underrepresentation of Nashville and other urban centres in Tennessee, while Chief Justice Warren's memorable assertion in *Reynolds* that "Legislators represent people, not trees or acres"[1] cleverly captured the subject matter of the Court's two seminal decisions in 1964 governing congressional and state legislative apportionment.

Yet Warren's colourful assertion was part of an argument that was based on a much more fundamental dichotomy—the distinction between the representation of "people," on the one hand, and the representation of interests, communities, and political subdivisions, on the other. The crux of Warren's argument was that "neither history alone, nor economic or other sorts of group interests, are permissible factors in attempting to justify disparities from population-based representation. Citizens, not history or economic interests, cast votes."[2] The importance of this focus on "people" became increasingly apparent as the Court came to insist on a very stringent standard of population equality even if, in order to meet that standard, the representation of interests, communities, and political subdivisions, as well as the attainment of other legitimate goals such as compact districts, had to be sacrificed. The Court's insistence on near-perfect "equality of numbers" was illustrated in the Court's 1969 *Kirkpatrick v. Preisler* decision, and even more vividly in the Court's 1983 *Karcher v. Daggett* decision, both decisions mocked by dissenting justices who wondered if the Court might not soon insist that a congressional district line be drawn down the middle of an apartment-house corridor.

In sharp contrast to the standard enforced by the United States Supreme Court, courts in both Canada and Australia have taken a much more tolerant view of population discrepancies, recognizing that representation in a democracy involves more than counting "mere numbers." Although it is doubtful that Americans would accept the wide population differences that are accepted by the courts in these two democracies, many American scholars have echoed the dissenting opinions of Justices Harlan and Stewart in *Reynolds* and companion cases, and have argued that the mathematical exactness required by the Supreme Court detracts from, rather than contributes to, the goal of "fair and effective representation."[3]

Why Equal Population Districts?

Even granting that "people" must be the subject of representation and that equal population districts must be constructed to the exclusion of all other goals, the additional question remains—to what purpose? Exactly *what* will be equalized when equal population districts are in place? One way of answering that question is to focus on elections and voters; what must be equalized is the "value" of the vote cast by individual district voters—the value must not be "debased" or "diluted." The other way is to focus on district residents and on what happens after the election; what must be equalized is representation in the broadest sense.

The difference between the two perspectives was clearly illustrated in Australia in 1974 when voters were asked in a referendum to change the intrastate apportionment base for the federal Parliament from "electors" to "people." The Labor Government which proposed the change—presumably for partisan advantage—argued that "Votes are cast by electors, but they are cast for people, for all the Australian people." Defenders of the status quo, whose views prevailed, argued that "Equal numbers of electors . . . is democratic. Equal numbers of people regardless of whether they are voters is undemocratic."

Borrowing from Madison's usage in *Federalist* 10—and ignoring the polemics of the Australian referendum—we may refer to the voter/election perspective as one that emphasizes the "democratic" theory of representation; and the people/postelection perspective as one that emphasizes the "republican" theory of representation. This paper argues that by choosing the demo-

cratic theory rather than the republican theory the Court encountered consequences and problems which could have been avoided. Before examining the
roots of that choice, and the consequences which stemmed from it, we need first
to describe more fully the republican theory of representation.

The Republican Perspective

As shown by historian Gordon Wood,[4] both the republican and democratic
theories of representation have firm roots in American history. Indeed, the
ratification conflict between the Federalists and the anti-Federalists was in
major part an argument over these two competing viewpoints. Speaking for the
Federalists, Madison argued that a republican form of government is one in
which representatives "refine and enlarge the public views." Although Madison
was critical of gross malapportionment, and while he favoured a liberal
franchise,[5] he stressed that it was a republican government, not a voter-directed
"democracy," that the Framers had constructed. As he noted in *Federalist* 54,
the extent of popular participation would vary widely from state to state.

The American colonists had, of course, rejected the argument that they
were "virtually represented" in the English Parliament. However, as both Wood
and John Ely[6] have argued, that rejection did not stem from the conviction that
persons can be represented only if they are permitted to participate in the
election process. Rather, the colonists' argument was based on the assertion
that they were not part of one, homogeneous English society and polity, and
hence no one in Parliament was capable of representing their interests. This
same "republican" view of representation—that people can be represented even
if they are not given the franchise—was articulated again in 1866 when the 14th
Amendment was adopted with its provision for the representation of "people"
rather than "voters."[7]

In view of the fact that the republican theory of representation may be
inferred from the wording of the 14th Amendment, that the Constitution refers
to the "republican form of government," and that, as Alexander Bickel has
argued,[8] the republican theory has a firm place in the American political
tradition—emphasizing that the legislature is a "relatively independent, deliberate decision-making" institution rather than "an animated voting machine"—the
Supreme Court could easily have chosen to make that perspective the centrepi-
ece of its early apportionment decisions. Had the Court done so, the purpose of
equal population districts would have been stated simply as the equalization of
ratios of representative per person so that each person has an equal "share" of
a legislator's consideration as the legislator performs the role of spokesperson
for constituents, "refiner of views," and provider of services.

The Democratic Perspective

It is possible, of course, to comb through plaintiff briefs and Court apportionment decisions to find passages compatible with the republican perspective.[9]
But those hints pale beside the much more prominent and repeated passages

in the Court's opinions that reflect the "democratic" perspective. Malapportionment is unconstitutional, the Court said repeatedly, because persons living in overpopulous districts have the "value," the "worth," the "weight," the "power," the "effectiveness," and the "strength" of their votes "diluted" or "debased"; their votes are not "counted" equally. Plaintiffs in *Baker* complained that the unequal population districts in Tennessee resulted in the "debasement of their votes"[10] and Solicitor General Cox's brief in this case similarly equated Tennessee's districting with "giving one twenty-fifth of a vote to citizens in the eastern half of the State and one vote to those in the western half."[11] Following that lead, Douglas's concurring opinion in *Baker* defined the question before the Court as being "the extent to which a State may weight one person's vote more heavily than it does another's,"[12] and noted the fact that "a single vote in Moore County . . . is worth 19 votes in Hamilton County . . . "[13] The two leading malapportionment decisions in 1964 continued the same reasoning. In his *Wesberry* decision, Justice Black equated Georgia's unequally populated congressional districts with a statewide election in which "votes of inhabitants of some parts of a State . . . could be weighted at two or three times the value of the votes of people living in more populous parts of the State . . . "[14] Warren's *Reynolds* decision applied similar arithmetic to Alabama's legislative districts, arguing that malapportionment is equivalent to allowing voters in some parts of a state to vote "two, five, or 10 times for their legislative representatives, while voters living elsewhere could vote only once."[15]

Tracing the Roots: Scholars and Advisory Groups

The Court's focus on the rights of voters, rather than the representation of inhabitants or persons, stemmed in part from the fact that the plaintiffs in the early cases were themselves voters, and that they chose as their tactic the claim that their voting rights were being denied under the equal protection clause of the 14th Amendment. Yet the Court's choosing to define equal representation in terms of vote "value," "worth," and so forth can be traced back much further than these early court briefs. Indeed, that formulation may be seen in Justice Black's dissenting opinion in *Colegrove v. Green* in 1946 when he argued that votes cast in overpopulous congressional districts in Illinois were less "effective" and carried less "voting power" than votes cast in less-populous districts.[16]

However, much more conspicuous than Black's dissent were the writings of academic scholars and advisory groups. A report published in 1950 by a committee of scholars appointed by the American Political Science Association recommended that congressional districts be equal in population because unequal districts "seriously violate a basic principle of democracy, that every vote should have the same weight, as nearly as possible."[17] In 1962 an advisory committee appointed by Congress likewise recommended in connection with state legislative elections that "each man's vote must count the same as every other man's vote."[18] A report sponsored by the Twentieth Century Fund and also published in 1962 appears to have been especially influential. Carrying the title *One Man–One Vote,* the report urged that "One man's vote must be worth the same as another's."[19] Also in that same year, scholars Paul David and Ralph Eisenberg published a volume of statistical tables entitled *Devaluation of the Urban and Suburban Vote.*[20] The volume presented data for all states showing that, for example, a vote cast for a state representative in an overly populous district was worth only 50% of what it "should be" if all districts were equal in population, while a vote cast in a sparsely populated district might be worth 200% of what it should be. These percentages, calculated for every state, were given wide circulation when they were published by *Congressional Quarterly Weekly.* Finally, Andrew Hacker's book *Congressional Districting,* published in 1963, followed the same formula, equating equal population districts with equally weighted votes and presenting a table showing for each state the "Value of Votes in Smallest District Compared to One Vote in Largest."[21]

With such seeming unanimity among scholars, public officials, and concerned citizens that equal population districts are justified in terms of equal vote worth, it is hardly surprising that the briefs presented by plaintiffs and by Solicitor General Cox relied on that rationalization, or that Justices Black and Warren did likewise in their seminal 1964 decisions. The problem was that the "vote value" justification had never been clearly defined, and it was subject to various interpretations.

Are equal-size districts desirable because each person's vote will have an equal impact on the outcome of a district election, or perhaps a statewide election? Or are equal population districts desirable because all voters, other things being equal, will then have an equal "share" of a representative's attention and consideration and thus, through that representative, an equal voice in the legislature. By the latter interpretation, terms like "equal value" and "equal worth" are used in a qualitative sense to refer to the potential benefits derived from representation after the election, regardless of the outcome of that election. As such, this latter interpretation of vote worth is very close to what I have labelled here as the republican perspective of representation, differing only in the sense that it speaks of voters rather than of people, or citizens, or constituents.

A strong case can be made that the academic writings and reports referred to above intended this latter, qualitative interpretation of terms like vote "worth," rather that a quantitative reference to the ability of a vote to affect election outcomes. To begin with the APSA Committee report, it is hard to believe that a committee of distinguished scholars would have failed to define vote "weight"—mentioned only once in the report—if the committee intended that term to be interpreted in a narrow quantitative sense. Indeed, one of the members of the committee, Laurence Schmeckebier, had published a book on congressional apportionment in 1941 in which he also used the terms "weight" and "power," but in their qualitative sense. He pointed out that the total number of voters who participated in House elections in Kansas was 20 times the number who participated in Mississippi, even though both states sent a seven-member delegation to the House of Representatives. Thus, the author reasoned, the "power" or the "weight" exerted by each voter in Mississippi was 20 times the power or weight exerted by each voter in Kansas. In other words, for Schmeckebier the unit of analysis was the statewide electorate and the statewide delegation, not the individual voter in each district, and his concern was the unequal voter-representative ratios and the impact of those inequalities on influence exerted in Congress and in the electoral college.[22]

It is also clear that the concept of "vote devaluation" as used in the title of David and Eisenberg's volume was *not* intended to refer to the diminished ability of a vote cast in an urban or suburban district to determine election outcomes. The authors explained in their introduction that their percentage calculations referred to the "relative values of the *right* to vote" in rural and urban areas (emphasis added), a formulation clearly indicating that the authors' argument was that the participation of each voter should be equally meaningful, equally valuable, and equally worthwhile in terms of expected benefits, at least to the extent that equal population districts can contribute to such equality. No mention is made in their comprehensive introduction to election outcomes.

Because of its apparent influence on the Court,[23] the report of the scholars assembled by the Twentieth Century Fund, and published under the title *One Man–One Vote*, merits close scrutiny. When that report asserted that "One man's vote must be worth the same as another's"—an assertion repeated almost verbatim by Justice Black in his *Wesberry* decision two years later—it seems clear that the authors were not making a quantitative statement. Despite its title, the report's message was a simple one—that only "people" should be represented since "acres do not vote; nor do trees"—an eye-catching assertion also repeated almost verbatim two years later, this time by Chief Justice Warren in *Reynolds*. As the following passage makes clear, the phrase "one man–one vote" used in the title was no more than a slogan to refer to equal population districts:

> The history of democratic institutions points compellingly in the direction of population as the only legitimate basis of representation today . . . As transportation and communications are revolutionized, the logic of separate representation for geographic strongholds disappears. The cry of "one man, one vote" heard today in the emerging new lands of Asia and Africa is no more than a reflection of democratic philosophy learned from the West.[24]

In summary, the background literature, despite its vocabulary, was not advancing a theory of fair representation defined in terms of the quantitative weight, power, worth, value, or effectiveness of a vote in determining election outcomes. Rather, the various writings intended to state no more than that districts should be equal in population for the reason similar to the one advanced in a resolution introduced in the Oregon legislature in 1951 calling for equal-population congressional districts: that with some districts containing "nearly twice the population of other districts . . . , each voter inside the larger district ... has only half the voice in Congress of each resident of the smaller districts ... "[25] The goal is representational voice, not electoral power.

Yet, as has been seen, in its 1964 seminal decisions the Court likened voters in overpopulated districts to voters being able to vote more than once, to votes being counted more than once, to votes being weighted to increase their value. Malapportionment "contracts the value of some votes and expands that of others."[26] With statements like these being endlessly repeated, the conclusion seemed inescapable that the Court was saying that the measure of fair apportionment is the equal ability of the individual voter to affect the district election outcome.

The early plaintiffs and authors of court opinions were not the only ones who misinterpreted the scholarly literature. Political scientist Ruth Silva interpreted Schmeckebier's book, referred to earlier, as advancing the theory that all voters should have equal "electoral power in choosing a legislator,"[27] and she testified before a federal court that that theory of vote value was the only theory of fair representation that was accepted by political scientists.[28]

Tracing the Roots: *Gray v. Sanders*

Robert Dixon argued in his celebrated book[29] that the probable explanation for the Court's basing its apportionment decisions on a quantitative-vote-value rationale was the nature of the first major apportionment case that came before it after *Baker v. Carr*, but before *Wesberry* and *Reynolds*. The case, *Gray v. Sanders*, involved not a district election system but rather a statewide at-large system, Georgia's county-unit method for the election of governor and U.S. senator. Like the Presidential Electoral College, under Georgia's unit system each county was allotted a certain number of unit votes, all of which were cast on behalf of the candidate receiving the plurality of popular votes cast in the county. Since the number of unit votes allotted per county did not reflect the size of the respective county populations, plaintiffs in the case argued that a popular vote cast in a sparsely populated county was given more weight in determining the statewide outcome than a vote cast in a more heavily populated county. Agreeing with the plaintiffs, the Court articulated a reasoning that became the hallmark of the Court's later apportionment decisions:

> How then can one person be given twice or ten times the voting power of another person in a *statewide* election merely because he lives in a rural area ...? The conception of political equality from the Declaration of Independence to Lincoln's Gettysburg Address ... can mean only one thing — one person, one vote (emphasis added).[30]

The slogans "one man–one vote," or "one person–one vote," were thus given birth, but now, in contrast to the Twentieth Century Fund report, were being used in a decidedly quantitative sense to refer to the ability of a person's vote to determine an election outcome. Even better was Justice Stewart's formulation in his concurring opinion, "one voter, one vote within a given constituency";[31] in the case at hand, the constituency being the entire state.

To add to the confusion, and even more seriously, the apportionment cases that followed *Gray* did not involve at-large elections in which popular votes were weighted. They concerned district elections in which popular votes were counted equally within each district and which thus met the standard of "one voter, one vote within a given constituency." Yet, ignoring the distinction between at-large and district elections, Justice Black in *Wesberry* and Justice Warren in *Reynolds* cited hypothetical illustrations of weighted votes cast in statewide elections ("two or three times"; "two, five, or 10 times") and applied them to district elections. In doing so they advanced a theory of equal representation which was very different from the one applied in *Gray*, as Justice Stewart argued in his dissent,[32] and even more radically different from the one contained in the scholarly literature from which the terms weights, worth, power, and "one man-one vote" were apparently derived.

Australian and Canadian Comparisons

All this is not to say that the quantitative approach to district vote value is necessarily flawed. Indeed, that theory of representation is precisely the one that Australia has adopted, and which Australians accurately describe as the theory of "one vote-one value." (The term "one man-one vote" is used to mean exactly that—allowing each person to vote only once.[33]) Thus a recent report published by the Commonwealth government carries the title *One Vote, One Value* and defines malapportionment as occurring when "the number of voters *required to elect a member of parliament* varies between electorates" (the Australian term for districts; emphasis added).[34] As shown more fully below, the Australian High Court has likewise explicitly defined equal apportionment in terms of the ability of district voters to affect district election outcomes. The difference between Australia and the United States, then, is that the United States Supreme Court has never explicitly explained its justification for equal population districts in terms of election outcomes; it has never given that theory its proper label—one vote-one value; and, as discussed below, it has not followed through with the requirements that that theory imposes.

A conspicuous feature of Canada's two major legislative apportionment court decisions—one regarding legislative boundaries in British Columbia (1989) and the other legislative boundaries in Saskatchewan (1991)—is that both borrow heavily from the vocabulary used by the American courts, making liberal use of the terms "vote power," "vote weight," "vote worth," "vote value," and "vote dilution," as well as the phrase "one person-one vote." Like the American decisions, moreover, these terms are never explicitly defined. Yet in one important respect the two Canadian decisions differ markedly from the two initial American decisions, *Reynolds* and *Wesberry*, and the decisions that stemmed from them: both of the Canadian decisions advance a rationale for reasonably equal population districts which focuses on postelection equality of representation, not election-day outcomes.

The two Canadian decisions explicitly recognize two roles of an elected representative, one being the legislative role and the other the ombudsman role. Reasonably equal population districts are justified in terms of those two roles. Population equality helps to insure (1) that the legislative "voice" of all citizens is equal; (2) that the burden of ombudsman is shared equally among all representatives; and (3) that the likelihood of parliamentary majorities reflecting electoral majorities is maximized.[35] Both Canadian decisions, therefore, indicate that the author, Justice McLachlin, uses the terms "power," "weight," and so forth in the same loose, qualitative sense as the American scholars referred to earlier, and that she did not intend to refer to a voter's ability to affect district election outcomes.[36] If that interpretation is correct, the theory of representation embraced by Canadian courts clearly differs from the one adopted by courts in Australia.

Consequences

Robert Dixon's purpose in pointing out the misuse by the Court of the *Gray* case precedent was to buttress his argument that legislative apportionment cases were not about voting rights, but about representation, and that the complexities of representation requires recognition of factors beyond the counting of "mere numbers." But the consequences of the vote-value line of reasoning have gone well beyond that one observation.

First, the Court left itself open to the charge that it was unrealistic, even naive. In view of the fact that less than one-third of a district's population usually participates in legislative elections, a definition of fair representation that excludes mention of the nonvoting majority seems strange indeed. The vote-value perspective is also vulnerable to the charge, made by Bickel[37] and others, that it "ignores the laws of probability," since the probability of an individual's single vote determining the result of a district election is infinitesimally small. Finally, what usually matters most in an election is not what happens at the individual district level but what happens at the aggregate level across all districts, a fact which the Court came to acknowledge when it shifted its attention from individual to group representation.

The second and most far reaching result of the Court's focusing on the value of a district vote was that subsequent plaintiffs were able to claim that an apportionment scheme may have the effect of depriving a racial or political minority group of its ability to elect the group's preferred candidates from districts in which they are concentrated. If there was any doubt what the Court intended to say in *Wesberry* and *Reynolds,* that doubt was removed once the Court ruled, first in 1965 (*Fortson v. Dorsey*) and again in 1971 (*Whitcomb v. Chavis*), that a multimember district scheme would violate the 14th Amendment if it operated "to minimize or cancel out the voting strength of racial or political elements of the voting population"; and when the Court began to interpret the Voting Rights Act of 1965 to require that apportionment schemes in areas covered by the act be designed to make the votes of racial minorities "effective" (*Allen v. State Board*). As the logical extension of that interpretation, the Voting Rights Act itself was amended in 1982 with the provision that, in areas where the act applied, districting schemes should enable racial minorities "to elect representatives of their choice." The impact of this restatement of the vote-value perspective can be seen most recently in the past summer's struggle in New York City over the design of the new city council, as blacks, Hispanics, Asians, Jews, and gays each demanded districts designed to facilitate the election of the groups' preferred candidates. One federal district court judge has described this development as a replacement of the republican form of government by a "tribal" form of government.[38]

A final consequence of the Court's focus on the equalization of vote value has been the incompatibility of that goal with the Court's acceptance of raw population figures for the construction of legislative districts. The problem was clearly pointed out by Chief Justice Barwick of the High Court in Australia, a country where, as already noted, the intrastate apportionment base is registered voters:

> I am unable to accept the view that mere equality of numbers of people in a division provides equality of voting value. One has only to contrast the situation of a voter in an electoral division in which there is a high proportion of children and teenagers under the age of 18 with a voter in an electoral division with an equal number of people in which there is a negligible proportion of children and of such teenagers to realize that mere equality of numbers, all other considerations aside, will not ensure equality in voting value.[39]

In 1972 a majority of the United States Supreme Court acknowledged the validity of this argument when it pointed out in the case of *Gaffney v. Cummings* that legislative districts vary widely in the number of persons (a) who are of age, (b) who are citizens, (c) who are registered, and (d) who actively vote (pp. 747–48). In addition, the Court came to recognize the inadequacy of raw census counts when it began to decide cases arising under the Voting Rights Act: a district must include a 65% black (or Hispanic) population in order to compensate for a higher mobility and a larger number of children in black communities, as well as for a lesser inclination of blacks to register and to vote. When the Court agreed to consider partisan seat-vote ratios in cases involving charges of partisan gerrymandering, it likewise recognized the need to look at the worth of the vote cast by those who actually vote.[40]

These concessions notwithstanding, the Court has shown no inclination to change the apportionment base either to the potential electorate, i.e., those of voting age, or to the actual active electorate as measured, say, by the number of registered voters or by total votes cast in recent elections.[41] Thus the incongruence between the Court's vote-value/vote-dilution definition of fair representation, and the Court's use of raw population counts for measuring conformance with that definition, continues. What's more, the incongruity has been magnified by two developments which have occurred since the Court's initial apportionment rulings—the increase in the number of noneligible aliens, and the unequal incidence of the decline of voter participation.

Conclusion

In 1988 the City of New York asked the Supreme Court to accept a redesigned Board of Estimate constructed on the probability calculations of lawyer-mathematician John F. Banzhaf III, calculations showing the relative ability of voters to determine district election outcomes, and the relative ability of a district's elected legislator to affect voting outcomes on the board. The Court was thus forced to face, more explicitly than ever before, the question of whether or not the vote-value argument advanced in *Reynolds* should be interpreted as referring to the ability of a voter to affect outcomes, either election outcomes or legislative outcomes. In a unanimous decision, the Court firmly distanced itself from that interpretation. It held that *Reynolds* did no more than establish the principle of equal population districts in order "that legislators will be elected by, and represent citizens in, districts of substantially equal size." The *Reynolds* decision, the Court said, had nothing to do with election or legislative outcomes.[42]

Whether this assertion should be seen as a revision of *Reynolds*, or simply a clarification, is by no means clear. What is clear is that had the assertion been made earlier the problems and entanglements that have been identified in this paper would have been avoided. The number of persons per district would have been the same, but the Court would not have legitimized one theory of representation to the near exclusion of others, and it would not have left itself vulnerable to charges of naiveté, inconsistencies, and to having helped foster a "tribal" form of government.

Notes

1. P. 562.
2. P. 537–38.
3. Critics of the strict standards imposed by the Supreme Court include Robert Dixon, Malcolm Jewell, and Abigail Thernstrom. See Dixon, *Democratic Representation* (New York: Oxford University Press, 1968); Jewell, "Commentary," in Nelson Polsby, ed., *Reapportionment in the 1970s* (Berkeley: University of California Press, 1971); Thernstrom, *Whose Votes Count?* (Cambridge: Harvard University Press, 1987).
4. Gordon Wood, *Representation in the American Revolution* (Charlottesville: University of Virginia Press, 1969).
5. Anthony Lewis, "Legislative Apportionment and the Federal Courts," *Harvard Law Review* 61 (1958): 1073.
6. John Ely, *Democracy and Distrust* (Cambridge: Harvard University Press, 1980), 82–83.
7. *Congressional Globe*, 22 January 1866, 356. Dixon argues (see n.3, 187–92) that, contrary to the opinion of Justice Black in *Wesberry*, it is far from clear that the Framers intended that congressional districts be equal in *population*. However, what is beyond question is that the Framers could not possibly have intended that districts be equal in the number of *voters*, since the extent of the franchise was to be left to the states. See below.

8. Alexander Bickel, *Politics and the Warren Court* (New York: Harper & Row, 1965), 183.
9. Possible meanings of the Court's early decision are discussed in Bernard Grofman and Howard Scarrow, "The Riddle of Apportionment: Equality of What?" *National Civic Review* 70 (1981): 242–54.
10. P. 186.
11. P. 23.
12. P. 243.
13. P. 245.
14. P. 8.
15. P. 562.
16. P. 569.
17. APSA Committee, "The Reapportionment of Congress," *American Political Science Review* 45 (1951): 154.
18. Advisory Commission on Intergovernmental Relations, "Principles for Reapportionment: Recommendations," reprinted in Howard Hamilton, ed., *Legislative Apportionment* (New York: Harper & Row, 1964), 117–23.
19. Twentieth Century Fund Conference of Research Scholars and Political Scientists, *One Man–One Vote* (1962), 3, as reprinted and paginated in Glendon Schubert, ed., *Reapportionment* (New York: Charles Scribner, 1965), 42–45.
20. Paul David and Ralph Eisenberg, *Devaluation of the Urban and Suburban Vote* (Charlottesville: University of Virginia, Bureau of Public Administration, 1961).
21. Andrew Hacker, *Congressional Districting* (Washington, DC: The Brookings Institution, 1963), 3.
22. Laurence Schmeckebier, *Congressional Apportionment* (Washington, DC: The Brookings Institution, 1941), ch. 7.
23. Dixon, *Democratic Representation* (see n.3), 286.
24. Twentieth Century Fund, *One Man–One Vote*, 4–5, as paginated in Schubert. See also n.40.
25. Quoted in James Todd, "The Apportionment Problem Faced by the States," *Law and Contemporary Problems* 27 (1962): 331.
26. *Wesberry*, 7.
27. Ruth Silva, "The Population Base for Apportionment of the New York Legislature," *Fordham Law Review* 32 (1963): 2 n.8.
28. Dixon, *Democratic Representation* (see n.3), 204–5.
29. Ibid., 176ff.
30. Pp. 379, 381.
31. P. 382.
32. *Lucas v. Colorado*, 712.
33. Joan Rydon, "'Malapportionment'–Australian Style," *Politics* 3 (1968): 133–47.
34. Parliament of the Commonwealth of Australia, *One Vote, One Value*. Report Number One of the Joint Standing Committee on Electoral Matters (Canberra: Australian Government Publishing Service, 1988), 15.
35. For a background of Canadian practice, see John Courtney, "Parliament and Representation: The Unfinished Agenda of Electoral Redistributions," *Canadian Journal of Political Science* 21 (1988): 675–90.
36. The two cases are *Dixon v. British Columbia*, [1989] and *Reference re Electoral Boundaries Commission Act*, [1991]. The latter decision, rendered by the Supreme Court of Canada, differed from the earlier decision in that it took a more tolerant

view of wide population disparities among districts, stressing the importance of "effective and fair representation" over the goal of strict population equality.

37. Bickel, *Politics and the Warren Court* (see n.8), 184.
38. *Kirksey v. Board,* 155-56.
39. *Ex. rel. McKinlay,* 606.
40. The Twentieth Century Fund report (see n.19) expressly took no position on what should constitute the apportionment base, saying that the question should be subject to future research (p. 7). That recommendation provides additional evidence that the report was not intended to be interpreted in a quantitative, vote-value sense (see above).

    The Court has acknowledged the legitimacy of a state confining its apportionment base to the eligible electorate, omitting aliens and persons accused of crimes (*Burns v. Richardson*). There are many historical precedents the Court could have cited had it ordered apportionment to be based on the size of the eligible electorate. Historical precedents are discussed in Howard Scarrow, "One Voter, One Vote: The Apportionment of Congressional Seats Reconsidered," *Polity* 22 (1989): 253-68.
41. Schmeckebier proposed such changes in the apportionment base in his 1941 volume *Congressional Apportionment* (see n.22).
42. In 1970 the Court had also been confronted with Banzhaf's theory as it applied to determining the relative power of voters to determine outcomes in single-member districts and multimember districts. Although the Court dismissed the argument that, according to that theory, voters in multimember districts exercised disproportionate power to determine district outcomes, the Court did not deny that its apportionment decisions had been designed to equalize the ability to affect those outcomes (*Whitcomb v. Chavis,* 144-45). The 1988 decision is *Board of Estimate v. Morris.*

Table of Cases

Allen v. State Board of Elections, 393 U.S. 544 (1969).
Attorney General (Ex. rel. McKinlay) v. Commonwealth, 7 ALR 593 (1975).
Baker v. Carr, 369 U.S. 186 (1962).
Board of Estimate v. Morris, 489 U.S. 688 (1988).
Burns v. Richardson, 384 U.S. 73 (1966).
Colegrove v. Green, 328 U.S. 549 (1946).
Davis v. Bandemer, 478 U.S. 109 (1986).
Dixon v. British Columbia (Attorney General), [1989] 35 B.C.L.R. (2d) 273.
Ex. rel. McKinlay, 7 ALR (1975).
Fortson v. Dorsey, 379 U.S. 433 (1965).
Gaffney v. Cummings, 412 U.S. 735 (1973).
Gray v. Sanders, 372 U.S. 339 (1960).
Karcher v. Daggett, 462 U.S. 725 (1983).
Kirkpatrick v. Preisler, 394 U.S. 526 (1969).
Kirksey v. Board of Supervisors of Hinds County, Miss., 554 F. 2d 139 (1977).
Lucas v. Forty-Fourth Colorado General Assembly, 377 U.S. 713 (1964).
Reference re Electoral Boundaries Commission Act, (1991) 81 D.L.R. (4th).
Reynolds v. Sims, 377 U.S. 533 (1964).
Wesberry v. Sanders, 376 U.S. 1 (1964).
Whitcomb v. Chavis, 403 U.S. 124 (1971).
YMCA v. Lomenzo, 238 Fed. Supp. 916 (1965).

COMMENTARY

JOHN C. COURTNEY

UNIVERSITY OF SASKATCHEWAN

In his paper Howard Scarrow distinguishes between the alternate purposes served by constructing districts of equal populations. One focuses on elections and voters, with the ultimate objective of equalizing the "value" of the vote, so that each voter has an equal opportunity along with every other voter to affect the district election outcome. The other is concerned with district residents and what happens *after* the election. What must be equalized for this latter group is representation in its broadest sense, each person having the opportunity to enjoy an equal "share" of a legislator's time and services. Scarrow labels the first of these alternatives the "democratic" option, and the second the "republican." Jennifer Smith in her Commentary has drawn much the same distinction when she notes that McLachlin II (Norman Ruff's useful categorization) failed to distinguish between the two principal reasons for having elections in the first place: voting and being represented.

Robert Frost's evocative phrase about "The Road Not Taken" might be used to summarize American experience with redistricting over the past three decades. But it occurred to me, after reading the earlier papers and the two now under discussion, that the same observation also helps to distinguish the Canadian experience with electoral boundary readjustments from the American. Robert Dixon's 1968 analysis of reapportionment and redistricting in the United States described his country's approach to drawing boundaries as "kaleidoscopic," amounting to constantly changing patterns of "new cases, new doctrines, new possibilities, and new insights follow[ing] each round of experience."[1] The history of U.S. court decisions since *Baker v. Carr* in 1962 bears out his assessment. It is a story of "firsts," of what is "new" on the redistricting agenda. Like so many other things American, it is *arriviste*, having moved with the times from the early heady days of "one person–one vote," through disputes over "racial" gerrymandering to recent contests alleging "partisan" districting.

Judges have now become regular players in the seemingly unending game of redistricting politics. The questions they are asked to settle seem at first blush to know no bounds. One of the messages implicit in the papers by Professors Grofman and Scarrow is that there may be few broadly defined social and political issues that American courts will not be called on to address in future debates over redistricting. That the law may be so mature as to have reached an advanced stage of senility, as Bernard Grofman suggests, will be no guarantee that allegedly aggrieved parties will stop turning to the courts when their perceived interests are affected.

That so far has not been the case in Canada. With the notable exception of the 1991 *Saskatchewan Reference* and the 1986 and 1989 *Dixon* cases in British Columbia, courts have not been turned to by aggrieved electors to protect the equality of voting power. Part of the explanation for this no doubt derives from the relatively recent adoption of the Charter and its guarantee of democratic rights. Yet section 3 certainly gave rise to speedy challenges to electoral laws on one front—the franchise—as prisoners, the mentally handicapped, the unenumerated, and, indeed, judges themselves sought as Canadian citizens to overturn at both federal and provincial levels their denial of the right to vote. But one person–one vote did not become a similar rallying cry for Canadians with the arrival of the Charter. Ted Morton accurately described the distinction in these terms: the United States has followed the road to the "right to an equal vote" and Canada the one to the "equal right to a vote."

Part of the explanation for the different roads taken in Canada and the United States on the matter of voter equality must surely be found in the way in which electoral boundary readjustments have been handled in the two countries. In the same year that the U.S. Supreme Court rendered its decisions in *Reynolds v. Sims* and *Wesberry v. Sanders* (1964), the Canadian Parliament adopted legislation that effectively removed redistribution from the hands of the politicians. By establishing and deploying 10 (now 11) independent electoral commissions after each decennial census to redistribute electoral districts, Canada has effectively depoliticized and federalized the process. Cries of gerrymandering, once so familiar at all levels of Canadian politics, have rarely, if at all, been heard about federal redistributions since the new process came into place. By creating a separate federal commission for each province and the Northwest Territories, in preference to one for the country as a whole, Canadians have designed a system much more likely to be attuned to local concerns and interests. That is a significant departure from American experience, where redistricting, as the two papers remind us, is a highly partisan activity played out by one governor, two parties, and both houses in each of 50 states.

Clearly American ingenuity knows no bounds. To have done so much on so many fronts in so short a time through a court system not noted for its speed is truly remarkable. Few, if any, would have imagined what progeny *Baker v. Carr* would have produced in three decades. In all likelihood, the U.S. is the better for it (undoubtedly American lawyers are), but one of the messages I get from Professors Scarrow and Grofman is that the future is clouded. Who knows what supposed electoral injustices lurk in the hearts of voters, parties, and advocacy groups? It may be true, as Bernard Grofman tells us, that *Bandemer* so far has no teeth. But let us suppose teeth soon appear: what shape and character will they assume and for whose benefit will they be used? Even allowing for the differences between the way Canadians and Americans go about redefining district boundaries (and they are substantial), one point that Canadians might take from America's experience with partisan gerrymandering (and indeed from *Baker v. Carr* itself) is that nothing is immutable. What is judged to be nonjusticiable one day may be acceptable to the court the next.

There is a sense in which this has become a "tiger-by-the-tail" issue in the United States. Once it started, there was no stopping it. So far, as I noted previously, that is far from the case in Canada. The useful tripartite analogue and developmental metaphor that Professor Grofman employed to describe the degree of legal maturity in each of the three categories of gerrymandering (one person–one vote, racial, and partisan) serve to highlight a remarkable difference between the two countries. Canadian courts have yet to address the second and third of these topics, and we are little beyond the toddler stage on the first—one person–one vote. Mudpies so far have been thrown in only two provinces, and formed but not yet tossed in a third. This is not to say that cases, alleging, for example, electoral boundary discrimination against minority language groups, Natives, and ethnic minorities in large urban centres (with its consequent legislative underrepresentation) might not be launched in Canada. If they are, I have no doubt that they will be as an extension, as it were, of the McLachlin II decisions rather than as a product of the same sorts of minority-underrepresentation cases resulting in the U.S. from the strict application of the one person–one vote doctrine. Bob Richards and Thom Irvine concluded that a distinct possibility as a result of the *Saskatchewan Reference* case is that the "one person–one vote" concept could be found at some future point to be *unconstitutional* in Canada because it fails to reflect the variety of considerations needed to ensure a system of effective representation. If they are correct, a more marked contrast to the American experience is difficult to imagine.

Both the Grofman and Scarrow papers serve to remind us that the debate over fair districting has brought to the surface an age-old question of whether the number of citizens, voters, or general population should serve as the denominator for the whole exercise. There seems to be no compelling case for abandoning total population figures, largely for what I take (at least implicitly) from the papers to be an adherence to Burkean representational norms. Congressmen, senators and state legislators are elected to serve and to represent *all* of their constituents, not simply the voters or citizens of their district. It is not inconceivable that the same question could come up in Canada, given the reference to "citizens" in section 3 of the Charter. Professor Scarrow tells us that Australians, with their policy of "one vote–one value," have gone the opposite route to the one Canada has employed at the federal level and the majority of the provinces. On the matter of the adequacy of decennial population counts, Bernard Grofman has alluded to the difficulties that the larger, more-urbanized states face in the apportionment process as a result of the systematic undercounting of the poor, the homeless, and racial minorities. Judged by most standards, the Canadian census is a great deal more complete and reliable than its American counterpart.

Howard Scarrow tells us that Americans at an earlier time in their history faced a choice over the kind of representational grounding they used to defend fairly constructed districts made up of basically equal populations. The distinction he draws between "democracy" and "representation," between electors and the people, is akin to a debate between Rousseauian will and Burkean reason, with the representational focus in one on what happens before an election and in the other on what happens after. That this has "tribalized" the process of designing legislative districts in the United States is something Canadians ought to be mindful of if they choose to push their electoral boundary readjustment process in that direction. Madam Justice McLachlin's references in the majority decision in the Saskatchewan case to "vast, sparsely populated territories," "citizens with distinct interests," "minority representation," and "cultural and group identity" suggest that Canada may at some point extend the process of compartmentalizing some of its electoral districts beyond that of an economic community of interest.

One final lesson from the American experience is the clear and undisputed need for comprehensive and readily understood contributions from the social sciences. The case for accurate and fair statistical measures, for expert witnesses, and for thoughtful, reflective analyses on both the process and content of electoral boundary readjustments has been amply demonstrated over the past three decades in the United States. I have no doubt that with time and the likelihood of further court challenges, Canadians can match their American colleagues on those scores. But we have a long way to go—especially in light of the difficulties we have noted so far in this conference with what it is that Canadians mean by the phrase "community of interest."

Notes

1. *Democratic Representation: Reapportionment in Law and Politics* (New York: Oxford University Press, 1968), 7.

COMMENTARY

WARD ELLIOTT
CLAREMONT MCKENNA COLLEGE

I suppose, as an invited veteran of the "reapportionment revolution" in the United States, that I should start by offering my condolences to the judges in the audience, and my congratulations to the lawyers and political scientists. If American experience is any guide, a vast opportunity for professional befuddlement lies ahead for judges, and a vast opportunity for professional employment lies ahead for lawyers and political scientists. This conference calls up memories of the high-water days of political science in the United States in the late 1960s and early 1970s. Political science was still the master science; it had not yet been displaced in that role by economics; and it prided itself on spearheading our "reapportionment revolution." Professional meetings in those days often offered gala displays of group chest-thumping and assertion of jurisdiction. We knew how to draw boundaries, all right, and they were big, inclusive ones, of our own turf.

One of the memories, a public-law panel at the American Political Science Association, stands out in my mind as especially pertinent to today's discussions. Several of our superstars—Walter Murphy, Glendon Schubert, and Ted Becker—had just returned from long visits to far-off lands and were eager to share the news: everyone in Ruritania was fascinated with our path-breaking public-law innovations, but they were decades behind us in their knowledge of the frontier. No one had heard of Jerome Frank, cue theory, or scalograms. Vast fields were ripe for tillage, if not pillage, by American public-law visitors spreading enlightenment no less authoritatively than our envied, globe-girdling colleagues in political-development and area studies. Perhaps we, too, could travel the world on grants, diffusing innovation to the untutored, embarking them on "Journeys Toward Progress."

I wondered aloud afterward whether this could be so. It seemed to me that public law was either a culture-fast game like baseball, much the same from one

196

country to another—in which case we would be studying the minor leagues—or it was a culture-saturable game like football/soccer/rugby—in which case we didn't know enough about the host-country cultures to tell them anything new about their own brand of public law. I suspect that the football analogy is the more pertinent, and I have to wonder how exportable our United States experience is, even to our nearest neighbour.

To that caution I should add two others. I do not propose to discuss what the United States Framers thought about "democratic" representation (of voters), as opposed to "republican" (of voters and nonvoters). Nor do I propose to discuss how exactly equal each district should be—such decisions in the United States were entrusted to lawyers, their motto being "Why be half-safe?" Thus, our equality requirements are far more stringent than they need to be about measurables. Could it be because they have to compensate for their lack of stringency about unmeasurables?

Instead, let me take up some questions raised by Howard Scarrow. Did American reapportionists in the 1950s and 1960s confuse the total population with the voting or voting-eligible population? The answer is yes, all the time. Did they confuse voting-rights questions with representation questions? Yes, all the time. Were these confusions intentional? The first confusion was probably not intentional; the second was at least partly so. The reapportionist justices—Brennan, Douglas, Black, and Warren—were very hesitant to define what they were talking about, or where it might come from in the U.S. Constitution. As often in the Warren era, one had to go to the Frankfurter or Harlan dissent, or to the briefs, to figure out what the majority really meant.

When Warren in *Reynolds v. Sims* did get around to defining the right, he used words like "vote" or "voting" interchangeably with "representation," but three or four times more frequently—most likely because it sounded less open-ended and quagmirelike. It spared the Court the task of addressing intractable complexities like the "effectiveness" of a vote, or the eccentricities of a checks-and-balances system where nobody's vote is ever equal, but where there is a vague hope, more often justified than not, that the inequalities would balance each other out. You may have an in with Nancy Reagan's astrologer, but I have one with her hairdresser. Warren mixed up his concepts enough to address the task at hand, but not enough, he hoped, to sustain Frankfurter's objection that he was getting in over his head.

Would it have helped to define the right in a more "Republican" way? I wonder. Who does a representative represent? Everyone who voted for him? Everyone in his party? Everyone who voted, including those who voted against him? Everyone eligible to vote in the last or next election? Every citizen in the district, regardless of eligibility? Every person in the district, regardless of citizenship or residency status? Tourists? Prisoners? College students? Conventioneers? People with green cards? Unenumerated illegal aliens?

We are toddlers on these questions, to borrow a term from Bernard Grofman. I see no strong reason to pick any one of these definitions to the exclusion of all the others, and no clear reason why a court should impose one, absent a clear constitutional mandate, where a more representative body (however defined) might have other ideas.

Bernard Grofman's paper, and his edited book, *Political Gerrymandering and the Courts,* discuss various ways of going beyond population equality and attempting to safeguard or equalize the effective votes of racial and partisan groups. The spectrum of willingness to intervene might be sketched at five levels. At the bottom would be the Felix Frankfurter position: courts should stay out of areas where they will always be toddlers. One rank up would be the Peter Schuck position: courts should be tough on district size but ignore other forms of vote dilution, including every kind of gerrymander. Two ranks up would be the Bruce Cain–Daniel Lowenstein position: courts should be tough on district size and on racial gerrymanders for blacks, Puerto Ricans, and Hispanics, but they should ignore partisan gerrymanders, and gerrymanders involving other minorities. This is more or less the consensus of American courts today. Three ranks up would be the position of Bernard Grofman himself, and a dozen other political scientists in *Political Gerrymandering and the Courts:* courts should be tough on every kind of gerrymander, as long as it is egregious enough. The highest level of intervention, advocated by the McGovern Commission and by sociologist Herbert Gans in the 1970s, and still a sentimental favourite with some political scientists, is to have someone order proportional representation.

Neither of the two extremes has many active advocates today. The "reapportionment revolution" is too well accepted to recur to Frankfurter's position. Proportional representation was political science's gift to Weimar Germany, the Fourth French Republic, and the Italian government today. In retrospect, it was the kiss of debility and death; it produced volatile, schismatic governments which represented interests beautifully but could not get them to form stable coalitions that could govern. It has fallen from favour among political scientists and is too far from the American mainstream for even the most daringly activist jurist to "discover" in the original understanding of the Equal Protection Clause.

Most of the debate in the United States is between the Cain-Lowenstein position and the Grofman position, with Grofman holding the high ground in logic, but Cain and Lowenstein politically ascendant. Of the two views, I am more sympathetic to Grofman's than to Cain's or Lowenstein's, but I am not convinced that Grofman's "twelve flags and three whistles" and "interocular testing" have been, or can be, made sufficiently clear and coherent to make courts something other than toddlers with gerrymanders. To me, the best practicable position for the United States is that of Peter Schuck. Our checks and balances are at their weakest in boundaries questions. The haves always draw the boundaries at the expense of the have-nots. One anomalous result of *Baker v. Carr* was to force legislators to revise and update old gerrymanders, whether they wanted to or not—without forcing them to be fair to the have-nots.

This process has produced safe districts wonderful for incumbents of both parties, not so wonderful for challengers or for getting new things done. Many think that it has polarized the two parties, stalemated action, and forced heavy resort to clumsy initiatives.

But checks and balances have been given less credit than they deserve, even in California. At any given time, half the states are divided between the two parties, making egregious abuse by one party (but not by incumbents) difficult or impossible. California is probably our worst case of partisan gerrymandering, but for two of the last three censuses, control of the state was divided. The truly egregious pillage took place during the 1980s, giving Democrats half again as many seats per vote as Republicans. But this advantage appears to have been a wasting asset. It was not enough, it seems, to make the state a perpetual Democratic fiefdom. The governor and the Supreme Court are Republican, and the latest court-drawn district plans seem to give both parties an equal shot at the state assembly and congressional delegation.

Of course, our experience with separation of powers, or checks and balances, is scant comfort to a Canadian audience, to whom such things are as strange and foreign as American football. For Canadians, as I understand it, the only protections are inertia, a sense of fair play, and a less-contentious disposition than is the American norm. Every Canadian I have talked to this weekend tells me that these, too, are wasting assets. For your sake, I hope that they are not. I opened with congratulations and condolences for opening up the little boundaries question. I close by wishing you good luck, not only on the little boundaries question, but on the big one, too. You will need it for both.

THE CHARTER OF RIGHTS AND FREEDOMS AND ELECTORAL VALUES

Chartering the Electoral Map into the Future

KENT ROACH
UNIVERSITY OF TORONTO

The Supreme Court's decision to uphold Saskatchewan's electoral boundaries was, for many, "surprising and disturbing."[1] In a country just waking up to the new role of its judiciary, the Saskatchewan decision even drew heavy editorial criticism. For the Saskatoon *Star Phoenix*, the decision was "a disappointment to those who had hoped the court would put an end to the Tories' crass political ploy to retain power." Playing the role of H.L. Mencken to the Court's naiveté, the *Star Phoenix* noted that while some judges in Ottawa may have thought overrepresentation of rural voters was about "group identity," it really "has everything to do with politics and power."[2] In an editorial that would have made its founder George Brown proud, the (Toronto) *Globe and Mail* warned the decision had given a "seal of approval" to "rampant inequity in the weighting of Canadians' votes" and argued that rural and northern voters "should not be accommodated by, in effect, handing out free votes to recognize cultural and group identity, or giving people a 50-per-cent voting bonus for living in underpopulated areas in the age of telephones, electronic media and advanced transportation."[3] If the nation's editorial writers are any indication, many had hoped that the Court would enforce a one person–one vote standard and believed that this would guarantee fairness and equality in the distribution of seats and the districting of ridings.

I will argue that the Court's decision is not surprising in light of recent doctrinal developments and institutional concerns that are leading the Supreme Court to adopt a more deferential posture to many of the policy issues that it confronts in Charter adjudication. I will suggest that the decision not to overturn Saskatchewan's boundaries also accords with the Court's understanding of equality rights under section 15 of the Charter. Having unanimously rejected the values of formal and individualistic equality in its leading

200

Andrews[4] decision, it is not surprising that the Court did not champion the one person-one vote principle.

I will then explain why on balance I do not find the Court's decision overly disturbing. Districting decisions within a range of relative equality of voting power are ones about which reasonable people can disagree. Most deviations from equal-population standards can be supported by legitimate policies to promote effective representation. The Saskatchewan legislation, for example, finds support in the traditional policy of promoting effective representation of rural interests. Some found it easy to detect and condemn partisan motivations in the legislation, but the American experience suggests that attempts by the judiciary to supervise partisan districting are problematic at best. Finally, even if the Supreme Court had required Saskatchewan to produce ridings with equal populations, that would not have ensured that everyone in the province would receive effective and equal representation. In the Canadian context, such a requirement may well have aggravated the underrepresentation of some of our most vulnerable minorities.

It would be a mistake, in my view, to assume that the Court's deferential posture toward the Saskatchewan boundaries necessarily spells the end of Charter considerations in districting. The Court's explicit concern about effective representation and its implicit determination to interpret the right to vote in accord with its interpretation of equality rights under section 15 may force it to invalidate districting decisions that have the effect of diluting the voting power of geographically concentrated minority groups. The decision will also lead the Court to defer to Charter-inspired administrative and legislative attempts to maximize the voting strength of minority groups. A decision that today benefits rural residents of Saskatchewan will support and perhaps mandate affirmative districting[5] in the future. This prospect is, in my view, again neither surprising nor disturbing. I will suggest that it continues Canadian antimajoritarian electoral traditions, satisfies our constitutional standards of equality, and suits our political culture.

It's Not So Surprising

The Supreme Court's six to three decision that the Saskatchewan boundaries did not violate section 3 of the Charter reflects many of the tensions that our highest court is experiencing in interpreting the Charter. The majority decision of Justice McLachlin demonstrates a tendency for the Court in the past few years both to place definitional limits on some Charter rights and to defer to the legislature's balancing of competing policy interests. In turn, the dissent of Justice Cory reflects an earlier experience under the Charter in which rights were interpreted in an expansive manner and governments were forced to meet rigorous standards of justification under section 1.

It is difficult to pinpoint the turning of the tide in Charter adjudication. Two cases at a fairly early stage of Charter adjudication provided a hint of what was to come and have relevance in the districting context. Although the decisions were conservative in preserving features of Canadian life that pre-date the Charter, it is noteworthy that they were written by the two judges who are perceived as the most liberal and activist members of our highest court in the last decade.

In the *Separate Schools Reference*, the Court upheld increased religious funding to Roman Catholic denominational schools under section 93 of the Constitution Act, 1867, in the face of Charter challenges on the basis of freedom and equality of all religions. In an opinion written by Justice Wilson, the Court stated that the Charter was never intended to invalidate other provisions of the constitution that provided for "special or unequal educational rights for specific religious groups in Ontario and Quebec."[6] The Court recognized for the first time that the Charter has a potential to challenge other constitutional traditions, and in order to conserve the past, it reasoned that the Charter was not intended to disrupt such traditions. Dicta in this case also suggest that the courts recognized that the Charter could be used to challenge constitutional provisions that guarantee effective representation in the House of Commons for less-populous provinces such as Prince Edward Island, the Yukon, and the Northwest Territories. The Ontario Court of Appeal, at least, stated that it would not allow the Charter to nullify these entrenched departures from representation by population.[7]

In *R. v. Edwards Books*, Chief Justice Dickson found that although Sunday closing laws infringed religious liberties, they were justified under section 1 as legitimate measures to provide for a common pause day. He stated that the courts must judge the legislature's balancing of interests in a deferential and pragmatic fashion and stated that "[i]n interpreting and applying the Charter I believe that the courts must be cautious to ensure that it does not simply become an instrument of better situated individuals to roll back legislation which has as its object the improvement of the condition of less advantaged persons."[8] For the first time, the Court acknowledged that invalidation of legislation under the Charter could hurt the lives of the disadvantaged and suggested that they could, in appropriate circumstances, apply less-exacting standards under section 1.

In subsequent years, the Court has at crucial junctures continued down the path marked by these two case. It has defined the extent of Charter rights in a more-limited fashion when it believed it necessary to preserve what it saw as important features of life b.c. (before [the] charter). In interpreting section 3 of the Charter to protect relative as opposed to absolute parity of voting power in the Saskatchewan decision, for example, Justice McLachlin was able to rely on a decision that excluded the right of unions to strike from the right to freedom of association on the basis of the Court's perception of the historical meaning of that term.[9] As the Court has sought to impose definitional limits on at least some Charter rights, the question of the intent of the framers of the Charter has become, in some contexts, as important as the interpretative edict of giving constitutional rights a broad and generous interpretation. Thus, both Justice

McLachlin's majority judgment and the concurring opinion of Justice Sopinka stressed that there was no evidence, either in the wording of section 3 or in the relevant debates surrounding its enactment, that it was intended to alter the modified form of representation by population that Canadians had before the enactment of the Charter.[10] Note that this reasoning is conservative in assuming that there must be evidence that the Charter was intended to change the legal and political framework into which it was introduced.

The Court has embellished its deferential use of section 1 in *Edwards Books* to save legislative policies such as restrictions on advertising aimed at children, mandatory retirement, and the criminalization of hate literature.[11] Although the majority judgment never reaches the question of whether Saskatchewan could justify its boundaries under section 1, it is clear that Justice McLachlin was influenced by the increased deference the Court has demonstrated in its scrutiny of governments' justifications for infringing Charter rights. For example, in *Irwin Toy,* the Court held that a general-reasonableness standard should govern state attempts to justify decisions that involve the allocation of scarce resources. The Attorney General of Saskatchewan successfully argued that the allocation of electoral boundaries "concerns questions about the entitlements of one group of electors *vis à vis* those of other electors" and as such did not involve either "a confrontation between the state and individuals" or a situation "where there are demonstrably right or wrong answers."[12] Justice McLachlin appeared to accept this logic and fuse section 1 and section 3 considerations in reasoning that: "[t]his Court has repeatedly affirmed that the courts must be cautious in interfering unduly in decisions that involve the balancing of conflicting policy considerations."[13] Thus her judgment stands as an example of both the recent tendency to place definitional limits on Charter rights and to defer to the state's balancing of interests under section 1.[14]

If the majority's judgment is representative of a new and more deferential approach to the Charter, the dissenting judgment is also typical of an older tradition of Charter activism. Justice Cory's dissent does not spend much time interpreting the right to vote or attempting to define and place limits on the equality of voting power that is protected by that right. Instead the judgment moves quickly to the question of justification and in particular the question of whether the impugned provisions infringe equality of voting power as little as possible. There Justice Cory applies the *Oakes* proportionality test rigorously. Nullification of legislation follows from the Court's ability to envision the government pursuing its objectives in a less-intrusive manner.[15] Thus, for Justice Cory, "a comparison of the 1981 map to that of 1989 convinces me that there has been such an infringement."[16]

One development which, in my view, places the Court's new approach to Charter adjudication in its best light was its decision in *Andrews* not to interpret the equality rights in section 15 of the Charter as a general guarantee of equal treatment in law for all individuals. The Court in *Andrews* rejected the view, popular among the courts of appeal until that time, that equality rights were designed to ensure that similarly situated entities were treated the same. Rather the Court held that equality rights were designed to protect enumerated and analogous groups from suffering further discrimination and disadvantage.[17] Thus, the Court placed a unifying interpretation on the whole of the text of section 15; affirmative action programs that were approved under section 15(2) were seen as an example of the differential treatment that equality required. In keeping with the recent tenor of Charter decisions, *Andrews* required judicial deference to government initiatives that treated people differently but either did not harm disadvantaged groups or were designed to improve their conditions. On the other hand, it contemplated an active role for the Court in responding to laws or programs that in their purpose or effect harmed disadvantaged groups.

It is strange that section 15 did not play more of an explicit role in the Saskatchewan case. The reference to the Court of Appeal simply asked whether the boundaries were consistent with the Charter. The parties limited their submissions to the right to vote and freedom of expression, but their time would have been well spent researching the section 15 jurisprudence. It appears that those who forget the struggle over the interpretation of equality rights are destined to repeat it. In fact, the decisions of the Court of Appeal and the Supreme Court played out at an unconscious level the previous struggle that ended with *Andrews*. The Court of Appeal stressed the value of the formal equality of each individual, stating that "no person's portion of sovereign power exceeds that of another."[18] Equality is achieved through the similar treatment of individuals; there is no room for group rights except as an anonymous aggregation of individuals and their rights.[19] In contrast, Justice McLachlin's judgment shares the same group and sociological approach to equality that characterized *Andrews*. Thus, she mentions the legitimacy of respecting cultural and group identity in the districting process and concludes:

> Factors like geography, community history, community interests and minority representation may need to be taken into account to ensure that our legislative assemblies effectively represent the diversity of our social mosaic.[20]

This approach means that an individual's right to vote is not violated by simply demonstrating differential treatment in the districting process. As in *Andrews*, it is recognized that sometimes genuine equality will require differential treatment.

In short, the editorial writers who were surprised with the Supreme Court's decision to uphold Saskatchewan's boundaries had not been closely watching the evolution of Charter adjudication. The Court had already demonstrated its willingness to impose definitional limits on Charter rights and to defer to the state's balancing of interests in the distribution of scarce resources. Moreover, the Court had rejected the values of formal and individualistic equality in favour of a more sociological and group-based approach which legitimized preferential treatment of the disadvantaged in the interests of equality. Given these trends, the fact that the Court deferred to Saskatchewan's distribution of ridings and did not require all individuals to be treated the same under a one person–one vote standard is not surprising.

It's Not So Disturbing

For the most part, the nation's editorial writers wanted the Court to follow the American example and implement one person–one vote. They assumed that such a standard would treat individuals fairly, prevent partisan districting, and guarantee equality. Saskatchewan's decision to overrepresent the rural population in its electoral map was dismissed as another self-interested, crassly partisan move by another unpopular Canadian government. Although the Saskatchewan boundary legislation may not be admirable or public-spirited, I will suggest that the cure of equal-population standards would have been worse than the disease.

The Supreme Court was sharply divided on the merits of the impugned boundaries. Justice McLachlin took on the allegations of partisan distribution made both in the popular press and by counsel and concluded that the addition of seats in Regina, Saskatoon, and Prince Albert in the 1989 electoral map "belies the suggestion that the 1989 Act was an unjustified attempt to adjust boundaries to benefit the governing party."[21] She admits that the map over-represents rural as opposed to urban ridings on the basis of population but suggests that this is justified in part by servicing considerations, including "difficulty in transport and communications."[22] In making these conclusions, Justice McLachlin ignored evidence submitted by the respondent that in the last election before redistribution, the governing Conservatives won 32 of 34 rural ridings and only 6 urban ridings.[23] Moreover, she accepts without question some contested and empirically verifiable assumptions about the difficulty for members to service rural as opposed to urban ridings.[24] In seeking to minimize the shortcomings of the Saskatchewan legislation, Justice McLachlin engaged in questionable political science.

Justice Cory's dissent accepted the need for some differential treatment of rural as opposed to urban ridings but made no reference to allegations of partisan distribution. He did suggest that the 1989 legislation's "mandatory rural-urban allocation may have prevented the Commission from taking sufficient account of the diminishing rural population and the corresponding urban growth of the province," adding specifically that on the basis of its population Saskatoon would be entitled to another member.[25] In the end, however, Justice Cory's decision to invalidate the boundaries revolved around the fact that the 1981 map provided proof positive that boundaries could be drawn in a better fashion. This conclusion is, in my respectful view, questionable political science *and* constitutional law because it begs the normative question.

The problem with Justice Cory's reasoning is that he does not explain why the 1981 map should set the constitutional standard. As Robert G. Dixon argued: "[t]he key concept to grasp is that there are no neutral lines for legislative districts . . . every line aligns partisans and interest blocs in a different way different from the alignment that would result from putting the line in some other place."[26] Given that there are no neutral boundaries, it is not clear why, as a matter of political theory or constitutional law, the 1981 map should be preferred to the 1989 map. Both respect relative equality of voting power; there is little explanation of why a +/- 15% tolerance from equal-population standards respected in 1981 is better than the +/- 25% tolerance respected in 1989. The 1981 standards would give the growing cities slightly more representation, but why is this good? All other things being equal, similar treatment has a value in a democracy but, as was recognized in *Andrews*, it may in some contexts be antithetical to genuine equality. Justice Cory criticizes the Saskatchewan legislation for "shackling" the boundary commission, but given the assumption that there are no neutral boundaries, it would have been more appropriate to praise the legislature for its candour. If urban residents didn't like the policy behind the distribution, they knew who to vote for in the next election.

Even if the Court had enforced equal-population standards within the limits set by enumeration data and the timing of elections, this would not guarantee that the electoral map would not produce partisan advantages. In fact, the requirement that ridings have equal populations in the United States has made partisan gerrymandering easier because it has devalued the significance of natural and political boundaries that mark out communities of interests. American courts are now struggling with the second-generation problems of such partisan gerrymandering without much success. In *Davis v. Bandemer*,[27] a majority of the United States Supreme Court held that an apportionment plan could be invalidated if plaintiffs were able to show partisan intent and effects but then divided sharply on the implementation of the test. In dissent, Justice O'Connor raised the valid point that, in judging whether a districting scheme had partisan effects, the only plausible baseline would be the percentage of popular vote that each party enjoyed. This would require the courts to introduce elements of proportional representation into the Anglo-American framework of single-member geographic ridings. She distinguished policing the partisan effects of districting as less manageable and less warranted than supervising the effects of districting on minorities, primarily because of the changing political allegiances of the population at large.[28]

In general, a decision to overrepresent rural voters as opposed to urban voters would not raise concerns about discrimination. Unequal treatment in itself does not violate section 15 of the Charter as it has been interpreted by the Supreme Court. There must be a finding that the unequal treatment will result in discrimination and this means that the group on the short end of the challenged legal distinction will usually have to be one that suffers or is vulnerable to more systemic political, legal, or social discrimination.[29] Urban as opposed to rural residents would not usually meet this criteria; they are generally more numerous than those in rural and remote areas and, in the absence of empirical evidence to the contrary, it seems reasonable to assume that urban residents enjoy easier access to the machinery of politics: their member, government offices, and the media.[30]

What makes Saskatchewan a somewhat difficult case, however, is that urban residents in that province have historically been a minority and, on the basis of the data before the Supreme Court, they continue to be a minority with 47.6% of the population and under the challenged boundaries, 43.9% of the seats. Moreover, rural residents have not traditionally been a minority and they now form a bare majority of the population and have 53% of the seats.[31] This alone would not be disturbing; on the admittedly crude basis of numbers, urban residents have only a slightly better claim to being a vulnerable minority than men! However, the rural/urban polarization of support for the Progressive Conservatives and NDP in the 1986 election raises the spectre of urban residents being rendered a permanent minority in the legislature and hence vulnerable to systemic political and legal discrimination at the hands of a solidly Conservative rural majority. Fortunately, however, the increasing growth of Saskatchewan's urban centres as well as the changeable political allegiances of rural residents mitigates the possibility of a rural stranglehold on power. To be sure, there has been some recent and controversial policies to benefit rural residents, but it is difficult to believe that urban residents, as well represented as they are,[32] are vulnerable to systemic political and social discrimination.[33]

Section 15 analysis also helps to explain a curious consensus between the Court of Appeal and the Supreme Court that most of the editorial writers neglected to mention. Despite the support it gave to the one person-one vote principle, the Court of Appeal held that the two largest deviations from equal-population standards in the electoral map[34] were justified under section 1 because in these northern areas "[t]he exigencies of geography, very sparse population and communication warrant deviation from the ideal."[35] This conclusion is somewhat suspect on the Court of Appeal's own reasoning; it had emphatically rejected similar arguments about the difficulty of servicing rural ridings.[36] In the Supreme Court, both Justices McLachlin and Cory agreed that substantial deviations were justified in the North to ensure effective representation of these remote and sparsely populated regions. This consensus about the need for special treatment of the North reflects Canadian electoral traditions; the sparsely populated and remote territories have always been represented in the House of Commons in numbers much greater than their population alone demands. Most provincial electoral maps also overrepresent the northern parts of provinces from the perspective of one person-one vote.[37]

Special treatment of the North also finds support in the Court's approach to equality rights. In *Andrews*, it was recognized that equality often requires differential treatment in order to prevent further disadvantage to disadvantaged groups and, in a subsequent case, the Court was cautious not to close a person's province of residence as potentially an analogous ground of discrimination.[38] The jurisprudence under the human rights code that was incorporated in *Andrews* reveals how often similar treatment can perpetuate disadvantage and reinforce barriers to full participation. People who live in the Yukon and the Northwest Territories and the northern regions of provinces are faced with systemic barriers to political participation. They live farther away from the government and the levers of political power. Even if their remoteness could be overcome with technology, northern residents would still be vulnerable to discrimination because they are a tiny minority who often have different aspirations for their lives and their communities than those in the south.[39] Aboriginal people also make up a significant portion of the population of the North, compounding the potential that such territories will be, at best, neglected and, at worst, exploited in a majoritarian system. Enforcing equal-population standards to give the vulnerable minorities in the North even less representation would only make their situation worse.

In rejecting the one person–one vote standard, the Supreme Court was well aware of the disproportionate and disadvantaging effects that its application could have on minorities. Instead it opted for the principle of effective representation within the contours of relative equality of voting power, making specific allowance for minority representation. It is ironic how much the Court's understanding of the need for genuine equality and effective representation resembles the opinions of Robert Dixon, one of the most perceptive critics of the American one person–one vote cases. Throughout his life, Professor Dixon warned that failure to recognize that equal-population standards did not guarantee effective representation would lead Americans to adopt "a majoritarian, numbers-dominated system which tends to 'pay off' only for large groups."[40] In the years since their "reapportionment revolution," Americans have had to recognize the need to represent minorities more effectively and have used their Voting Rights Act to prevent the dilution of the voting strength of African-Americans and Hispanic-Americans. Canadians seem to have heeded Professor Dixon's concerns from the start.

Chartering the Future

Does the deferential approach taken by the Supreme Court spell an end to Charter considerations in districting decisions and judicial review over them? A focus on section 3 of the Charter and its requirement for relative equality of voting power may well lead to the conclusion that most Canadian electoral maps are "Charter-proof" and this is at least one aspect of Canadian political life that will not be affected by the Charter. If we look at section 15 of the Charter, however, I think the story is different. In order to understand where we may be heading, it will be instructive to examine the American experience of courts invalidating districting decisions that result in the dilution of the votes of geographically concentrated minorities.

The judicial career of Felix Frankfurter stands as an example of how a deferential approach to the districting process can be combined with a concern for the effect that districting decisions have on vulnerable minorities. Justice Frankfurter is best known for his counsel that courts ought to stay clear of "the political thicket"[41] raised by apportionment. Less well known, but equally important, is that he felt compelled to wade into the political thicket to hold that an Alabama law that redrew the boundaries of the City of Tuskegee to exclude its black population was an unconstitutional attempt to "single out a readily isolated segment of a racial minority for special discriminatory treatment."[42]

The American experience in dealing with discriminatory districting has some relevance in Canada. American courts have been confronted with a great variety of discriminatory districting practices. These include the use of at-large voting and geographically large multimember districts to dilute the voting strength of geographically concentrated minorities (stacking), the drawing of boundaries to ensure that minorities are kept in a minority status in a number of ridings where on the basis of their population they could form a majority in at least one riding (cracking), and the drawing of boundaries to give a minority group a large percentage of the population in one riding whereas different boundaries would give the minority group a majority in two or more ridings (packing).[43] In Canadian federal and provincial systems, a potential exists for districting decisions to dilute minority voting strength by packing and especially by cracking. In some Canadian municipalities, at-large voting may diminish the opportunities for geographically concentrated minorities to elect representatives of their choice through stacking.[44]

The potential for either discriminatory or affirmative districting in the United States has, of course, been constrained by the constitutional imperative of equal-population standards. Within these constraints, however, American courts have encouraged what one commentator recently termed "compensatory majoritarianism."[45] After the Saskatchewan decision, a potential exists in Canada for a more robust form of compensatory antimajoritarianism.

American courts have at various times been hostile to the notion that minorities had group rights to "safe seats." In 1971, the Supreme Court overturned the finding of Judge Otto Kerner that a multimember district in the Indiana legislature deprived African-Americans concentrated in Indianapolis's inner city effective political representation.[46] In 1980, the Court upheld an at-large voting scheme in Mobile, Alabama, holding that under the Bill of Rights the plaintiffs must show that the voting scheme was devised with a discriminatory intent not just a discriminatory result.[47] This decision was effectively reversed in 1982 when Congress amended the Voting Rights Act to make it illegal for districting practices to result in the infringement of voting rights.[48] This amendment has now been interpreted to invalidate districting schemes in situations where a bloc voting majority will "usually be able to defeat candidates supported by a politically cohesive, geographical insular minority group."[49] This has led to criticisms by dissenting judges and commentators that the results test has de facto created a right for minorities to have their ballots given maximum strength defined as election of their members and that this constitutes unfair affirmative action.[50] In Canada, however, affirmative action appears much less controversial than in the United States and in any event finds approval under section 15(2) of the Charter. Likewise, as under the Voting Rights Act, a Canadian plaintiff will only have to demonstrate the discriminatory effects not intent of a districting practice.[51]

A problem that the Americans have encountered that Canadians may well experience is the competitive nature of the affirmative districting process. Remember that drawing the boundaries is not neutral but an exercise in distributing political power. In a pluralistic society many groups compete for political power and, especially in our urban areas, many geographically concentrated racial, ethnic, and linguistic groups live in close proximity. A leading American case demonstrates these problems. In the early 1970s, concerns arose that black and Hispanic people had been packed in several Brooklyn and Manhattan ridings and thus their voting power minimized. The subsequent redistricting attempted to maximize the number of districts where African-Americans and Puerto Ricans would hold the balance of power but was met with charges within the two communities that the new boundaries placed previously safe seats in jeopardy. Moreover, the new boundaries were challenged on constitutional grounds by a Hasidic Jewish community who argued that the new boundaries, by dividing their community into two districts (cracking), unfairly diluted the voting strength of its members. The new boundaries were eventually upheld, with the majority of the Supreme Court holding that racial considerations and numerical quotas were allowable under the Voting Rights Act.[52] Boundary commissions and courts may be faced with competitive claims that pit a disadvantaged group against another disadvantaged group over where boundaries are drawn. On the other hand, conflict is not inevitable and disadvantaged groups may find the prospects of coalitions among themselves preferable to conflict.

As always, Canadians must approach the American experience with caution. Most minority-vote-dilution litigation in the United States has centred on the use of at-large voting at the local level, with its obvious effect of diluting the votes of geographically concentrated minorities, particularly African-Americans. In addition, American voter registration procedures have chronically deterred minority political participation and their two-party system may make racial bloc voting more likely. A history of both majority and minority groups voting as antagonistic blocs has been central to the American jurisprudence because it is thought that only then are:

> Minorities ... both unable to elect their choices to office and unable to form coalitions with whites for the election of candidates favored by the minority community. Further, white officials are free to ignore the needs and interests of the minority community, since white voters control the elections. Minority voters, as one court put it are 'frozen into permanent political minorities destined for constant defeat at the hands of the controlling political majorities.'[53]

In Canada, we know that minority groups are not represented in the legislatures in proportion to their population, but we do not know whether there is such antagonistic bloc voting with its potential of freezing minorities out of political influence.

Litigation alleging discrimination in districting remains a possibility in Canada. Such cases will not be easy to litigate but our section 15 jurisprudence, with its focus on discriminatory effects as opposed to purposes, will ease the burden of proving a constitutional violation. Because the Saskatchewan case recognizes the legitimacy of departures from equal-population standards to facilitate minority representation, litigation can focus on both how populous ridings are and where boundaries are drawn. It may not be necessary to show a history of antagonistic bloc voting, but only that a particular districting decision has the effect of disadvantaging a concentrated minority by, for example, decreasing the likelihood that they will receive services sensitive to the particular needs of their members. Minority groups may not have to show that they could have a majority of the population in a riding but only that whatever significance they could have, should not be diminished by packing or cracking.

Discriminatory districting litigation will not always succeed. Governments may be able to argue that courts should be deferential to the choices made by legislatures and boundary commissions because distribution and districting involves the allocation of scarce resources. Even if a court does find that a particular districting practice violates section 15 and the government has not justified the violation under section 1, it will face some difficult remedial problems. Courts may be unwilling to create boundaries to facilitate minority representation themselves, but they may find a way to remand the issue back to the boundary commissions and legislatures with some guidance as to how they can comply with section 15.[54]

Even if this type of litigation never emerges or is not successful, we may see districting commissions and legislatures making conscious efforts to maximize minority-group voting strength. There is some reason to believe that the very "discrete and insular" groups that are protected under section 15 will, because of these characteristics, be in a good position to lobby commissions and legislatures for safe or even guaranteed seats.[55] Even so, such minority groups, once elected, remain in the minority and face possible prejudice from the majority.[56] At present, there is discussion at the federal level and in some provinces about legislative initiatives that will provide seats for aboriginal people in proportion to their population.[57] These proposals contemplate going beyond geographic ridings and creating a separate voters' list. Since, however, the Supreme Court has affirmed that there must be only relative equality of voting power and that minority representation is a legitimate reason for departing from equal population standards, there are increased opportunities to draw the boundaries of existing ridings to encourage the representation of geographically concentrated minority groups. The approval given Saskatchewan's two northern ridings suggests how much Canadian courts are prepared to tolerate departures from equal-population standards and how this may facilitate representation of geographically concentrated aboriginal people.

Some may believe that the Saskatchewan decision leaves us with the worst of both worlds. It allows legislatures room within the wide confines of relative equality of voting power to try to obtain partisan advantage while these same generous standards and the threat of section 15 litigation will encourage "affirmative gerrymandering." My answer to these critics revolves around antimajoritarian Canadian electoral traditions, the Court's interpretation of equality rights, our present minoritarian political culture, and the prospects of alternative forms of promoting minority representation.

First, Canada has never been able to live with the unmitigated majoritarian principle of "rep by pop" and recent attempts to renew Confederation point in the direction of more not fewer departures from majority rule.[58] George Brown's principle of "rep by pop" was insufficient to create this country, and insistence on unmitigated majoritarianism remains a recipe for its fracture. To be sure, "rep by pop" received some recognition at Confederation but it was also set off through the institutions of federalism, the Senate, and group considerations in the formation of the Cabinet. In large part because of the failure of the Senate to represent regional interests, "rep by pop" has been qualified in the House of Commons to ensure that the less-populous provinces and territories maintain effective representation through the devices of the Senate Floor Rule and the "grandfather" clauses.[59] Affirmative districting was even recognized in the British North America Act of 1867 as the members of some predominantly anglophone ridings in the Québec legislature received a veto over changes in the composition of their ridings.[60] This type of protection may not have been justified at Confederation, but I think that the anglophone minority of Québec would have a strong section 15 case today that ridings should not dilute their voting strength by cracking or packing. Francophone minorities in other provinces such as New Brunswick would also have strong cases. Unfortunately, in some provinces, they would no longer have the concentrated numbers to make affirmative districting a realistic possibility.

Second, the Supreme Court has adopted a concern for effective representation from many of the same concerns that led it in *Andrews* to reject formal equality and identical treatment. The Saskatchewan legislation did not treat urban residents as favourably as rural residents but that does not mean that there is no one in the legislature to speak and lobby for urban interests. Once we move away from the rural/urban split in Saskatchewan, most of the beneficiaries of affirmative districting are more vulnerable than rural residents in Saskatchewan while those disadvantaged by such districting may be even better represented than the urban residents of Saskatchewan.

Third, it should be acknowledged that the pressures in Canadian political culture that are leading to demands for a more representative executive and judiciary are also relevant in the formation of legislatures. The modern trend is toward ensuring that minorities have proportional representation in all the institutions of government. Alan Cairns has described the growth of a new minoritarian Canadian political culture with many minority groups demanding rights and attaching themselves to the Charter, and section 15 in particular, to advance these rights.[61] Canada has never been ruled by "rep by pop" because of the need for effective representation of provinces and communities; today the effective representation of minority groups deserves the same recognition. Indeed racial, cultural, linguistic, and religious identities would seem to be part of contemporary definitions of communities of interest.

Whatever its potential, affirmative districting cannot ensure effective representation for all of those disadvantaged groups that are protected under section 15. It can only protect minorities that are both politically and geographically cohesive and large enough in number to influence election results in local, provincial, or federal constituencies. This may benefit some racial, ethnic, religious, and linguistic minorities and some unenumerated but analogous groups such as the economically disadvantaged and the gay community. It will be easier for a minority group to make a difference in elections at the local level or in less-populous provinces because the population needed to influence the election of a member will be smaller. Affirmative districting will not benefit more diffuse disadvantaged groups such as women, the disabled, and the elderly, or minority groups who are not concentrated in a riding in sufficient numbers to influence the outcome of a election. What may be needed to encourage increased representation of these groups is, in a sense, the reverse of affirmative districting, through adjustments to the populations of single-member ridings. That is, larger multimember ridings or proportional-representation systems may encourage parties to run tickets that are balanced, especially in terms of gender.[62] Another alternative is guaranteed seats for members of disadvantaged groups based on separate voters' lists.[63]

Affirmative districting is not a panacea for our contemporary concerns about the nature of representation in our legislatures and governments. In some contexts, however, I think it could encourage a politics at the constituency level that is sensitive to the concerns of minorities. This local politics may lead to members doing a better job of servicing diverse communities. If affirmative districting encourages parties to run minority candidates and if they are elected, our legislatures may better reflect our social mosaic. Even this (and for that matter more radical innovations such as guaranteed seats with separate voters' lists) will not guarantee that governments will be responsive to the disadvantaged.[64] It may, however, enable their voices to be better heard in our legislatures.

The Court's judgment in the Saskatchewan case legitimizes affirmative districting by recognizing minority representation as an approved reason for departures from equal-population standards. Section 15 litigation may in some contexts require affirmative districting by holding that districting practices that dilute a minority's voting strength have discriminatory effects.[65] To my mind, affirmative districting is not an alien or divisive innovation. It has roots in the past and particularly in the traditional concept of community of interest which also rejects a majoritarian demand for equal-population standards. It looks to the future, and in particular contemporary understandings of equality rights, to encourage minority representation within the framework of territorial representation.

Affirmative districting and active encouragement of women and minorities by political parties may allow Canada to respond to demands for more representative legislatures without moving toward separate seats allotted on the basis of gender, race, ethnicity, age, language, or disability. Such a departure from territory as a basis of representation would produce a competitive demand by any excluded disadvantaged group for its own seats. Moreover, as my colleague Katherine Swinton has suggested in her essay in this volume, separate seats stress one-dimensional understandings of identity and difference. In contrast, affirmative districting allows the continued aggregation of interests that territorial representation encourages.[66] Separate seats would create an incentive for representatives to ignore the concerns of voters who, because of their personal characteristics, are not their constituents. This might create a more responsive politics at the constituency level, but it would make politics much more difficult and divisive in the legislature. Nevertheless, Canada may be heading in the direction of separate seats and the Court's decision in the Saskatchewan case suggests that the courts might defer to such legislative attempts to facilitate minority representation.

Conclusion

Shortly after the Warren Court laid down the one person–one vote rule, Carl Auerbach noted in the "Reapportionment Cases," that "[i]t is paradoxical for the judicial activists, who extol the Court as the protector of minorities, to praise it for helping to excise the power of minorities to curb majority rule in our state legislatures."[67] A few years later, Alexander Bickel criticized the one person–one vote rule for depriving "discrete groupings and interests, regional, racial and other, of direct representation" and making impossible the use of "the method of federalism" in the construction of legislatures.[68] In the intervening years, the one person–one vote standard has remained one of the Warren Court's most popular and obeyed precedents while others of a more anti-majoritarian tenor have been resisted and eroded.[69] One person–one vote did not, however, bring about a politics more responsive to minority concerns and recent efforts under the Voting Rights Act have been directed to ensuring effective minority representation within the framework set by electoral districts with equal populations.

In the Saskatchewan case, our Supreme Court has rejected strict equal-population standards and sanctioned electoral ridings with unequal populations in the interest of effective representation, including the representation of communities and minorities. It is, in my view, not surprising or disturbing that our most antimajoritarian institution has not reached out to augment the political power of urban residents. If the Court continues to be genuinely concerned with effective representation, it can remain faithful to its antimajoritarian role. This concern will require invalidation of voting restrictions on groups such as

214

prisoners and the homeless and may require invalidation of districting decisions that dilute the voting strength of geographically concentrated minorities. Nevertheless, in a country with antimajoritarian electoral traditions and effective demands for legislatures and boundary commissions to produce policies designed to facilitate the representation of minorities, the Court's antimajoritarian role will at times require it to stay its hand. This is what the Court did in the Saskatchewan case and what I suspect it will do again in the future.

Notes

1. *Reference re Electoral Boundaries Commission Act (Sask) ss. 14, 20* (1991) 81 D.L.R. (4th) 16 (S.C.C.); "What Your Vote's Worth," *The Globe and Mail,* 7 June 1991, A14.
2. "Power Politics Still in Force," Saskatoon *Star Phoenix,* 8 June 1991, C9. For accounts that stress the partisan motivations and implications of the impugned legislation, see M. Rasmussen and M. Stobbe, eds., *Devine Rule in Saskatchewan* (Saskatoon: Fifth House Publishers, 1991), 63-64; J. Pitsula and K. Rasmussen, *Privatizing a Province: The New Rights in Saskatchewan* (Vancouver: New Star Publishing, 1990), 255.
3. "What Your Vote's Worth" (see n.1), A14. See also "A Sparkling Dissent," *The Toronto Star,* 12 June 1991.
4. *Andrews v. Law Society of British Columbia,* [1989] 1 S.C.R. 143.
5. In the American context often referred to as "affirmative gerrymandering," I prefer the term districting because, as will be discussed, the distinction between gerrymandering and districting is largely a matter of evaluation. Likewise in the Canadian context, I could also use the term "nondiscriminatory districting" to refer to attempts to ensure that districting decisions do not adversely affect geographically concentrated minority groups.
6. *Reference re an Act to Amend the Education Act (Ontario)* (1987), 40 D.L.R. (4th) 18, 60-61.
7. *Reference re an Act to Amend the Education Act* (1986), 25 D.L.R. (4th) 1 at 54 (Ont. C.A.). On the prospects of Charter review of ss. 51 and 51A of the Constitution Act, 1867, see K. Roach, "One Person-One Vote? Canadian Constitutional Standards for Electoral Distribution and Districting," in D. Small, ed., *Drawing the Map: Equality and Efficacy of the Vote in Canadian Electoral Boundary Reform* (Toronto: Dundurn Press, forthcoming); K. Swinton, "Federalism, Representation, and Rights" in this volume.
8. *R. v. Edwards Books and Art,* [1986] 2 S.C.R. 713, 779.
9. *Reference re Public Service Employees Relations Act,* [1987] 1 S.C.R. 313, 403-4.
10. *Reference re Electoral Boundaries Commission Act* (see n.1), 20-21, 36-37. It is interesting to note that the Court has not accepted similar arguments in other contexts that they believe are within "the inherent domain of the judiciary." For example, there is no evidence that anyone thought s. 7 of the Charter would regulate the principles of liability in the substantive criminal law and there is some evidence that it was intended only to provide procedural protections. *Reference re B.C. Motor Vehicles* (1985), 24 D.L.R. (4th) 536 (S.C.C.).
11. *Irwin Toy v. Québec* [1989] 1 S.C.R. 927; *McKinney v. University of Guelph* (1990)

76 D.L.R. (4th) 545 (S.C.C.); *R. v. Keegstra* (1991) 61 C.C.C. (3d) 1 (S.C.C.).

12. Factum of the Appellant Attorney General of Saskatchewan, para. 138, p. 56, Supreme Court of Canada file 22345.

13. *Reference re Electoral Boundaries Commission Act* (see n.1), 39.

14. In several important speeches, Justice McLachlin has articulated her own judicial philosophy as one that requires a certain amount of judicial deference toward the legislature and aims at cooperation among these two institutions. See B. McLachlin, "The Charter: A New Role for the Judiciary?" *29 Alberta Law Review* (1991): 540; B. McLachlin, "The Role of the Court in the Post-Charter Era: Policy-Maker or Adjudicator," 39 *UNB Law Journal* (1990): 39.

15. This manner of Charter interpretation resembles that championed by my colleague David Beatty who argues that the Court embraced this approach in some early Charter cases but has increasingly departed from it. See Beatty, *Talking Heads and the Supremes: The Canadian Production of Judicial Review* (Toronto: Carswell, 1990). It will be apparent that I agree with some of Beatty's empirical observations about the behaviour of the Supreme Court but do not share his normative conclusions that the recent more deferential approach is unconstitutional or even bad.

16. *Reference re Electoral Boundaries Commission Act* (see n.1), 26.

17. For commentary supportive of *Andrews*, see W. Black and L. Smith, "Case Comment," 68 *Canadian Bar Review* (1989): 591. For commentary critical of the decision, see Beatty, *Talking Heads and the Supremes* (see n.15), 73 n.6.

18. *Reference re Electoral Boundaries Commission Act (Sask.) ss. 14, 20* (1991) 78 D.L.R. (4th) 449 at 460 (Sask. C.A.).

19. As the Court of Appeal stated: "And what applies at the level of the individual applies at the level of the group. If one constituency of voters, 5,000 in number let us say, is entitled by law to elect one representative, while another, numbering 10,000, is entitled to no more, then obviously it cannot be said each is being accorded their democratic rights. The rights of the latter are debased," ibid., 461. Even the Court of Appeal's decision to hold that two northern ridings were justified under s. 1 of the Charter is not connected to the need for effective representation of distinct regional groups, ibid., 481.

20. *Reference re Electoral Boundaries Commission Act* (see n.1), 36.

21. Ibid., 42.

22. Ibid., 44.

23. Respondent's Factum, para. 57, p. 21, Supreme Court of Canada file 22345 (results of 1986 election).

24. Increasingly heterogenous urban ridings may very well present their own servicing problems.

25. *Reference re Electoral Boundaries Commission Act* (see n.1), 25–26. In the 1986 election, 8 of 10 Saskatoon seats were won by the NDP, often by large margins. See *Canadian Parliamentary Guide 1989*, 1089.

26. R.G. Dixon, "Fair Criteria and Procedures for Establishing Legislative Districts," in Grofman, Lijphart, McKay, and Scarrow, eds., *Representation and Redistricting Issues* (Lexington: D.C. Heath, 1985), 7–8.

27. 478 U.S. 109 (1986).

28. Ibid., 155–56. See also, L. Tribe, *Constitutional Law*, 2d ed. (Mineola: Foundation Press, 1988), 1082-84; P. Schuck, "The Thickest Thicket: Partisan Gerrymandering

and Judicial Regulation of Politics," 87 *Columbia Law Review* (1987): 1325, for commentary that supports Justice O'Connor's position.

29. *R. v. Turpin* (1989) 48 C.C.C. (3d) 8 at 34 (S.C.C.).

30. Kent Roach, "Reapportionment in British Columbia," 24 *UBC Law Review* (1990): 92-93.

31. *Reference re Electoral Boundaries Commission Act* (see n.1), 42.

32. It can be expected that policies to favour rural interests such as the decentralization of the civil service will be balanced by other policies to attract the urban vote such as the government's recent role in enticing Crown Life to relocate in Regina.

33. There are disadvantaged people living in the cities but the disadvantages they suffer from the impugned distribution of ridings are at most indirect. There is little reason to think that adding a few members would result in better representation of disadvantaged groups in the cities. As will be discussed in the next section, however, minorities, including the economically disadvantaged, might have a legitimate constitutional claim if the boundaries of ridings in urban areas were drawn to diminish their influence in elections.

34. The northern ridings of Athabasca and Cumberland with variations from the 1986 electoral quotient of -37.3% and -28.1% respectively. *Reference re Electoral Boundaries Commission Act* (see n.18), 470.

35. Ibid., 481.

36. Attempts to justify unequal districts under s.1 for reasons of quality of service are vulnerable to arguments that the government can and should address servicing issues directly (travel allowances, free phone lines, etc.) and not through the districting process.

37. *Campbell v. Canada (Attorney General)* (1987) 21 B.C.L.R. (2d) 130 aff'd (1988) 25 B.C.L.R. (2d) 101 (B.C.C.A.); Patrick Boyer, *Election Law in Canada* (Toronto: Butterworths, 1987), 107ff; G. Dacks, "Political Representation in The Northwest Territories," in J. Johnston and H. Pasis, eds., *Representation and Electoral Systems: Canadian Perspectives* (Scarborough: Prentice-Hall Canada, 1990), 143-44.

38. *R. v. Turpin* (1989) 48 C.C.C. (3d) 8 (S.C.C.). Note that the discrimination claim in *Turpin* was that those accused of murder in all provinces except Alberta were victims of discrimination. There is little reason to believe that Parliament would subject accused people in the vast majority of the country to systemic prejudice as opposed to those in Alberta. The case may have been different if the accused were from the Territories where, by virtue of *Criminal Code* provisions, juries are composed of only 6 people whereas in the rest of Canada they have 12 people. See *R. v. Emile* (1988) 42 C.C.C. (3d) 408 (N.W.T.C.A.), holding that the 6-person jury violates s. 15. Since *Turpin*, however, the Supreme Court has backed off the notion that a person's province of residence could be an analogous ground of discrimination, at least in the context of criminal law. See *R. v. S. S.* (1990) 77 C.R. (3d) 273 (S.C.C.).

39. See generally, Thomas Berger, *Northern Frontier, Northern Homeland: The Report of the Mackenzie Valley Pipeline Inquiry* (Ottawa: Supply and Services, 1977); A.C. Hamilton and C.M. Sinclair, *Report of the Aboriginal Justice Inquiry of Manitoba* (Winnipeg: Queen's Printer, 1991), 227-37.

40. R.G. Dixon, "The Warren Court Crusade for the Holy Grail of 'One Man-One Vote,'" *Supreme Court Law Review 219* (1969): 268. See also, R.G. Dixon, *Democratic Representation: Reapportionment in Law and Politics* (New York: Oxford University Press, 1968).

41. *Colegrove v. Green* 328 U.S. 549 at 556 (1946); *Baker v. Carr* 369 U.S. 186 at 226 (1962).
42. *Gomillion v. Lightfoot* 364 U.S. 339 at 346 (1960).
43. See generally, F. Parker, "Racial Gerrymandering and Legislative Reapportionment," in C. Davidson, ed., *Minority Vote Dilution* (Washington: Howard University Press, 1984), 85, who uses the evocative terms "stacking," "cracking," and "packing." See also, *Wright v. Rockefeller* 376 U.S. 552 (1964); *Allen v. State Board of Education* 393 U.S. 544; *White v. Regester* 412 U.S. 755 (1973); *United Jewish Organization v. Carey* 430 U.S. 144 (1977); *Connor v. Finch* 431 U.S. 407 (1977); *Rodgers v. Lodge* 458 U.S. 613 (1982).
44. At-large voting schemes were adopted in some municipalities to diminish the influence of minority groups in ward systems: N. Maveety, *Representation Rights and the Burger Court* (Ann Arbor: University of Michigan Press, 1991), 102. Although s. 3 of the Charter only protects the right to vote in federal and provincial elections, at-large schemes could be challenged under s. 15 of the Charter.
45. Ibid., 123. See also, B. Grofman, "What Happens After One Person–One Vote?" in this volume.
46. *Whitcomb v. Chavis* 403 U.S. 124 (1971). Judge Kerner had chaired the National Advisory Commission on Civil Disorders arising out of inner-city riots in 1968 in which he stated that America was "moving toward two societies, one black, one white—separate and unequal." See A. Thernstrom, *Whose Votes Count? Affirmative Action and Minority Voting Rights* (Cambridge: Harvard University Press, 1987), 69–70.
47. *Mobile v. Bolden* 446 U.S. 55 (1980).
48. Voting Rights Act, 42 U.S.C. #1973, s. 2.
49. *Thornberg v. Gingles* 106 S.Ct. 2752 at 2766 (1986). For a fuller discussion of both this case and a district-specific approach to racial gerrymandering, see B. Grofman, "What Happens After One Person–One Vote?" in this volume and literature cited therein.
50. *Thornberg v. Gingles*, 2790–92 per Justice O'Connor; Thernstrom, *Whose Votes Count?* (see n.46); D. Wells, "Against Affirmative Gerrymandering," in *Representation and Redistricting Issues* (see n.26), 77.
51. *Andrews v. Law Society of British Columbia* [1989] 1 S.C.R. 143.
52. Justice White noted that the redistricting left white majorities at both the county and state levels, stating "there was no fencing out of the white population from participation in the political processes of the county, and the plan did not minimize or unfairly cancel out white voting strength . . . even if voting in the county occurred strictly according to race, whites would not be underrepresented relative to their share of the population." *United Jewish Organization v. Carey* 430 U.S. 144 at 165–66 (1977). Such reasoning would also be relevant under the *Andrews* approach to equality, although the Jewish community could also make claims under s. 15 of the Charter.
53. Parker, "Racial Gerrymandering and Legislative Reapportionment" (see n.43), 108.
54. Roach, "Reapportionment in British Columbia" (see n.30), 93–101.
55. M. Olson, *The Logic of Collective Action: Public Goods and the Theory of Groups* (Cambridge: Harvard University Press, 1965); B. Ackerman, "Beyond *Carolene Products,*" 98 *Harvard Law Review* (1985): 713.
56. D. Farber and P. Frickey, "Is *Carolene Products* Dead? Reflections on Affirmative

THE CHARTER AND ELECTORAL VALUES

Action and the Dynamics of Civil Rights Legislation," 79 *California Law Review* (1991): 703-6.

57. "A Place in the Mainstream," *The Globe and Mail*, 29 May 1991, A5; L. Marchand et al., *Aboriginal Electoral Districts: The Path to Electoral Equality* [Ottawa]: The Committee for Aboriginal Electoral Reform (1991).

58. A reformed Senate would temper majority rule and recent proposals have suggested that an elected upper house should effectively represent not only regional minorities but women and various ethnic and racial minorities. Section 3 of the Charter would not apply to elections for an upper house because it applies only to elections for the House of Commons and the provincial assemblies. Section 15 would still apply but it allows and may even require differential treatment to aid disadvantaged groups. On voting rights and the Senate, see generally, F.L. Morton and R. Knopff, "Does the Charter Mandate 'One Person, One Vote'?" Research Study 7.1, Research Unit for Socio-Legal Studies, University of Calgary, 1991.

59. K. Swinton, "Federalism, Representation, and Rights," in this volume.

60. Constitution Act, 1867 (U.K.), 30 & 31 Vict., s. 80.

61. A. Cairns, *Disruptions: Constitutional Struggles from the Charter to Meech Lake* (Toronto: McClelland & Stewart, 1991) D. Williams, ed.

62. This has been the European experience. M. Steed, "The Constituency," in *Representation and Electoral Systems* (see n.37), 198. On the other hand, multimember ridings have often been challenged by geographically concentrated African-American groups in the United States as a dilution of their voting strength.

63. See Christine Boyle's proposals for dual male and female members for ridings or at-large voting with guaranteed representation for women. C. Boyle, "Home-Rule for Women: Power Sharing Between Men and Women," 7 *Dalhousie Law Journal* (1983): 790.

64. L. Guiner, "The Triumph of Tokenism: The Voting Rights Act and the Theory of Black Electoral Success," 89 *Michigan Law Review* (1991): 1077.

65. Section 15(2) allows governments to implement affirmative-action measures should they choose to do so. On the other hand, identical treatment of groups in some contexts may violate the equality rights of s. 15(1) and lead to purposive remedies that resemble activities that could be justified under s. 15(2).

66. K. Swinton, "Federalism, Representation, and Rights," in this volume.

67. C. Auerbach, "The Reapportionment Cases: One Person, One Vote–One Vote, One Value," *Supreme Court Law Review* 1 (1964). Along similar lines, R.G. Dixon concluded in the early 1970s that: "[r]eapportionment has transferred political power to the suburbs, but minority representation is undervalued or precarious under the predominantly majoritarian cast of the rulings." Dixon, "The Court, The People, and 'One Man, One Vote'," in N. Polsby, ed., *Reapportionment in the 1970s* (Berkeley: University of California Press, 1971), 8.

68. A. Bickel, "The Supreme Court and Reapportionment," in *Reapportionment in the 1970s* (see n.67), 72.

69. Many of the Warren Court's decisions protecting civil and due-process rights have been resisted by governments and eroded by the subsequent decisions of the Burger/Rehnquist Court. In contrast the one person–one vote cases were quickly obeyed and quite popular. G. Baker, *The Reapportionment Revolution* (New York: Random House, 1967), 40. Subsequent courts have eased the one person–one vote standard in state legislatures, but maintained it in vigour for congressional districting.

Canada's Constitutional Mosaic: Boundaries in Dispute

DOUG WILLIAMS
DEPARTMENT OF JUSTICE CANADA[1]

All the social sciences are submerged biographies of the silent majority of humanity: the peasant, the artisan, the immigrant, the slave, women, and (in our case) that basic irreducible unit of representative politics, the voter. All of them, even as mere numbers, have surfaced in the human sciences as part of a long and slow democratization of values in a period whose ideologies were often . . . hostile to these aspirations.

— Judith N. Shklar

The beginning of wisdom in comparative constitutionalism consists in the realization that the appropriate division of labor between legislature and judiciary must, to a large extent, be indigenous to each country and must depend on that nation's experience with and faith in the operation of each branch.

— Paul C. Weiler

Introduction

Conceptualizing the movement and merits—or otherwise—of Canada's constitutional order has developed into more than a small cottage industry of scholarly articles and books. Something closer to the image of a sprawling industrial park of constitutional commentary more accurately describes the scope, the sophistication, and the vitality of scholarship on the Canadian Constitution since 1982. And there can be little doubt that it was the inclusion of the Charter of Rights and Freedoms in Canada's constitutional order that has prompted this much-to-be-welcomed outpouring of theoretical reflection and debate. In my view, this recent addition to our constitutional discourse represents the greatest transformation in Canadian political thought since Confederation.[2] More important for the present discussion, few areas of legislation and public policy illuminate this deep transformation in our national self-understanding more effectively and in such a timely manner than that of electoral redistribution.

The following discussion primarily takes place on the playing field of political philosophy. Such an approach seems appropriate not only in light of my professional training, but more importantly, because the merits of *any* serious argument about voting "weight" ultimately turn on several fundamentally disputed points of political philosophy. No one understood this better than Felix Frankfurter in his powerful dissent in the landmark *Baker v. Carr* decision. In opposition to those about to initiate a still-turbulent period of court-led redistribution in the United States, Frankfurter wrote:

> Talk of "debasement" and "dilution" is circular talk. One cannot speak of "debasement" or "dilution" of the value of the vote until there is first defined a standard of reference as to what a vote should be worth. What is actually asked of the court in this case is to choose among competing bases of representation— ultimately, really, among competing bases of political philosophy.[3]

That a similar train of thought has come to orient the Supreme Court of Canada's interpretation of the content of Charter rights was forcefully stated by Dickson, J. (as he then was) in *R. v. Big M Drug Mart Ltd.* where he observed:

> In my view this analysis is to be undertaken, and the purpose of the right or freedom in question is to be sought by reference to the character and the larger objects of the *Charter* itself, to the language chosen to articulate the specific right or freedom, to the historical origins of the concepts enshrined, and where applicable, to the meaning and purpose of the other specific rights and freedoms with which it is associated within the text of the *Charter*. The interpretation should be, as the judgment in *Southam* emphasizes, a generous rather than a legalistic one, aimed at fulfilling the purpose of the guarantee and securing for individuals the full benefit of the *Charter*'s protection. At the same time, it is important not to overshoot the actual purpose of the right or freedom in question, but to recall that the *Charter* **was not enacted in a vacuum,** and must therefore, as this Court's decision in *Law Society of Upper Canada v. Skapinker* ... illustrates, be placed in its proper linguistic, philosophic and historical contexts.[4]

It should not be surprising, then, that Madam Justice McLachlin was impressed by the same "broad and purposive approach" when writing on behalf of the six-to-three member majority in the Supreme Court's recent reference case on the Saskatchewan government's electoral redistribution.[5] Ultimately, I intend to argue that in addressing the issue of electoral representation in the manner it has, the Supreme Court of Canada demonstrates an abiding respect for many enduring features of its traditional constitutional order and distinctiveness. Against the view of many, I accordingly contend that the *principled*

221

concerns brought to bear upon the issue of electoral boundaries by the Supreme Court's majority provide compelling evidence *against* the alleged "Americanizing" influence of the Charter—at least insofar as the country's understanding of representation is concerned.

Chartering Boundaries

An instructive example of the changes wrought by the Charter upon our constitutional identities and the character of the country's public philosophy can be gleaned from comparing recent controversies over the court cases of British Columbia and Saskatchewan with an earlier debate on redistribution in the House of Commons in 1974, prior to the proclamation of the Representation Act of that year.

On two occasions in 1974, the House debated issues concerned with devising a new formula for redistributing federal electoral seats. On 11 January 1974, the House Leader (at the time, Mr. MacEachen) introduced a suspension bill (C–208), ordering a halt to the redistribution process then underway until January 1975 so "that the system of readjusting representation in the House of Commons, including the method of determining the number of Members for each province established by Section 51 of the British North America Act [could] be referred to the Standing Committee on Privileges and Elections" for extensive review and public discussion. As things turned out, shortly thereafter Parliament was dissolved and the ensuing election prevented the committee from studying the problem in any further detail. However, on 20 February, prior to the dissolution of Parliament, the government's proposals—the so-called "amalgamation formula"—were laid before the Standing Committee on Privileges and Elections by the Leader of the House.[6]

Following the intervening election, on 2 December 1974 the Hon. Mitchell Sharp (who succeeded Mr. MacEachen as House Leader) moved second reading of a bill based on the earlier proposals. The legislation passed quite easily, receiving Royal Assent on 20 December.[7] Shortly thereafter, Professor Mallory drew attention to an especially noteworthy feature about the debate on both these occasions: "the House seemed scarcely aware that it was debating a constitutional change of major importance."[8] Unlike previous changes in electoral redistribution, The Representation Act, 1974, was not described as an amendment to the British North America Act at all. As Mallory observed, whether intentional or otherwise, this had the effect "of distracting attention from the fact that the bill was a constitutional amendment of some importance."[9]

I intend to argue that one inevitable and salutary consequence of the addition of the Charter to our political order has been to preclude virtually any such "distracting" effect in the future when constitutional issues are at stake. Quite the contrary, as citizens and elites have learned to work their constitution in the post-Charter era, the overwhelming impact of such activity has been to elevate its visibility and the *principled* level of constitutional discussion, to deepen its entanglement in matters of everyday life and far-reaching concern, and to catalyze a healthy public debate about alternative bases of citizenship and democracy in Canada.

Of special interest in the context of the post–Meech Lake experience of constitutional renewal, Mallory ultimately explained the lack of serious public discussion of the redistribution issue in 1974 as "a good example of the 'closed politics' of a past age which would not have understood participatory democracy."[10] This experience stands in marked contrast to the level and volume of serious public discussion—indeed controversy—surrounding the judiciary's recent involvement in determining electoral boundaries in British Columbia and Saskatchewan.

To cite but one of many available examples, shortly after the Supreme Court of Canada's ruling on the Saskatchewan government's reference appeal, the former Attorney General of British Columbia, Bud Smith, argued before the annual meetings of the Commonwealth Parliamentary Association that "we should do all we can to keep the courts out of the issue, almost entirely. The question of effective representation is simply none of their business."[11] According to Mr. Smith, the Charter of Rights and Freedoms represents a "Franco-American system of law" and is conceptually incompatible with British parliamentary tradition.

Several things are problematic about the intellectual foundations of the former BC Attorney General's criticisms of the Supreme Court's involvement in the issue of effective representation. In the next part of this paper, I will situate and attempt to refute the allegation concerning the fundamental incompatibility between the Charter and parliamentary tradition within a larger body of commentary, an interpretive community best described as captives of a polarized, dichotomous way of thinking and an insufficient historical understanding of political traditions, rights, and the nature of democratic government.

I also intend to argue that the recent experience with the politics of electoral redistribution in Canada has continued to extend and deepen, rather than impede, the vitality of discussion in Canada of what Shklar referred to at the outset of this paper as the "long and slow democratization of values"[12] in much the same fashion as occurred during the Meech Lake process, a process understandably of more visibly recognized constitutional change. Governments were forced to appreciate that the "closed politics" of traditional executive federalism had become unacceptable to many Canadians during the Meech Lake process. The constitutional order had, as Alan Cairns classically observed, ceased to be exclusively an affair of governments, citizens having come to demand a more active hand in shaping their constitutional futures in the post-Charter era.[13]

Distinct traces of a significantly enhanced role of Canadian citizens in the process of electoral reform are everywhere to be found in the recent judicial cases in British Columbia and Saskatchewan—in the initiation of litigation itself, in the mobilization of bias and support, in their characteristic post-Charter, postmodern (meaning widely consumed, fragmented, frequently sensationalistic) media exposure, and in patterns of interveners before the courts, to name only the most obvious dimensions. Charting electoral boundaries in the post-Charter era, thus yet again, has opened the constitution up for public discussion and wider participation in an unprecedented manner.[14]

In significant respects, the struggle over electoral boundaries, like the prior Meech Lake experience, represents a contest between long-standing champions and critics of the Charter of Rights and Freedoms—and not just with respect to its specific effects on particular jurisdictions, groups, and individuals, but with its larger symbolic dimension and long-term institutional impact in mind as well. In the conclusion to this admittedly speculative paper, I will engage this debate arguing that, at least insofar as the question of redistributing electoral boundaries is concerned, recent experience provides more than a little evidence for the emergence of what Weiler has termed an indigenous variety of "comparative constitutional wisdom." Such a wisdom would be indicative of a creative political artistry, increasingly able to define an appropriate division of labour between the legislative branch of government and the judiciary, respectful of the history and merits of each body and the interests they *ideally* are intended to serve.[15] That Canada may finally be working itself toward the type of constitutional mosaic appropriate to its complex history and its increasingly dynamic nature is this paper's animating assumption.

Constitutional Change in a Distinct Society

Since the idea of entrenching a charter of rights first arose at the federal level, constitutional discussion has often succumbed to what has been characterized in another context as the "fallacy of misplaced polarities." In the 1960s, Giovanni Sartori rightly pointed out that much of the work in the field of comparative political development was dominated by a series of misleading dichotomies such as "modernity" and "tradition," obscuring fundamental dimensions of politics in political systems situated at both ends of the spectrum. Dimensions of modernization in formerly "traditional" societies, as well as strong remnants of traditional behaviour in allegedly opposite "modern" states, were equally misunderstood.

The view of the former BC Attorney General, that the question of effective representation is simply "none of [the court's] business," and a good deal of the so-called "populist" challenge to entrenching the Charter of Rights and Freedoms, are predicated on a similar kind of polarized thinking. This habit of thought has assumed several different forms. The underlying common denominator to each of these variations is the belief in the fundamental incompatibility of judicial supremacy and parliamentary government.

On such a view, "the ballot box is the people's ultimate mechanism for controlling the shape of government policies . . . [And] in Canada, voting is also how citizens have traditionally influenced 'rights' issues such as abortion, capital punishment, and language."[16] By contrast, Canadians do not elect judges. They are appointed to tenured positions from which they can be removed only on grounds of personal misbehaviour—a category that excludes the direction of and underlying rationale of their rulings. And this indepen- dence, what Weiler describes as "this absence of accountability to the general public," stands at the very heart of the judicial office in Canada.

Small wonder, then, that criticisms of the judicial appointments process have assumed significant new proportions in the post–Charter era. For while such detachment from popular influence is apparently desirable in judges adjudicating the fate of an individual under an established legal framework ("Is so-and-so actually guilty of fraud or murder?" for example), it is not as clear that such an absence of accountability is appropriate once judges are obliged to confront directly issues involving deep moral and philosophical concern such as the Charter embodies. Indeed, criticism in this respect recently has run so deep as to provoke questions about the very legitimacy of the Canadian judiciary.[17] Happily, this is a debate beyond the scope of the present discussion.

But it underscores a basic philosophical debate about the nature of democratic government in Canada in the post-Charter period. To what extent is the Court's obligation to rule on important issues of entrenched rights fundamentally in- compatible with a healthy respect for the legislative will of the people as manifest in Parliament and the provincial legislatures? Those who define the terrain of the debate as involving a stark contrast between the American (or "Franco-American") tradition of a "rights conscious" citizenry and an activist judiciary, on the one hand, and the Canadian tradition of parliamentary democracy and "rule by the people," on the other, suggest just such an incompatibility. Before exploring the contrary view, a few specific aspects of the "populist" critique of the Charter and the judiciary's new role of adjudicating conflicts involving fundamental moral and political values merit further attention.

One of the most persistent criticisms of the Charter has been that judicial rule would undermine "a sense of community" and make it more difficult to generate social policy that reflects "community values."[18] A related concern was that it would encourage having recourse to "a quick judicial fix over the arduous and unpredictable demands of politics," reinforcing allegedly unnatu- ral habits of passivity and docility among citizens.[19] More pointedly, the charge has been made that the Charter has confused the Canadian notion of democ- racy: "We have come to imagine that democracy has more to do with the protection of individual rights than with rule by the people."[20] And it is increasingly common to find these specific sorts of charges rolled up into a broader thesis about how these alleged antidemocratic effects of the Charter represent yet a further step in "Americanizing" Canadian habits of thought and institutions.

In short, whether presented in the form of a heated polemic or a probing philosophical analysis, there is no shortage of support for the view that, in entrenching the Charter in the constitutional order, we have jeopardized our distinctiveness as a political community, having grafted what Charles Taylor has popularized as an alien "atomistic" variety of individualism and "rights seeking" consciousness onto our more indigenous "communitarian" and "participatory" public philosophy. The Charter thus construed has dramatically increased the general likelihood of litigiousness and spearheaded a more general "judicialization" and "legalization" of the political process. Canadians can be expected to increasingly call upon the law and the judiciary to stifle—indeed "trump"—the more authentic Canadian model of political participation, the central pillar of which is parliamentary sovereignty.[21]

In my opinion, a number of the stark contrasts evident in this train of thought—especially the juxtaposition of individual rights and "rule by the people"—are examples of committing the constitutional and philosophical equivalents of the "fallacy of misplaced polarities." As such, this "populist" critique of the Charter obscures fundamental historical and political realities about the nature of rights, unwittingly underestimates the strength and depth of the Canadian political tradition itself, and, finally, frequently burdens discussion of constitutional change with unnecessary and misleading simplifications. While it may be true that a "concern for the individual is the defining characteristic of liberalism, not of democracy,"[22] this really misses several fundamental points about rights in *any* system of limited, democratic governance.

When one explores the *principled case for democratic government*, it supports not the pure majoritarian form, but instead a regime itself limited by constituent moral principles and ideals. One of the most important of these ideals is that of placing some restraints on the legitimate scope of majority will: "limitations that flow from a decent respect for the fundamental rights of the individual."[23] *Democracy as an ideal* fundamentally must reflect as great a concern for the protection of minorities as it does for allowing its majorities to rule through elected delegates. The alternative is to reduce the meaning of democratic government to the *de facto* view that whatever policy the majority of a community wants, it is entitled to—regardless of the costs and burdens that policy may impose on a dissenting minority.

The delegated nature of modern governance provides an equally significant ground of support for the international movement toward entrenching fundamental, judicially enforceable rights in constitutional agreements and comparable covenants, of which the Canadian Charter of Rights and Freedoms is but one recent example. Consider the case of the administration of criminal justice. In such a field, the basic challenge is to effectively balance the shared collective need for effective crime control and the individual's claim to personal liberty. It goes without saying that a legislative body of *any* variety—parliamentary or congressional—is structurally incapable of resolving this tension in a specific situation. The very best a legislative body can achieve in this context is to express a particular mood, declaring perhaps that the powers of arrest "must be exercised only on reasonable grounds, taking account of the relevant circumstances."[24]

Of necessity, in the pre-Charter era, ultimate responsibility to make administrative decisions in a specific criminal case fell to various public officials (police, prosecutors, prison and parole board officers, etc.). Such officers not only generally operated with little public visibility but naturally expressed a bureaucratic perspective "inherently tilted against claims of civil liberty infringement."[25] With the Charter in place, ultimate authority over reconciling such claims falls to the court–an institution with no commitment to either side of the dispute and, perhaps more significantly, conducting its proceedings in *full public view*, each side obliged to present its case in a public hearing reported by the media. Notwithstanding other issues in the criminal justice area which may be in dispute, it is hard to see how giving authoritative voice to appointed judges instead of, say, various appointed police officials or parole officials is an erosion of Canadian democracy.[26]

As the reach of the state extends ever deeper into the everyday lives of citizens throughout the world, a totally natural response has been to seek correspondingly greater security against potential abuses of such delegated authority, even that expressed through majorities in representative bodies. No one perhaps expressed this concern more clearly than Alexander Hamilton in the famous *Federalist* 78, when he observed that: "It is not otherwise to be supposed that the Constitution could intend to enable representatives of the people to substitute their *will* to that of their constituents. It is far more rational to suppose that the courts were designed to be an intermediate body between the people and the legislature in order, among other things, to keep the latter within the limits assigned to their authority."[27]

It is more than a little logical, and not to be attributed to the strength of American exports, that as the "administrative state" has increased its demands and burdens upon its citizens, they in turn have sought refuge in the protection of institutions of remedy, appeal, and restraint.[28] Courts fulfil these tasks in ways other institutions are ill-equipped to perform. In the context of public law, a government of the day might be tempted to enact laws that hamstring the opposition party in an election, by perhaps trying to dilute the integrity of the vote through the malapportionment and/or gerrymandering of constituencies, or through measures designed to muzzle the press. It is hard to figure out how judicial review over such matters, requiring elected officials simply to adhere to some of the basic underlying moral principles of a democracy, detracts from or frustrates the citizenry's self-rule.[29]

To be sure, challenging the traditional practices of executive federalism and parliamentary government to execute their responsibilities in more accountable, representative ways undoubtedly *complicates the democratic process*. But to blame this important transformation in the traditional "pillars" of Canadian constitutionalism on importing yet another bad, foreign idea from the United States profoundly underestimates the international appeal and moral force sustaining such a modification to our traditional pattern of government. Perhaps even more disturbing, the so-called populist critique of the Charter equally underestimates the strength of Canada's indigenous political tradition and the distinctiveness of its current constitutional order. Before concluding with a few remarks about how, in my opinion, the Supreme Court's recent ruling on the Saskatchewan government's appeal concerning electoral redistribution represents a paradigm of this distinctiveness—an indigenous variety of constitutional wisdom—several comments about political change in the context of Canada's overall constitutional order seem appropriate.

Political traditions are learned habits of association. As such, the longer their performance, the greater the likelihood of their survival notwithstanding necessary modification in the face of change. In concluding, I will suggest that we may increasingly want to conceptualize the constitutional order, like our society's class, power, and ethnic structures as John Porter once classically expressed them, as a mosaic.[30] Before doing so, however, it may be helpful to recall just how distinctive, how uniquely Canadian, the Charter of Rights and Freedoms has helped the larger constitutional order to become, even in more traditional terms.

Suffice it to say that anyone the least bit familiar with both the history and nature of a country like Canada will recognize the fact that the typical "rights" case will nearly always present a difficult moral choice between individual claims and community needs. In the present context, this becomes manifest in the dilemma of reconciling the representation of people, considered as individuals, with the ideal of representing a variety of other interests, typically congealed in particular places and communities scattered throughout Canada's diverse, unevenly inhabited terrain.

We sometimes tend to lose sight of the fact that the Canadian Charter is, in fact, far more sensitive and candid than the American Bill of Rights in reconciling the responsibility of protecting an individual's fundamental legal and democratic rights with other aspects of the constitutional order, as articulated through the tradition of parliamentary government. The caveat with which the Charter begins—the section 1 declaration that its guarantees are to be subject "to such reasonable limits . . . as can be demonstrably justified in a free and democratic society"—is but one of many features conveying the explicitly complex blend of majoritarian and minoritarian interests simultaneously being addressed in the Constitution.[31] To this general reminder of the need to balance the interests of majorities and minorities in the Constitution, we might also recall various specific protections and guarantees extended to majorities and minorities in the very same part of the Charter (for example, as in section 15). And an even more obvious, albeit still controversial, legacy of the Charter's distinctive quality is evident in the *non obstante* or "notwithstanding clause" of section 33.

Amidst all this evidence to the contrary, it is less than fully clear why so many commentators have insisted on viewing the role of the Charter in Canadian political life as such an alien import. The ideals underlying its initial design and, by and large, its subsequent impact on the overall constitutional order to date provide more than ample support for viewing our most recent "constitutional experiment" as at least a modest success in reconciling the

traditional claims of parliamentary government with the more recent, interna-
tionally driven demand for the protection of minorities and an entrenched body
of rights.[32]

New Boundaries: Electoral Redistribution as a Paradigm of Canada's Constitutional Mosaic

As should be clear by now, this paper has been much less concerned with the
redistribution of specific electoral boundaries in a particular province than with
the underlying train of thought appropriate for reflecting upon the issue in the
context of enhancing the prospects of democracy in Canada in the post-Charter
era. Against those who feared that the introduction of the Charter into such
areas of public policy as have traditionally fallen under the jurisdiction of
Parliament and the provincial legislatures would generate a greater sense of
docility and apathy, it has been suggested that subjecting the issue of electoral
redistribution to the process of judicial review has significantly enhanced the
level of interest, the quality of debate, and the public's role in the matter.[33] If
responsiveness to citizens' interests and demands is to stand as a significant
measure of the health of a political order in the "participatory age," then I would
suggest that the judiciary's recent role in the issue of redistributing electoral
seats is a paradigm case of healthy constitutional balancing between the
legislative majority will of the people and the judicial branch's interest in and
responsibility for protecting the interests of potentially vulnerable minorities.

Specifically, in upholding the Saskatchewan government's electoral boundary scheme, the Supreme Court of Canada not only recently reaffirmed its
intention to interpret the rights guaranteed and protected in the Charter in
historical and philosophical contexts unique to the country, but more significantly, it did so with regard to the issue that perhaps better than any other takes
us to the very heart of the distinctiveness of Canada's political traditions. For
in concluding that an individual's "parity of voting power, though of prime
importance, is not the only factor to be taken into account in ensuring effective
representation," Madam Justice McLachlin gave strong voice to the range of
considerations distinguishing the difficulties of representing Canadians from,
say, their neighbours to the south. Representing people and places, if you will,
in a country as geographically dispersed and as unevenly and generally thinly
populated as Canada, and in the midst of significant new immigration and
mobility trends, suggested to the Court that the purpose of section 3 of the
Charter[34] was not to ensure "equality of voting power *per se*, but the right of
effective representation."[35]

Notwithstanding the Charter, the Supreme Court went on to confirm that ours,
indeed, is a representative democracy, the contours of which fall very much within
the traditional jurisdiction of provincial legislatures and Parliament to reconfigure,
provided the deviations from voter parity are justified. Factors like geography,
community history, community interests, and minority representation, the judgment goes on to argue, "may need to be taken into account to ensure that our

legislative assemblies effectively represent the *diversity of our social mosaic.*"[36] These, the Court goes on to point out, are but some of the examples of "considerations which may justify departure from absolute voter parity in the pursuit of more effective representation; the list is not closed."[37]

Nothing could be further from this train of thought concerning electoral redistribution than current American thinking and practice, where what Robert Dixon once decried as the "higher math" of the matter has become so complex as to lead the courts to impose stricter numerical tests of voter equality than the statistical reliability of the U.S. Census can even sustain![38] And this might have come as less of a surprise had various critics of the Charter taken the time to appreciate how differently configured and deeply embedded in a unique prior constitutional order our entrenched rights were from those of the United States.

As alluded to earlier, future students of Canadian constitutionalism may find it useful to think of the constitutional order as a complex, moving mosaic. Picture this mosaic as a series of multicoloured tiles and mirrors suspended beneath the three pillars of the constitutional order as a whole—federalism, parliamentary government, and the Charter.[39] Imagine these three pillars, as well, configured like a pyramid, beneath which this evolving mosaic (or constitutional culture) perpetually moves. Domestic and international transformations periodically force the suspended mosaic to shift its movement and motion, but those pillars of governance beneath which it hangs derive from "a living tree capable of growth and expansion within *its natural limits.*"[40] At least insofar as we have elected to represent ourselves, an indigenous stock of comparative judicial wisdom would seem to have taken firm root in Canada. Thinking this all through in terms of a variegated mosaic in motion—with vertical, horizontal, and temporal planes all simultaneously at play—might begin to do justice to the political artistry our times increasingly demand.

Notes

1. The views expressed in this paper are solely those of the author; they do not necessarily reflect the policies or views of the Government of Canada or the Department of Justice. The author would like to thank Mirella D'Avanzo and Robin Rostad for their assistance in preparing this paper, as well as Lynn Smith, Christopher Manfredi, and Cynthia Williams for comments on an earlier version of the paper which was presented at the conference on "Drawing Boundaries: Legislatures, Courts and Electoral Values," jointly sponsored by the College of Law and the Department of Political Studies of the University of Saskatchewan, held 8–9 November 1991 in Saskatoon.
2. For a fuller discussion of the issues involved in studying Canadian political thought, see Cynthia and Doug Williams, "Ideas and Identities in Canadian Political Life," in A. Gagnon and J. Bickerton, eds., *Canadian Politics: An Introduction to the Discipline* (Peterborough: Broadview Press, 1990), 196–228 and the references therein.
3. 369 U.S. 186, 7 L.Ed. (2d) 1962, 734.
4. [1985] 1 S.C.R. 295, 344, emphasis added.

5. *Reference re Electoral Boundaries Commission Act (Sask), ss 14, 20* (1991) 81 D.L.R. (4th) 16 (S.C.C.).

6. For helpful background to and analysis of the Amalgam Method and formula, see J.R. Mallory, "Amending the Constitution by Stealth," *Queen's Quarterly* 82 (Autumn 1975): 394–401; M.L. Balinski and H.P. Young, "Parliamentary Representation and the Amalgam Method," *Canadian Journal of Political Science* 14/4 (1981): 797–812; and J. Courtney, "The Size of Canada's Parliament: An Assessment of the Implications of a Larger House of Commons," in P. Aucoin, ed., *Institutional Reforms for Representative Government,* Vol. 38 of the Research Studies of the Royal Commission on the Economic and Development Prospects for Canada (Toronto: University of Toronto Press, 1985); J. Courtney, "Some Thoughts on Redistribution," *Canadian Parliamentary Review* (Spring 1986): 18–20; and J. Courtney, "Parliament and Representation," *Canadian Journal of Political Science* 21/4 (1988): 675–90.

7. The complete proposals and projected alterations to existing ridings appear in *Canada. House of Commons Standing Committee on Privileges and Elections: Minutes of Proceedings and Evidence,* 3 (9 April 1974): 3, 27–33, 145.

8. Mallory, "Amending the Constitution by Stealth" (see n.6).

9. Ibid., 398.

10. Ibid., 400.

11. Quoted in Jody Paterson, "Put Curb on Judges to Avoid Elite Rule, Parliamentarians Warned by Smith," Victoria *Times-Colonist,* 13 August 1991, A3.

12. Judith N. Shklar, "Redeeming American Political Theory," *American Political Science Review* 85/1 (1991): 4.

13. See Alan C. Cairns, "Citizens (Outsiders) and Governments (Insiders) in Constitution-Making: The Case of Meech Lake," *Canadian Public Policy,* Supplement 14 (1988), reprinted in Douglas E. Williams, ed., *Disruptions: Constitutional Struggles from the Charter to Meech Lake* (Toronto: McClelland and Stewart, 1991). More extended discussion of the decline of citizens' deference throughout the world and of the international dimensions and influence of rights discourse can be found in Max Kaase, "The Challenge of the 'Participatory Revolution' in Pluralist Democracies," *International Political Science Review* 5/3 (1984); Neil Nevitte, "New Politics, the Charter and Political Participation," (mimeo) in H. Bakvis, ed., *Representation, Integration, and Political Parties in Canada* (Toronto: Dundurn Press, 1991 forthcoming), a Research Study of the Royal Commission on Electoral Reform and Party Financing; Cynthia Williams, "The Changing Nature of Citizen Rights," in Alan C. Cairns and Cynthia Williams, eds., *Constitutionalism, Citizenship and Society in Canada* (Toronto: University of Toronto Press, 1985), Vol. 33 of the Research Studies of the Royal Commission on the Economic Union and Development Prospects for Canada; and Doug Williams, *Problems of Governance, Political Participation and the Administration of Justice in an Information Society* (Ottawa: Department of Justice, Research and Development Directorate, 1991).

14. Compare recent experience with the situation described by R.K. Carty: "If, historically, Canadian concepts of representation have rejected precise criteria for boundary revisions, and especially any strict application of numerical equality, the recent revolution in electoral mapmaking indicates that this element of the (elite) political culture has not significantly changed." "The Electoral Boundary Revolution in Canada," *American Review of Canadian Studies* 15/3 (1985): 282.

Tensions brought to the surface during the recent redistributions in British Columbia and Saskatchewan suggest significant changes in both the elite and mass political cultures insofar as issues of representation are concerned.

15. Paul Weiler, "Rights and Judges in a Democracy: A New Canadian Version," *University of Michigan Journal of Law Reform* 18/1 (1984): 74-75.

16. Ibid., 65.

17. For helpful introductions to this debate, compare: David M. Beatty, *Talking Heads and the Supremes: The Canadian Production of Constitutional Review* (Toronto: Carswell, 1990), especially part 3; Patrick Monahan, *Politics and the Constitution: The Charter, Federalism and the Supreme Court* (Toronto: Carswell, 1987), especially part 2; Keith Banting, *Federalism and the Supreme Court of Canada: Competing Bases of Legitimation*, prepared for the Ontario Law Reform Commission Conference on the Nomination of Persons for Judicial Appointment, 14-15 September 1989; and Alan C. Cairns, "Who Should the Judges Be? Canadian Debates about the Composition of a Final Court of Appeal," prepared for the Fourth Berkeley Seminar on Federalism, 19-20 April 1990.

18. These two phrases respectively come from a paper written by Professor G.P. Brown of Carleton University (distributed by the Manitoba Government at the First Ministers' Conference on the Constitution in September 1980); and Sterling Lyon, "Notes for a Statement on the Entrenchment of a Charter of Rights," First Ministers' Conference on the Constitution, 9 September 1980, p. 6. For a thoughtful discussion of such a sentiment in the context of the long-standing dichotomy and "basic tension between liberty and community" in Canada, see Robert C. Vipond, *Liberty and Community: Canadian Federalism and the Failure of the Constitution* (Albany: State University of New York Press, 1991), especially 1-3, 191-97.

19. This view was argued a year ago in a stinging polemic by Robert Martin, "The Charter and the Crisis in Canada," in David E. Smith, Peter MacKinnon, and John C. Courtney, eds., *After Meech Lake: Lessons for the Future* (Saskatoon: Fifth House Publishers, 1991), 126.

20. Ibid., 122.

21. Representative of the more polemical approach are Michael Mandel, *The Charter and the Legalization of Politics in Canada* (Toronto: Wall and Thomson, 1989), and Robert Martin, "The Charter and the Crisis in Canada" (see n.19); an elegant though similarly motivated philosophical discussion can be found in Charles Taylor, "Alternative Futures: Legitimacy, Identity and Alienation in Late Twentieth Century Canada," in *Constitutionalism, Citizenship and Society* (see n.13), 183-229. The fact that these critics of the Charter represent the so-called "left" of the Canadian political spectrum, while those mentioned earlier (see n.17) are identified with conservative ideology, may suggest that the roots of "populism" in Canada are more complex and differentially inspired than elsewhere.

22. Martin, "The Charter and the Crisis in Canada" (see n.19), 122.

23. Weiler, "Rights and Judges in a Democracy" (see n.15), 68.

24. Ibid., 66.

25. Ibid.

26. For an informative discussion of the interpretive impact of the Charter on the administration of criminal justice, see Kent Roach, "The Charter and the Criminal Process," in J. Gladstone, R.V. Ericson, and C.D. Shearing, eds., *Criminology: A Reader's Guide* (Toronto: University of Toronto Press, 1991), especially 200-2.

27. In Alexander Hamilton, James Madison, and John Jay, *The Federalist Papers*, edited with an Introduction by Clinton Rossiter (New York and Scarborough: Mentor Books, 1961), 467.

28. For interesting discussions of the growth and nature of the "administrative state," compare Paul Pross, "Space, Function, and Interest: The Problem of Legitimacy in the Canadian State," in O.P. Dwivedi, ed., *The Administrative State in Canada: Essays for J.E. Hodgetts* (Toronto: University of Toronto Press, 1982); and Alan C. Cairns, "The Past and Future of the Canadian Administrative State," *University of Toronto Law Journal* 40 (1990): 319–61.

29. For a particularly clear statement of this thesis, see J. Ely, *Democracy and Distrust* (Cambridge: Harvard University Press, 1989), especially chapter 5.

30. See John Porter, *The Vertical Mosaic* (Toronto: University of Toronto Press, 1965).

31. For helpful discussions of the presence of these two sorts of interests and rights in the Charter, compare F.L. Morton, "Group Rights Versus Individual Rights in the Charter: The Special Cases of Natives and Québecois," in N. Nevitte and A. Kornberg, eds., *Minorities and the Canadian State* (Oakville: Mosaic Press, 1985); David Elkins, "Facing Our Destiny: Rights and Canadian Distinctiveness," *Canadian Journal of Political Science* 22/4 (December 1989): 699–716; and the articles contained in a special issue of the *Canadian Journal of Law and Jurisprudence* 4/2 (July 1991), especially the introduction by Michael McDonald, "Should Communities Have Rights? Reflections on Liberal Individualism."

32. For an early discussion of the Charter's influence in this context, see Alan C. Cairns, "The Canadian Constitutional Experiment," *Dalhousie Law Journal* 9/1 (1984), reprinted in Douglas E. Williams, ed., *Constitution, Government, and Society in Canada* (Toronto: McClelland and Stewart, 1988), chapter 8.

33. As Ronald Dworkin once put the matter, the process of judicial review transfers issues of fundamental rights "from the battleground of power politics to the forum of [moral and legal] principle." See "The Forum of Principle," 56 *NYU Law Review* (1981): 518.

34. Section 3 reads: "Every citizen of Canada has the right to vote in an election of a member of the House of Commons or of a legislative assembly and to be qualified for membership therein."

35. *Reference re Electoral Boundaries Commission Act* (see n.5), 35.

36. Ibid., 36 (emphasis added).

37. Ibid.

38. For helpful discussions of this experience, compare Nelson W. Polsby, ed., *Reapportionment in the 1970s* (Berkeley: University of California Press, 1971); Charles Redenius, "Representation, Reapportionment, and the Supreme Court," *Political Studies* 30/4 (1982); and F.L. Morton and Rainer Knopff, "Electoral Distribution and the Courts: Does the Charter of Rights Require 'One Person, One Vote'?" (Calgary: Research Unit for Socio-Legal Studies, 1991).

39. For an early elaboration on these three "pillars" of Canadian constitutionalism, see Cynthia Williams, note 13; and for a discussion of several other metaphors we might consider in conceptualizing Canada's constitutional order, see Doug Williams, "Meisel's Postcards: or Notes Toward a Constitutional *Colimaison*," a paper presented at the Conference in Honour of John Meisel, "Canada's Century: Governance in a Maturing Society," held at Queen's University in April 1991.

40. These, of course, are Lord Sankey's famous words in *Edwards v. Attorney-General of Canada*, (1930) A.C. 124, 136.

COMMENTARY

CHRISTOPHER P. MANFREDI
MCGILL UNIVERSITY

It is by now almost platitudinous to declare that the Charter of Rights and Freedoms has had a profound impact on Canadian political life. Nevertheless, it remains important to measure that impact in specific cases and issue areas. Such is the task undertaken by Kent Roach and Doug Williams with respect to the *Saskatchewan Electoral Boundaries Reference* (1991). Roach's principal objective is to challenge the conventional wisdom that the Supreme Court's decision in this case was "surprising and disturbing"; Williams's concern is with what this case reveals about the populist critique of Charter decision making evident in the work of commentators like Michael Mandel and Robert Martin. For both Roach and Williams, the political impact of the *Saskatchewan Reference* was not nearly so large as many believe, and it is to this proposition that my comments are directed.

According to Roach, the decision upholding the constitutionality of Saskatchewan's electoral boundaries was not surprising in view of the Court's recent tendency to interpret rights more narrowly and to defer to the legislature's balancing of competing policy considerations. These tendencies became evident in several Charter decisions: the *Separate Schools Reference* (holding that the Charter does not invalidate other constitutional provisions); *Edwards Books and Art* (holding that courts should defer to legislative policy balancing that favours disadvantaged groups); and the *Alberta Labour Reference* (holding that freedom of association does not guarantee a constitutional right to strike). In Roach's view, Justice McLachlin's decision in the Saskatchewan case that the right to vote guaranteed by section 3 of the Charter does not entail "equality of voting power"[1] is similarly narrow and deferential.

There are at least two reasons, however, to question this interpretation. First, although the decision might be deferential in a narrow, technical sense (since the Court upheld the districting plan), it still contains elements of the broad and

234

purposive interpretive method evident in the Court's most activist decisions. Indeed, it is necessary to distinguish carefully between judicial deference and judicial restraint. Courts may defer to specific policy choices while simultaneously expanding their own political power. Perhaps the best example of this phenomenon is the Supreme Court's decision in *Operation Dismantle* (1985). In this case, the Court deferred to the Cabinet's decision to allow cruise-missile testing while simultaneously rejecting the "political questions" doctrine, which would have excluded such policy choices from judicial review altogether.

The second reason for reconsidering Roach's interpretation is that Justice McLachlin's decision to define the "right to vote" as really meaning the right to "effective representation" does not constitute a particularly narrow interpretation of section 3. To the contrary, the narrowest interpretation of the right to vote would seem merely to mean the right to enter a voting booth once every four or five years and mark an "X" on a piece of paper. Even this interpretation of section 3 would leave ample opportunity for judicial review, since existing legislative incursions on this right would need to be justified under section 1. At most, one can characterize McLachlin's decision as a narrow interpretation of the "right to effective representation."

By transforming the relatively straightforward word "vote" into the indeterminate phrase "effective representation," Justice McLachlin's majority judgment is, in fact, an activist decision that lays the groundwork for a powerful and continuing judicial role in supervising the electoral system. Although McLachlin conceded that one precondition for "effective representation" is "relative parity of voting power,"[2] she intimated that defining the right to vote in terms of absolute voter parity would actually be an overly restrictive interpretation of section 3. Implicit in her judgment is the view that the Court has more important things to consider in implementing section 3 than simply guaranteeing adherence to the one person–one vote standard.

It is thus correct to suggest that those who advocate greater judicial supervision of the electoral process need not be overly alarmed at the Court's reluctance to declare Saskatchewan's electoral boundaries unconstitutional. The open-ended nature of the newly declared collective right of various groups to "effective representation" guarantees an abundance of constitutional litigation in the future. In particular, the Saskatchewan decision opens up two lines of inquiry that raise significant questions about the normative legitimacy and institutional capacity of the Court's exercise of its constitutional review powers under section 3. If the establishment of judicially manageable standards of a quantitatively defined right to effective representation is difficult, then this is doubly so for a qualitatively defined version of that right. Moreover, a qualitatively defined right to effective representation presents numerous remedial puzzles. For example, it is not inconceivable that the Court might find it necessary to order that a certain number of seats in a legislature be reserved for groups whose historical exclusion from the political process have made them "discrete and insular minorities."

The possibilities for judicial activism within the framework established by the *Saskatchewan Reference* indicate the importance of considering the issues raised by Doug Williams. Like Roach, Williams suggests that this decision does not deserve the level of criticism it has received, largely because it reflects Canadian political culture. More generally, Williams's purpose is to challenge the "populist" critique of Charter adjudication, which is based on two propositions: first, that the Charter imports an alien (i.e., American) notion of individual rights into Canadian political discourse, thus corrupting Canada's more communitarian political culture; second, the Charter undermines the traditional structure and practice of parliamentary democracy. Williams's response to these propositions is that the populist critique misstates the nature of rights and the balance between individuals and community, and that it underestimates the strength of Canada's indigenous political traditions and the distinctiveness of the current constitutional order.

Williams is correct to assert that the populist critique is partially misplaced, but not for the reasons he offers. What the Charter actually imports into Canadian political discourse is a late-20th-century *corruption* of American political principles in which *judicial supremacy* has replaced *constitutional supremacy*. This view can be summarized in the following syllogism: the constitution is the supreme law; the judiciary is the authoritative voice of the constitution's meaning; therefore, the judiciary is the source of supreme law. The corruption consists in the widespread acceptance of the minor premise, and is best reflected among Canadian cases in the Supreme Court's *B.C.G.E.U.* decision of 1988. In this decision, the Court argued that the Charter could not be used to close British Columbia courts because the Charter is meaningless without operating courts, and democracy ceases to exist if the Charter is meaningless.

The original American understanding of the relationship among courts, the constitution, and the more overtly political branches of government is best expressed by Alexander Hamilton's description in a passage from *Federalist* 78 (quoted by Williams) of courts as an *intermediate* body between the people and the legislature. Although Hamilton conceded the power of courts to review the constitutionality of legislation, he saw this power as being legitimately exercised only under very narrow circumstances. Moreover, in *Federalist* 81 he made it clear that judicial usurpations of legislative authority could, and should, be remedied by the simple expedient of impeachment. In the original institutional design of the U.S. Constitution, the judiciary, executive, and legislature were co-equal branches of government, each with coordinate authority to interpret the Constitution.

The consequences of ignoring this original view in favour of importing the modern American conception of judicial power are especially troubling when one conceives of constitutional adjudication as involving judicial guardianship of fundamental moral principles, which appears to be the view implicit in Justice McLachlin's electoral boundaries judgment. One reason that this is troubling is that it is an inaccurate description of most Charter decisions. Charter cases are only rarely about fundamental rights, and almost never about fundamental moral principles. Instead, they usually involve policy disputes whose resolution is centred around the least-restrictive-means branch of the *Oakes* test. A second reason to worry about this trend is its belief in the idea that judges are moral philosophers. It is a profoundly odd notion to believe that elevation to a nation's highest court transforms someone into a moral philosopher. There is nothing in legal training or the practice of law that imparts superior judgment in this area. Indeed, the image of members of the Canadian Court as moral philosophers, sitting in judgment about the fundamental principles of our political regime, borders on the absurd.

Notes

1. 81 D.L.R. (4th), 35.
2. Ibid.

COMMENTARY

JON H. PAMMETT
CARLETON UNIVERSITY

Equality of voting strength or worth as a standard for establishing constituency boundaries has the advantage of simplicity and of "fairness" as a test of its face validity. Such a division is reasonably easy to accomplish, if we accept the caveat that the equality can never be exact because of deaths, population movements, etc. It has the disadvantage of being an absolute; if this standard is accepted, it is not easy to talk in any terms other than those of absolutes, or to maintain a position that any deviation from absolute equality of constituency size is acceptable.

Once a criterion other than equality of voting power is accepted as a proper basis for drawing boundaries, as is now the case in Canada after the Supreme Court decision on the Saskatchewan boundaries, we are into very murky territory, because absolutes are not present. Nevertheless, we must recognize that the history of constituencies is replete with instances of boundary drawing that are not based on equality. Foremost among these have been efforts to represent localities of unequal size. The philosophical justification for so doing, however, has been so intimately involved with the efforts to gain partisan advantage that it is difficult to disentangle the two.

The establishment of territorial constituencies for electoral choice goes back to the Attica of 508 BC, when the reorganization of Kleisthenes divided the territory into about 170 demes, communities with definable geographic localities. These were, however, combined further into larger subunits, and finally into 10 tribes, essentially artificial units. Some of the particular combinations of demes (which formed the basis of the sortitions) have led to speculation that this was the "first gerrymander," as the districts appear to have favoured the Alkmeonid family and their allies, who lived in a number of different spots.

In the Roman Republic, one of the two voting assemblies, the *comitia tributa*, reflected the organization of the Roman state into 35 local districts, again called tribes. Only 4 of these were in Rome proper, and this was not adjusted when the population of the city grew. Rather, new citizens were added to rural tribes, even if their residence was elsewhere. Voting took place by tribe, and only in Rome (where elections were not permitted on market days). Those who could afford to come to Rome, or who lived there already, composed the tribe for electoral purposes. Prominent families and candidates manipulated this system ruthlessly, even after the secret ballot was introduced in 139 BC, which permitted simultaneous voting. Thus, the territorial divisions served to support a politics of personal gain for both leaders and followers.

Both Canada and the United States inherited a system of constituencies from Britain, where their design was intimately linked to their representative function. Counties were the preserve of large landowners, peers, country gentlemen; these worthies, fired by noblesse oblige, were charged with taking care of their districts. Boroughs were of various sorts but were represented by local patrons and officials, with the same charge. Parliament was to be composed of men of substance, responsible for their locality and usually resident in it, well situated to be the channel of benefit to that specific area.

Drawing constituency boundaries in ways that deviate from equality of population has had two purposes, which we may label empowerment and distribution. To take the latter first, it can be argued that "coherent" local areas, which may be quite different in size and population, have specific needs for government services, largesse, and patronage. The most effective distribution of benefits thus requires the drawing of local boundaries to reflect "community of interest," in which "interest" is given a direct material interpretation. An empowerment purpose for drawing boundaries makes the assumption that group representation can be achieved by tailoring constituencies to reflect the predominance of such groups in a local area.

Can cultural, racial, or ethnic groups realistically expect to be empowered by the drawing of local constituency boundaries to reflect their existence? The operations of a parliamentary system of government with executive dominance makes one sceptical of this possibility. Does a smaller-than-average population (producing a more "coherent" constituency) enhance the chances of getting the representative into Cabinet? This seems doubtful; in fact, it might work in reverse. Are we to assume that "community of interest" is important because of all the free votes MPs engage in, and the assumption that MPs, being delegates, will be better able to vote the way their coherent rather than incoherent riding wants? The empowerment purpose for unequal representation seems to assume a potency for local MPs and MPPs that simply does not exist.

The most logical explanation seems to be that the Supreme Court feels that effective representation depends on the distribution of local benefits. To the extent that "taking care of the local district" is the prime function of a representative, and that "taking care" involves the procurement of local patronage, then a doctrine of "effective representation" makes some sense as the criterion for the establishment of constituency boundaries. To the question raised by the *Saskatchewan Reference* case, and by many of the papers at this conference, "what does effective representation mean?" it provides a possible answer. Effective representation consists of the provision of the maximum amount of direct material benefit for a local area. In order to establish the nature of the most desirable benefit (which is presumed to vary with the needs of local areas), it is necessary to employ "community interest" as a criterion for establishing the appropriate boundaries.

Does this mean that the personal problems of constituents are better dealt with in smaller, or more "coherent," constituencies? It might, if office staff is constant in size. But why do some constituents deserve better service than others? The Supreme Court makes reference to rural voters making more demands on their representatives. This may be so, but if this doctrine is extended to encompass many different groups, will the allocation of resources to satisfy local demands be augmented to the point where many more people are better served? And, although many would argue that the American congressman fulfills precisely the role of local provider, is the MP in the modern parliamentary system in a good position to do so? Cabinet control of the levers of patronage leaves little room for independent action by the local member.

However, need we be so sceptical and vaguely negative about the Supreme Court's new doctrine of effective representation based on the distribution of local patronage. Different kinds of electoral politics contain within themselves the seeds of their own modification. The electoral politics of issues and opinions, which has dominated federal and provincial politics in Canada for much of this century, is one without social roots or personal contact.[1] Its discontents are those of distance and meaninglessness. Its superficiality and reliance on merchandising and business-derived advertising techniques have been accompanied by "consumer resistance" in the form of public disinterest in politics and cynicism about politicians. A politics of personal or small-group gain is difficult to sustain as well because of the pervasive atmosphere of corruption it engenders, and the difficulties of operating it on a large scale; that's why we left it behind, to a large extent, at the beginning of this century. But never completely. And perhaps it is time for a more overt recasting of politics to take account of the particularistic, to bend the boundaries, to give more special favours. This might do more than any reform of Parliament or provincial legislatures to revive the powers of local members. Maybe the Supreme Court is actually on to something.

Notes

1. For an elaboration of the analysis alluded to here, see Jon H. Pammett, "A Framework for the Comparative Analysis of Elections Across Time and Space," *Electoral Studies* 7/2 (1988): 125–42. An application to Canada has been made in Jon H. Pammett, "The Meanings of Canadian Elections," paper prepared for "Canada's Century: Governance in a Maturing Society—A Conference in Honour of John Meisel," Queen's University, April 1991.

Contributors and Editors

DAVID J. BERCUSON, FRSC, is Professor of History and Dean of Graduate Studies at the University of Calgary. He has published extensively in the area of Canadian military and labour history.

R.K. CARTY is an Associate Professor in the Department of Political Science at the University of British Columbia who served as a consultant to a recent electoral boundary commission in BC. Recent publications include *Grassroots Politicians: Party Activists in British Columbia* (co-author) and *Leaders and Parties in Canada: Experiences of the Provinces* (co-editor).

BARRY COOPER is Professor of Political Science at the University of Calgary. He has published in the area of Canadian political thought and Western political philosophy. Together with David Bercuson he is the co-author of the controversial bestseller, *Deconfederation: Canada Without Quebec.*

JOHN C. COURTNEY is Professor of Political Studies at the University of Saskatchewan. In 1990–91 he was the William Lyon Mackenzie King Visiting Professor of Canadian Studies at Harvard University.

MUNROE EAGLES is Assistant Professor of Political Science and a Research Scientist with the National Center for Geographic Information and Analysis (NCGIA) at the State University of New York at Buffalo. He has recently authored two research studies for the Canadian Royal Commission on Electoral Reform and Party Financing, and has published articles in *Political Geography Quarterly* (1988), the *British Journal of Political Science* (1989), and the *European Journal of Political Research* (1991).

WARD ELLIOTT is a Professor of Government at Claremont McKenna College (California) and the author of *The Rise of Guardian Democracy* and articles and reviews on voting rights and reapportionment. He has also written on smog, traffic, and population policy. He is a member of the Society for Preservation of Middle Class; the Claremont Bicentennial Power Lawn Mower Drill Team; and the Pumpkin Papers Irregulars.

RONALD E. FRITZ is Associate Professor of Law at the University of Saskatchewan. Although his research interests had primarily been in the areas of family law and insurance law, he developed a personal interest in the Saskatchewan redistribution process flowing from the 1987 provincial legislation. Subsequent to making an individual submission to the Saskatchewan Electoral Boundaries Commission, he became an incorporator, director, and officer of the Society for the Advancement of Voter Equality (SAVE) and aided SAVE's counsel in the preparation and presentation of SAVE's position in the Saskatchewan Electoral Boundaries Reference case.

241

BERNARD GROFMAN is Professor of Political Science and Social Psychology at the School of Social Sciences, University of California, Irvine. His major fields of interest are in American politics, comparative election systems, and social choice theory. His current research is on mathematical models of group decision making and focuses on small group behaviour (especially juries) on the one hand, and electoral behaviour (especially reapportionment) on the other. He is also involved in modelling individual and group information processing and decision heuristics.

JANET HIEBERT is an Assistant Professor of Political Studies at Queen's University and was a Research Coordinator for the Royal Commission on Electoral Reform and Party Financing.

THOMSON IRVINE, B.A. (Hons., Sask.), LL.B. (Queen's), LL.B. (Laval), LL.M. (Yale), is a former Law Clerk at the Supreme Court of Canada. He is currently a Crown Solicitor with the Constitutional Law Branch, Public Law & Policy Division, of the Saskatchewan Department of Justice.

RAINER KNOPFF, Professor of Political Science at the University of Calgary, was the founding editor of the Canadian Journal of Law and Society, and has written widely in the areas of public law and Canadian political thought. Recent publications include *Charter Politics* (1992), co-authored with F.L. Morton, and *Human Rights and Social Technology: The New War on Discrimination* (1989).

PETER MACKINNON is Dean and Professor of Law at the University of Saskatchewan. He is a former president of the Canadian Association of Law Teachers, and a current Bencher of the Law Society of Saskatchewan. He was appointed Queen's Counsel in 1990.

CHRISTOPHER P. MANFREDI is Assistant Professor, Department of Political Science, McGill University. He has published articles on the Charter of Rights and Freedoms in the *Canadian Journal of Political Science, Canadian Public Administration*, and the *American Journal of Comparative Law.*

F.L. MORTON is an Associate Professor of Political Science at the University of Calgary. His research on constitutional law, courts, and civil liberties has been published in Canada, the United States, Britain, and France. He is co-author with R. Knopff of *Charter Politics* (1992) and editor of *Law, Politics and the Judicial Process in Canada* (1984).

JON H. PAMMETT is Professor and Chair of the Political Science Department at Carleton University, Ottawa. He has written extensively on elections in Canada and elsewhere, and is co-author of *Absent Mandate: Interpreting Change in Canadian Elections.*

MURRAY RANKIN is a partner in the law firm of Arvay Finlay, Victoria and Vancouver, BC. He has been a Professor of Law at the University of Victoria and was counsel for the Government of the Yukon in its Supreme Court intervention in the *Carter* case.

ROBERT G. RICHARDS holds an LL.B. from the University of Saskatchewan and an LL.M. from Harvard University. He was Director of Constitutional Law in Saskatchewan from 1985 to 1990 and has extensive litigation experience in the constitutional field. He presently practises with MacPherson, Leslie & Tyerman in Regina.

CONTRIBUTORS AND EDITORS

KENT ROACH is an Assistant Professor of Law at the University of Toronto, Faculty of Law, and a former Law Clerk for Madam Justice Bertha Wilson of the Supreme Court of Canada. In addition to articles and casebooks in the fields of criminal justice and constitutional litigation, he is the author of two essays on distribution, districting, and the Charter published in the *University of British Columbia Law Review* and Volume 11 of the *Research Studies* of the Royal Commission on Electoral Reform and Party Financing.

NORMAN J. RUFF is an Assistant Professor of Political Science at the University of Victoria and a specialist in British Columbia politics. Recent works include "Pacific Perspectives on the Canadian Confederation" in Douglas Brown, ed., *Canada: The State of the Federation, 1991* (1991) and "Continuity and Change: Party Activists, 1973–87" in D. Blake, R.K. Carty, and L. Erickson, *Grassroots Politicians: Party Activists in British Columbia* (1991). Together with W. Ross, he made six submissions on electoral redistribution to the Fisher Commission 1987–88 and is currently working on a comparative study of electoral reform.

ANDREW SANCTON is an Associate Professor of Political Science at the University of Western Ontario and director of the Local Government Program. He has recently written "Local Government Reorganization in Canada since 1975," a research report published by the Intergovernmental Committee on Urban and Regional Research.

HOWARD A. SCARROW is Professor of Political Science at the State University of New York at Stony Brook. His chapter on "Apportionment, Districting, and Representation in the United States" appears in Volume 11 of the *Research Studies* of the Royal Commission on Electoral Reform and Party Financing.

DAVID E. SMITH, FRSC, is Professor of Political Studies at the University of Saskatchewan. His most recent publications include *Jimmy Gardiner: Relentless Liberal* (1990), co-authored with Norman Ward, and (forthcoming) *Building a Province: A History of Saskatchewan in Documents* (1992).

JENNIFER SMITH is Associate Professor of Political Science at Dalhousie University. She is currently a member of the Nova Scotia Electoral Boundaries Commission.

KATHERINE SWINTON is a Professor at the Faculty of Law of the University of Toronto and is cross-appointed to the Department of Political Science. Her teaching and research interests include Canadian constitutional law, federalism, and equality in employment. Her most recent book is *The Supreme Court and Canadian Federalism: The Laskin-Dickson Years* (1990).

DOUG WILLIAMS is Senior Research Officer in Public Law with the Department of Justice in Ottawa. He formerly taught political theory, Canadian politics, and Women's Studies at Queen's University, McGill University, and the University of Victoria, and is the author of *Truth, Hope and Power* (1988), a number of articles on the philosophy of the social sciences, film, and political analysis, as well as the editor of *Constitutionalism, Government and Society in Canada* (1988), *Disruptions: Constitutional Struggles from the Charter to Meech Lake* (1991), and of *Political Theory by Other Means* (1991).

Bibliography

Books and Articles

Ackerman, B. 1985. "Beyond *Carolene Products.*" 98 *Harvard Law Review* 713.

Advisory Commission on Intergovernmental Relations. 1964. "Principles for Reapportionment: Recommendations." Reprinted in *Legislative Apportionment,* edited by Howard Hamilton, pp. 117-23. New York: Harper & Row.

APSA, Committee Report. 1951. "The Reapportionment of Congress." *American Political Science Review* 45.

Archer, Keith. 1990. "Voting Rights in Alberta Under the *Electoral Boundaries Commission Act, 1990.*" Manuscript. University of Calgary.

Auerbach, C. 1964. "The Reapportionment Cases: One Person, One Vote-One Vote, One Value." *Supreme Court Law Review* 1.

Balinski, M.L., and H.P. Young. 1990. "Fair Electoral Distribution." In *Representation and Electoral Systems: Canadian Perspectives,* edited by H. Paul Johnston and H. Pasis, pp. 240-44. Scarborough: Prentice-Hall.

——. 1981. "Parliamentary Representation and the Amalgam Method." *Canadian Journal of Political Science* 14: 797-812.

Bickel, Alexander. 1965. *Politics and the Warren Court.* New York: Harper & Row.

——. 1971. "The Supreme Court and Reapportionment." In *Reapportionment in the 1970s,* edited by N. Polsby. Berkeley: University of California Press.

Birch, A.H. 1964. *Representative and Responsible Government.* Toronto: University of Toronto Press.

British Columbia. 1984. *First Report of the British Columbia Electoral Commission.*

British Columbia, Legislative Assembly, Select Standing Committee on Labour, Justice and Intergovernmental Relations. 1989. *Minutes.*

Cain, Bruce E. 1984. *The Reapportionment Puzzle.* Berkeley: University of California Press.

Cairns, Alan C. 1988. "Citizens (Outsiders) and Governments (Insiders) in Constitution-Making: The Case of Meech Lake." *Canadian Public Policy* Supplement 14. Reprinted in *Disruptions: Constitutional Struggles from the Charter to Meech Lake,* edited by Douglas E. Williams. Toronto: McClelland and Stewart, 1991.

Canada. 1991. *Shaping Canada's Future Together: Proposals.* Ottawa: Minister of Supply and Services.

Carty, K.C. 1985. "The Electoral Boundary Revolution in Canada." *American Review of Canadian Studies* 15/3: 273-87.

Clark, William A.V., and Peter A. Morrison. 1991 forthcoming. "Demographic Paradoxes in the Los Angeles Voting Rights Case." *Evaluation Review.*

Congressional Globe. 22 January 1866.

Courtney, John C. 1988. "Parliament and Representation: The Unfinished Agenda of Electoral Redistributions." *Canadian Journal of Political Science* 21: 675-90.

——. 1986. "Some Thoughts on Redistribution." *Canadian Parliamentary Review* 9:18-20.

——. 1985. "Theories Masquerading as Principles: Canadian Electoral Boundary Commissions and the Australian Model." In *The Canadian House of Commons: Essays in Honour of Norman Ward,* edited by John C. Courtney, pp. 135-72. Calgary: University of Calgary Press.

BIBLIOGRAPHY

Dahl, Robert A. 1986. *Democracy, Liberty and Equality.* Oslo: Norwegian University Press.

Dauer, Manning J., and R.G. Kelsay. 1955, 1956. "Unrepresentative States." *National Municipal Review* 44, 45.

David, Paul, and Ralph Eisenberg. 1961. *The Devaluation of the Urban and Suburban Vote.* Charlottesville: University of Virginia Press.

Davidson, Chandler. 1984. *Minority Vote Dilution.* Washington, DC: Howard University Press.

Dawson, R. MacGregor. 1935. "The Gerrymander of 1882." *Canadian Journal of Economics and Political Science* 1: 197–221.

Dixon, Robert G. 1968. *Democratic Representation: Reapportionment in Law and Politics.* New York: Oxford University Press.

———. 1982. "Fair Criteria and Procedures for Establishing Legislative Districts." In *Representation and Redistricting Issues,* edited by Bernard Grofman et al. Lexington: Lexington Books.

———. 1969. "The Warren Court Crusade for the Holy Grail of 'One Man–One Vote.'" *Supreme Court Law Review* 219.

———. 1990. "What is Gerrymandering?" In *Representation and Electoral Systems: Canadian Perspectives,* edited by H. Paul Johnston and H. Pasis. Scarborough: Prentice-Hall.

Ely, John. 1980. *Democracy and Distrust.* Cambridge: Harvard University Press.

Farber, D., and P. Frickey. 1991. "Is *Carolene Products* Dead? Reflections on Affirmative Action and the Dynamics of Civil Rights Legislation." 79 *California Law Review* 685.

First Report: Report of the Royal Commission on Electoral Boundaries for British Columbia, December 1988. 14 July 1989.

Grofman, Bernard, ed. 1990. *Political Gerrymandering and the Courts.* New York: Agathon Press.

Gudgin, Graham, and Peter Taylor. 1979. *Seats, Votes and the Spatial Organization of Elections.* London: Piori.

Guiner, L. 1991. "The Triumph of Tokenism: The Voting Rights Act and the Theory of Black Electoral Success." 89 *Michigan Law Review* 1077.

Hacker, Andrew. 1963. *Congressional Districting.* Washington, DC: The Brookings Institution.

Hamilton, Alexander, James Madison, and John Jay. *The Federalist Papers,* edited by and with an Introduction by Clinton Rossiter. New York and Scarborough: Mentor Books, 1961.

Hook, Sidney. 1962. *The Paradoxes of Freedom.* Berkeley: University of California Press.

Katz, Richard S. 1980. *A Theory of Parties and Electoral Systems.* Baltimore: Johns Hopkins University Press.

Levesque, Terrence J., and Kenneth H. Norrie. 1979. "Overwhelming Majorities in the Legislature of Alberta." *Canadian Journal of Political Science* 12: 451–70.

Lewis, Anthony. 1958. "Legislative Apportionment and the Federal Courts." *Harvard Law Review* 61: 1073.

Lijphart, Arend. 1990. "Criteria of Fair Representation." In *Representation and Electoral Systems: Canadian Perspectives,* edited by H. Paul Johnston and H. Pasis, pp. 201–6. Scarborough: Prentice-Hall.

———. 1990. "The Political Consequences of Electoral Laws, 1945-85." *American Political Science Review* 84: 481–96.

Long, S.A., and F.Q. Quo. 1972. "Alberta: One-Party Dominance." In *Canadian Provincial Politics: The Party Systems of the Ten Provinces,* edited by M. Robin, pp. 1–26. Scarborough: Prentice-Hall.

MacLachlin, B. 1991. "The Charter: A New Role for the Judiciary?" 29 *Alberta Law Review* 540.

———. 1990. "The Role of the Court in the Post-Charter Era: Policy-Maker or Adjudicator." 39 *UNB Law Journal* 39.

Mallory, J.R. 1984. *The Structure of Canadian Government,* rev. ed. Toronto: Gage.

Martin, Robert. 1991. "The Charter and the Crisis in Canada." In *After Meech Lake: Lessons for the Future,* edited by David E. Smith, Peter MacKinnon, and John C. Courtney. Saskatoon: Fifth House Publishers.

Maveety, N. 1991. *Representation Rights and the Burger Years*. Ann Arbor: University of Michigan Press.

Montgomery, Bryon J. 1990. *Annexation and Restructuring in Sarnia–Lambton: A Model for Ontario County Government?* Local Government Case Studies #4. London, Ontario: University of Western Ontario Department of Political Science.

Morton, F.L. 1987. "The Political Impact of the Canadian Charter of Rights and Freedoms." *Canadian Journal of Political Science* 20: 31–55.

Olson, M. 1965. *The Logic of Collective Action, Public Goods and the Theory of Groups*. Cambridge: Harvard University Press.

Parker, F. 1984. "Racial Gerrymandering and Legislative Reapportionment." In *Minority Vote Dilution*, edited by C. Davidson. Washington, DC: Howard University Press.

Parliament of the Commonwealth of Australia. 1988. *One Vote, One Value*. Report Number One of the Joint Standing Committee on Electoral Matters. Canberra: Australian Government Publishing Service.

Pasis, Harvey E. 1990. "Electoral Distribution in the Canadian Provincial Legislatures." In *Representation and Electoral Systems: Canadian Perspectives*, edited by H. Paul Johnston and H. Pasis. Scarborough: Prentice-Hall.

Porter, John. 1965. *The Vertical Mosaic*. Toronto: University of Toronto Press.

Qualter, Terence H. 1970. *The Election Process in Canada*. Toronto: McGraw-Hill.

Rae, Douglas W. 1967. *The Political Consequences of Electoral Laws*. New Haven: Yale University Press.

Report of the 1989/90 Electoral District Boundaries Commission: Northwest Territories.

Report of the U.S. Senate Committee on the Judiciary on S. 1992. 1981.

Roach, Kent. 1990. "Reapportionment in British Columbia." *University of British Columbia Law Review* 79: 93–101.

Royal Commission on New Zealand's Electoral System. 1986.

Ruff, Norman. 1990. "The Cat and Mouse Politics of Redistribution: Fair and Effective Representation in British Columbia." *BC Studies* 87: 48–84.

Ruff, Norman, and William Ross. 1988. "Reflections and Refinements: An Appraisal of the Preliminary Report of the Royal Commission on Electoral Boundaries," submission to the Fisher Commission (Victoria).

Rydon, Joan. 1968. "'Malapportionment'–Australian Style." *Politics* 3: 133–47.

Sancton, Andrew. 1990. "Eroding Representation-by-Population in the Canadian House of Commons: The Representation Act, 1985." *Canadian Journal of Political Science* 23: 441–57.

Schmeckebier, Laurence. 1941. *Congressional Apportionment*. Washington, DC: The Brookings Institution.

Schubert, Glendon, and Charles Press. 1964. "Measuring Malapportionment." *American Political Science Review* 58: 302–27.

Sharman, Campbell. 1984. "The Strange Case of a Provincial Constitution: The British Columbia Constitution Act." *Canadian Journal of Political Science* 17.

Shklar, Judith N. 1991. "Redeeming American Political Theory." *American Political Science Review* 85/1.

Silva, Ruth. 1963. "The Population Base for Apportionment of the New York Legislature." *Fordham Law Review* 32.

Smiley, Donald, and Ronald Watts. 1985. *Intrastate Federalism in Canada*. Toronto: University of Toronto Press.

Smith, Henry Nash. 1950. *Virgin Land: The American West as Symbol and Myth*. New York: Vintage.

Smith, Jennifer. 1991. "Representation and Constitutional Reform in Canada." In *After Meech Lake: Lessons for the Future*, edited by David E. Smith, Peter MacKinnon, and John C. Courtney. Saskatoon: Fifth House Publishers.

Steed, M. 1990. "The Constituency." In *Representation and Electoral Systems: Canadian*

BIBLIOGRAPHY

Perspectives, edited by H. Paul Johnston and H. Pasis. Scarborough: Prentice-Hall.

Still, Jonathan W. 1990. "Political Equality and Election Systems." In *Representation and Electoral Systems: Canadian Perspectives*, edited by H. Paul Johnston and H. Pasis, pp. 21-27. Scarborough: Prentice-Hall.

Taylor, P.J. 1985. "All Organization is Bias: The Political Geography of Electoral Reform." *The Geographical Journal* 15.

Taylor, P.J., and R.J. Johnston. 1979. *Geography of Elections*. London: Croom Helm.

Todd, James. 1962. "The Apportionment Problem Faced by the States." *Law and Contemporary Problems* 27.

Turner, Frederick Jackson. 1893. "The Significance of the Frontier in American History." *Annual Report of the American Historical Association.*

Twentieth Century Fund Conference of Research Scholars and Political Scientists. 1962. *One Man–One Vote.* Reprinted and paginated in *Reapportionment*, edited by Glendon Schubert, pp. 42-45. New York: Charles Scribner, 1965.

Victoria *Times-Colonist.* 13 August 1991.

Ward, Norman. 1963. *The Canadian House of Commons: Representation*, 2d ed. Toronto: University of Toronto Press.

———. 1967. "A Century of Constituencies." *Canadian Public Administration* 10: 105-22.

Weiler, Paul. 1984. "Rights and Judges in a Democracy: A New Canadian Version." *University of Michigan Journal of Law Reform* 18/1.

Wells, D. 1982. "Against Affirmative Gerrymandering." In *Representation and Redistricting Issues*, edited by B. Grofman et al. Lexington: D.C. Heath.

Wirth, Louis. 1964. "Rural-Urban Differences." In *Louis Wirth on Cities and Social Life: Selected Papers*, edited by Albert J. Reiss. Chicago: University of Chicago Press.

Wood, Gordon. 1969. *Representation in the American Revolution*. Charlottesville: University Press of Virginia.

Zeran, Bonnie J. 1991. "Should Peel's Regional Chairman be Directly Elected?" Unpublished Diploma in Public Administration research paper, University of Western Ontario.

Law Cases

Canada and Commonwealth

Andrews v. Law Society of British Columbia, [1989] 1 S.C.R. 143.

Australia (Attorney General) v. Commonwealth (1975), 135 C.L.R. 1, 50 A.L.J.R. 279, 7 A.L.R. 593 (Aust. H.C.).

Campbell v. Attorney General of Canada (1988), 49 D.L.R. (4th) 321 (B.C.C.A.).

Carter v. Saskatchewan (Attorney-General), S.C.C., decision rendered 6 June 1991, unreported at time of writing, draft judgment.

Dixon v. British Columbia (Attorney General), [1986] 7 B.C.L.R. (2d) 186.

Dixon v. British Columbia (Attorney General), [1989] 35 B.C.L.R. (2d) 273.

Edwards v. Attorney General of Canada, [1930] A.C. 124.

Ex. rel. McKinlay v. Commonwealth (1975), 7 A.L.R. 593.

Hoogbruin v. British Columbia (Attorney General), [1986] 70 B.C.L.R. 1, 2 W.W.R. 700, 24 D.L.R. (4th) 718 (C.A.).

Irwin Toy v. Québec, [1989] 1 S.C.R. 927.

Operation Dismantle v. The Queen, [1985] 1 S.C.R. 441.

Penikett v. Canada (1987), 45 D.L.R. (4th) 108 (Y.T.C.A.).

R. v. Big M Drug Mart, [1985] 1 S.C.R. 295.

R. v. Boundary Commission for England, Ex Parte Foot and Others, [1983] 1 All E.R. 1099 (C.A.)

R. v. Edwards Books and Art, [1986] 2 S.C.R. 713.

R. v. Keegstra, [1991] 3 S.C.R. 697.

R. v. Oakes, [1986] 1 S.C.R. 103.

R. v. Turpin (1989), 48 C.C.C. (3d) 8 (S.C.C.).

Reference re an Act to Amend the Education Act (1986), 25 D.L.R. (4th) 1 (Ont. C.A.).

Reference re an Act to Amend the Education Act (Ontario) (1987), 40 D.L.R. (4th) 18 (S.C.C.).

Reference re Electoral Boundaries Commission Act (Alberta), #9103–0081–AC, 21 November 1991 (unreported).

Reference re Electoral Boundaries Commission Act (Sask.) (1991), 81 D.L.R. (4th) 16 (S.C.C.).

Reference re Provincial Electoral Boundaries, [1991] 3 W.W.R. 593 (Sask. C.A.), 90 Sask. R. 174, 78 D.L.R. (4th) 449 *(sub nom. Reference re Electoral Boundaries Commission Act)*.

Reference re Provincial Electoral Boundaries, [1991] 5 W.W.R. 1 (S.C.C.), 81 D.L.R. (4th) 16, *(sub nom. Reference re Electoral Boundaries Commission Act)*.

Reference re Public Service Employees Relations Act (Alta), [1987] 1 S.C.R. 313.

Reference re Representation in the House of Commons, [1903] 33 S.C.R. 475 (S.C.C.).

Reference re Representation of Prince Edward Island in The House of Commons, [1903] 33 S.C.R. 594 (S.C.C.).

Reference re Saskatchewan Electoral Boundaries (unreported at time of writing), Sask. C.A., decision rendered 6 March 1991, file no. 639, draft judgment.

Reference re Section 27 of the Judicature Act, R.S.A. (1980), Chapter J–1, unreported, file #9103–0081–AC, draft judgment.

Reynolds v. Attorney General British Columbia (1984), 53 B.C.L.R. 394, 5 W.W.R. 270, 11 D.L.R. (4th) 380 (C.A.).

Thomson Newspapers Ltd. v. Canada (1990), 76 C.R. (3d) 129 (S.C.C.).

United States

Allen v. State Board of Education, 393 U.S. 544 (1969).

Badham v. Eu (N.D. California, No. C–83–1126, dismissed 21 April 1988).

Baker v. Carr, 369 U.S. 186 (1962).

Bandemer v. Davis, 478 U.S. 109 (1986).

Board of Estimate v. Morris, 489 U.S. 688 (1988).

Brown v. Thomson, 462 U.S. 835 (1983).

Burns v. Richardson, 384 U.S. 73 (1966).

City of Mobile v. Bolden, 446 U.S. 55 (1980).

Colegrove v. Green, 328 U.S. 549 (1946).

Connor v. Finch, 431 U.S. 407 (1977).

Federation for American Immigration Reform (FAIR) et al. v. Philip M. Klutznick, 486 F. Supp. 564 (1980).

Fortson v. Dorsey, 379 U.S. 433 (1965).

Gaffney v. Cummings, 412 U.S. 735 (1973).

Garza v. County of Los Angeles, U.S. 9115 F. 2d 763 (1990).

Gingles v. Edmisten, 590 F. Supp. 345 (1984).

Gomillion v. Lightfoot, 364 U.S. 339 (1960).

Gray v. Sanders 372 U.S. 339 (1960).

Karcher v. Daggett, 462 U.S. 725 (1983).

Kirkpatrick v. Preisler, 394 U.S. 526 (1969).

Kirksey v. Board of Supervisors of Hinds County, Miss., 554 F. 2d 139 (1977).

Lucas v. Forty-Fourth Colorado General Assembly, 377 U.S. 713 (1964).

Republican Party of Virginia v. Wilder, Civ. No. 91–0424–R (W.D. Va., 1991).

Reynolds v. Sims, 377 U.S. 533 (1964).

Ridge v. Verity, Civ. No. 88–351 (W.D. Pennsylvania, 1991).

Thornberg v. Gingles, 478 U.S. 30 (1986).

U.S. v. Marengo County Commissioners, 731 F. 2d 1546 (11th Cir., 1984).

Wesberry v. Sanders, 376 U.S. 1 (1964).

BIBLIOGRAPHY

Whitcomb v. Chavis, 403 U.S. 124 (1971).
White v. Regester, 412 U.S. 755 (1973).

Additional Reading

Alker, Hayward R., Jr., and Bruce M. Russett. 1964. "On Measuring Inequality." *Behaviourial Science* 9: 207-18.

Banting, Keith. 1989. *Federalism and the Supreme Court of Canada: Competing Bases of Legitimation.* Prepared for the Ontario Law Reform Commission Conference on the Nomination of Persons for Judicial Appointment, 14-15 September.

Beatty, David M. 1990. *Talking Heads and the Supremes: The Canadian Production of Constitutional Review.* Toronto: Carswell.

Beitz, Charles R. 1988. "Equal Opportunity in Political Representation." In *Equal Opportunity,* edited by Norman E. Bowie, pp. 155-76. Boulder: Westview Press.

Berger, Thomas. 1977. *Northern Frontier, Northern Homeland: The Report of the Mackenzie Valley Pipeline Inquiry.* Ottawa: Supply and Services.

Boyle, Christine. 1983. "Home-Rule for Women: Power Sharing Between Men and Women." *Dalhousie Law Journal* 7: 790-809.

Cairns, Alan C. 1984. "The Canadian Constitutional Experiment." *Dalhousie Law Journal* 9/1. Reprinted in *Constitution, Government, and Society in Canada,* edited by Doug Williams, chap. 8. Toronto: McClelland and Stewart, 1988.

——. 1979. *From Interstate to Intrastate Federalism.* Kingston: Queen's Institute of Intergovernmental Relations.

——. 1990. "The Past and Future of the Canadian Administrative State." *University of Toronto Law Journal* 40: 319-61.

——. 1990. "Who Should the Judges Be? Canadian Debates about the Composition of a Final Court of Appeal." Prepared for the Fourth Berkeley Seminar on Federalism, 19-20 April. *Canadian Journal of Law and Jurisprudence,* 4/2, special edition. July 1991.

Clarke, Harold. 1978. "Determinants of Provincial Constituency Service Behaviour: A Multivariate Analysis." *Legislative Studies Quarterly* 3/4 (November).

Coulson, Michael. 1983. "Reforming Electoral Distribution." *Policy Options* 4: 25-28.

Courtney, John C. Forthcoming. "Discrimination in Canada's Electoral Law." In *Discrimination in the Law in the Administration of Justice,* edited by Walter Tarnopolsky and Joyce Whitman. Toronto: Carswell.

——. 1992. "Parliamentary Representation: Electoral Redistributions." In *Comparative Political Studies: Australia and Canada,* edited by Malcolm Alexander and Brian Galligan. Melbourne: Longmans Cheshire.

——. 1985. "The Size of Canada's Parliament: An Assessment of the Implications of a Larger House of Commons." In *Institutional Reforms for Representative Government,* edited by P. Aucoin. Toronto: University of Toronto Press.

Eagles, Munroe. 1992. "Enhancing Relative Vote Equality in Canada: The Role of Electors in Boundary Adjustment." In *Drawing the Map: Equality and Efficacy of the Vote in Canadian Electoral Boundary Reform,* edited by D. Small. Toronto: Dundurn Press. *Research Study* for the Royal Commission on Electoral Reform and Party Financing.

Elkins, David. 1989. "Facing Our Destiny: Rights and Canadian Distinctiveness." *Canadian Journal of Political Science* 22/4 (December): 699-716.

Francis, R. Douglas. 1989. *Images of the West: Responses to the Canadian Prairies.* Saskatoon: Western Producer Prairie Books.

Grofman, Bernard. 1985. "Criteria for Districting: A Social Science Perspective." *UCLA Law Review* 33/1 (October): 77-184.

——. 1992 forthcoming. "An Expert Witness Perspective on Continuing and Emerging Controversies in Voting Rights Case Law: From One Person, One Vote to Political Gerrymandering." *Stetson Law Review.*

——. 1981. "Fair and Equal Representation." *Ethics* 91/3 (April): 477–85.

——. 1990. "Toward a Coherent Theory of Gerrymandering: *Thornberg* and *Bandemer*," in *Political Gerrymandering and the Courts*, edited by B. Grofman, pp. 29–63. New York: Agathon Press.

——. 1991. *Voting Rights, Voting Wrongs: The Legacy of Baker v. Carr*. A Report of the Twentieth Century Fund. New York: Priority Press.

Grofman, Bernard, et al. 1985. "The 'Totality of Circumstances Test' in Section 2 of the 1982 Extension of the Voting Rights Act: A Social Science Perspective." *Law and Policy* 7/2 (April): 209–23.

Grofman, Bernard, and Lisa Handley. 1992 forthcoming. "Identifying and Remedying Racial Gerrymandering." *Journal of Law and Politics*.

Grofman, Bernard, and Howard Scarrow. 1981. "The Riddle of Apportionment: Equality of What?" *National Civic Review* 70/5 (May): 242–54.

Grossman, Lawrence. 1967. "'Safe Seats': The Rural-Urban Pattern in Ontario." In *Voting in Canada*, edited by John C. Courtney, pp. 99–103. Scarborough: Prentice-Hall.

Handley, Lisa. 1991. "The Quest for Voting Rights: The Evolution of a Vote Dilution Standard and Its Impact on Minority Reporting." Ph.D. Dissertation, George Washington University.

Harrison, Dick. 1977. *Unnamed Country: The Struggle for a Canadian Prairie Fiction*. Edmonton: Hurtig.

Hawkes, D., and B. Morse. 1991. "Alternative Methods for Aboriginal Participation in Processes of Constitutional Reform." In *Options for a New Canada*, edited by R. Watts and D. Brown, pp. 178–86. Toronto: University of Toronto Press.

Jewell, Malcolm. 1971. "Commentary." In *Reapportionment in the 1970s*, edited by N. Polsby. Berkeley: University of California Press.

Johnston, H. Paul, and Harvey E. Pasis, eds. 1990. *Representation and Electoral Systems: Canadian Perspectives*. Toronto: Prentice-Hall.

Kaase, Max. 1984. "The Challenge of the 'Participatory Revolution' in Pluralist Democracies." *International Political Science Review* 5/3.

Lowenstein, Daniel Hays. 1990. "*Bandemer's* Gap: Gerrymandering and Equal Protection." In *Political Gerrymandering and the Courts*, edited by B. Grofman. New York: Agathon Press.

Lyons, W.E. 1969. "Legislative Redistricting by Independent Commissions: Operationalizing the One Man-One Vote Doctrine in Canada," *Polity* 1: 429–59.

——. 1970. *One Man-One Vote*. Toronto: McGraw-Hill.

McCubbins, Matthew D., and Thomas Schwartz. 1988. "Congress, the Courts and Public Policy: Consequences of the One Man, One Vote Rule." *American Journal of Political Science* 32: 388–415.

McDonald, Laughlin. 1992 forthcoming. "The Effects of the 1982 Amendments of Section 2 of the Voting Rights Act on Minority Representation." In *Controversies in Minority Voting*, edited by B. Grofman and C. Davidson. Washington, DC: The Brookings Institution.

McDonald, Michael. 1991. "Should Communities Have Rights? Reflections on Liberal Individualism." *Canadian Journal of Law and Jurisprudence* 4/2 (July).

Mahew, David R. 1971. "Congressional Representation: Theory and Practice in Drawing the Districts." In *Reapportionment in the 1970s*, edited by N. Polsby, pp. 249–85. Berkeley: University of California Press.

Mallory, J.R. 1975. "Amending the Constitution by Stealth." *Queen's Quarterly* 82 (Autumn): 394–401.

Mandel, Michael. 1989. *The Charter and the Legalization of Politics in Canada*. Toronto: Wall and Thomson.

Monahan, Patrick. 1987. *Politics and the Constitution: The Charter, Federalism and the Supreme Court*. Toronto: Carswell.

Morton, F.L. 1985. "Group Rights Versus Individual Rights in the Charter: The Special Cases of

Natives and Quebecois." In *Minorities and the Canadian State,* edited by N. Nevitte and A. Kornberg. Oakville: Mosaic Press.

Morton, F.L., and R. Knopff. 1991. "Does the Charter Mandate 'One Person, One Vote.'" Research Study 7.1. University of Calgary Research Unit for Socio-Legal Studies.

Nagel, S.S. 1972. "Computers and the Law and Politics of Redistricting." *Polity* 5: 77–93.

Nevitte, Neil. 1991 forthcoming. "New Politics, the Charter and Political Participation." In *Representation, Integration, and Political Parties in Canada,* edited by H. Bakvis. Toronto: Dundurn Press.

Norrie, K., R. Simeon, and M. Krasnick. 1986. *Federalism and the Economic Union in Canada.* Toronto: University of Toronto Press.

Owram, Doug. 1980. *Promise of Eden: The Canadian Expansionist Movement and the Idea of the West, 1856–1900.* Toronto: University of Toronto Press.

Pammett, Jon H. 1988. "A Framework for the Comparative Analysis of Elections Across Time and Space." *Electoral Studies* 7/2: 125–42.

——. 1991. "The Meanings of Canadian Elections." Paper prepared for "Canada's Century: Governance in a Maturing Society–A Conference in Honor of John Meisel." Queen's University.

Pasis, Harvey E. 1983. "Achieving Population Equality Among the Constituencies of the Canadian House, 1903–1976." *Legislative Studies Quarterly* 7: 111–15.

——. 1987. "The Courts and Redistribution." *Canadian Parliamentary Review* 10: 8–9.

——. 1972. "The Inequality of Distribution in the Canadian Provincial Assemblies." *Canadian Journal of Political Science* 5: 433–46.

Polsby, Nelson W., ed. 1971. *Reapportionment in the 1970s.* Berkeley: University of California Press.

Pross, Paul. 1982. "Space, Function, and Interest: The Problem of Legitimacy in the Canadian State." In *The Administrative State in Canada: Essays in Honour of J.E. Hodgetts,* edited by O.P. Dwivedi, pp. 107–29. Toronto: University of Toronto Press.

Qualter, T.H. 1967. "Representation by Population: A Comparative Study." *Canadian Journal of Economics and Political Science* 33: 246–68.

Redenius, Charles. 1982. "Representation, Reapportionment, and the Supreme Court." *Political Studies* 30/4.

Roach, Kent. 1991. "The Charter and the Criminal Process." In *Criminology: A Reader's Guide,* edited by J. Gladstone, R.V. Ericson, and C.D. Shearing, pp. 200–2. Toronto: University of Toronto Press.

——. 1991 forthcoming. "One Person–One Vote?: Canadian Constitutional Standards for Electoral Distribution and Districting." In *Drawing the Map: Equality and Efficacy of the Vote in Canadian Electoral Boundary Reform,* edited by D. Small, pp. 15–23 (mimeo). Toronto: Dundurn Press.

Ruff, Norman, and William M. Ross. 1989. "Towards a More Equitable Distribution of Seats in British Columbia." *Canadian Parliamentary Review* 12: 21–23.

Sancton, A. 1973. "The Application of the 'Senatorial Floor' Rules to the Latest Redistribution of the House of Commons: The Peculiar Case of Nova Scotia." *Canadian Journal of Political Science* 6: 56–64.

——. 1975. "The Representation Act, 1974." *Canadian Journal of Political Science* 8: 467–69.

Schuck, P. 1987. "The Thickest Thicket: Partisan Gerrymandering and Judicial Regulation of Politics." 87 *Columbia Law Review* 1325.

Taagepera, Rein, and Matthew Shugart. 1989. *Seats and Votes: The Effects of Determinants on Electoral Systems.* New Haven: Yale University Press.

Taylor, Charles. 1985. "Alternative Futures: Legitimacy, Identity and Alienation in Late Twentieth Century Canada." In *Constitutionalism, Citizenship and Society in Canada,* edited by A. Cairns and C. Williams, pp. 183–229. Toronto: University of Toronto Press.

Thernstrom, A. 1987. *Whose Votes Count?* Cambridge: Harvard University Press.

Tribe, Lawrence. 1988. *American Constitutional Law,* 2d ed. Mineola: Foundation Press.

Tufte, Edward R. 1973. "The Relationship Between Seats and Votes in Two-Party Systems." *American Political Science Review* 67: 540–54.

Vipond, Robert C. 1991. *Liberty and Community: Canadian Federalism and the Failure of the Constitution.* Albany: State University of New York Press.

Williams, Cynthia. 1985. "The Changing Nature of Citizen Rights." In *Constitutionalism, Citizenship and Society in Canada,* edited by A. Cairns and C. Williams. Toronto: University of Toronto Press.

Williams, Cynthia and Doug. 1990. "Ideas and Identities in Canadian Political Life." In *Canadian Politics: An Introduction to the Discipline,* edited by A. Gagnon and J. Bickerton, pp. 196–228. Peterborough: Broadview Press.

Williams, Doug. 1991. "Meisel's Postcards: or Notes Toward a Constitutional *Colimaison.*" Paper presented at the Conference in Honour of John Meisel, "Canada's Century: Governance in a Maturing Society," held at Queen's University (April).

——. 1991. *Problems of Governance, Political Participation and the Administration of Justice in an Information Society.* Ottawa: Department of Justice, Research and Development Directorate.

Wollock, Andrea J., ed. 1980. *Reapportionment; Law and Technology.* Denver: National Conference of State Legislatures (June).

Zagarri, Rosemarie. 1987. *The Politics of Size: Representation in the United States, 1776–1850.* New York: Cornell University Press.